TRACKER MANUAL

A practical guide to animal tracking in southern Africa

TRACKER MANUAL

A practical guide to animal tracking in southern Africa

Alex van den Heever
Renias Mhlongo
Karel Benadie
Ian Thomas

Above, left to right: Cheetah, front left paw; lion track in sand; yellow-billed hornbill foot.

Published by Struik Nature
(an imprint of Penguin Random House South Africa (Pty) Ltd)
Reg. No. 1953/000441/07
The Estuaries No. 4, Oxbow Crescent, Century Avenue, Century City, 7441

PO Box 1144, Cape Town, 8000 South Africa

Visit **www.struiknature.co.za** and join the Struik Nature Club for updates, news, events and special offers.

First published in 2017
Second edition 2024
10 9 8 7 6 5 4 3

Copyright © in text 2017, 2024: Alex van den Heever
Copyright © in photographs 2017, 2024: Alex van den Heever or as indicated alongside images
Copyright © in illustrations 2017, 2024: Alex van den Heever and Ian Thomas
Copyright © in published edition 2017, 2024: Penguin Random House South Africa (Pty) Ltd

Front cover: Hyaena front left foot © Ian Thomas
Half-title page: Lion track in dried-out mud © Ian Thomas
Title page spread: Leopardess dropping down a huge rock face © Ian Thomas

Publisher: Pippa Parker
Managing editor: Roelien Theron
Editor: Natalie Bell
Design concept: Janice Evans
Design: Gillian Black
Proofreader: Emsie du Plessis

Reproduction by Studio Repro

Printed and bound in China by 1010 Printing International Ltd

MIX
Paper | Supporting responsible forestry
FSC® C016973

All rights reserved. No part of this publication may be reproduced, stored in a retrieval system, or transmitted, in any form or by any means, electronic, mechanical, photocopying, recording or otherwise, without the prior written permission of the copyright owner(s).

978 1 77584 774 8 **(Print)**
978 1 77584 775 5 **(ePub)**

Mapula
Trust

The Publishers and Authors extend grateful thanks to the Mapula Trust for their generous support of this publication.

Making illegal copies of this publication, distributing them unlawfully or sharing them on social media without the written permission of the publisher may lead to civil claims or criminal complaints.
Protect the communities who are sustained by creativity.

Contents

Foreword	**7**
Preface	**8**
Acknowledgements	**9**
Introduction to tracking	10
Practical tracking	13
Reading tracks and signs	17
Track morphology	31
About this book	42
Animals' tracks and signs	**44**
Carnivores	44
Large mammals	94
Antelopes	131
Small mammals	195
Primates	243
Hares & rodents	251
Amphibians & reptiles	268
Birds	289
Insects & other invertebrates	340
Theory for trackers	**354**
Animal track comparisons	**358**
Glossary	**368**
Bibliography	**370**
Index	**373**

Foreword

It is a pleasure to be writing an introduction to this informative and beautifully presented manual on tracking by Alex van den Heever, Renias Mhlongo from the Lowveld and Karel 'Pokkie' Benadie from the Great Karoo, with illustrations by Ian Thomas.

Since the inception of the Tracker Academy in January 2010, I have had the immense pleasure of working closely with the trainers of the Academy. My task as part of the academic staff has been to supplement – and link animal tracking skills to – ecological thinking … to recognise and understand the connections between the spoor of the animal and the animal itself – its biology, its behaviour, its evolutionary adaptation to its surroundings and, not least, to make sense of the social and psychological significance of wild animals in the lives of human beings. Whether we realise it or not, to identify the track of an animal is to enter into a relationship with that animal, and as every ranger and wildlife guide will confirm, we can learn a lot about ourselves from the wild – if we are open to it.

In keeping with the ecological theme, I believe it is important to draw attention to the link between tracking skills, life and leadership skills. Put differently, the manner in which you track a wild animal is, in principle, no different to the way you keep track of your life, including your relationships and your career. Both depend for their success on one's capacity to focus and to scan – to pay attention to detail and processes on the one hand, and to see the bigger picture and understand consequences on the other. Tracking and situation analysis are the same thing. They are both about problem solving: collating the facts and making decisions.

This is a unique tracking manual. It puts you 'into the skin' of the trainees. Everything you read and measure is a reflection not only of the spoor that they will come to recognise and describe, but an indication of the standard that has been set for Tracker Academy's deserved recognition by the Field Guide Association of South Africa (FGASA) and the Culture, Art, Tourism, Hospitality and Sport Sector Education and Training Authority (CATHSSETA) as a legitimate training facility for future guides and trackers.

Finally, the privilege of working with approved expert trackers such as Renias Mhlongo and Pokkie Benadie simply cannot be measured. I am both humbled and grateful to be associated with the Tracker Academy. Alex, Renias, Karel and Ian can be very proud of this manual.

Dr IAN McCALLUM

Preface

Tracker Academy is a training division of the South African College for Tourism, which operates under the auspices of the Peace Parks Foundation. We train unemployed people in traditional animal-tracking skills for employment in the conservation industry. Most of our students come from rural villages near wildlife areas in southern Africa. Through donor funding we offer training bursaries to 32 candidates per annum, to study our formally accredited Tracker Skills programme.

Tracker Academy's overarching vision is to restore indigenous knowledge in Africa. Our aim is to demonstrate that ancient tracking skills have relevance for modern conservation efforts. We strive to contribute to the current knowledge of tracking by unearthing new discoveries. Many of the descriptions of tracks and signs in this field guide are transcriptions of verbal records from Karel Benadie and Renias Mhlongo, the Academy's two founding trainers. Further contributions from these and other expert trackers are anticipated, as we endeavour to create a living repository of indigenous knowledge.

Tracker Academy is the first specialist tracker school in South Africa to have its training programme formally accredited by the Culture, Art, Tourism, Hospitality and Sport Sector Education and Training Authority (CATHSSETA).

With 1,500 hours on foot practising tracking skills and about 150 encounters with large animals, our students develop a high degree of tracking competency during their year of training. This sets the Academy's courses apart from many other short 'bush skills' courses.

Since inception of the Academy in 2010, some 90% of our tracker graduates have been successfully deployed in permanent jobs across the ecotourism, wildlife protection and research sectors of the conservation industry.

A small number of skilled trackers remain in Africa, and the few who do possess these traditional skills are disappearing fast. It would be an indictment of modern conservation to lose this important element of indigenous knowledge.

*Founding trainers of Tracker Academy, **left to right**: Karel Benadie, Renias Mhlongo and Alex van den Heever.*

ALEX VAN DEN HEEVER
www.trackeracademy.co.za

Acknowledgements

The late André Kilian's idea for this book was to create a living repository of indigenous tracking knowledge. Gaynor Rupert and the Rupert Nature Foundation stepped in and provided generous funding to make the first edition of the *Tracker Manual* a reality. Then owing to popular demand, Pippa Parker at Struik Nature invited us to write a second edition. I am writing during the Christmas holidays and I'd specifically like to thank my dear wife Pippa, and our daughters Bella and Sophie, for allowing me the time to write this updated edition – I will make it up to you!

My very special thanks go to Ian Thomas for his continued support and mentorship over the last two decades, and for creating the new illustrations of tracks for this edition. Ian is a passionate, focused and meticulous naturalist whose influence on this book and the Tracker Academy cannot be overstated. Time with Ian taking track photos in the bushveld is my best! There is always great humour paired with incredible insights – and both in equal measure.

Thank you to Dave Hood, Kara Heynis (Lory Park), Maggie Newman, Tarry Myers, Mike Bridgeford, Aeiden Swan, Alex Sliwa, Stephanie Venske, Sean Matthewson, Brian and Chantelle Rode, Rob Gess, Sal Roux, Siphiwe Mandleni, Mark Lautenbach, Seth Vorster, Thulani Sibuyi, Etienne Oosthuizen, Chris Roche, Byron Serrao, Sylvie Geerkens, Jonathan Geall, Lucien Beaumont, Darren Pietersen, David Dampier, Andrea Campbell, Simon Stobbs, James Tyrrell, Joe Grosel, Derek Engelbrecht, Kevin Murray, Warren Pearson, Lawrence Wietz, Don Heyneke and Michael Bosman, who graciously offered their track and animal images.

Gratitude goes to Professor Marcus Byrne who provided valuable information on some tracks of insect species. David Hood, Thomas Imrie and Grant Hine provided feedback on the initial draft of the book. To Dr Ian McCallum, thank you for writing such a great Foreword, and for your ongoing and unique contribution to Tracker Academy – it is most appreciated.

To the landowners of Samara, Londolozi, Tswalu Kalahari Reserve, Singita, Phinda, EcoTraining, Gorongosa National Park and African Parks Network, thank you for making your properties available for the collection of much of the material. We would also like to offer special thanks to the Peace Parks Foundation – under whose auspices Tracker Academy operates – for the ongoing support.

Thank you to Robert Hlatshwayo, Norman Chauke and Innocent Ngwenya, certified Lead Trackers, for your committed assistance in providing track measurements and photos as well as constantly challenging the accuracy of our track descriptions and measurements.

And to our two tracking experts, Karel and Renias, who provided the impetus, knowledge and inspiration for this manual – which will no doubt be of great value to all future Tracker Academy students – thank you for sharing your knowledge and skills. Let's not forget Janetta Bock-Benadie, Karel's lovely wife, who has constantly supported the process.

Finally, a special word of thanks to the many wild animals who left their signs for us to study, photograph and record.

ALEX VAN DEN HEEVER

Introduction to tracking

In essence, tracking is the knowledge and skills required to recognise, interpret and follow animal signs. The constant merging of the rational mind with our imagination to interpret the 'evidence' left behind makes tracking one of the most complex forms of proficiency in the world of wildlife.

Tracking skills enable one to know what animals are doing without seeing them, allowing trackers to witness the secret lives of animals. Like any skill, tracking can be trained and evaluated to a high degree of competency. Its application has relevance in the ecotourism, wildlife protection, education and animal monitoring sectors of the conservation industry.

An ancient skill

Traditional tracking skills evolved in Africa thousands of years ago for reasons of survival. However, with rapid urbanisation, people no longer required the services of traditional hunter-gatherers so that, over the past 60 or so years, tracking skills have disappeared at an alarming rate.

That said, there are still a few exceptionally talented trackers among us, working at private game reserves and national parks, tracking animals daily for the benefit of guests, or to monitor game or conduct anti-poaching patrols. This is relatively intensive tracking – the original hunter-gatherers would not have tracked lions, for instance, with anything like the same frequency and determination – and has resulted in the emergence of some uniquely skilful practitioners.

Profile of a tracker

Tracking requires one to be physically fit and able, and to have good eyes, an imagination, a good memory and the ability to think rationally. The best trackers in the world have something extra – the ability to assimilate all the evidence around them and to combine this with their intimate knowledge of local wildlife. Interestingly, many expert trackers are also excellent mimics of both animal and human behaviour, which gives weight to the idea that they are particularly keen observers of behavioural traits.

The most talented trackers are always inquisitive, constantly learning and steadily honing their skills over many years. Tracking an antelope for instance, for hours in the heat of the day is tremendously difficult. The tracker must seek to understand the nature of the animal being pursued: What does it eat? What habitat does it prefer? Where is it going? And why?

Trackers follow a lion trail.

James Tyrrell

■ INTRODUCTION TO TRACKING

Ju/'hoansi trackers track a porcupine near Xai Xai, Botswana.

With answers to these questions, the tracker can start to predict the animal's movements. As Renias Mhlongo says, 'You must put the animal in your heart'.

Over time, trackers get to know the influence of the landscape and its vegetation, the season, the time of day and how this may relate to the animal being trailed. At this point, tracking becomes intuitive, but it is not a mystical activity, as some assume. Rather, good tracking skills are the result of years of painstaking practice in the field and a close understanding of the natural environment. Expert trackers therefore demonstrate exceptional ecological literacy in their quest to understand that which they pursue.

In addition to a tracker's knowledge of the wilderness, interpreting tracks and signs requires the ability to analyse objectively the smallest physical details. For example, the track difference between the track of a subadult white rhino and an adult black rhino is relatively small – mostly a matter of subtle differences in proportions, and two lobes on the posterior edge, as opposed to one. Some people have natural analytical skills, while others must develop them over time.

Successful tracking also involves being able to switch rapidly from taking in the broader context to observing minute details – a matter of 'zooming in and out'. This can be extremely tiring, especially during long, hot days, and it requires all the senses. By assimilating all available information, trackers can form a mental image of animals and their activity in a particular area. It's important to avoid focusing solely on one animal, which can cause one to miss other signs along the way. For example, a tracker following a black rhino in the thicket may easily miss the subtle alarm call of a shrike, indicating the presence of a leopard lying under a bush nearby.

The expert tracker is entirely familiar with the rules of tracking but always guided by the senses. Although it may appear mystical to the novice, tracking is a legitimate skill like any other, which over time can be mastered to a high degree of competence.

The ability to switch one's attention continually from examining the minutiae of detailed signs to seeing animals within the broader context of the landscape contributes to tracking success.

Trailing animals

While tracking describes the knowledge and skills required to recognise, interpret and follow animal signs, trailing is the skill required to follow a trail of diverse animal signs until the animal is found, much like an investigator searches for evidence to build a case and catch a perpetrator. Furthermore successful trailing requires a tracker to integrate the track evidence with the landscape and broader environment in order to interpret an animal's movements and whereabouts.

Today's trackers

Only those who practise trailing daily are able to assimilate this ancient African pursuit. Practice must be consistent and repetitive, with focused engagement. Trackers should target specific areas for improvement, push their limits, and request immediate feedback. This pursuit requires a commitment to lifelong learning and refinement.

Historically, hunter-gatherers trailed animals to hunt and feed themselves. Wildlife was hunted not for trophies, but for human sustenance and survival. However, since about the 1960s, traditional hunters have had less reason and opportunity to trail and hunt animals.

Today, the skill of trailing is required for the most part by professional trackers employed in the ecotourism and wildlife protection industries. Discerning travellers secure the services of trackers to find wild animals during safari game drives. In other areas, field rangers trail animals for protection in anti-poaching efforts. They also collect data for scientific research.

Tracking requires one to be physically fit and able, to have good eyes, an imagination, a good memory and the ability to think rationally.

Practical tracking

Some of the best followers of animal trails are those who have spent years practising the skill. Those who have worked as cattle herders or subsistence hunters in their youth have always been at a particular advantage. However, this is not to suggest that those without any tracking experience cannot learn to track with equal competence.

Typical behaviour

The first requirement is to learn about animal behaviour, such as social structure, habitat and diet preferences. Once you understand the general behaviour traits of a species, you can begin to delve deeper into the specific behaviour of individuals. For example, at Londolozi there was a female leopard that hunted greater cane rats in two specific areas. If her tracks started off in the direction of one of these favourite hunting grounds, her whereabouts could reliably be predicted.

We know that most animals – particularly soft-footed ones such as lions and leopards – take the path of least resistance: they use existing routes through bush, and their movements are generally logical. Following an aardvark, however, could make you dizzy as it meanders in and out, sometimes going in circles. It helps to know that this is typical aardvark behaviour, as it repeatedly visits a series of ant and termite colonies in its search for food. Establishing an animal's intentions can help one anticipate its next move.

Seasonality

Seasonality also plays an important role when following animal trails. Animals such as elephants will frequent certain reliable drinking sites during the dry winter, and these paths become well defined. In the hot summer months, leopards in Sabi Sands spend more time in trees and on top of termite mounds in the mid-afternoon, to take advantage of the breeze. If one follows rhinos regularly enough, their territorial boundaries and favourite wallows soon become obvious. Knowledge of such behavioural patterns, combined with local knowledge of a particular area, can greatly enhance the efficiency and success rate of trailing and finding animals.

Evidence of a leopard having dragged a carcass

PRACTICAL TRACKING ■

Substrate
The type of substrate has a bearing on tracks. Take the time first to establish what *undisturbed* ground and vegetation looks like; disturbances, ranging from small and nondescript to obvious, can then be recorded. Sandy soils are notorious for making tracks look either smaller or bigger, depending on the depth of the sand. Tracks in mud usually appear bigger. On harder ground, the full extent of the track is seldom visible. With these factors in mind, the tracker must assess the track size, shape, texture and colour, which changes according to its age (freshness). Fresh tracks may appear darker than the surrounding soil, or lighter, depending on the substrate. As the track ages, so its colour will return to that of the surrounding soil, making older tracks more difficult to follow. Texture can also be a determining factor: for example, an adult rhino track is often recognisable only by the unique texture of its sole imprint. In extreme situations, animal tracks are represented by nothing more than faint little scuff marks on the ground, the size, shape and colour of which become key.

Evidence
It is important to investigate all the available evidence when studying animal signs. Spend time looking around for more tracks or signs before you make a decision. One particular track or dropping may be difficult to identify, yet the animal could have left a clearer sign close by. Take note of even small disturbances on the ground and in the vegetation. These may include dislodged stones, discoloured or loosened soil, broken twigs or branches, bruised or bent grass, soil on top of short grass, hairs embedded in flattened buffalo dung or in a bush, urine marks, mud clods, mud scrapings on trees, territorial scrapings and stripped leaves.

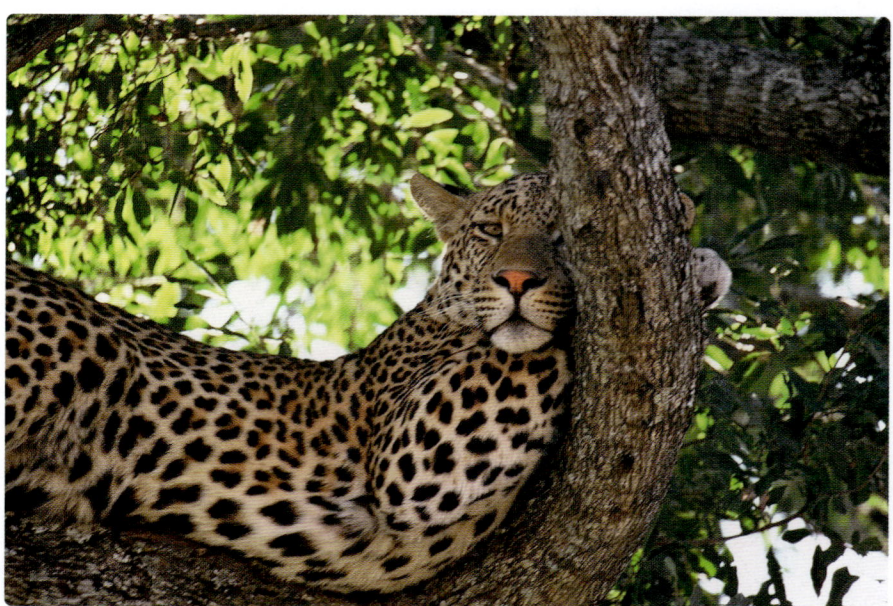

In the hot summer months, leopards spend more time up trees, enjoying the breeze.

Trackers investigate the freshness of a lion dropping.

Gait
Interpreting an animal's gait can give valuable insight into what it is doing or where it may be going. For example, a gait indicating that a lion is moving quickly could mean that it intends to link up with other members of the group, or it may have heard or detected a territorial rival. A slow-moving predator may be on the lookout for prey, or even in the process of stalking its prey.

Other creatures
Birds and other animals can help a tracker to stay on the trail or give an idea of general activity in the area. For example, tracks of zebra running in a certain direction may indicate the presence of hunting lions. Impala grazing calmly in a clearing could mean that the lions have already passed. Bird alarm calls are clear indicators of predators, particularly leopards. For example, white-crested helmetshrikes make a faint clicking sound when they see a leopard. Some birds give different alarm calls for different predators, such as the grey go-away bird, which produces a shorter, high-pitched call for an owl, and a longer, more drawn-out call for a leopard.

Individuals
Knowing the 'personalities' of individuals and their likely response to being approached on foot is also of benefit to a tracker, especially from a safety perspective. Bear in mind that the bush is fraught with potentially dangerous situations, although experienced trackers have surprisingly few dangerous encounters with animals. For six years, on a daily basis, seasoned tracker Karel Benadie followed trails of black rhinos – a particularly temperamental species to encounter on foot – without having any life-threatening experiences. Acute awareness is the key to safety.

PRACTICAL TRACKING

Looking for evidence

It's important to take in the whole scene. Novice trackers tend to focus on the ground in the hope of *seeing* tracks. However, this significantly reduces both their field of vision and their awareness, and can lead to uncomfortably close brushes with potentially dangerous animals. As soon as you lift your eyes and broaden your field of vision, it becomes possible to 'read' the terrain. It is surprising how many disturbances on the ground, including tracks, droppings and feeding signs, can be seen from a distance of up to 10 metres. Fresh leopard droppings in the middle of a natural game path are easily seen at a distance, instantly confirming that one is on this animal's trail, and even making it possible to predict where the animal may have gone next.

Novice trackers tend to get frustrated when they cannot see tracks. They walk faster and faster, hoping to cover as much ground as possible in order to spot at least some signs. This only increases the chance of missing important evidence.

In such a situation, it is best to stop, take a deep breath and return to the place where the last confirmed track was seen. From this point, you can reflect on where the animal is likely to have come from, what it was doing, in which direction it may have gone and along which path. Spend time investigating whether there could be a partial or obscured track on the ground. If the ground is too hard to show tracks, then move on to softer, more impressionable substrate up ahead.

Another option is to walk slowly in a series of arcs, looking for evidence. Be aware, however, that moving too slowly could mean that you never actually catch up with the animal that you are following.

The idea is to maintain a steady pace, but be guided by the terrain and substrate. Open country with soft sand means that you can move more quickly, while tracking in a riverine thicket where tracks and signs are not so obvious will require that you move more slowly. Novice trackers should begin by tracking slowly; with experience, they will develop a pace that suits their particular tracking style.

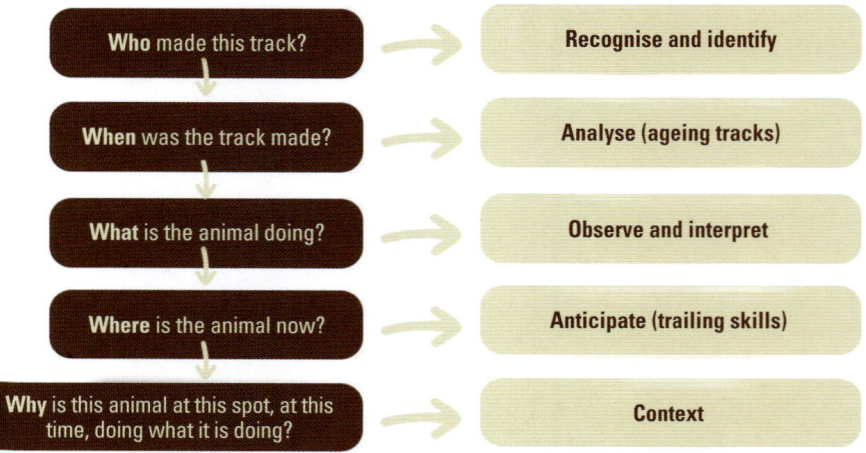

The art of tracking may be summarised with five overarching questions.

Reading tracks and signs

Animal tracks and signs are the basic building blocks of tracking, akin to the alphabet of a language that a tracker must learn before being able to read and comprehend the signs that animals leave.

Tracks and signs encompass all evidence of the presence of animals in a particular area. Among these are visible animal tracks (spoor), signs of feeding, feathers, bones, hairs, urine, territorial marking signs, pastings, droppings, hooves, horns and skeletons, as well as scents and calls – these are all essential investigative clues for a tracker; they function as clues to help construct each animal's narrative. Bird alarm calls are inextricably linked to predator movements too and are vital to a tracker's knowledge base.

Size, shape and gait

Every single track is unique: track sizes and shapes vary according to sex, age, physical condition and most importantly, the substrate (soil). No two individuals of the same species leave the same footprint. Differing gaits, such as when an animal accelerates, trots, bounds, runs, skids and turns, also create many track variations, which will be explored later on in this chapter. Aged animals, or those with injuries, regularly create tracks that are atypical. Expert trackers usually notice these subtle differences – and it is dynamics such as these that make tracking a challenging yet exciting skill to learn.

Substrates

Certain substrates, such as a thin layer of soft silt, can provide a near-perfect track impression. However, other substrates such as gravel or loose sand can obscure the process. In fact, obscure tracks are more common in the field, and a deductive process is often required to interpret the clues. It helps a tracker to disqualify animals that could not have caused the particular track or sign – this significantly reduces the list of potential 'suspects'.

Seldom does one find a clear track in the bush. Obscurities are the norm. Substrates have a great impact on the track impression – soft sand versus stony ground gives rise to very different impressions. Below are four variations of a lion track on different substrates

Hard granitic soil

Soft sand

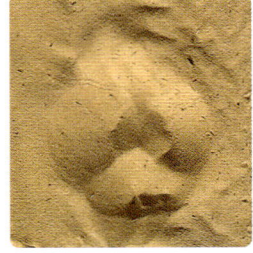

Wet sodic soil

Soft alluvial soil

The type of substrate has a profound impact on track appearance.

TRACK IDENTIFICATION KEY

When you encounter a track, you can narrow the search options by considering the following questions:

Is it an insect, bird, reptile, amphibian or mammal track?
- Be sure you make the distinction.

Which way is the track facing?
- Spend time determining which way the animal was headed.

What is the true length of the track?
- Carefully measure from the tips of the claws/toes/hooves to the very posterior (back) edge of the main pad.
- Is soil or sand making the track look bigger or smaller than it really is?
- Some species have a proximal pad behind the main pad, e.g. mongooses; if this pad shows in the track, make sure you find this and include it in your measurement.

If it's a hoof track:
- What is the shape of the hooves?
- Is it an even- or odd-toed ungulate?
- Are the cloven hooves situated tightly together, or are they splayed apart?
- Are the hoof edges straight, concave or convex?
- Where is the widest point of the hoof?

Does it have toes?
- How many toes?
- Are the toes situated tightly together, or are they splayed?
- What is their shape and size?
- Are the toes arranged symmetrically or not?

Does it have claws?
- How long are the claws?
- How many claws can you see?

Does it have a main pad?
- What is the shape of the main pad, and is it symmetrical or asymmetrical?
- Does the main pad look segmented?
- Does the main pad have two or three lobes on the posterior edge?

Where in the landscape is this animal?
- Are you near water, in a clearing, in a riverbed, in a woodland, on a rocky outcrop? The answer will help eliminate certain species that do not occur in that particular area.

What is the animal's behaviour?
- Is it walking, trotting, bounding or galloping?
- Is it in a group or solitary?
- Is it marking territory, digging, stalking, sleeping or feeding?
- What is it feeding on?
- Did it move during the day or night?
- How fresh is this track?
- Did any other species cross the track?

Are there droppings?
- What is the overall shape of the droppings: are they pellet-shaped, long and cylindrical or large balls?
- What is the detail of the shape: is it pointed on one side or round on both sides?
- What is the density – how easily does it break apart?
- What size are the droppings?
- What colour are the droppings?
- What do they consist of – grass, twigs, vegetable matter, insect fragments, meat, bone or skin?
- Where are the droppings found – near water, in thick cover, in an open area, on top of a small bush?

■ READING TRACKS AND SIGNS

Deduction and logic
Successful track identification is a deductive process where the tracker uses all the rules to reach a logical conclusion.

For example: hyaena tracks show claw marks whereas lion tracks do not, as shown in the photos below, with the hyaena track on the left and a lion print on the right.

Hyaena track   **Lion track**
Claw mark

Track identification is a deductive process.

Recording track data
Professional trackers must demonstrate a high level of observer reliability when collecting track-based data in the field for scientific research. Various methods for recording an animal's track include photography, illustration and measuring footprints.

Knowing the individual features of a track is crucial to accurate measuring. Below are two common measurements. Gauging the length and width of an individual toe, cloven hoof or main pad is helpful for differentiating between sexes and individuals within a species.

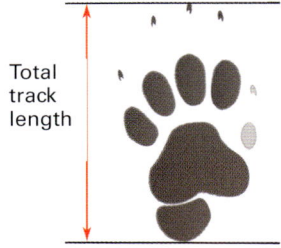

Total track length

Total track width

Determining track ages
Ageing tracks is an imperfect science with many variables at play. It is beneficial to keep recent weather conditions in mind when analysing a track's age, therefore trackers are advised to observe and record daily climatic conditions and seasonal variations.

Factors to consider when interpreting a track's age:

- **Time of day** Tracks age slower at night when the air is still and the relative humidity is higher. Conversely, tracks age faster during the day when the temperature is higher and wind is more prevalent.
- **Heat** Tracks lose moisture quicker in hot, dry conditions, and deteriorate quicker without moisture. Therefore, the rate of track ageing changes considerably at noon and early afternoon. Take note of these changes throughout the year.
- **Humidity** Tracks age slower (remain fresher) in humid conditions when the moisture content in the air is high. The slower the moisture loss from the substrate, the longer the track is preserved.
- **Wind** Air currents cause tracks to lose their definition and colour. The drying, eroding effect of wind causes track edges to become brittle.
- **Rain** Wet weather quickly reduces the clarity and definition of a track, particularly in sandy soils.
- **Type of substrate** Tracks age faster in soft, loose, dry sand than in wet, moist substrate. Damp clay can be very misleading as it preserves track definition for longer.
- **Animal behaviour** Everyday, familiar wildlife activities can give trackers insight into track age. For example: in summer animals will seek out a shady refuge in the midday heat. Their resting place can provide clues as to where

READING TRACKS AND SIGNS

the shade was, and therefore reveal the approximate time they were in that place. The same is true for animals seeking warmth in winter.

- **Other animals** Different tracks may help to age a track. For example: when a nocturnal animal (such as a genet) leaves tracks on top of those of a diurnal animal (such as a rhino), this may mean that the rhino walked that night, or earlier.

Genet tracks over rhino footprint

CASE STUDY: AGEING BOOT TRACKS

These six photographs were taken in Kruger National Park in July, over two days, every five hours, during the day. Generally, weather conditions in Kruger are stable and cool in July, with relatively high humidity.

WEATHER CONDITIONS
- **Average humidity:** 65%
- **Daytime temperature:** 26° C
- **Average windspeed:** 4.7km/h
- **Rainfall:** 0mm

GENERAL NOTES
- Tracks age quickly in early October when the humidity is low (<55%) and the temperature is high (>30° C), assuming no inclement weather.
- Tracks also age quickly from late August to early September in Kruger, as traditionally this is the windy period of the year, combined with rising temperatures.
- Tracks age slowest in April when humidity is still high (>70%) and the temperature is relatively cool (±26° C), assuming no inclement weather. High humidity and moderately low temperatures cause tracks to age slowest.

TRACKER'S FIELD NOTES
- At 65%, the average humidity was higher than the average for July in Skukuza (58%).
- The boot track's edges become less defined and start to crumble over time.
- The first notable period of ageing takes place five to 10 hours after the track was made (between 12:00 and 17:00 on Day 1, in photo 3).

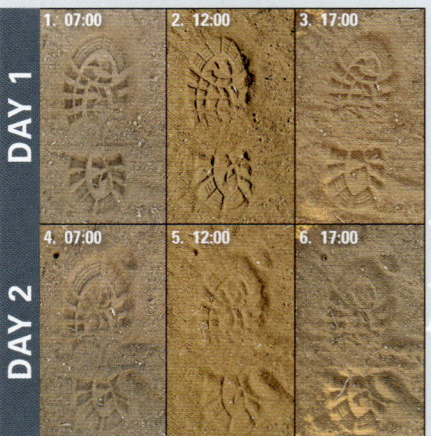

Photos taken in midwinter (July). Noting environmental conditions is key to accurate ageing of tracks.

- The second notable period of ageing takes place overnight: a scrub hare has moved partially over the boot track (photo 4), most probably causing dust to settle on top the boot track.
- Slightly cloudy weather on Day 2 (photo 5, 12:00) significantly reduces the contrast and shadow of the track.
- Late afternoon (photo 6, 17:00) produced the worst track definition, when compared with 07:00 and 12:00 on the same day.
- After 24 hours, the rate of track ageing was surprisingly slow, possibly due to higher humidity.

READING TRACKS AND SIGNS

Animal gaits

An animal's gait describes both the manner of locomotion and the pattern of footsteps at various speeds. Most animals use a variety of gaits, depending on required speed, the need to manoeuvre, the type of terrain and the energy usage preferences of the species. Other factors that influence gait are anatomy, age, and energy and health levels. Each specific gait has an optimum speed at which the energy consumed per metre is less than the cost of changing the gait. For example, a fast walk eventually becomes less energy efficient and more tiring than a slow trot, hence the animal will make a change in gait.

Gaits help trackers to understand an animal's speed and type of movement, and therefore to infer its possible behaviour. For example, it is possible to determine that a lioness is intent on linking up with the rest of the pride, from her sudden change in direction and trotting gait.

In some cases, even if the track is obscure, evidence of an animal's gait may be a strong clue to its identity. For example, a scrub hare has a distinctive bounding gait.

Essential terminology associated with animal gaits

Although most gaits have specific names and descriptions, it is sometimes difficult to differentiate them while tracking. The gaits listed below have been simplified to those that are relevant to tracking.

- **Stride** is the cycle of locomotion by the same foot, measured from a position on a track to the same position on the next track made by that foot. Stride length increases with speed.
- **Straddle** is the distance between the footfall of left and right feet, measured between the outside extremities of the tracks. An imaginary line midway between the straddle extremities is known as the **straddle centre**. Straddle size narrows as speed increases.
- **Register** (**partial** or **direct**) refers to when the hind foot is placed directly or partially on top of the track made by the front foot, during locomotion.
- **Understep** refers to when the hind foot registers directly behind the front foot.
- **Overstep** occurs when the hind foot registers directly in front (ahead) of the front foot.

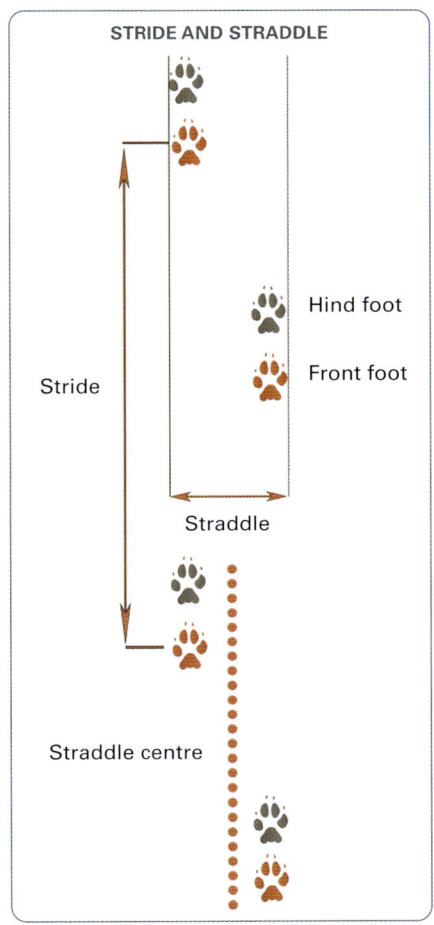

STRIDE AND STRADDLE

Stride

Hind foot
Front foot

Straddle

Straddle centre

READING TRACKS AND SIGNS

Walking

When walking, animals move each foot independently of the others. For a moment, two feet may become airborne simultaneously – the instant the animal picks up its front foot and the hind foot lands. The hind foot may register either behind (**understep**), directly on top of (**direct register**), or ahead of the front foot (**overstep**). Where the hind foot lands in relation to the front foot depends on three factors: body length, leg length and speed. Generally, the hind foot lands progressively further forward with speed.

Key characteristics
- Stride is short.
- Straddle is wide.
- Hind foot registers either behind, on top of, or in front of the front foot.

WILD DOG WALKING

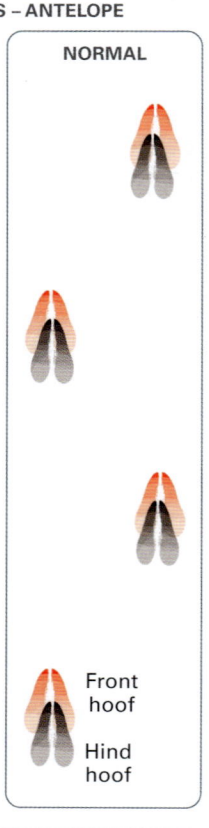
WALKING GAITS – ANTELOPE
SLOW / NORMAL
Front hoof / Hind hoof

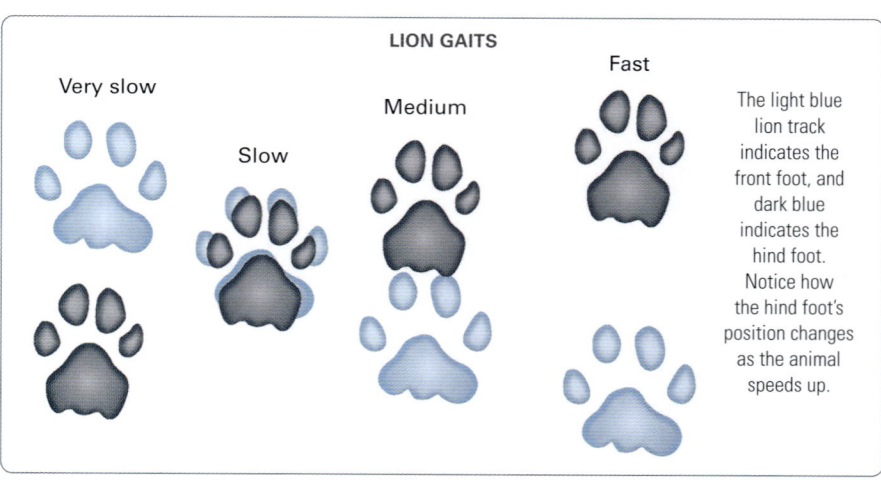
LION GAITS
Very slow, Slow, Medium, Fast

The light blue lion track indicates the front foot, and dark blue indicates the hind foot. Notice how the hind foot's position changes as the animal speeds up.

READING TRACKS AND SIGNS

Trotting

As soon as the energy cost of a fast walk becomes inefficient, animals break into a trot. The effort of this gait is evenly distributed over all four legs, so trotting is well suited to travelling over uneven terrain for long distances. While trotting, diagonally opposite front and hind legs move simultaneously, creating a repeating pattern of paired footprints. The animal is briefly airborne in the moment just before one set of diagonally opposing feet lands and the other set pushes off. As the animal starts to speed up, so the stride length increases proportionally. Speeding up causes the animal's weight to become increasingly transferred to the front of the foot, and its toes or cloven hooves begin to splay more. This results in less defined track impressions, as well as more displaced soil or sand (scuffing). Predators' claw marks may become exaggerated when they move faster. The further the hind foot lands ahead of the front foot, the faster the animal is trotting. A slower trot is depicted by a direct register and a shorter stride.

Key characteristics
- Stride is longer than in walking.
- Straddle is narrower than in walking.
- Hind and front foot pairs register close to each other.
- Two-beat rhythm: each set of four footfalls sounds like two beats as front and hind pairs land simultaneously.

WILD DOG TROTTING

A drawback with trotting is that, at a certain speed, the hind leg collides with the front foot on the same side. To counter this, animals make use of two variations of trotting, the **side-trot** and the **straddle-trot**. Species such as jackals, wild dogs, domestic dogs and foxes make regular use of these trotting variations.

1 Side-trotting

The trotting animal turns its body at a slight angle to the direction of travel. The trail produced by a side-trot shows both front feet registering on one side of the straddle, and the two hind feet landing on the other. Trotting at an angle prevents collision between the hind and front feet, which would happen when these animals reach a certain speed.

TROTTING GAITS – JACKAL

TROT	SIDE-TROT

Front foot / Hind foot	Front foot / Hind foot

23

READING TRACKS AND SIGNS

Key characteristics
- Stride is longer than in walking.
- Straddle is narrower than in walking.
- Hind feet register ahead of front feet.
- Hind feet register on one side of the straddle, and front feet on the other.

2 Straddle-trotting

Another way to avoid the hind foot colliding with the front is to bring the hind foot out wider with each step, to avoid it colliding with the front foot.

Loping

Loping is an energy-efficient, natural gait in which the animal is momentarily airborne.

There are two variations on the lope; in this gait, the animal places its feet in either of the following sequences:

- **Rotary lope:** front left, front right, hind right, then **hind left**; the feet register in a clockwise motion around the body.
- **Transverse lope:** front left, front right, hind left, then **hind right**; the lope usually gives rise to a three-beat rhythm because the two feet (front and hind) in the middle of the sequence land simultaneously.

TROTTING GAITS CONT. – JACKAL

STRADDLE-TROT

LOPING GAITS – ANTELOPE

■ READING TRACKS AND SIGNS

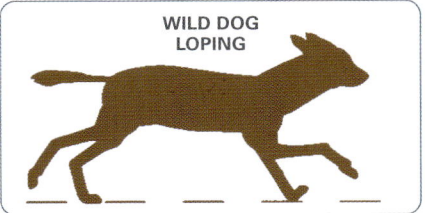

Depending on the speed of the lope, the hind foot will land behind (slower speed) or register on top of or next to the front foot (faster speed). Otters typically lope.

Key characteristics
- Stride is longer than in trotting.
- Straddle is narrower than in trotting.
- Footfalls make a three-beat rhythm.
- Track pattern: **front**, hind and front, **hind**.
- One hind foot always registers alongside (partial register) or directly on top of a front foot.
- In each four-track sequence, one pair of front and hind are positioned closely together.

Galloping – transverse (or normal)

Galloping is the fastest and most tiring form of locomotion. With each stride, the animal completely loses touch with the ground. The cadence (frequency of steps per minute) of the legs is very high and can easily be increased if necessary. The galloping stride length is significantly increased from that of the trotting or loping gaits.

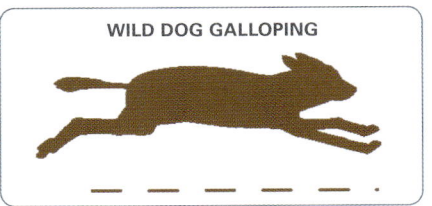

Otter loping gait

READING TRACKS AND SIGNS

There are two variations on the gallop:
- **Transverse gallop** (the most commonly seen gallop): front left, front right, hind left, then hind right. Both front and hind feet tracks register at the same angle, across the straddle centre.
- **Rotary gallop**: front left, front right, hind right, then hind left, in a circular fashion around the body. The two front feet register at a different angle (diagonally) to the hind feet, across the straddle.

The distance between each four-track sequence in a series grows with speed, and four-track sequences are repeated with greater frequency the faster the animal gallops. When galloping at full pace, all the animal's footprints register in one line along the straddle centre.

Key characteristics
- Stride is very long.
- Straddle is very narrow.
- Footfalls make a four-beat rhythm.
- Track pattern: hind feet register beyond front feet, i.e. front, front, hind, hind.
- Both hind feet register beyond both front feet.
- Cadence (number of steps per minute) is high.

Bounding

The track diagrams of bounding tree squirrel and hare show how each animal's explosive hind legs propel it upwards and forwards off the ground. A bounding animal lands on its two front legs, followed thereafter by the hind legs, which come over and around, striking the ground ahead of and on either side of the front feet. Animals such as hares, squirrels and mongooses frequently make use of the bounding gait.

Squirrels tend to place their front feet very close together, sometimes partially on top of each other. Mongooses tend to place their front feet one beyond the other (see diagram on p. 27).

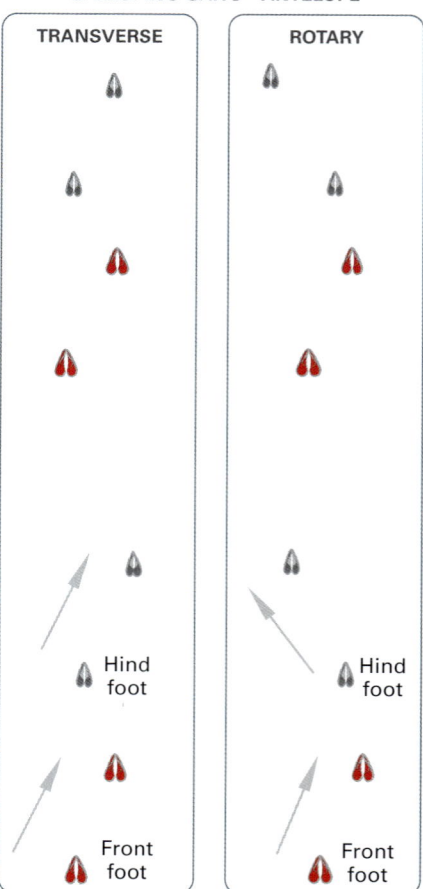

GALLOPING GAITS – ANTELOPE

Hare bounding

Tarry Myers

■ READING TRACKS AND SIGNS

Key characteristics
- Track pattern reveals repeated four-track sequences in a T- or Y-shape.
- Front feet (red in diagram) register one in front of the other and hind feet (grey) parallel ahead of front feet.
- Note the position of the front feet.

BOUNDING – MONGOOSE

Hind feet

Front feet

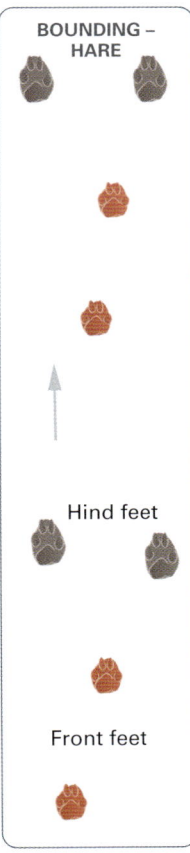

BOUNDING – HARE

Hind feet

Front feet

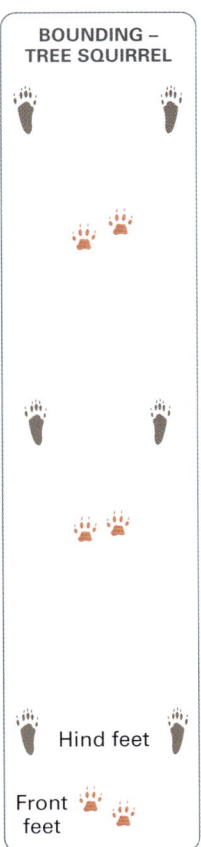

BOUNDING – TREE SQUIRREL

Hind feet

Front feet

Ground squirrel bounding

READING TRACKS AND SIGNS

Hopping
A hopping animal picks up its front feet and propels itself forward with its hind feet, landing first on the front feet and then the hind. The hind feet register behind the front. Some rodent species hop.

Key characteristics
- Repeated four-track sequences
- Hind feet land behind the front feet.
- Box shape

Bipedal hopping
Bipedal hopping uses only two legs for locomotion. The bipedal hopping gait is produced by two energetically explosive hind legs propelling the animal forward. Tracks show both hind feet registering together (typically in parallel). The distance between sets of tracks depends on the speed at which the animal is moving. Animals such as springhares and bushbabies hop, as well as many bird species.

Pronking/stotting
In Afrikaans, to 'pronk' means to show off or flaunt. This bouncing gait occurs when an animal pushes off the ground and lands with all four feet simultaneously. It is seen regularly with springbok and impala; maximum height is the desired result. Although the purpose of pronking has not been identified, springbok have been observed pronking during the first seasonal rains and in the presence of predators. The reasons for this behaviour could be excitement, agitation, or an attempt to demonstrate physical prowess to rivals within the herd or to predators.

HOPPING AND PRONKING GAITS

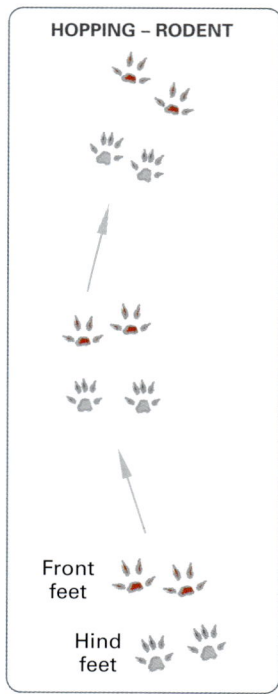

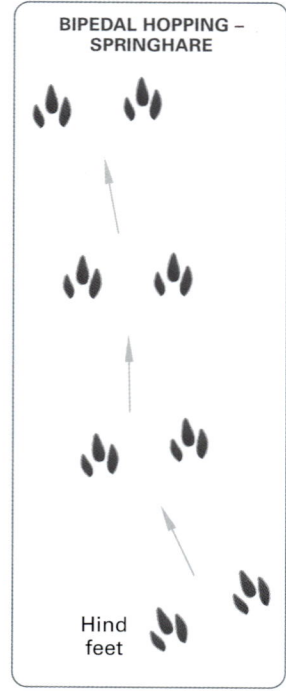

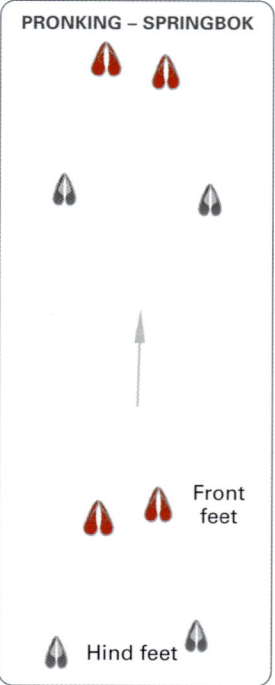

■ READING TRACKS AND SIGNS

Droppings (scat)

Droppings (or scat) provide trackers with information about an animal's diet. Waste matter can help identify a species, and it provides useful information about an animal's relationship with the environment. Trackers are enabled to identify a predator's preferred prey species by examining the contents of droppings.

Droppings can vary considerably in size, texture, colour and shape; an animal's age, health and seasonal diet (availability of food) can also have a profound effect on the appearance of its droppings. Trackers must consider the following when examining scat and piecing evidence together: colour, shape, diameter (width), texture, contents, odour, location, tracks.

An animal's scat can easily have more than one shape, making interpretation difficult. The information tabulated here functions as a guide; it is not prescriptive.

COMMON SCAT SHAPES AND FORMS

Tubes and cylinders are produced in the lower gut, mainly produced by animals feeding on a diet of fruit and fibre; also produced by meat eaters.

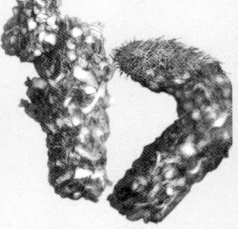
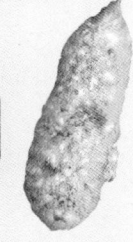

Porcupine   Genet   Cape clawless otter   Baboon

Twisted scat appears curled and contorted – generally caused by skin and hair in the droppings.

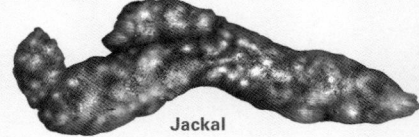

Jackal

U-shaped scat is bent backwards on itself, as the name suggests, caused by long hairs and skin.

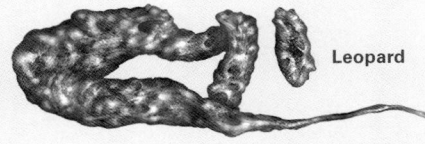

Leopard

Segmented scat is partitioned, either partially or completely.

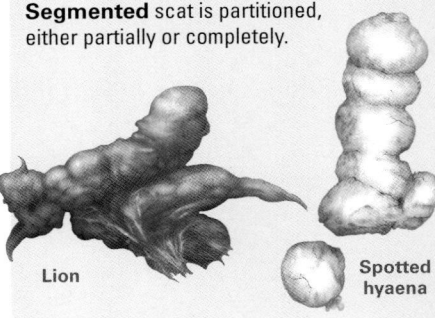

Lion   Spotted hyaena

Blobs and squirts are produced in the caecum (lower intestine); this form is commonly seen in grass eaters and some carnivores, where quantities of blood are consumed.

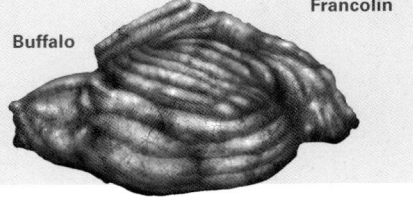

Francolin

Buffalo

READING TRACKS AND SIGNS

COMMON SCAT SHAPES AND FORMS

Tapered scat reduces in thickness towards one or both ends.

White-tailed mongoose

Blunt ends means 'rounded' towards both ends – the opposite of tapered.

Vervet monkey

Pellets are produced in the lower gut of animals that feed predominantly on grass and fine vegetation.

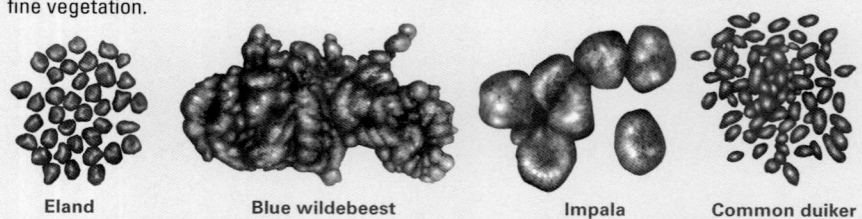

Eland　　Blue wildebeest　　Impala　　Common duiker

Other shapes

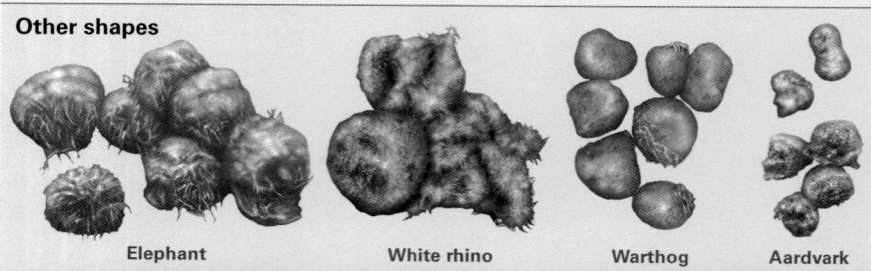

Elephant　　White rhino　　Warthog　　Aardvark

All dropping images by Jonathan Geall

TYPICAL SCAT SHAPES

	Pellets	Tubes & cylinders	Twisted	Segmented	Blunt ends	Tapered	U-shaped	Blobs & squirts
Cats (felids)		✓		✓	✓	Occasionally	Occasionally	Occasionally
Dogs (canids)		✓	✓		Occasionally	✓		Occasionally
Hyaena		✓		✓	✓			Occasionally
Antelope (ungulates)	✓							
Hares	✓					✓		
Primates		✓						✓
Mongoose		✓						
Squirrel	✓					Occasionally		
Porcupine		✓				Occasionally		
Honey badger		✓		Occasionally				
Birds								✓
Reptiles		✓						✓

Track morphology

Track morphology refers to the form, shape or structure of animal footprints and how to recognise and 'read' the various features of a track. The appearance of a track impression is directly influenced by the structure and shape of the animal's foot, the animal's movement (gait), and the type of substrate on which the track is produced.

Form follows function

The form or shape of an animal's body is directly linked to its function and purpose. Animals' feet and legs have evolved to fulfil a specific function in a particular environmental niche. That function allows the animal to thrive, hence the evolution of form represents a race for energetic efficiency, to survive.

A zebra's single and light, reinforced hoof allows it to gallop – at speed – away from predators, over hard and uneven terrain.

A lion's soft-padded foot enables it to tread lightly and quietly when stalking its prey, while its strong flexible paws have sharp, hooked claws for gripping and holding its prey.

TRACK MORPHOLOGY

STEM TETRAPODS AND THE ORIGIN OF FIVE DIGITS

Some of the earliest tracks in the fossil record help today's trackers understand the extent to which animal feet have evolved over millennia.

The primitive vertebrate called a stem tetrapod (or limbed fish) is considered to be a common ancestor of all later four-legged vertebrates including mammals, birds, reptiles and amphibians. All known remains of these four-limbed fish have been dated towards the end of the Devonian Period (380–360 million years ago). Devonian stem tetrapods had more toes than their descendants, with known species having six, seven or eight toes per foot. During the Carboniferous Period (359–300 mya) all tetrapods had five toes on each of their front and hind feet. This foot morphology coincided with these animals becoming more terrestrial, as they ventured out of the water and onto land, eventually evolving into land-dwelling animals.

Today, all vertebrates are considered to have five digits, even though some digits may be absent, reduced, redundant, or have changed position. Even bats and whales have bony remnants of five digits. A horse has a single toe, but in its early embryonic stages, its limb buds have five little 'condensations', showing an evolutionary link to other tetrapods. Scientists do not know the reason for five digits and no environmental pressure has been identified that favours five digits on four-legged animals.

Tutusius umlambo is a species of Devonian tetrapod found near Makhanda (Grahamstown), South Africa, by the palaeontologist Rob Gess, who formally described it in 2018. The genus was named in honour of the late Archbishop Desmond Tutu.

Previously all Devonian tetrapods were found in areas that had been tropical, leading to the belief that these were exclusively tropical animals. But South Africa was situated in the Antarctic Circle during the Devonian Period, providing sufficient evidence to overturn earlier beliefs about the distribution of these animals.

About 385 million years ago, a stem tetrapod left tracks on Valentia Island, one of Ireland's most westerly points. This fossilised trail gives insight into how animals' feet have evolved.

Two tetrapod fossils found in South Africa in 2018: Umzantsia amazana *(left) and* Tutusius umlambo *(right). Both resembled a reptile–fish hybrid, with crocodile-like head and legs, and fishy fin-like tail.*

■ TRACK MORPHOLOGY

Foot postures

Three types of foot posture are recognised in mammals: plantigrade, digitigrade and unguligrade.

Each mammal species has a particular foot posture, which has an impact on the track it leaves. These foot postures play a crucial role in determining the weight distribution, locomotion style and overall morphology of the feet, ultimately influencing the distinctive characteristics observed in animal tracks.

THREE FOOT POSTURES

Key

humerus (arm bone)
radius–ulna (forearm bones)
carpus (wrist)

metacarpus (palm bones, cannon, splints)
phalanges (toes, finger bones, pasterns, coffin bones)

Plantigrade: the most primitive of all three postures e.g. human, baboon, porcupine Walks with toes, carpals and tarsals flat on the ground **Benefits:** strong stance, climbing, gripping	**Front leg of baboon** 	**Baboon tracks**   Front left Hind left The entire surface of the foot makes contact with the ground during locomotion. The animal places the heel down first, then rolls forward along the length of the foot and pushes off with its toes. This produces a track that reveals the full extent of the heel, sole and toes.
Digitigrade: most terrestrial members of order Carnivora e.g. dog, cat Walks on its toes with carpals and tarsals (wrist and heel) raised **Benefits:** stealthy movement, explosive running and jumping	**Front leg of jackal** 	**Jackal tracks**   Front left Hind left The phalanges (digits, toes and fingers) touch the ground, while the ankle (tarsal bones) and wrist (carpal bones) are raised and protected by the carpal and tarsal pads (commonly known as main pad).
Unguligrade: the most advanced of all three postures e.g. zebra, horse, antelope Walks on its toenails (hooves) **Benefits:** greater potential for speed and stride length; energetically efficient	**Front leg of zebra**	**Burchell's zebra tracks** Front left Hind left Only the hoof meets the ground. The animal walks on the very tips of its toes (like a balancing ballerina), which are protected by hooves (effectively walking on its toenails). The hooved tracks cut deep into the soil due to their relative weight, creating conspicuous impressions on the ground.

TRACK MORPHOLOGY

Feet, form and function

The various components of a track are conventionally referred to by the same terms as the corresponding parts of the animal's foot. For the purposes of this book, animal tracks have been divided into four broad categories:
- paws with soft pads
- hard hooves
- bird feet
- other animals' feet, including insects.

Soft-padded feet of a lion

TELLING LEFT FROM RIGHT FEET

It is easy to detemine which tracks have been made by left and right feet if a trail of footprints is visible. The method we use applies to both soft-footed and hooved animals.

1. Place one of your hands at the base of the track.
2. The aim is to ensure that your third finger (the longest on your hand, technically digit number 3) corresponds with the longest toe or hoof in the track (also digit number 3).

Telling left from right

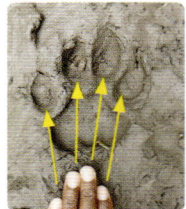 

Left: Track made by left foot of a lion
Right: Track made by left hoof of a wildebeest, shown with the index and middle finger of the left hand

3. Match your finger number 3 with the track's toe number 3. Change hands if needed to ensure the longest digits match up. Your left hand means it's a left paw or hoof print.

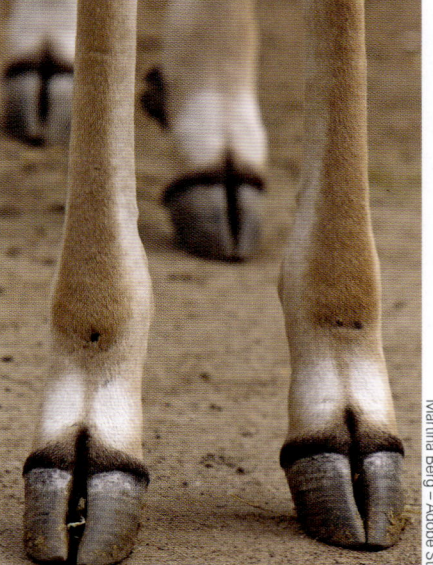

Cloven hooves of a kudu

Raven feet

34

■ TRACK MORPHOLOGY

Paws with soft pads

All carnivores and rodents have paws with soft pads, also known as digitigrade or plantigrade. Their feet can be discussed in terms of the following four components:

1 The **main pad** (the large pad behind the toes in, for example, dog and cat tracks) is known as the **metacarpal** pad in front tracks and the **metatarsal** pad in hind tracks. Features such as the number of lobes on the distal (leading edge) and proximal (back edge) sides of this pad are important.

2 Toes (or **digital pads**) and their shape and position can help differentiate front from hind tracks. Toes are always numbered from the inside (corresponding to our big toe or thumb), which is toe number 1, to toe number 5 on the outside. In most animals that display only four toes, toe number 1 is absent – either because it is situated too high up (e.g. dewclaw or false hoof) to leave an impression under normal conditions, or because there isn't one – as in feline hind legs.

3 Claws are not consistent features: the young of some clawed animals may not show claws in their tracks at all, and animals like cats and genets whose claws don't typically mark may extrude their claws on slippery surfaces or when running.

4 Proximal pads lie behind the main pad (posterior edge). They are called carpal pads in front tracks and tarsal pads in hind tracks. Also sometimes referred to as 'wrist pads'.

All the feet of animals that fall into the 'paws with soft pads' group have at least some and sometimes all of these features. For instance, the porcupine shows all of these features, whereas wild dogs lack proximal pads, and the springhare may show just toes and claws, which are inseparable in their particular tracks.

PAWS WITH SOFT PADS

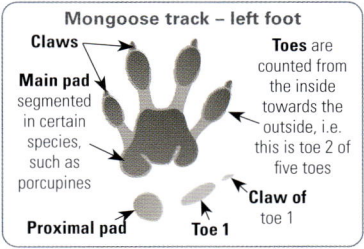

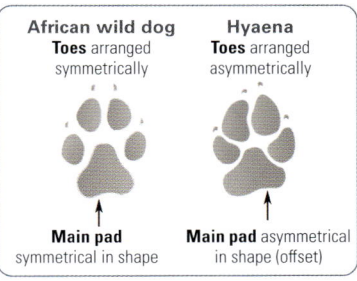

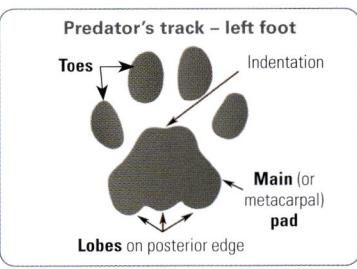

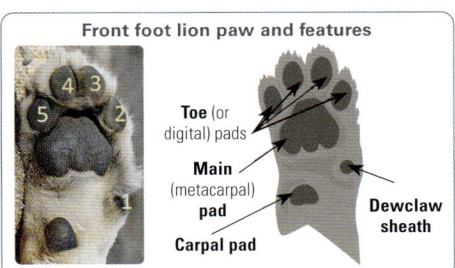

Note: Sometimes the pads of the front tracks are generically referred to as palmar pads and those of the hind tracks as plantar pads. This terminology is often used to refer to tracks of species where the proximal and main pads cannot easily be differentiated, such as monkey and baboon tracks.

TRACK MORPHOLOGY ■

CAT CLAW MECHANISM
By IAN THOMAS

A cat's claws are both useful and formidable. They are used to seize prey, provide grip when pouncing or climbing, and to gash an opponent. To be effective they need to be hooked and pointed. If the claws were continually in the protracted (extended) position then they would be exposed to scraping on rough ground. This wear and tear would dull the sharpness and reduce the hook. A mechanism allows a cat to keep its claws sheathed and retracted while in the relaxed state, which in turn maintains the claw's curve and sharpness when protracted.

It is crucial that the claws are stable when in the protracted position. This is partly determined by the overall strength of the paw, but also by how firmly it rests on the second toe bone of the paw when in the protracted position.

Cats have a dewclaw on the inside of, and slightly above, the front paws. This claw seldom touches the ground and so receives less wear and tear; it tends to be sharper and longer than the others.

The figures below show a simplified, lengthwise view through a cat's paw, illustrating the structure that allows a cat to retract the claws when relaxed and protract them when flexed.

Figure 1 shows a section through a relaxed, passive paw. The claw is retracted and sheathed, and rests to the side of the second toe bone. It is held in this position by two elastic ligaments (labelled in diagram). One of these ligaments can be seen in this view and a second ligament, in its extended position, is visible in Figure 2. There are slings (purple in diagram) that hold the tendons (labelled in diagram) in position. A muscle that attaches to a sling is shown in red-orange.

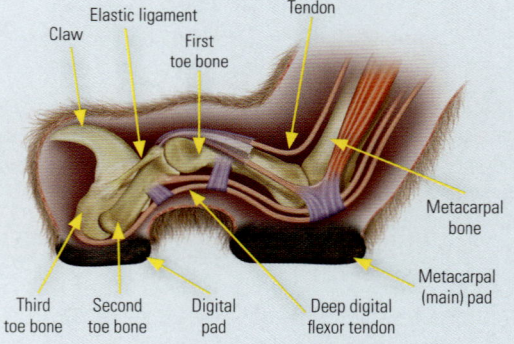

Figure 2 shows a section through a protracted or flexed paw. Muscles that attach to the two upper tendons (pale orange) have contracted, causing the bones in the paw to straighten, lengthen, broaden and stiffen. The contraction of the deep digital flexor tendon has rotated the third toe bone (onto which the claw is attached) forward and down – the claw no longer rests to the side of the second toe bone, but now sits firmly on a notch on the front of it.

Now the claw is out, unsheathed and ready to hook into something.

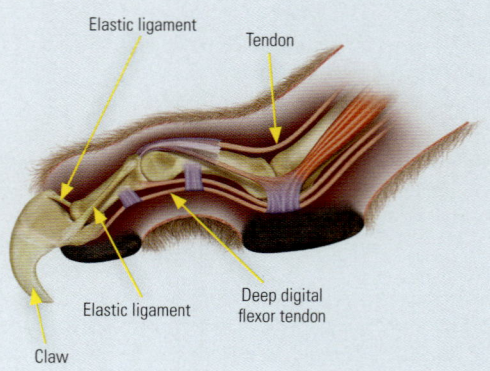

■ TRACK MORPHOLOGY

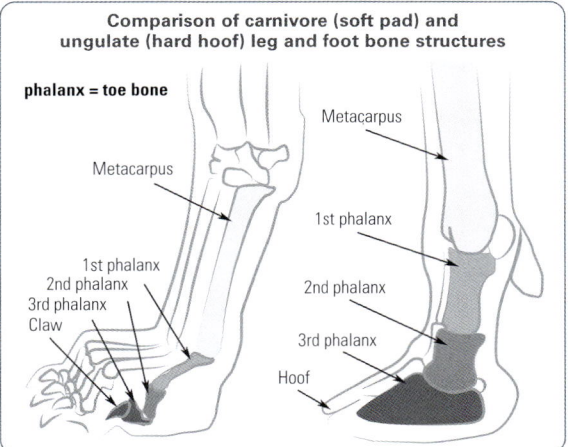

Comparison of carnivore (soft pad) and ungulate (hard hoof) leg and foot bone structures

phalanx = toe bone

HARD HOOVES

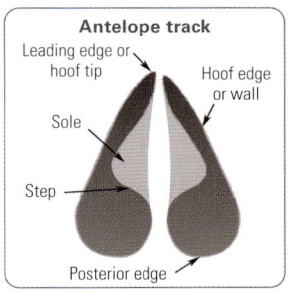

Antelope track

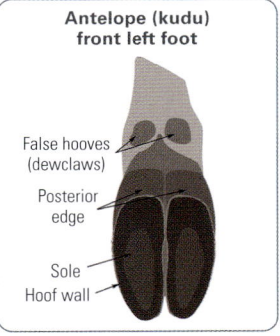

Antelope (kudu) front left foot

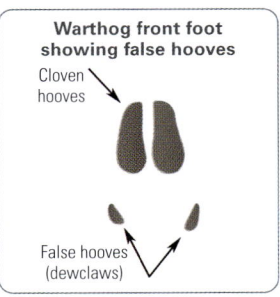

Warthog front foot showing false hooves

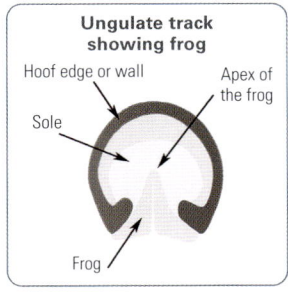

Ungulate track showing frog

Hard hooves

Hooves are modified claws, and hooved animals (or ungulates) are essentially walking on their toes and claws (unguligrade). The central area of an antelope hoof is called the sole. In antelope, it is the outer edge of the track – the 'hoof wall' or 'hoof edge' – that marks most prominently, as it is the hardest part. The sharper front portion terminates in the hoof tips; the back or 'posterior edge' slopes backward, and can make tracks that penetrate deeper into soft substrate appear much larger.

Antelope have two weight-bearing hooves, and two dewclaws (known as 'false hooves') situated higher up the leg. In some species these may mark in certain conditions, such as while the animal is running or in very soft substrates, whereas they almost never mark in other species and therefore their presence can be an important identification feature.

Antelope hoof

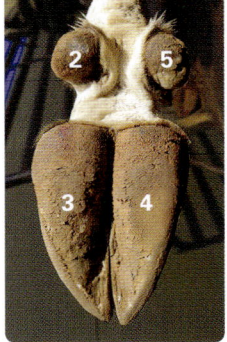

Note the false hooves on this gemsbok's foot.

Toe **1** is absent.

Toes **2** and **5** have migrated up the leg and effectively become redundant – seen here as **false hooves**.

The two **cloven hooves** represent toes **3** and **4**.

TRACK MORPHOLOGY

WHAT IS A 'STEP' IN A HOOVED TRACK?

In certain very clear substrates, the ridge between the sole and the hardened area of the posterior edge gives rise to a 'step', depicted by a light grey line or shading in the track drawings. The step runs transversely to the central ridge, delineating the proximal area of the hoof, which marks more deeply than the rest of the hoof. Examples of antelope that show a step are: steenbok, wildebeest, sable, red hartebeest, tsessebe and waterbuck.

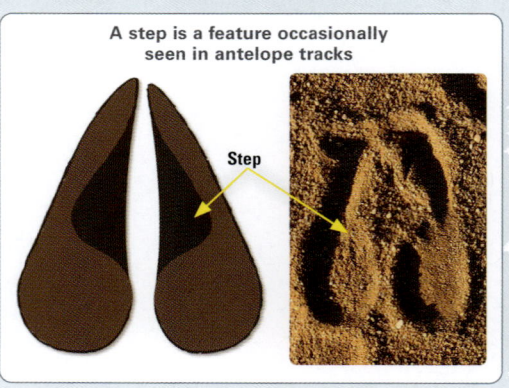

A step is a feature occasionally seen in antelope tracks

Some animals, such as rhinos and hippos, have hooved toes and a sole that's made up of soft cartilaginous tissue, which also makes contact with the ground. The triangular-shaped 'frog' in zebra and horse hooves extends from the posterior edge to a point (the apex) in the middle of the hoof, and acts as a shock absorber as the foot makes contact with the ground.

Birds' feet

The feet of birds have up to four toes and associated claws. Their toes are long and narrow, and not easily confused with any mammal tracks. Sometimes a central metatarsal pad may show. Birds' toes are made up of soft, scaly pads. Because birds are so lightweight, it is often the case that on hard substrates, only their claws leave an impression.

Other key identification features of bird feet are the angles at which individual toes are arranged, the gait (hopping, running or walking), the presence of webbing, and whether the bird drags its toes or walks pigeon-toed and so on.

Common bird foot structures

Dactyly is the term used to describe the arrangement of digits on hands and feet. The number and configuration of toes in bird tracks is important for recognising the differences between bird tracks so that a correct identification can be made. Knowing the dactyly of birds gives trackers insight in terms of a bird's behaviour and preferred habitat.

Numbering of birds' toes always begins with toe number 1, the hind toe, also called the hallux (technical term).

Male crested francolin left foot — Metatarsal spur

Speckled mousebird foot

Aeiden Swan

■ TRACK MORPHOLOGY

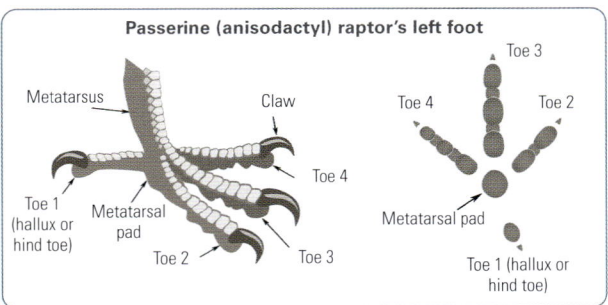

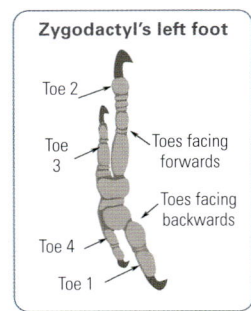

BIRD FOOT STRUCTURES SEEN IN THE FIELD

Anisodactyl Most perching birds are anisodactyl, with three toes reaching forwards and one backwards, e.g. starlings, doves, larks, crows, raptors.

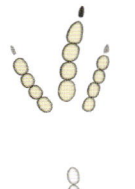

Red-winged starling

Syndactyl These birds have feet that show toes 3 and 4 (the middle and outer of the forward-facing toes) partially fused together, e.g. kingfishers, hornbills and bee-eaters.

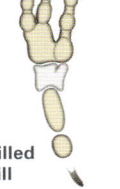

Yellow-billed hornbill

Didactyl The two-toed ostrich is the only didactyl in the world. The large inner toe is toe 3, and the smaller outer toe is toe 4.

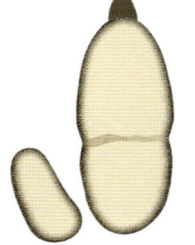

Ostrich

Tridactyl These birds have three toes; toe 1 (the hallux) is absent, e.g. ground birds such as bustards, korhaan, coursers, thick-knees and buttonquails.

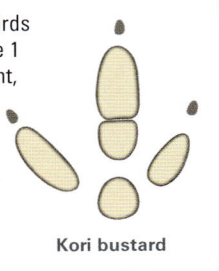

Kori bustard

Zygodactyl These are climbing birds with two toes facing forwards (toes 2 and 3) and two facing backwards (toes 1 and 4), e.g. owls, coucals, woodpeckers, parrots, lovebirds and cuckoos.

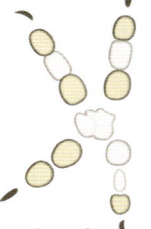

Spotted eagle-owl

Heterodactyl This foot structure is unique to the trogon family. It is similar to the zygodactyl: toes 1 and 2 face backwards, and 3 and 4 face forwards.

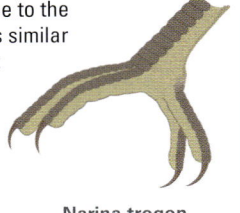

Narina trogon

TRACK MORPHOLOGY

BIRD FOOT STRUCTURES SEEN IN THE FIELD, CONTINUED...

Pamprodactyl This is an unusual foot structure where all four toes can rotate and face forwards, enabling the bird to hang upside down, e.g. mousebirds and some swifts.

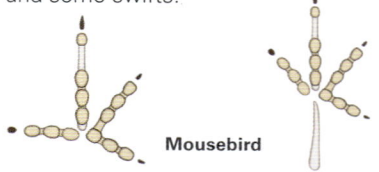

Mousebird

Palmate These birds have webbed toes, e.g. geese, ducks, gulls and penguins.

Semipalmate These birds have partially webbed feet, e.g. herons, crakes, sandpipers, plovers, pied avocet and hamerkop.

Totipalmate All four toes are connected by webbing, e.g. pelicans, darters and cormorants.

Lobate Each of the toes is independently webbed, e.g. coots, grebes and finfoots.

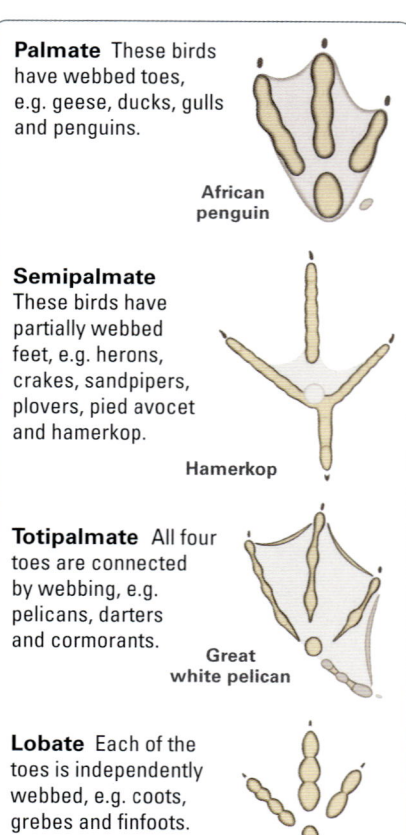

African penguin

Hamerkop

Great white pelican

Coot

The African jacana has extraordinarily long toes that assist the bird in navigating around its aquatic home.

Bird calls and tracks

Expert trackers are always listening to bird calls to help them understand the activity around them. For example, the shrill call of a starling from a position low in a bush may indicate that a snake is nearby, while a shrike may sound the alarm to signal the presence of a leopard in a thicket. Or oxpeckers may call from a group of buffalo. Knowing the activity in the surrounding bush is vital to walking safely in the wild.

Bird tracks can be helpful in determining the age of an animal's track. For example, a lion track on top of a fresh francolin trail would be an indication that the lion moved that same morning, as opposed to the previous evening.

CASE STUDY

A bush party goes tracking at dawn in winter. Their tracker finds a rhino track with a superimposed trail of a meandering dove. Their tracker knows that doves are not active at night or very early on cold mornings. This tells them that the rhino most likely was in that area in the hours of the previous night, afternoon or even earlier.

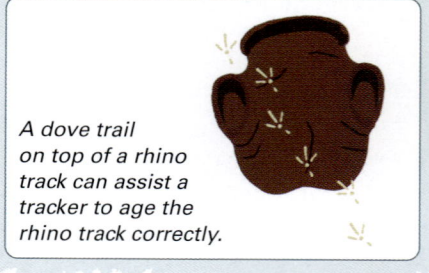

A dove trail on top of a rhino track can assist a tracker to age the rhino track correctly.

■ TRACK MORPHOLOGY

Tracks of other animals

Apart from tracks made by the three major groups described (paws with soft pads, hard hooves, and birds), trackers must also consider the tracks of reptiles and amphibians (they have toes with claws and associated foot pads and/or drag marks), as well as those of insects and other arthropods.

The terminology used to describe these animal tracks is less well developed, but as the individual tracks diminish in size and their features become less discernible (as for most insects), the pattern of the track becomes increasingly relevant.

INSECT'S LEG

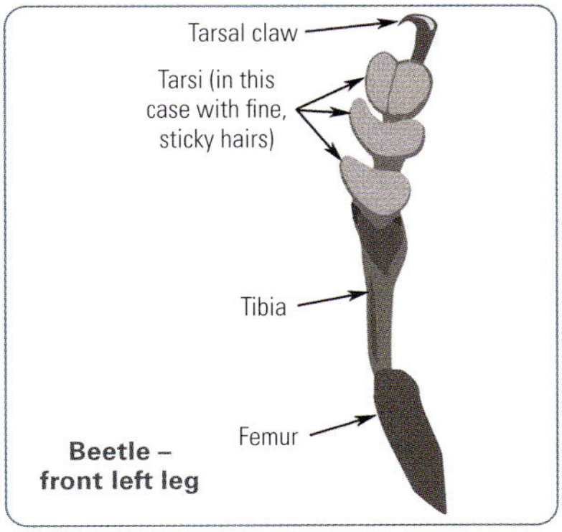

Tarsal claw
Tarsi (in this case with fine, sticky hairs)
Tibia
Femur

Beetle – front left leg

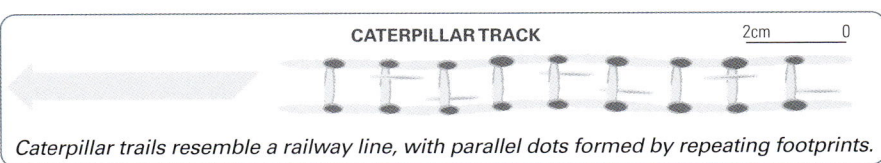

CATERPILLAR TRACK 2cm 0

Caterpillar trails resemble a railway line, with parallel dots formed by repeating footprints.

Péringuey's adder uses a sidewinding motion to move across a soft sand dune south of Swakopmund, Namibia.

About this book

The **Introduction to tracking** provides useful background information about the origins of tracking and matters concerning the tracking environment. The structure of various tracks and signs is discussed, with explanations of essential terminology and typical animal gaits. There is a useful list of key questions that enable users to identify tracks effectively.

In the **Animals' tracks and signs** section species that are easily confused have been grouped together in each chapter for quick reference. Thus, taxonomic order is not followed for all species. For instance, the striped polecat and most of the mongooses are both carnivores and small mammals, but they appear in the **Small mammals** chapter. Each account gives a brief description of the animal's preferred habitat and likely distribution, followed by information in point form under a series of headings:
- Habits
- Burrow or den
- Feeding and diet
- Droppings
- Territorial behaviour
- About the track/Track and other signs.

The track lengths provided in this book were measured in near-perfect conditions. However, several factors can influence the accuracy of track measurements, including variations in soil or substrate texture, the age of the tracks, and the animal's gait. It is essential to remember that track measurements should be understood in this context. Animals are not identical, so there is also size variance in each individual animal.

The information about behaviour includes material relevant to tracking.

For some of the larger animals, there is additional information about their gait, male versus female tracks and front versus hind tracks. For those species regularly trailed by trackers, such as lion, the description presents what one is likely to see and experience when following a trail; however, these accounts are not designed to teach

Pangolin

Springbok

■ ABOUT THIS BOOK

Tracker students conduct track surveys as part of their training.

one how to track and find an animal – that comes with practice in the field.

For most species, there is a **Can be confused with ...** box, detailing those animal tracks that are most similar to, and can most easily be mistaken for, the species that has left the tracks and signs under scrutiny. See the **Track comparisons** pages at the back of the book. These tables are also available on the Tracker Academy website; scan this QR code:

Each species account has track drawings and photographs of typical prints. The track drawing measurements may differ slightly from those described in the text, as a range of measurements is taken in the field. The drawings represent a near-perfect track – what one may see when an animal steps on a faultless substrate, which is hard underneath with a thin covering of soft, fine soil. Areas of a track that are shaded in light grey depict those features that are not commonly imprinted on a substrate, such as dewclaws, etc.

A **Glossary** at the back of the book explains the correct terminology and biological terms.

Tracker following a hyaena trail

MAMMALS ■ Carnivores

Lion
Panthera leo

Africa's largest and most charismatic carnivore – males can weigh up to 225kg. Lions have disappeared from about 95% of their original range and it is estimated that there are only around 20,000 wild lions remaining in Africa (2021). In the wild, males seldom live longer than 12 years, as injuries sustained from continual fighting with rival males reduce their longevity.

Lions typically inhabit grassland and woodland savanna, although they may be found in forested areas.

Habits
- Lions prey on medium-sized to large ungulates, with hunts co-ordinated and led by experienced females.
- Usually nocturnal, hunting by night and resting by day; sometimes up and about on cool days, particularly in winter.
- Gregarious, typically living in prides of one to six adult males and three to six related females with young. Pride sizes vary depending on availability of prey.
- Young nomadic males start to challenge resident pride males for dominance at four to seven years of age.
- Lions habitually roar just after sunset and at dawn. It is possible to differentiate between the male and female roar, although the difference is subtle.

Feeding and diet
- Feed on impala, warthog, wildebeest, zebra, buffalo and occasionally giraffe, hippo and young elephants. Prey such as porcupines is taken in desperation.
- Display much aggression when feeding at a kill. Adult males dominate the carcass while females compete with the cubs, which may starve in lean times.
- Hyaena clans may challenge lions for their kills and, if in superior number, are known to rob them successfully of the carcasses they have caught.
- The prey's greenish stomach contents, bone fragments, the odd hoof, clumps of hair and much flattened grass are indicative of a kill.

Lioness bringing down a young blue wildebeest calf

MAMMALS ■ Carnivores

Droppings
- Droppings are segmented, with blunt ends, 32–40mm in diameter. They vary from light to dark, depending on the amount of meat and/or bone and hair consumed.
- Dark (sometimes black) droppings, loose in consistency, are produced after a meal consisting of large amounts of flesh, blood and innards.
- Bone fragments, hooves and hair are commonly found in lion droppings.
- When large amounts of skin have been eaten, droppings may have a twisted and knotted shape.
- Once dry, droppings may turn white (similar to the scat of hyaenas) if large amounts of bone have been consumed.
- Lion droppings are produced close to kills and randomly throughout their territory, as opposed to hyaena droppings, which are often produced in latrines.

Lion droppings

Territorial behaviour
- A social species, moving about in prides of anything between four and 25 individuals: one can generally expect to find several sets of lion tracks, although males may travel singly while marking or seeking out new territory.
- Although territorial overlapping does occur, males, and indeed prides, will fiercely defend their territory against rivals.
- Males mark territory by scraping the ground with their hind feet and spraying urine. This often occurs adjacent to natural game paths or roads, and usually near a prominent bush (and can look very similar to hyaena scrapings).
- Following a territorial scrape the animal may scent-mark a bush nearby by rubbing its face among the branches. Lions in the southern Kruger National Park commonly use a magic guarrie bush (*Euclea divinorum*) for this purpose.

Lioness claw marks on a leadwood tree (Combretum imberbe)

- One may find evidence of their wet, sticky urine; given that the urine dries relatively quickly, this can be helpful in determining the age of the tracks.
- Roaring is also an important part of territorial advertising and display, as well as being used for communication.
- Lions have been noted to roar regularly after a rainstorm, presumably to re-establish territorial occupation; however, this has not yet been verified in a behavioural study.

MAMMALS ■ Carnivores

- Ongoing, repeated roaring throughout the night could indicate a territorial dispute between males, or possibly a successful takeover.
- Lions will claw trees to scent-mark with their interdigital toe glands, sometimes clawing the same tree repeatedly. The striking visual effect of claw marks may also have a territorial marking function. Another reason for this behaviour may be to sharpen their claws.
- Rolling in buffalo and hippo dung is common; this is thought to be for territorial marking and/or for social reasons.

About the track

- Track shows a broad main pad and four large oval toes. Claw marks usually do not show unless the lion is running, abruptly changing direction, jumping or stepping in mud.
- Toe number 1 (which is situated high up on the leg) and the dewclaw do not show in the track.
- In most substrates, one can see evidence of the three diagnostic lobes on the posterior edge of the main pad.
- The main pad is more symmetrical when compared with that of the hyaena.
- The main pad slopes down ever so slightly to the outside of the track.

Front versus hind track

- Front foot is broader, to carry the significant weight of the head and chest. The front feet are used for gripping and holding, afforded by the larger surface area.

Male lion hind foot track in wet sand

Male lion front and hind track

MAMMALS ■ Carnivores

Lion cub tracks, with toes marginally broader and more splayed than those of leopard tracks

Tracks of a three-month-old lion cub

- The front foot main pad is broader on the leading edge, when compared with that of the hind foot.
- The front foot toes are slightly more splayed than those of the hind foot, where they are arranged more tightly together – making the hind track marginally narrower.
- The hind foot main pad will often appear sharper (more angular) on the posterior edge, and the three lobes are often more defined than on the front foot.
- The front feet often land facing outwards slightly, which is true for many of the large-chested cats of both sexes.

Lion gaits

- A lion's gait can vary widely. While the animal is walking very slowly, its hind foot will land behind the front foot. With a very slight increase in pace (perhaps while it's stalking) its hind foot track will register on top of the front foot. Once it starts to speed up to a medium pace, the hind foot lands just ahead of the front foot. As the animal accelerates, the hind foot will land further and further ahead of the front foot, to a maximum distance of 120mm, before the lion finally breaks into a trot.
- For a regular walking gait, the average distance between the front and hind feet is 2–25mm. This measurement was taken from three prides of lionesses walking along a road.

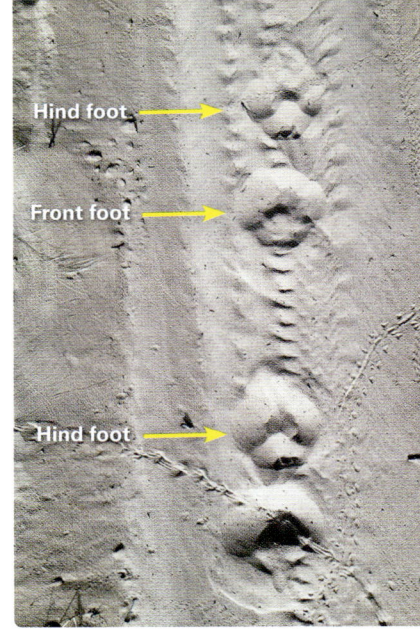

Male lion gait: this animal was moving quickly. Notice the broader front feet.

47

MAMMALS ■ Carnivores

- Front and hind tracks of the same side (left or right) will register together, either slightly to the left or right of the straddle centre, in a normal gait.
- Should the lion start to trot, the tracks become less clear. Once the lion starts galloping, it transfers its weight onto its toes. Signs of galloping show only toe and claws marks, with no main pad showing. (See p. 25 in the Introduction.)

Male versus female

- Track lengths measured at Londolozi Game Reserve show the track of a male lion's front foot to be 138mm and hind foot 141mm. The lioness front track is 127mm and hind foot 116mm.
- The adult male's toes are broader than the female's, and rounder than her more oval toes.
- The dimensions of one male lion's toes showed that the right hind foot's toe number 3 is 37mm long and 23mm wide, and that toe number four is 31mm long and 24mm wide.
- The main pad on the adult male lion is fuller, broader and less angular than on the lioness.
- Dominant male lions often strut, flicking their front feet in a particular manner that is unique to the male lion – a swagger of sorts. When the front foot strikes the ground in this way (i.e. not cleanly) the track can be obscured.

Following lion trails

- When tracking a pride, keep note of the number (and sex ratio) of the component animals, bearing in mind that an individual, or even a group, may join the pride almost unnoticed.

Lion and lioness tracks

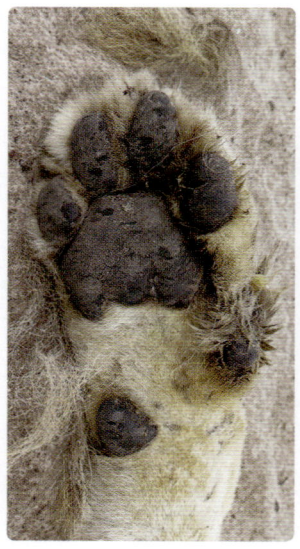

Male lion front foot

Male lion hind foot

MAMMALS ■ Carnivores

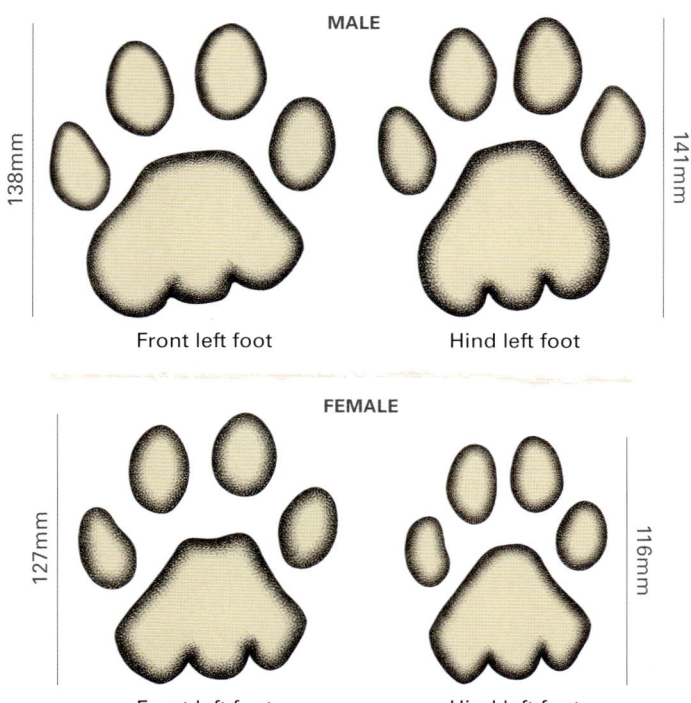

- Lions' social structure is dynamic, so it's vital to understand their behaviour in order to track and find them safely and consistently.
- Male lion interactions, e.g. territorial disputes, can exacerbate their aggression towards trackers on foot.
- At night, expert trackers will take note of lion vocalisations (roars) and their intensity, including hyaena calls and distress calls from prey. Having a mental picture of happenings during the night is very helpful to trackers when they set out the following morning.
- Coalition males (often pairs) may split up in the evenings to patrol territory on their own, reuniting at dawn. Larger male coalitions of four or five individuals may spend long periods apart, seldom coming together.
- Male lions may cover distances of several kilometres in a single night. While patrolling, they will use roads and natural game paths, taking short cuts where necessary. Regular calling and scent-marking may indicate an intention to link up with other members of the pride, or perhaps alert the pride to the presence of a rival male.

A lion trail still visible through grass that is wet with dew

MAMMALS ■ Carnivores

Tracks of a pride of lions crossing a riverbed

Evidence of a lion having rolled in hippo droppings

- Tracking lions requires one to read the terrain carefully: these animals invariably take the easiest route – the path of least resistance – moving along game paths or through openings between thickets.
- One of us (Renias Mhlongo) believes the best way to learn to track lions is to do so barefoot; because humans are also soft-footed, a tracker's choice of route through the bush would tend to be the same as that of lions.
- As the morning heats up, lions will look for a suitable place to rest, ultimately settling for the day.
- One seldom sees perfectly clear tracks along a trail: the main pad and toes will often create little disturbances or scuff marks in the soil, which show up as a slightly different colour. The ability to recognise the faint outlines of a lion track improves dramatically with regular, long-term practice.
- When moving through tall grass, lions leave a slight trail of bent grass, which can successfully be followed. However, other animals such as zebra leave similar-sized trails, so one needs to look carefully for specific tracks on the ground, often partly hidden by vegetation.

Fresh lion signs showing residual sand from a lion having stepped on the log

Lion hairs stuck fast in hippo droppings

MAMMALS ■ Carnivores

Experience with lions on foot

- When encountered at a safe distance in an open area, lions usually stand up and face the tracker. They may growl at this point, or drop their head and flatten their ears – simply giving a warning. If the tracker backs off, lions will usually relax again. Stopping and staring at the lion could precipitate a charge.
- If encountered close-up, in thick bush, lions are more likely to charge, with ears flattened, making lots of noise, lashing their tail, and with a fixed focus on the human.

Male lion marking territory

- In either scenario, more aggressive lions will make a mock charge – first approaching the tracker, growling, and finally charging, stopping just a few metres away.
- It is important to note that lions sleep very soundly during the day, and may easily be stumbled upon in long grass or in thick bush if the trackers are not cautious and vigilant.
- If a lion charges, the golden rule is to stand still until it has stopped. Shouting or throwing something at it during a charge could unnerve an aggressive animal.
- Lionesses with cubs, and wounded lions are potentially very aggressive.
- It is vital to note that vigilance and knowledge of local lion behaviour is the first line of safety when tracking these animals on foot. The more experience and knowledge of local prides, the better a tracker becomes at predicting their behaviour.
- Note that lions from other areas of Africa, with individual personalities and having had different interactions with humans, will behave differently when encountered by people on foot. The above experiences are described from encounters in the southern Kruger National Park, Kalahari, Sabi Sands and northern KwaZulu-Natal.

Can be confused with ...

- *Lion cub tracks can be confused with those of **leopards**; a lion cub's toes are marginally broader and slightly more splayed than the leopard's. The middle lobe of the lion cub's main pad posterior edge appears to be more clearly defined (sharper with steeper edges) than on the leopard.*
- *The lion territorial scrape can look very similar to that of the **hyaena**.*

Leopard
Panthera pardus

This large, stocky cat is golden-yellow in colour with black and gold rosettes (fused spots).

With a very wide tolerance of habitat – from high in the mountains down to the coastal plains and even into the fringes of cities – the leopard is Africa's most revered and widespread big cat.

Habits
- Nocturnal and diurnal, but tends to nocturnal behaviour when disturbed by humans.
- They are solitary, unless a female has cubs or a mating pair is seen together.
- Regarded as 'stalker-pouncers' – the chase being not much more than 40m.
- Unless disturbed, they feed on the ground until the carcass is lighter, then hoist it into a tree, out of reach of larger predators such as lions and hyaenas, to finish feeding. Certain individuals hoist kills more regularly than others.
- Leopards more frequently make use of evergreen trees, into which they hoist their prey, particularly in areas where they compete with hyaenas, vultures and other large predators, as the trees offer cover all year round.
- During hunting, mothers leave their cubs in the safety of a well-hidden den. Tracks of a female leopard in and out of a thicket could indicate the presence of a den site.

Den
- Dens are usually relatively inaccessible – holes in termite mounds, rocky outcrops or in dense thickets.
- Females reuse the same den sites for successive generations of cubs.

Feeding and diet
- Their diet consists of small to medium-sized antelope, as well as ground birds, pythons, monitor lizards, fish, rodents and even insects.
- Male leopards appear to feed on the ground more regularly. However, no two leopards behave in the same way, each individual's behaviour being influenced by the presence of larger predators in the vicinity.

Leopard with python kill

MAMMALS ■ Carnivores

- An adult leopard will feed on an impala carcass for two to three days, leaving periodically to rest or drink water.
- Leopards will pluck fur from a carcass before they begin feeding. Bits of fur can often be found below large trees, indicating the presence of a kill.

Droppings

- Droppings vary in colour from light brown to black. They may be loose, or firm and segmented. They taper at one end and commonly contain hair.
- Leopard droppings measure about 32mm in diameter.

***Left to right**: Female leopard droppings; leopard dropping containing cane rat hair; male leopard droppings*

Territorial behaviour

- Both males and females mark territories. They scrape the ground using their hind feet, releasing scent from interdigital toe glands. They also spray urine on prominent bushes.
- The leopard's call (or roar) is a rasping sound used to reaffirm territory and communicate its presence.
- A male's territory size at Londolozi Game Reserve is about 40km^2, and may include up to five different females within its range. Female territories recorded at Londolozi are some 15km^2. Leopard territories may overlap as much as 60%. Young females usually establish territory adjacent to that of their mother, and in one instance a youngster was observed taking over her mother's territory altogether.

Scraped earth where male leopard has scent-marked with its hind feet

MAMMALS ■ Carnivores

- As with all predators, leopards select territories with the greatest abundance of prey, cover, water and potential mates.
- Only as a last resort will leopards fight to defend their territory.

About the track

- The leopard track appears as a typical cat 'pug mark' showing four oval-shaped toes and a large main pad.
- Male leopards' tracks are larger than the females'. The 'Camp Pan' male leopard at Londolozi had a front foot length of 95mm and width of 93mm; the hind foot length was 100mm and width 91mm. This male's front foot toes were 3–7mm broader than those of a typical female.
- Female leopards' tracks are slightly smaller than the males' and their toes are narrower. The 'Tamboti' female leopard at Londolozi had a front foot length of 77mm and width of 73mm; the hind foot length was 80mm and width 65mm.
- There is significant variation in track dimensions for both sexes; tracks made by one particular female leopard were found to be very similar to those made by an average male.
- Claw marks do not show unless the animal steps in thick mud or it accelerates and runs.
- The main pad occasionally shows an indentation on the leading edge – not always visible in the field.
- The main pad posterior edge shows three relatively well-defined lobes, which usually appear clearer on the hind foot track.
- Males tend to have a slightly more bulging outer lobe on the posterior edge of the main pad, whereas females' main pads are more angular in this area of the track.
- The typical leopard gait (normal walk) shows the hind foot registering 20–40mm ahead of the front foot. However, when the animal is walking very slowly the hind foot will land behind the front foot. With a very slight increase in pace (or while

Leopard front and hind tracks

Notice the three well-defined lobes.

MAMMALS ■ Carnivores

Male leopard front foot track

Female leopard tracks

stalking) the hind foot will register on top of the front foot. With acceleration, the hind foot lands further and further ahead of the front foot.
- Front and hind tracks of the same side (left or right) will register together, either slightly to the left or right of the straddle centre, during a normal walking gait. If one stands back and views the track sequence from a distance, in the direction of travel, it is relatively straightforward to distinguish left from right feet.

Four-month-old leopard cub track

Following leopard trails
- Leopards are among the most difficult animals to track and find on foot. They are generally solitary, tread very lightly and often move in unpredictable directions – particularly when they are hunting. Leopards will make use of game paths and roads, but regularly move through long grass or thickets where their direction of travel is less obvious.
- Unless the substrate is very soft, it is virtually impossible to track a leopard by its spoor alone. Successful leopard tracking requires the tracker to be able to move quietly, rely on evidence and clues left behind, anticipate the animal's

MAMMALS ■ Carnivores

movements, interpret bird and other animal alarm calls, and to recognise exceptionally faint tracks on the ground.
- The most successful leopard trackers make extensive use of local knowledge of leopard behaviour and their territories.
- Listening to and interpreting alarm calls of birds, tree squirrels, vervet monkeys and antelope is a vital component of leopard tracking.
- Birds such as the white-crested helmetshrike, fork-tailed drongo, starling, grey go-away-bird, chinspot batis, black-backed puffback, Burchell's coucal, francolin and even Wahlberg's eagle will alarm at leopards. It is important to know these alarm calls.
- For a novice tracker, leopard tracks may be difficult to see: their small foot size and comparatively light weight result in often indistinct tracks. Usually, just the main pad makes a significant impression, with four indistinct toes showing.
- Should a tracker inadvertently walk towards a leopard, the animal will usually crouch, allowing the tracker to pass by completely unaware, possibly not more than a few metres away. Dominant males and females with cubs may growl loudly, and even mock charge the intruder, although they will more commonly turn and run away, grunting in irritation. A full charge is possible in areas where leopards are regularly hunted, or from females with young.

Leopard tracks in sand

- Leopards climb trees to take advantage of the breeze, particularly on hot summer's days. Or they will lie on well-vegetated and shady termite mounds. They also rest in riverine thickets and densely wooded areas, such as tamboti thickets.
- Leopards become active in the late afternoon for a few hours, and again in the early hours before sunrise – often resting for several hours at night.

Can be confused with ...

- *Leopard tracks can be confused with* **subadult hyaena** *tracks (which have claws), although hyaenas have a unique gait.*
- *Can also be confused with those of* **lion cubs**, *although lion cub tracks are broader and have a more distinct inset in the three lobes on the main pad posterior edge.*
- *The tracks can be confused with those of cheetah, although the latter usually show claw marks and more defined ridges and lobes on the main pad's posterior edge.*

MAMMALS ■ Carnivores

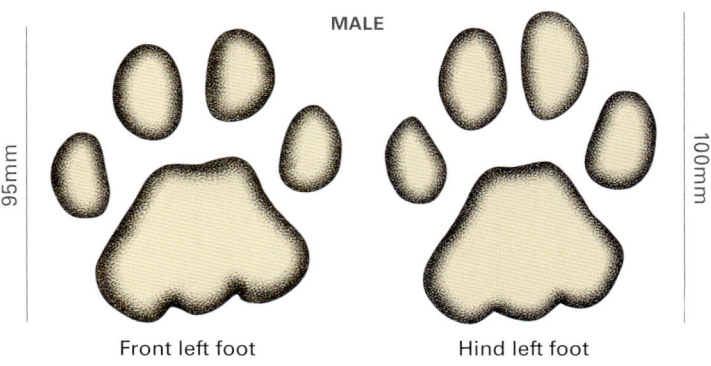

MALE

Front left foot — 95mm

Hind left foot — 100mm

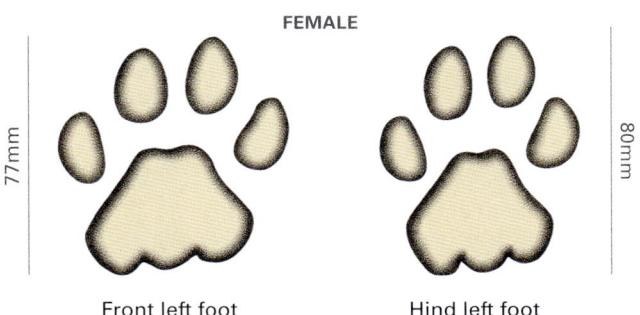

FEMALE

Front left foot — 77mm

Hind left foot — 80mm

- Claw marks on trees are indicative of where they have climbed. Leopards also claw trees as part of their territorial behaviour.
- Territorial marking such as scraping with their hind legs, usually next to a game path or road, is common behaviour for leopards.
- Hyaenas will follow leopards as they move, looking for leopard kills, so it is common to find hyaena tracks following leopard tracks. At Londolozi, hyaenas rob leopards of about 35% of their kills.

Blood trail marked by leopard dragging a carcass

MAMMALS ■ Carnivores

Cheetah
Acinonyx jubatus

The cheetah is considered the fastest land mammal on Earth. The specialised design of this cat includes a slender build, long legs, a deep chest and a small head with large nostrils. The cheetah's tail is thick and flat, acting as a counterweight that assists with balance when the animal changes direction at high speeds. It prefers open grassland. Listed as Vulnerable, they have disappeared from about 90% of their original range and it is estimated that there are only around 7,100 remaining in the wild (2021).

Habits
- Cheetahs occupy large home ranges, which, in the southern Kruger National Park, may be up to 200km^2.
- Diurnal, thereby avoiding competition with the larger nocturnal predators.
- Solitary, but they may live in sibling pairs or family groups of females and cubs. Males will form small coalition groups.
- Once a cheetah has identified suitable prey, it gives chase with a burst of speed, trips up and catches the prey, and finally kills the exhausted animal by throttling it. Speeds of 90–110km/h have been recorded, with a strike rate of around 50%.
- Mothers actively teach their cubs hunting and killing skills by knocking down prey without killing it to allow the cubs to 'practise'.
- Unlike the other large cats, cheetahs are unable to roar. Instead, they communicate by making bird-like chirps or tweets, and can purr loudly.

Evidence of a cheetah having chased an impala onto a log; notice the impala's fur.

Feeding and diet
- Cheetahs target small to medium-sized antelope such as steenbok and impala.
- At Samara Karoo Reserve, cheetah food preferences are springbok, young kudu and steenbok. At Londolozi bordering the Kruger National Park, impala and steenbok are the preferred choice of prey.

MAMMALS — Carnivores

- Cheetahs make use of an 'ankle-tap' with their dewclaw to trip up prey at high speed, often leaving a telltale cut on the prey's hind legs.
- Once they have killed their prey, they may initially pause to catch their breath. As with most predators, cheetahs start feeding between the hind legs and move towards the abdomen of the carcass.
- Bite marks show a width between the canines of 32–35mm, depending on sex and age.
- Few bones are consumed, and little of the skin, leaving most of the skeleton intact.
- Cheetahs lose a large proportion of kills to scavenging lions, hyaenas and leopards in areas where these predators occur in high densities; while feeding, they also remain alert to the presence of other predators, including vultures.

Droppings

- Short, cylindrical, segmented tubes, blunt at both ends, measuring about 30mm in diameter.
- Droppings vary from light green to black in colour.

Droppings vary from light green to black, and are dense and contain little hair.

Droppings on top of a boulder; cheetahs regularly deposit droppings on vantage points.

Territorial behaviour

- Cheetahs are not territorial, but scent-mark for social reasons, such as a male indicating his presence to attract females.
- They scent-mark by scraping with their hind feet and clawing tree trunks or spraying them with urine. A male cheetah was observed climbing into a tree to defecate and spray urine onto the branches.
- They tend to mark the same prominent trees on a regular basis.

About the track

- Track length at Samara Karoo Reserve: front foot 95mm and hind foot 105mm.
- The cheetah's track is typical of a large cat; however, unlike true cats, it cannot completely retract, or sheath, its claws. Claw marks can therefore usually be found in their tracks, although they don't always make clear impressions.
- The main pad has a slight indentation on the leading edge.
- The posterior edge has three well-defined lobes extending up the main pad, creating ridges that presumably provide added traction when the cheetah is chasing prey at high speed. These ridges are not as distinctive in leopard and lion tracks.

MAMMALS ■ Carnivores

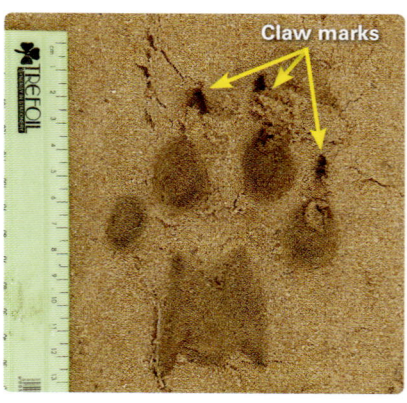

Cheetah track: notice the distinct lobes on the main pad's posterior edge.

Female cheetah hind foot track

- The hind foot main pad is square, or box-shaped, on the leading edge, and is marginally longer than on the front foot.
- At a normal walking gait, the hind foot registers 40–60mm in front of the front foot (overstep).

Cheetah paw

Following cheetah trails

- Due to their preference for open areas, cheetahs are not regularly trailed on foot. However, one can still learn about their movements and behaviour by following their tracks.
- In the Sabi Sands Game Reserve they move between open areas in search of suitable prey, particularly in the early morning and late afternoon.
- While hunting, cheetahs climb termite mounds and fallen tree stumps, spend a few minutes watching, and then proceed to the next vantage point.
- Cheetahs rest in the shade during the heat of the day, often in the middle of a clearing where visibility is good.
- They have been observed hunting in thickets at Samara Karoo Reserve in the Karoo and at Phinda Game Reserve in KwaZulu-Natal, where they have hunting excursions by moonlight.
- Research shows that vocalisations by lions and hyaenas assist cheetahs to avoid these competitors.

Female cheetah tracks: hind foot (top) and front foot (bottom) show overstep.

MAMMALS ■ Carnivores

Can be confused with ...

- The front foot tracks of a cheetah can be confused with **leopard** tracks; however, the absence of claw marks in the leopard's track, as well as its broader toes and main pad, separate the two species. In addition, the lobes and ridges on the leopard's main pad posterior edge are not as well defined as the cheetah's.
- Cheetah tracks can also be confused with those of the **African wild dog**, but the wild dog's toes are positioned symmetrically, unlike the cheetah's, and the wild dog's main pad is narrower and more triangular in shape.

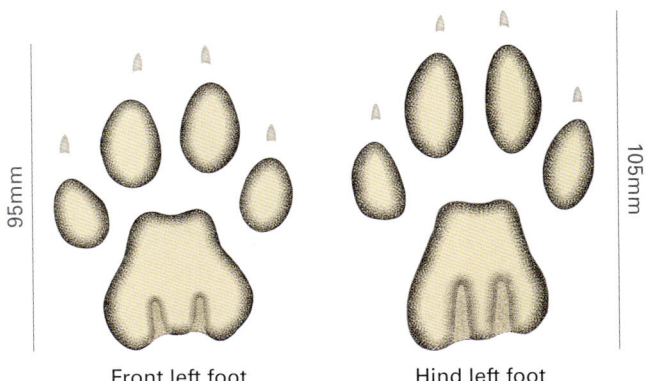

Front left foot   Hind left foot

Cheetah kill; note that the larger bones have not been eaten.

MAMMALS ■ Carnivores

Serval
Leptailurus serval

This 'leggy', slender, medium-sized cat is yellow with black spots. It has the largest ears of any cat and a relatively short tail. It prefers thick grassland and reedbeds near water.

Habits
- Servals are active in the late afternoon, at night and through to late morning.
- They are mainly solitary, but may be found in pairs.
- Cubs are born in dense vegetation, thick grass or abandoned aardvark burrows.
- Adults and young fall victim to larger predators and other animals; a group of buffalo was seen to horn and kill three cubs hidden in long grass.
- The serval hunts by stalking patiently through long grass, listening intently, and then leaping, using a distinctive and precise pounce, to trap the prey on the ground.
- It is capable of leaping 2–3m vertically and 3–4m horizontally from a stationary position.
- Servals communicate with high-pitched chirping, hissing, as well as quiet grunting sounds.

Feeding and diet
- The serval feeds on small mammals, mainly rodents, including vlei rats and mice. An opportunistic predator, it also preys on frogs, snakes, lizards, insects, fish and birds.
- With larger prey, the serval mostly avoids eating the organs, intestines, fur and feathers.
- It locates prey predominantly with its sense of hearing, but also by sight, and is known to snatch birds from the air and chase prey into water.

Droppings
- Serval droppings are surprisingly large, segmented, blunt and measure 20–22mm in diameter.
- Droppings are dark green to black in some cases, and contain lots of rodent hair. They are seldom covered.
- As droppings age and dry out they turn light grey in colour, similar to an old piece of steel wool.

Serval droppings

MAMMALS ■ Carnivores

Left and above: *The serval hind foot track – note the toes are situated well ahead of the main pad. The imaginary line drawn in the photo **(left)** between the toes and the main pad does not touch any segment of the track.*

Territorial behaviour
- Males and females scent-mark by spraying urine on prominent bushes.
- Servals have been recorded scraping the ground with their feet and spraying urine, but this is not common behaviour.
- After defecating they occasionally rake the droppings with their hind feet.

About the track
- Most track lengths are front foot 50mm and hind foot 45mm; however, one particular individual's tracks measured front foot 42mm, hind foot 45mm.
- The track shows four oval-shaped toes on each of its feet. Claw marks show when it is jumping, which it does regularly when hunting rodents in long grass.
- The posterior edge of the main pad has three fairly well-defined lobes.
- The serval's main pad is narrower and more pointed than that of the caracal, with which it is regularly confused, mostly on the leading edge of the main pad.
- It is possible to see the hind foot toes situated well ahead of the main pad. An imaginary line drawn between the toes

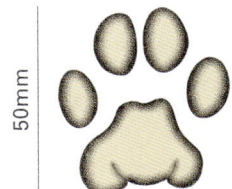
Front left foot

Hind left foot

and the main pad does not bisect any segment of the track; such a line cannot be drawn on a caracal's track. However, it is important to note that this feature is not always clearly evident if seen in hard substrate.
- A commonly used gait results in the hind foot registering about 45cm ahead of the front foot.

Above left and centre: Male serval front foot and front track; notice the similarity to the caracal front foot. *Above right:* Male serval hind foot; observe how narrow it is.

Can be confused with ...

- Serval tracks are easily confused with those of **caracal**. However, the caracal's hind track is 5–10mm longer; its main pad is significantly broader on the leading edge; its toes are slightly broader and front foot toes more splayed when compared to the narrower-set serval toes; its main pad is situated closer to the toes; and the front feet face slightly outwards.
- Serval and caracal droppings are similar in size and shape.
- The serval track is sometimes confused with that of a **young cheetah** due to its narrowness and its well-defined main pad lobes on the posterior edge of the track. The obvious difference is that the cheetah usually shows claw marks in its tracks.
- Serval tracks can be confused with the **African wild cat**, but the serval's track is some 20mm longer, with a main pad that is comparatively narrower on the leading edge. The wild cat's toes are rounder in shape.

Serval front foot track; claw marks show only when the animal is jumping.

MAMMALS ■ Carnivores

Caracal
Caracal caracal

The powerfully built caracal is the largest of Africa's small cats. It is mostly tan-coloured, with the underside of the chin and body being white, and with black ears that are tipped with long tassels of hair. Its short, powerful legs give it the exceptional ability to jump – it regularly catches birds in mid-air.

This animal can tolerate a wide range of habitats, from semi-desert to savanna grassland and scrubland, including riverine and densely wooded forests.

Behaviour
- Mostly nocturnal and solitary except during mating, or when females have kittens.
- Both males and females actively defend their territory; in particular, females defend their smaller range against other females.
- Caracals make use of the classic stalk–pounce method of catching prey.
- They have exceptional power and agility: using their muscular hind legs, they are capable of leaping 2–3m into the air, from a standstill, to catch birds and other prey.

Feeding and diet
- They hunt mice, reptiles, birds and small to medium-sized antelope, such as the young of bushbuck or springbok.
- Bite marks with a width of about 28mm (top canines) and 23mm (bottom canines) are usually found on either side of the prey's throat or spine. As with most feline predators, claw and scratch marks can be found on the prey's rump and flanks.
- In the Karoo, vervet monkeys often fall prey to caracal, and hence produce vociferous alarm calls for these cats.

Caracal territorial scrape

MAMMALS ■ Carnivores

Caracal droppings recently deposited   *Old droppings, turning to white*

Droppings
- Diameter of 22–25mm, cylindrical, partially segmented and occasionally tapered on one end.
- They turn white as they dry out.

About the track
- The track shows four relatively large oval toes on both feet. Hind foot claws are sometimes seen.
- Track lengths measured at Samara Karoo Reserve show front foot 50mm and hind foot slightly longer – 55mm.
- The main pad is broad with three distinctive lobes at the posterior edge.
- Characteristically, the outside toes on front and hind feet extend lower down on either side of the main pad. This is particularly true for the hind foot.
- The front foot main pad sometimes shows a slight indentation on the leading edge and is broader than that of the serval – with which it could be confused.
- Hair growing between the toes and main pad can partially obscure the track.
- At a normal walking gait, the hind foot registers partially on top of the front foot.
- As with leopard and lion, the broad-chested caracal's front foot often lands at a slight angle, pointing outwards.
- Evidence of protracted hind foot claw marks and splayed toes may indicate that the cat has launched itself after a bird.

Hind foot track   *Front foot track, slightly distorted by wet mud*

MAMMALS ■ Carnivores

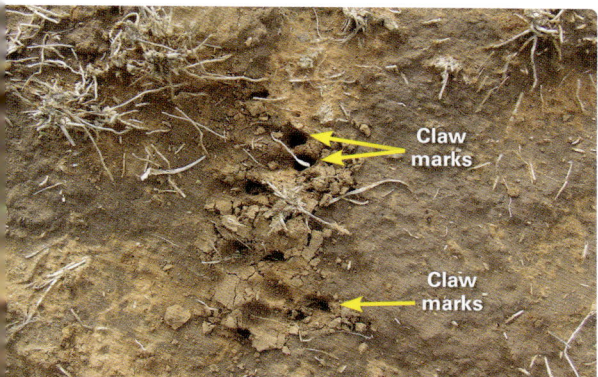

Above: Track of a leaping caracal – notice the hind feet with claws extended.
Left: Caracal galloping – notice the angle of the right front foot.

Caracal front and hind tracks

Can be confused with ...

- Caracal and **serval** tracks can easily be confused. The serval track is similar in length but narrower than that of the caracal; the toes on the serval hind foot are usually set further forward of the main pad, and the leading edge of the serval main pad is much narrower.
- **Female leopard** tracks are about 25mm longer. The toes and main pad of a female leopard are comparatively broader than those of the caracal.

Front left foot   Hind left foot

67

MAMMALS ■ Carnivores

African wild cat
Felis silvestris cafra

This small, sandy-coloured cat is similar in build to a domestic cat. It has reddish to black bands on its legs and tail.

It can tolerate a variety of habitats and occurs widely in southern Africa, where it prefers areas that offer good cover, such as *Senegalia* scrub and woodland, tall grass and riverine habitats. Where there is insufficient cover, the wild cat will shelter in holes dug by other animals, among rocks or under the roots of trees.

Habits
- Nocturnal and secretive.
- Solitary except during mating periods when several males may accompany a female.
- Terrestrial but a good tree climber when hunting or threatened.

Feeding and diet
- They hunt rodents, birds, hares and reptiles, as well as insects; prey detected mainly by sight and sound.
- Head and some innards of prey are often not consumed.

Droppings
- Droppings are segmented, occasionally tapered, light green to dark brown in colour and measure 18mm in diameter; partially covered.

Territorial behaviour
- Wild cats are highly territorial and mark their territory by spraying urine on small bushes. Covering their droppings no doubt also serves to demarcate their territory.

African wild cat droppings

Droppings and territorial scrapings

MAMMALS ■ Carnivores

Above and below: African wild cat front and hind foot tracks

African wild cat tracks imprinted in soft Kalahari sand

About the track
- The African wild cat's track shows four oval-shaped toes on both front and hind feet – very similar to that of the domestic cat.
- Tracks measured at Londolozi Game Reserve are front foot length 34mm and hind foot 37mm.
- The front foot is marginally broader but shorter than the hind foot. As with all true cats, claws are generally sheathed, so no claw marks are seen unless the animal is accelerating, running or jumping.
- The main pad posterior edge has three clearly distinguishable lobes – which is true for all the cats.

Front left foot   Hind left foot

MAMMALS ■ Carnivores

Can be confused with ...

- The African wild cat track can be confused with that of the **serval**; however, the serval's track is some 20mm longer, with a bigger gap between the main pad and the toes, and the main pad leading edge is narrower.
- It can also be confused with the **African civet**, but the civet's track is some 20mm longer, its toes are larger and rounder and its unsheathed claws will usually show, while the wild cat's mostly do not.

Left: Evidence of a wild cat having dragged a hare it had killed
Above: African wild cat front foot track

- The hind foot toes are more elongated than those of the front foot, and the main pad is narrower. The hind foot toes also lie well forward of the main pad. By contrast, the front feet outside toes are situated low down, flanking the main pad.
- In certain substrates, evidence of hair growing between the toes may be seen in the track.
- A commonly used gait results in the hind foot registering about 30cm ahead of the front foot.

Black-footed (small-spotted) cat
Felis nigripes

First documented in the Karoo in 1824, the black-footed cat is Africa's smallest wild cat – weighing less than 2kg. It is listed as Vulnerable on the IUCN Red List. It is found in the arid grasslands of South Africa, Botswana and Namibia, and prefers open habitats with some grass cover. This cat makes good use of abandoned aardvark burrows in which to take refuge.

Habits
- Solitary, secretive and nocturnal; hunting throughout the night.
- A mother usually gives birth to two kittens between September and April, after a gestation of 63 days. The young are weaned after two months.
- They are patient and effective hunters. An individual has been observed waiting outside a rodent den for about an hour, in readiness for an unsuspecting murid to emerge, whereupon it pounced with lightning speed.
- These cats make extensive use of abandoned springhare burrows as a refuge.

Feeding and diet
- Opportunistic hunters, they feed predominantly on rodents, shrews, reptiles, birds and insects, and will also scavenge.

Black-footed cat kill – an eastern clapper lark

MAMMALS ■ Carnivores

Droppings
- Dark coloured, segmented droppings, around 13mm in diameter and 55mm in length, not covered or deposited in middens. Droppings are similar to those of the small grey mongoose.

Territorial behaviour
- Territories are maintained by spraying urine, scent-rubbing and clawing. The size of their territory is not known.
- Can produce a loud meowing sound.

About the track
- Front foot track 25mm; hind foot 23mm.
- Track shows four oval toes, arranged in an arc, on both front and hind feet. The front foot track's toes are positioned forward of the main pad.
- The main pad shows three clearly defined lobes on the posterior edge.

Can be confused with ...
- The black-footed cat track is about 10mm shorter than that of the **African wild cat**.
- The black-footed cat has a broader main pad than the **genet** (the pad has three lobes on the posterior edge).

Captive black-footed cat dropping

Black-footed cat front and hind tracks

Front left foot

Hind left foot

Hind foot track

African wild dog
Lycaon pictus

Lex Hes

Considered the most efficient hunter in Africa, the African wild dog (or Cape hunting dog) possesses speed, stamina and excellent pack co-ordination. Each individual's mottled coat pattern is unique.

These dogs live on open savanna and bushveld, where they run in packs, hunting co-operatively. Wild dog populations require large conservation areas to remain viable. According to the IUCN Red List recorded in the last decade, there were 1,409 individuals left in sub-Saharan Africa. They are considered to be Endangered.

Habits
- Highly efficient pack hunters, with a hunting success rate of about 80%. They hunt in the early morning and late afternoon and are also known to be active in moonlight.
- Gregarious, living in packs of six to eight adults and many pups; packs numbering more than 25 have been recorded.
- The alpha pair in a pack breeds. If pups are born to a lower-ranking female they have a lower chance of survival, mostly due to starvation.
- A pack bonds through continual greetings and interactions, such as sniffing and licking each other. Both adults and pups enjoy play.
- Members of a pack co-ordinate their movements while hunting by means of chirping or squeaking sounds. They also make a drawn-out 'whoo, whoo, whoo, whoo' contact call that can be heard surprisingly far away.
- The pack trots continuously as they hunt, stopping only for a few seconds to listen, before continuing again.
- When adults return from a successful hunt, pups beg from them, nudging at the corner of their mouth, causing in the adults an automatic reflex action to regurgitate food for their offspring.
- In Kruger National Park, wild dogs occupy home ranges of 150–1,100km^2 in extent (Fuller et al, 1992), which the alpha pair mark with urine.
- Lions and hyaenas have a direct impact on wild dog populations by pirating their kills and eliminating their pups, often when they are still in the den.

Den
- In the southern Kruger National Park, wild dogs create underground dens in disused aardvark or warthog burrows in termite mounds, which they use for about three months.

MAMMALS ■ Carnivores

- Den sites may be changed every three to four weeks. If the den is disturbed by lions, the dogs will immediately move on.

Feeding and diet

- Wild dogs target mostly impala at Londolozi Game Reserve and in the southern Kruger National Park. Kudu, springbok, reedbuck and wildebeest are also favoured prey.
- Most of the carcass is devoured, leaving only the larger bones, neck and head.
- Prey – utterly exhausted after having been relentlessly chased, often for several kilometres – is quickly killed by being disembowelled.
- In the past, wild dogs were regarded as wanton killers, with a reputation for inflicting slow and painful death. They were, until recently, killed by farmers and conservationists.

Droppings

- Droppings are cylindrical and tapered at one end. Loose stools are common and they defecate randomly as they move. Light to dark brown, sometimes black, often contain hair and bones. They measure 25mm in diameter.

About the track

- Typically dog-like in appearance. A range of track lengths measured front foot 86–90mm and hind foot 77–82mm.
- The tracks show four toes with sturdy claws on both front and hind feet, the marks of which are usually visible.
- Characteristic are the two middle toes that lie parallel to one another, with a slight gap between them.
- The main pad is triangular in shape – the leading edge is narrow with no indentation.

Wild dog droppings

Tracks of a pack of wild dogs

MAMMALS ■ Carnivores

Wild dog front and hind tracks

Track showing parallel toes and triangular main pad

- The main pad's posterior edge has two symmetrical yet indistinct lobes.
- The front track is broader than that of the hind foot.
- The regular walking gait shows the hind foot registering behind or on top of the front foot.
- Trotting results in the hind foot registering on top of the front foot, but with a longer stride. As the animal speeds up, its hind foot lands further and further in front of the front foot, until it breaks into a gallop.

Can be confused with ...

- Wild dog tracks can be confused with those of the **spotted hyaena**; however, the hyaena's toe arrangement and main pad shape are not at all symmetrical, its outside toes being typically kidney-shaped, whereas the wild dog's toes are more uniform in shape.
- Wild dog tracks can also be confused with those of the **cheetah**, but the wild dog's toes are positioned symmetrically, unlike the cheetah's, and the wild dog's main pad is narrower and more triangular in shape.

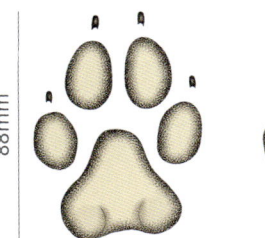
Front left foot

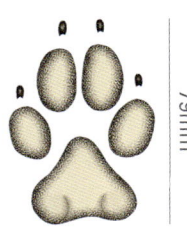
Hind left foot

MAMBALS ■ Carnivores

Black-backed and side-striped jackals
Canis mesomelas and *C. adustus*

The blacked-backed jackal (*Canis mesomelas*) (left) and its slightly larger cousin – the side-striped jackal (*C. adustus*) – are widely spread throughout southern, eastern and central Africa.

Industrious little canids, both are scavengers and successful hunters. Despite being victims of persecution by farmers and hunters for about 200 years, jackals endure well in the Karoo.

Habits
- Monogamous, jackals are both diurnal and nocturnal, although they are more active at night in areas where they are persecuted by hunters and farmers.
- Highly opportunistic hunters and scavengers; they will kill the young of small ungulates such as common duiker and steenbok.
- They produce a barking alarm call for leopards and lions.
- They vocalise throughout the night, making a howling sound to communicate with territorial rivals and with mates. Side-striped jackals also make a series of 'yaps'.

The remains of an ostrich nest raided by jackals

MAMMALS ■ Carnivores

Den
- In both the bushveld and the Karoo, jackals make use of abandoned aardvark holes in termite mounds in which to den and raise pups.

Feeding and diet
- Omnivorous, they target small mammals, insects, birds, reptiles, scorpions, spiders and fruits, and will raid ostrich nests for the eggs.
- During droughts, jackals successfully hunt and kill small and medium-sized antelope such as young impala, running them down, biting them on the flank, and slowly disembowelling them.
- Not always guilty, jackal tracks near a carcass do not necessarily mean they were responsible for the kill – they are prolific scavengers and quick to arrive at a carcass.
- For trackers to identify the predator responsible for a kill, they must make a careful assessment of the bite and/or claw marks on the carcass: claw marks on the rump and neck of the prey will rule out jackals as they are not able to kill in this manner. The surrounding area must also be assessed for other predators' tracks, signs of struggle, fur, skid marks, etc., to pinpoint the perpetrator – often a difficult task, particularly if vultures, hyaenas and others have all fed on the carcass.
- Width of jackal's canines: top 25mm, and bottom 22mm.

Droppings
- Droppings are partially segmented, often twisted and tapered at one end, sometimes U-shaped). They measure 18–22mm in diameter.
- Light brown, black and eventually turn white with age – contain hair, insect carapaces, berries, feathers and even bone fragments.
- Droppings usually deposited in an elevated position, off the ground, on top of a rock, bush or clump of grass.

Above and below: *Fresh and old droppings respectively, deposited on top of bushes*

Territorial behaviour
- Jackals defecate on top of small bushes, shrubs, rocks or clumps of grass – presumably to take advantage of air movement for dispersing the scent.
- They mark territory by urinating and scratching on the ground with both front and hind feet. They also roll on the ground, leaving hair in the vicinity.

MAMMALS ■ Carnivores

Above left: Black-backed jackal typical front foot track shows four toes; toe 1 and the dewclaw of the front foot do not make an impression.
Above right: Black-backed jackal's overlapping front and hind tracks – a normal walking gait
Right: Black-backed jackal front foot; the imaginary X formed by the lines shows the separation of the toes and main pad.

About the track

- There are no distinctive differences between the tracks of the black-backed jackal (*Canis mesomelas*) and the side-striped jackal (*C. adustus*); however, confirmed track photos of both species have been included.
- Black-backed jackal tracks measure front foot 60mm and hind foot 55mm; confirmed sizes for side-striped jackal tracks are not available.
- The jackal track shows four toes on front and hind feet – toe number 1 and the dewclaw of the front foot do not make an impression.
- The triangular-shaped main pad has three subtle lobes on the posterior edge, the middle lobe being the widest.
- The oval-shaped toes are situated well ahead of the main pad and have short, thick, relatively long claws.
- Positioning of the toes and overall symmetry are diagnostic: the two middle toes are situated well forward, parallel to each other. The outside toes are also situated approximately in line with each other – particularly evident on the hind foot.
- Several trackers have commented on the overall appearance of the hind foot's resemblance to the image of the stylised shape of a Christmas tree.
- A helpful ID tip is to draw an imaginary X through the track without touching any part of the toes or main pad.
- Jackals make extensive use of a trotting and side-trotting gait. (See p. 21 for informative descriptions of a variety of animal gaits.)

MAMMALS ■ Carnivores

Side-striped jackal tracks

Black-backed jackal tracks

Can be confused with ...

- Jackal tracks can be confused with **white-tailed mongoose**, although the mongoose's toes are significantly smaller and they are arranged in a semi-circular (arc) shape, whereas the jackal's two parallel middle toes sit forward and two outside toes slightly further back, and the track is generally more symmetrical.
- The jackal's toes are significantly bigger than those of the **aardwolf**, **Cape fox** and **bat-eared fox**.
- The droppings can easily be confused with those of the **caracal**; however, the jackal's droppings are often twisted and more segmented, plus they usually contain more hair and insect fragments than those of the caracal.

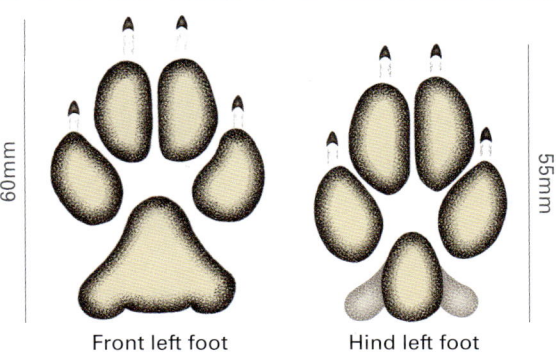

Front left foot   Hind left foot

79

MAMMALS ■ Carnivores

Bat-eared fox
Otocyon megalotis

The bat-eared fox has red-brown body fur, distinctively enormous black ears, black legs and a bushy, black-tipped tail.
　Inhabits open country with short grass in arid and savanna zones.

Habits
- Both diurnal and nocturnal; more regularly active in the day during winter.
- Playful, monogamous and gregarious, they travel in small groups of mating pairs and young.
- A number of groups may feed together at food-rich locations.

Burrow and resting sites
- Make use of abandoned aardvark holes as burrows, which measure up to 1m in depth and are kept perfectly clean.
- At Samara Karoo Reserve bat-eared foxes commonly rest up under familiar firethorn (*Searsia pyroides*) thickets.

Feeding and diet
- Mostly insectivorous: insects account for 80% of their diet. In the Great Karoo they seem to target harvester termites (*Hodotermes mossambicus*).
- Prodigious diggers, excavating narrow holes with their front feet in search of food.
- Their acute hearing enables them to detect the faintest of movements made by insect activity underground.
- They also eat small reptiles, scorpions, beetles, rodents, birds and eggs, and sometimes fruits, but do not kill domestic stock.

Droppings
- Partially segmented, cylindrical droppings, 16–18mm in diameter and very dark in colour – containing insect fragments and seeds.
- Deposited randomly throughout the range and in latrines.

Droppings are dark brown to black and contain fragments of their diet.

Typical gait

MAMMALS ■ Carnivores

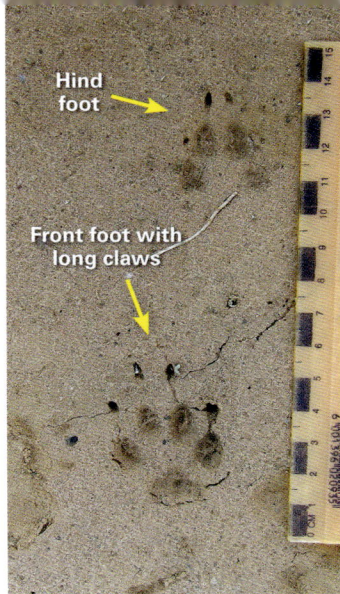

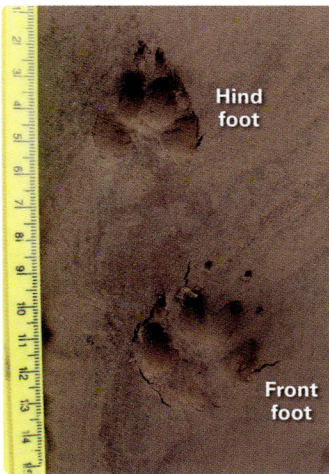

Far left: Bat-eared fox tracks
Left: Front and hind tracks – an overstep is a common bat-eared fox gait.

About the track
- The front foot track shows four toes; although it has five toes, toe number one does not make an impression. Track lengths are front foot 46mm, hind foot 42mm.
- Unusually long front foot claws are characteristic; they can strike 10–14mm in front of the toes, and mark clearly in most substrates.
- Front foot toes are more splayed than those of the narrower hind foot.
- The hind foot has four toes with shorter claws that are often curved slightly inwards.
- The hind foot shows a clear gap between the toes and main pad.
- The main pad is triangular shaped but is not always distinguishable due to the fur beneath the feet – especially hind foot.
- The typical trotting gait shows the hind foot registering close to the opposite side's front foot.

Can be confused with ...
- Bat-eared fox tracks are similar to those of the **Cape fox**; however, their front foot claws are longer and the toes are marginally smaller than those of the Cape fox.
- Although the bat-eared fox has less obscuring fur under its feet than the Cape fox, the presence of what fur there is may lead trackers to confuse bat-eared fox tracks with those of the **Cape hare** or **scrub hare**.

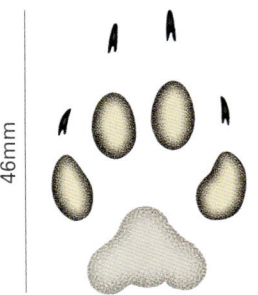
Front left foot
46mm

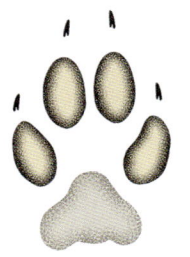
Hind left foot
42mm

81

MAMMALS ■ Carnivores

Cape fox
Vulpes chama

The Cape fox is slightly built and has a silvery grey back with buff and white underparts, and a large bushy tail with a black tip. It is also known as a draaijakkals, Afrikaans for 'turn jackal', for its tendency to make sudden turns when fleeing a threat.

It inhabits mainly open grassland with scattered thickets, as well as semi-desert scrub and fynbos. This poorly understood little carnivore is persecuted in farming areas, although its predatory impact on sheep stocks has been shown to be negligible.

Habits
- Cape foxes are predominantly nocturnal and particularly elusive. Their social structure is not well understood.
- They express alarm by means of high-pitched barks, especially when with their young, and are known to growl when threatened.
- Outside mating, males and females are found alone, foraging separately.

Burrow
- Burrows are used predominantly for breeding purposes.
- An active digger, it excavates its own burrow, but is also known to occupy other animals' burrows, such as those of yellow mongoose and springhare.

Feeding and diet
- Omnivorous; eats invertebrates, small rodents, young hares, reptiles and fruits.
- It is known to scavenge carrion, but rarely hunts large prey such as lambs.

Droppings
- The light green to grey-coloured droppings measure 15mm in diameter and up to 75mm in length.
- Droppings are cylindrical, unsegmented and usually tapered at one end.
- Occasionally deposited in an elevated position for territorial purposes, off the ground, on top of a rock, bush or clump of grass.

Cape fox droppings

About the track
- Track shows four toes on both front and hind feet. Although the front foot has five toes, toe number 1 and its claw do not make an impression.

MAMMALS ■ Carnivores

Cape fox front foot track

Cape fox front and hind tracks – notice the slightly broader front foot.

- Track measurements show front foot 47mm and hind foot 42mm in length.
- An inordinate amount of fur grows under the feet and between the toes, having a characteristic obscuring effect in the footprints and making it difficult to distinguish the main pad, especially in dry substrate.
- In a normal walking gait, the hind foot registers ahead of the front foot. The straddle trot is also common. (See p. 21 for more information about gaits.)

Can be confused with ...

- *Claw marks are evident in the track, although they are not as long as those of the **bat-eared fox**. The bat-eared fox's rounder toes are also more splayed than those of the Cape fox.*

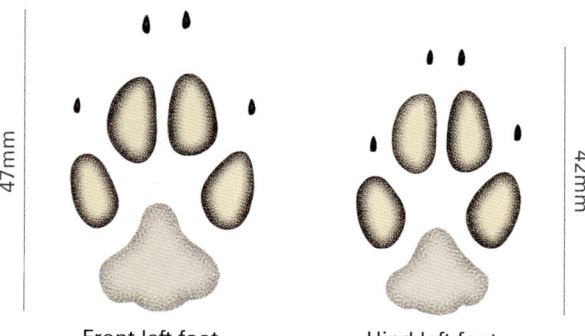

Front left foot   Hind left foot

MAMMALS ■ Carnivores

Aardwolf
Proteles cristatus

Similar in size to a jackal but with the characteristic hyaena shape, the aardwolf has erect ears and long, yellowish fur with a few thin black stripes on its sides and upper legs.
It prefers the semi-arid Karoo, grassland and savanna biomes of southern Africa.

Habits
- Socially monogamous (although sexually polygamous), nocturnal and secretive. Usually solitary but may be found in pairs.
- Males regularly guard the young while the females go out foraging.
- Rarely vocal, occasionally make a purring, barking or squealing sound.

Den
- They occupy and modify the burrows of springhares and aardvarks for up to eight weeks at a time.
- Spend an inordinate amount of time in their burrows (up to 19 hours per day), especially during cold spells.

Feeding and diet
- Insectivorous: they feed almost exclusively on snouted harvester termites (genus *Trinervitermes*), of which they can consume hundreds of thousands in a night.
- They locate termites using smell and sound, and lick them off the ground using their specially adapted broad tongue.
- These carnivores do not eat meat; in fact, most of their teeth (except canines and incisors) are significantly reduced.

Fresh aardwolf droppings

Droppings
- Unsegmented, cylindrical droppings with blunt ends are deposited and partially buried in middens.
- Droppings are surprisingly large and measure 40mm in diameter, dark, with a pine/eucalyptus odour; they consist mainly of sand and termite heads.

Territorial behaviour
- Territories are marked with anal gland scent on grass stems, called 'pasting'.

Aardwolf midden

MAMMALS ■ Carnivores

Left to right: Aardwolf front left foot with long claws; aardwolf hind foot; aardwolf track

About the track
- Track shows four toes with long claws on both front and hind feet.
- Track measurements taken in the Karoo were front foot 54mm and hind foot 45mm.
- Characteristically, their tightly fitting toes resemble a puzzle.
- The lengthened leading edge of the main pad fits in between the two outside toes, particularly on the front foot.
- The main pad posterior edge is asymmetrical, with the outside lobe extending further back than the inside one.
- Long, sturdy claws on all feet assist their prodigious digging efforts.
- Aardwolf have a unique gait where their hind leg swings across the centre line of movement and steps next to the front foot on the opposite side. For instance, the right hind foot will leave a track just behind the left front foot. Depending on the speed at which the aarwolf is moving, the hind foot can register behind, next to, or slightly on top of the front foot. This distinctive walking pattern sets this animal apart from cats.

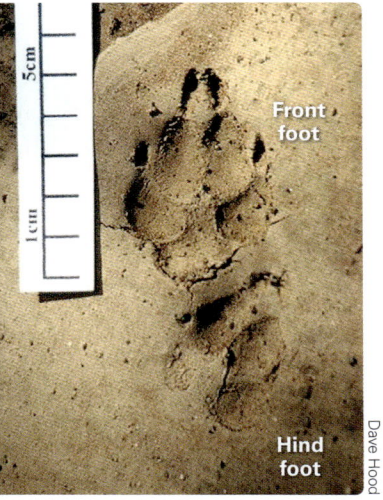

The main pad on the hind foot seldom makes a clear impression, especially in hard substrate.

Can be confused with ...
- The kidney-shaped outside toes resemble those of the **spotted hyaena**.
- The aardwolf track is 10mm smaller than that of the **black-backed jackal**, and its main pad is significantly narrower.

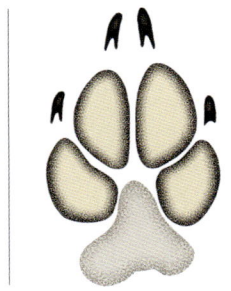 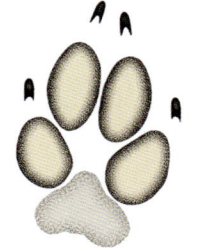

Front left foot   Hind right foot

85

MAMBALS ■ Carnivores

Brown hyaena
Hyaena brunnea

This scavenger has pointed ears and a dark brown shaggy coat with a cream-coloured mane that extends from the back of the neck across the shoulders. Its head and neck are grey, as are its legs, with dark horizontal stripes. There is little difference between the sexes, although males may be slightly bigger than females.

In southern Africa the brown hyaena is found in savanna grassland, semi-desert and desert.

Habits
- Nocturnal and more secretive than its larger spotted cousin, it typically forages alone.
- Its acute sense of smell enables it to find carcasses at considerable distances; one individual was observed successfully following a scent trail for well over 1km.
- Brown hyaenas are social animals that live in clans consisting of up to four adult males and six adult females and their young, with one territorial and dominant alpha male.

Den
- Den sites are usually well concealed in rocky areas on a hilltop or in remote sand dunes. Mills (1990) found that 94% of dens in the southern Kalahari were located in the dunes.
- Cubs are protected by the narrow entrance and tight side tunnels of the den.
- Occasionally surplus food, such as an antelope leg or horn, is brought back to the den.

An abandoned brown hyaena den with bone and porcupine quills

A brown hyaena den in the Kalahari

MAMMALS ■ Carnivores

Feeding and diet
- The brown hyaena is a poor hunter – live prey makes up only a small percentage of its diet.
- Mainly a scavenger, it feeds on carcasses killed by other animals.
- It will also eat insects, birds' eggs (especially ostrich eggs) and wild fruits.
- On the Namibian coast its staple diet is seals.
- It is known for taking food back to its den site, hence the evidence of bones, skulls, porcupine quills and hooves.

Droppings
- Fresh droppings are light to dark brown-green in colour and less segmented than spotted hyaena droppings; 28–38mm in diameter. The combination of consuming calcium-rich bones and the fermentation process in the caecum contributes to the white colouration of hyaena droppings.
- Droppings are deposited in territorial middens throughout their territory.
- Middens are created in slightly saucer-shaped depressions with a diameter of about 100cm – smaller than that of the spotted hyaena.
- In the Kalahari, droppings may contain seeds from the tsamma melon.

Fresh droppings turn white surprisingly quickly.

Old droppings

Territorial behaviour
- The brown hyaena produces a paste with its anal gland and deposits this on plant and grass stems along territorial borders as well as throughout its territory.
- The pale component of the paste is long-lasting and is said to convey the message of 'territory occupied' to intruders; the dark brown component lasts only a matter of days and is believed to convey social information to other members of the resident clan, such as breeding status.
- The brown hyaena deposits its scent pastes high on grass stalks or thin branches by walking over the vegetation.
- The clan co-operatively defends a territory.

Territorial scent pasting

MAMMALS ■ Carnivores

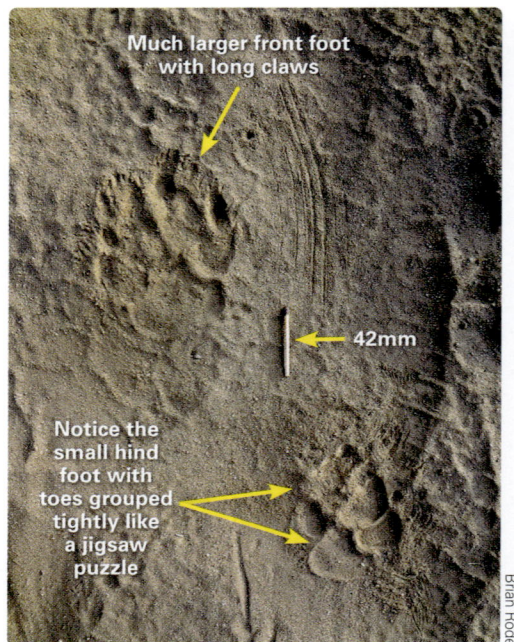

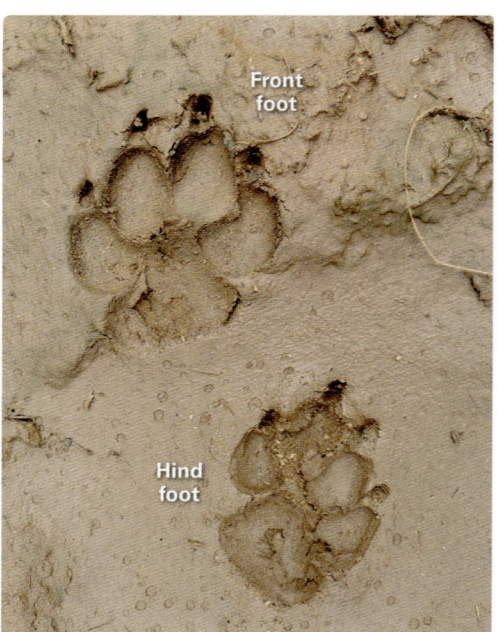

Top left: Brown hyaena's front and hind foot tracks showing tightly grouped toes
Top right: Tracks showing evidence of hair marks around the feet
Left: Near-perfect front and hind foot tracks of brown hyaena
Above: Male leopard track (**top left**) compared to the brown hyaena track (**bottom right**)

MAMMALS ■ Carnivores

About the track
- Track has four toes with thick claws on both front and hind feet.
- Tracks measured in the Northern Tuli Game Reserve in Botswana are front foot 97mm and hind foot 78mm.
- Characteristic are the kidney-shaped outside toes, similar to spotted hyaena tracks in this regard.
- The brown hyaena has a thick mat of hair around the foot, which often shows in the track, particularly in soft substrate.
- The toes are grouped tightly together, particularly on the hind foot – almost jigsaw puzzle-like.
- Heavy claw marks usually show up clearly in the track, although the extensive mat of hair around the feet can partially obscure them.
- Although the main pad posterior edge is asymmetrical, this is not as marked when compared with that of the spotted hyaena.
- A diagnostic feature of the track is the significantly smaller hind foot (up to 25mm shorter than the front foot) – unlike the spotted hyaena.
- Hyaenas (and aardwolf) have a unique gait where their hind leg swings across the centre line of movement and steps next to the front foot on the opposite side. For instance, the right hind foot will leave a track just behind the left front foot. Depending on the speed at which the hyaena is moving, the hind foot can register behind, next to, or slightly on top of the front foot. This distinctive walking pattern sets this animal apart from cats.
- As with all the hyaenas, the hind foot registers facing outwards at an angle of about 25 degrees to the front foot, which faces in the direction of the animal's movement.

Can be confused with ...
- *Tracks of brown and **spotted hyaena** can be confused. However, the brown hyaena shows a more notable size difference between the front and hind tracks. Evidence of hair often shows around the edges of the feet, which is absent in its spotted cousin. Brown hyaena front foot claws are longer than those of the spotted hyaena.*

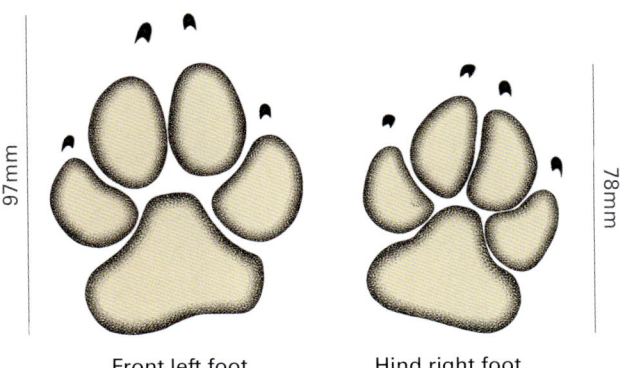

Front left foot   Hind right foot

MAMMALS ■ Carnivores

Spotted hyaena
Crocuta crocuta

This incredibly smart carnivore has light brown fur with dark brown spots that fade with age. Its massive jaws, powerful shoulders and front legs are all perfectly designed for tearing hides, ripping flesh and crushing the largest of bones. Females are larger than males.

The spotted hyaena inhabits most savanna habitat types; absent in dense forest and desert.

Habits
- Predominantly nocturnal, but also active during the day.
- Gregarious, they live in female-led (matriarchal) groups of 30 or more animals, depending on food availability.
- Females dominate males socially and stay together for life; they are the social nucleus of the clan.
- Extraordinarily good caretakers of the next generation, high-ranking females rear more cubs than subordinate females.
- They may travel up to 50km a night in search of food.
- Capable hunters but better known (sometimes wrongly) as scavengers that feed on medium-sized to large ungulates. They apply a more focused strategy in their hunting and foraging than many other carnivores: injured, aged or sick animals are selected and chased relentlessly over long distances at speeds of up to 55km/h.
- The female appears to have 'masculinised genitalia' with an elongated clitoris that forms a fully erectile structure through which it urinates, mates and gives birth. The vaginal labia are folded over and resemble the male scrotum – making it challenging to determine their sex.

Den
- They mainly use caves or disused aardvark holes in termite mounds in which to den.
- Although bones and skulls may be found near the den, this is not typical of the spotted hyaena – but is noticeable with the brown hyaena.
- In the southern Kruger National Park, dens in disused termite mounds are often situated in thickets or close to dry riverbeds.
- Spotted hyaena seldom brings leftover food back to the den – unlike brown hyaena.

A typical hyaena den site in a disused aardvark hole in a termite mound; the slopes of the mound are worn bare from the traffic.

MAMMALS ■ Carnivores

- Fresh and old tracks showing hyaenas moving back and forth on a well-used game path could well indicate the presence of a den.

Feeding and diet
- Spotted hyaenas are highly opportunistic hunters of medium-sized to large ungulates, but smaller prey, such as springhares, birds and reptiles, is also eaten.
- Clans of up to four have been recorded successfully hunting large animals like gemsbok and eland.

Spotted hyaena vomit, complete with butchered lamb bone from a lodge!

- They readily eat carrion, which they detect by smell, the sounds of other predators feeding, or by the distress calls made by prey being killed. Their senses of smell and hearing are particularly acute.
- If hyaenas outnumber lions by three (or more) to one, they are capable of stealing a carcass from them; however, they appear to show greater respect for dominant male lions.
- When challenging another predator for a carcass, the clan will converge and set up a chorus of high-pitched giggling and laughing calls.

Droppings
- Fresh droppings are dark green or brown but turn white as they dry, due to oxidation of the considerable quantity of bone (containing calcium) in their diet.
- Droppings are cylindrical, segmented with blunt ends, measuring 35–40mm in diameter.
- Spotted hyaena droppings are generally larger and a little more coarse in consistency than those of the brown hyaena.
- Occasionally a 'fur ball' is vomited up containing hair, bone fragments and hooves (even a Christmas decoration from a neighbouring tourist camp!).

Old droppings turn white surprisingly quickly.

Spotted hyaena's latrine site with scent-marking and old droppings

MAMMALS ■ Carnivores

Territorial behaviour
- Hyaenas scent-mark their territories by smearing grass stems with drops of strong-smelling, dark yellow (turning black) paste from their anal scent glands.
- They create latrines with pastings throughout their territory, and along territorial boundaries.
- The dry white droppings form an important visual territorial mark.
- In the Sabi Sands Game Reserve, spotted hyaenas defecate in latrines in a core area of 50–75m^2, but droppings may be deposited over a larger area beyond.

About the track
- Track lengths measured at Londolozi Game Reserve are front foot 106mm and hind foot 101mm.
- The track shows four toes with stout claws on both front and hind feet.
- Considerably less size difference between front and hind feet, unlike brown hyaena.
- The kidney-shaped outside toes are characteristic.
- The toes are grouped tightly together, and occasionally a distinctive ridge of soil forms between the toes and the main pad, with soil creating a 'peak' in the middle of the track – particularly evident in mud or wet sand. By contrast, leopard and lion tracks tend to show slightly larger gaps between their toes.

Above: The hyaena's hind foot lands at an angle slightly offset from the direction of travel.
Above right: A hyaena front left track – notice the kidney-shaped outside toes.
Right: The peak or ridge of sand in the middle of the track

Prominent 'peak' of sand sometimes forms between the toes and main pad

MAMMALS ■ Carnivores

- The main pad is asymmetrical in shape, with one of the two lobes on the posterior edge extending lower than the other.
- The front feet are generally larger, which no doubt supports the powerfully built forequarters that assist with functions such as gripping, crushing and tearing.
- It is assumed that the bigger females' tracks are larger than the tracks of males, although evidence is still being gathered.
- Hyaenas (and aardwolf) have a unique gait where their hind leg swings across the centre line of movement and steps next to the front foot on the opposite side. For instance, the right hind foot will leave a track just behind the left front foot. Depending on the speed at which the hyaena is moving, the hind foot can register behind, next to, or slightly on top of the front foot. This distinctive walking pattern sets this animal apart from cats.
- As with all the hyaenas, the hind foot will register facing outwards at an angle of about 25 degrees to the front foot, which faces in the direction of the animal's movement.

Spotted hyaena hind foot; notice two posterior lobes.

Can be confused with ...

- *The spotted hyaena track may be confused with that of the smaller **brown hyaena**. However, a brown hyaena's front foot claws are marginally longer and there's a notable size difference between its front and hind track (hind track of brown hyaena is 20mm smaller than the front). In soft substrate, the brown hyaena's track often shows a significant mat of hair around the edges of the feet, and its toes are more tightly arranged than those of the spotted. The main pad posterior edge of the spotted hyaena is less symmetrical in its form, with one lobe on the posterior edge extending lower than the other.*

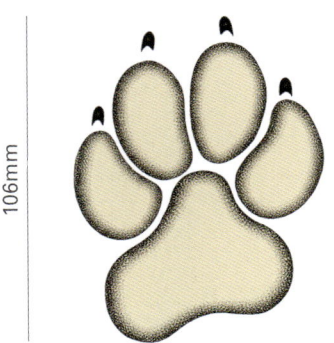

106mm   101mm

Front left foot   Hind right foot

MAMMALS ■ Large mammals

African elephant
Loxodonta africana

The largest living land mammal, an elephant bull may weigh up to 6,000kg. Mostly confined to protected areas, there are around 415,000 wild African elephants (2021), a number vastly lower than the 26 million that roamed the continent in the early 1800s, and particularly disheartening considering a loss of over 100,000 elephants in the last decade.

In southern Africa, elephants inhabit savanna woodland and grassland, which offer access to food, water and shade.

Habits
- Elephants are active at most times of the day and night, resting for short periods. They can move up to 30km per day in the dry season.
- Gregarious; each family unit is made up of about ten closely related females and calves led by a matriarch.
- Elephants frequent known feeding areas where water is accessible, their well-used paths often serving for hundreds of years.
- Using their front feet and trunk, elephants will dig for water in dry riverbeds.
- Elephants enjoy swimming on hot days, often submerging themselves entirely if the water is deep enough.
- They may rest standing up, but also sleep leaning against termite mounds, and occasionally they lie down.

Feeding and diet
- Predominantly browsers of a wide variety of plants (up to 130 plant species), they will also graze in the summertime.
- During the wet season, elephants eat fruits, leaves, shoots, seeds and seedpods.
- In the dry winter months they feed extensively on roots, bark and twigs, including those of the mopane tree (*Colophospermum mopane*), a vital component of the winter diet.
- They also browse on acacia (*Senegalia*) species, eating the leaves, bark and wood.
- African elephants use their tusks to strip bark off trees, so accessing the desirable cambium layer underneath.
- Elephants, particularly bulls, push over trees to access the roots, leaves and bark.

Elephant's foot; notice creases.

MAMMALS ■ Large mammals

Droppings
- Barrel-shaped, about 200mm in diameter, coarse and containing fibrous material such as small twigs, bark, leaves, and occasionally fruits.

Elephant droppings containing fruits of the marula tree (Sclerocarya birrea)

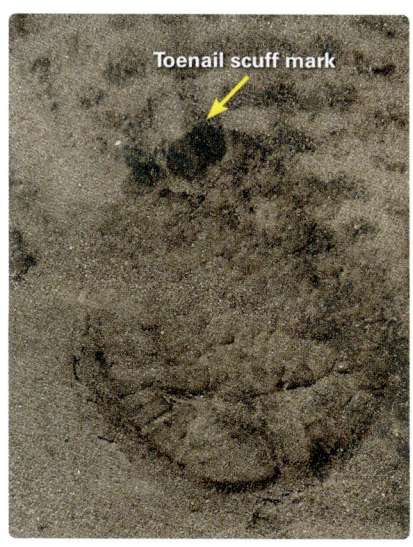

Elephant front track

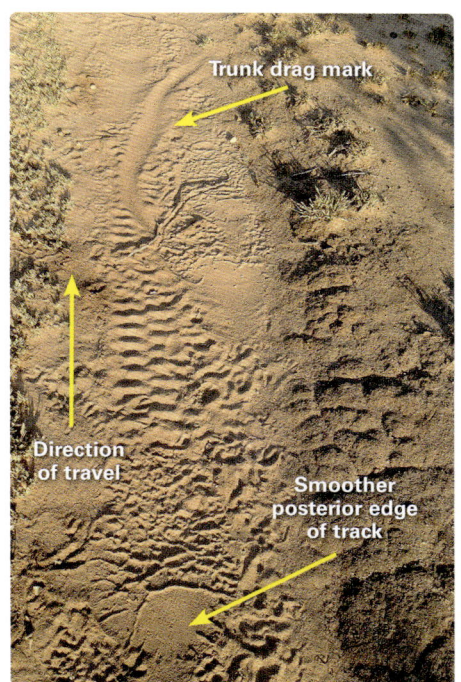

A clear and detailed elephant trail

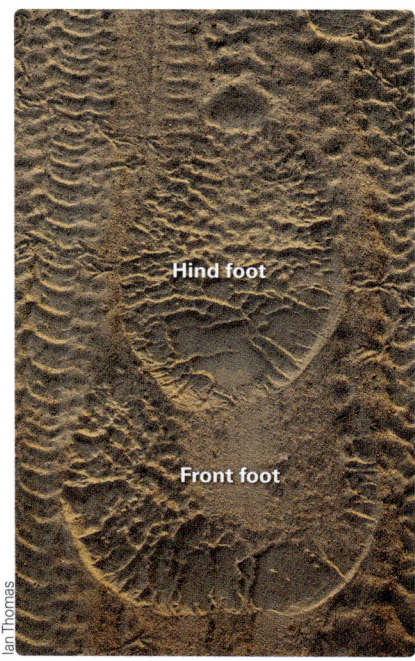

Elephant front and hind track; the hind track is narrower and more oval in shape.

MAMMALS ■ Large mammals

About the track
- Elephants' unmistakable large, round tracks have five indistinguishable toes on the front foot and four on the hind foot.
- Track lengths vary, as shown in the table below.

| ELEPHANT TRACK MEASUREMENTS: BULLS VERSUS COWS |||||
| Tracks measured from a sample of 20 bulls and 20 cows |||||
	Front foot length	Front foot width	Hind foot length	Hind foot width
An adult bull	**505mm**	**472mm**	**566mm**	**354mm**
Median measurement	475mm	355mm	502mm	318mm
An adult cow	**446mm**	**347mm**	**492mm**	**284mm**
Median measurement	427mm	332mm	480mm	308mm

- Front foot track is broad and round in shape, whereas the hind foot is narrower and more oval.
- The soles of the feet are rough and cracked, leaving a wrinkled pattern of cracks and creases in the track.
- There is a thicker layer of cartilage on the posterior edge, resulting in fewer cracks forming in this area of the track; noting this smoother section helps establish the direction in which the elephant is moving. Subtle scuff marks created by the toenails also help to indicate direction.
- The layer of cartilage under the feet cushions and distributes the weight of the animal, enabling it to move surprisingly silently.

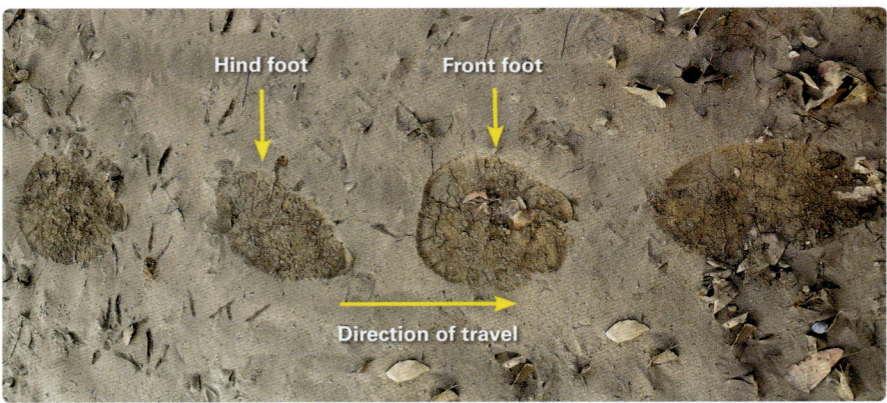

An elephant trail showing the direction of travel

MAMMALS ■ Large mammals

- Tracks are often accompanied by drag marks made by the trunk. Bull elephants in particular tend to drag their trunk, creating a serpentine trail.
- At a normal walking gait, the hind foot registers partially on top of the front foot. As the animal speeds up, so the hind foot registers progressively further forward, and at maximum speed, some distance in front of the front foot.
- Skinner's *Mammals of the Southern African Subregion* claims the circumference of the front foot multiplied by 2.5 equals the shoulder height.
- According to wildlife scientist Peter Apps, the length of the bull's hind foot multiplied by 5.8, and that of the cow by 5.5, equals the shoulder height.

Following elephant trails

- Elephants, particularly breeding herds, walk long distances and may be spread out over an extensive area if they are not moving with purpose. Range size varies relative to the availability of food and water – with a mean average of 880km^2 (Whyte, 2001) for breeding herds in the Kruger National Park.
- Trackers should be aware of the possibility of unknown herds, with unfamiliar traits and personalities, moving into an area under observation.
- Elephant signs include tracks, scuff marks, droppings, urine, a pungent musth odour (males), flattened grass, bark stripped from trees, chewed plant and wood material, small branches stripped of bark, felled trees, and mud smeared on leaves or rubbed on trees at a height of 2–3m above the ground.
- Trackers must ensure that they are following sufficiently 'fresh' signs, particularly when there is regular elephant activity in an area. It is easy to confuse new signs with older ones, so it is a good idea to touch and assess the moisture in such signs – bearing in mind that moisture evaporates very quickly, especially on a warm day.
- Foraging elephants usually do not follow natural game paths. They move at 3–10km/h, depending on whether they are feeding or not.
- The sounds of breaking branches or elephants' communicative 'rumbling' noises are often heard. That said, they can also be exceptionally silent, and may be stumbled upon quite unexpectedly. If disturbed, the entire herd will often stand dead still and listen quietly.

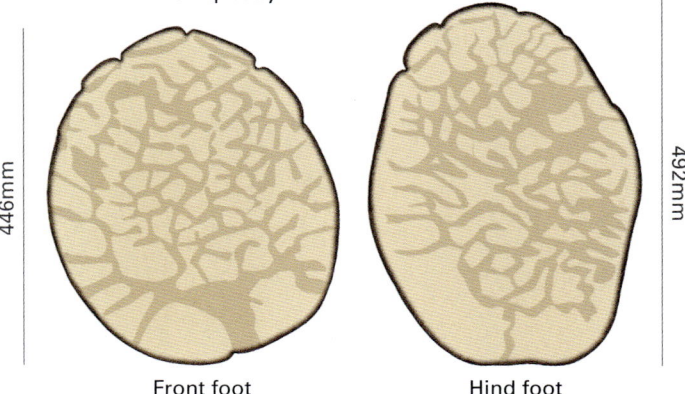

Front foot   Hind foot

MAMMALS ■ Large mammals

- Trumpeting, rumbling and squealing are sounds indicative of social interaction from within the herd; trackers approaching on foot should proceed with caution.
- Elephants enjoy wallowing in mud, using their front feet to kick and loosen soil to spray onto their back and behind their ears. Shallow divots of soil, as wide as their feet, are signs that elephants have passed this way, given that they are the only animals to practise this behaviour.
- Once bathed, they will rub against a mature tree to rid themselves of ectoparasites, leaving a thick layer of mud caked on the tree.
- If disturbed, elephants will turn to face the threat, head held high, ears out and tail lifted.
- They have an excellent sense of smell and hearing: it is therefore critical to know the wind direction when on foot in the vicinity. However, their eyesight is not particularly good; it is thought to be similar to that of humans, except that elephants have the advantage of height.
- In a serious confrontation, an elephant will put its head down, tuck its trunk away, flatten its ears against its body and charge without much noise.
- Bull elephants periodically enter a state of increased sexual activity, called musth: fluid drips from the penis (droplets can be seen with their tracks), giving off a pungent smell that lingers. During this state their testosterone levels are elevated, and as a result they become more aggressive and are to be respected and avoided.

A knob thorn tree (Senegalia nigrescens) *stripped of its bark by an elephant*

Muddy evidence of elephant rubbing on a tree

A hole dug by an elephant in a dry riverbed reveals a small pool of water.

Black (hook-lipped) rhinoceros
Diceros bicornis

This often cantankerous pachyderm weighs up to 1,200kg and has two horns that may be of similar length. The species is smaller than the white rhino and, as its name implies, has a triangular-shaped prehensile upper lip, used to browse leaves. Africa has lost 90% of its black rhino population; with a current population of some 5,600 animals (2021), the species is listed as Critically Endangered.

This rhino inhabits savanna woodland with thick bush that provides plenty of cover.

Habits
- Diurnal, most active in the early morning and late afternoon; tends to lie up in shade during the heat of the day.
- Solitary, but females are found with calves (up to three years of age) and with males during courtship.
- Partial to wallowing in mud and water in an attempt to cool down and rid themselves of ectoparasites.
- When on the move, calves walk behind their mother, not in front, as with the white rhino.
- Bulls fight aggressively over females in oestrus.
- Poor eyesight but acute senses of smell and hearing.
- A female black rhino with a calf may be very dangerous and may charge unexpectedly – they are best avoided.

Feeding and diet
- They browse on leaves and fruits.
- Occasionally they pull down large branches, and even push over medium-sized trees to access the leaves.
- They feed on a wide variety of plant species, with a preference for acacias (*Vachellia* and *Senegalia*), *Euclea* species and tamboti trees (*Spirostachys africana*) in southern Kruger National Park.
- Well known for tolerating poisonous plants such as the tree euphorbia.

Notice the acacia branches 'cut' at a 45-degree angle by black rhinos.

Droppings
- Diameter of 150–170mm, with fragments of small branches, short twigs and leaves. Occasionally a coppery colour. Often found kicked from a territorial scrape – so incomplete in terms of shape.

Black rhino droppings

MAMMALS — Large mammals

Black rhinos pull down branches to get at fresh leaves, much as elephants and eland do.

Note the angle of the rhino's bite when it feeds on small branches.

Territorial behaviour

- In territorial middens, males (and occasionally females) defecate, then kick and scrape their droppings using their hind feet.
- Females create shorter, less exaggerated scrapes.
- According to conservationist Dr Simon Morgan, black rhino bulls produce longer, more winding scrapes than the shorter, straighter scrapes of white rhino bulls.
- Youngsters have been observed imitating their mothers by kicking their droppings.
- Individuals passing through an area, or rhinos defecating away from a territorial midden, tend not to kick or scrape their droppings.
- Mature males also spray urine into bushes.
- Interestingly, where both species of rhino share a range, they occasionally make use of the same territorial midden.

Black rhino bull territorial mark – notice the long, sinuous scrape.

About the track

- This large, odd-toed ungulate's track has three distinctive toes – a large, wide middle toe and two smaller outer toes – with thick, sturdy toenails.
- Adult track measurements are front foot 240mm and hind foot 230mm, although smaller individuals' tracks of 200mm have also been recorded. Measurements of an adult bull desert-adapted black rhino (*Diceros bicornis bicornis*) show front foot 270mm and hind foot 260mm in length.
- The front track is marginally broader than the hind track, and its outside toes are situated closer to the middle toe.
- Telling left from right foot: the inside toe is situated further forward in the track than the outside toe. The middle toe slopes down towards the outside of the track.
- The sole contains a spongy pad of cartilage that cushions the foot from impact with the ground.
- The shape and appearance of the black rhino's footprint has been likened to the silhouette of a person wearing a pair of headphones.

MAMMALS ■ Large mammals

DESERT-ADAPTED BLACK RHINO (BULL) TRACK MEASUREMENTS

	Front foot length	Front foot width	Hind foot length	Hind foot width
1	270mm	260mm	260mm	240mm
2	260mm	240mm	240mm	230mm
3	230mm	225mm	215mm	195mm
Median measurement	260mm	240mm	240mm	230mm

- On hard ground, the large middle toenail is the only feature that makes an impression, along with a faint scuff mark.
- The normal walking gait shows the hind foot landing behind the front foot at a slight angle, or registering on top of the front foot when the animal is travelling faster.
- When the rhino runs or gallops, it transfers its weight forward onto its toes, resulting in the toenails digging deeper into the ground.

Following black rhino trails
- Black rhinos follow familiar trails to water holes, especially when water is scarce. They usually drink in the early morning and late evening.
- When browsing, rhinos walk from thicket to thicket, or grove to grove. At Phinda Game Reserve they appear to move from one tamboti (*Spirostachys africana*) thicket to the next.
- Clear tracks may not always be visible, in which case the tracker must look for other signs, such as trampled or bruised grass and plants, broken or 'cut' branches, wet mud on surrounding bushes, and a disturbed substrate.
- Trees and small bushes that black rhinos have fed on will typically have branches bitten off at a 45-degree angle.
- Black rhinos wallow in mud and then rub up against trees, rocks and stumps to rid themselves of ectoparasites. They also make extensive use of familiar rubbing posts, leaving them with perfectly smooth, shiny surfaces.
- Their movements can often be inferred from the landscape and time of day; for example, if

Black rhino front foot track

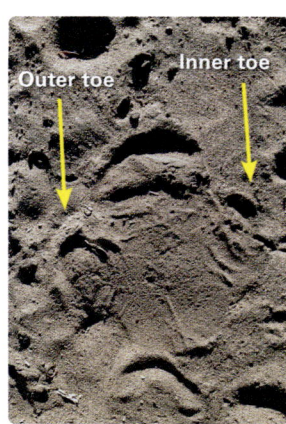

Black rhino hind foot track; notice the outside toes of the hind foot are positioned comparatively lower than those of the white rhino.

MAMMALS ■ Large mammals

following a fresh rhino trail mid-morning, one can assume that the animal is headed for shade in a dry riverbed or dense woodland. Knowing the direction from which the animal has come can also be a useful start for determining its intended direction.
- On hard ground, scuff marks might show where a rhino has slightly dragged its feet, exposing the darker soil beneath. Bare patches of soil can reveal almost imperceptible clues and are worth investigating closely.
- Both males and females leave urine and territorial scrape marks as they move; parallel scrape marks can be several metres in length.
- Sounds of a rhino sighing, snorting, stamping its feet (to rid itself of flies) or scraping its rough hide through a thorn bush are all noises commonly associated with tracking rhinos on foot.
- Oxpeckers (genus *Buphagus*) – birds that sit on rhinos to feed on external parasites – will call and occasionally fly up in alarm if a human or predator approaches. The alerted rhino will invariably turn to face the threat, and raise its head and snort, sometimes advancing to investigate.
- If bothered, it may charge. Black rhinos are well known for being short-tempered.
- It is vital to be aware of available cover or suitable trees for climbing when following a fresh black rhino trail.

Black rhino hind foot track

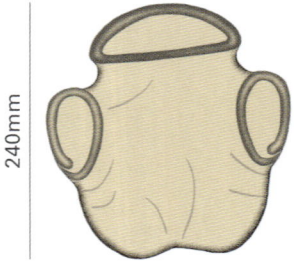

Front left foot

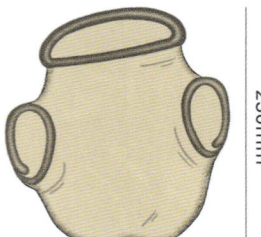

Hind left foot

Can be confused with ...

- *Compared with those of the **white rhino**, the black rhino's outside toes are smaller, narrower and are situated further from the middle toe. Black rhino tracks are 50–70mm shorter than white rhino tracks.*
- *In clear substrate, black rhino tracks (which reveal creases and lines that are unique to each individual) show fewer creases than those of white rhinos.*
- *The posterior edge of the black rhino track has a shallow indentation, while that of the white rhino is deeper and more distinct. The overall shape of the black rhino track is oval compared to the overall 'box' shape of that of the white rhino.*

White rhinoceros
Ceratotherium simum

Also known as the square-lipped rhinoceros, this is the second-largest land mammal, weighing up to 2,200kg. Despite its mass, it is surprisingly light on its feet and is known for its relatively docile nature. Having recovered from a population of a mere 100 individuals in the early 1900s, the 18,000 that remain in the wild in southern Africa (2021) are again under poaching pressure for their horn.

White rhinos prefer flat, open savanna grassland with available cover. They drink regularly and may trespass onto other rhinos' territories to access water.

Habits
- Predominantly diurnal, white rhinos are active in the early morning and late afternoon and sometimes at night. They usually drink water in the late afternoon to early evening.
- Gregarious, they form small groups of two to five females, subadults and young; dominant bulls are solitary and territorial.
- Adults and calves make growling, squealing and shrieking sounds when interacting. There is always an abundance of vocalisation when bulls approach mothers and their calves.
- When fleeing, the calves will run ahead of their mother.

Feeding and diet
- They prefer short, fresh grass and are selective grazers of grasses such as *Panicum maximum* and *Themeda triandra*.

Droppings
- As grazers, white rhinos produce large droppings that are relatively fine in texture, and measure about 170mm in diameter.
- Rhino dung is darker (becoming black with age) than elephant dung, which is brown and coarser in texture.

Cow and calf droppings; notice the mustard-coloured liquid dropping of four-week-old calf.

Territorial behaviour
- Territorial bulls spray urine, defecate and then scrape dung along the ground using their hind feet, leaving two striking drag marks. Territorial bulls make extensive use of middens throughout their territory, which often contain large piles of dung, both old and fresh.

MAMMALS ■ Large mammals

- During the summer months the middens become magnets for scores of dung beetle species.
- Territorial middens are usually located near water holes, next to roads and along natural game paths.
- Interestingly, young sausage trees (Kigelia africana) have often been noticed growing in white rhino middens in the Sabi Sands Game Reserve.
- Although females will defecate on or near territorial middens, they generally do not scrape their dung.
- Where both species share a range, black and white rhinos are known to make use of the same territorial midden.

Territorial bulls make use of middens, which often contain large piles of old as well as fresher dung. Interestingly, white and black rhinos may even share middens.

Young sausage tree (Kigelia africana) *growing out of a rhino midden*

About the track

- Track has three distinctive toes with thick, sturdy toenails: a large middle toe, with two smaller outer toes situated close to the middle one.
- A white rhino adult bull's front foot length has been measured at 290mm and hind foot 275mm.
- Samples of tracks from 22 bulls and 22 cows show that bull tracks are on average longer (by 20mm) and broader (by 15–20mm) than female tracks.

	Front foot length	Front foot width	Hind foot length	Hind foot width
WHITE RHINO TRACK MEASUREMENTS: BULLS VERSUS COWS *Tracks were measured from a sample of 22 bulls and 22 cows*				
An adult bull	**290mm**	**280mm**	**275mm**	**260mm**
Median measurement	294mm	287mm	278mm	269mm
An adult cow	**260mm**	**250mm**	**270mm**	**220mm**
Median measurement	275mm	265mm	268mm	247mm

MAMMALS ■ Large mammals

Far left: A typical white rhino track showing characteristic creases
Left: White rhino front and hind tracks

- The overall shape of the white rhino track is square, whereas the black rhino's is oval or circular.
- The sole contains a pad of spongy cartilage that, in soft substrate, may produce a track with a random pattern of small block-like creases; this print is unique to each rhino, and potentially helpful to trackers for monitoring individual specimens.
- The posterior edge has a distinctive indentation (two lobes), although this feature can be difficult to distinguish in hard substrate.
- On hard ground, the middle toenail is often the only feature that makes an impression, along with scuff marks.
- White rhinos sometimes drag their bottom lip along the ground, creating a 200mm-wide drag mark.
- A typical walking gait shows the hind foot registering just behind or partially on top of the front foot, with the feet facing outwards slightly.

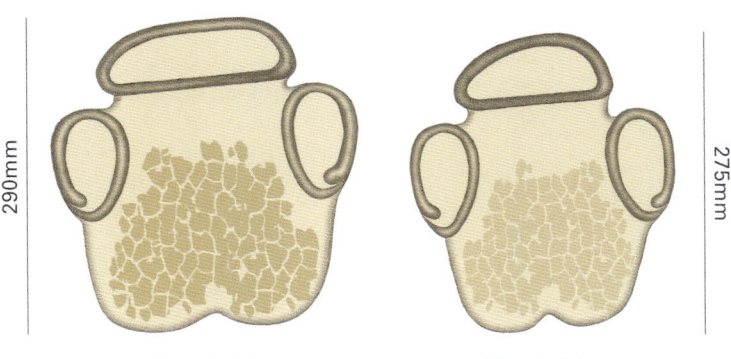

Front left foot　　　　　　　　Hind left foot

MAMMALS ■ Large mammals

Rhino rubbing post

White rhino bull tracks observed along a game path

- To determine left from right foot, note that the inside toe is situated slightly further forward than the outside toe. The middle toe angles down towards the outside of the track.
- Rhinos put more pressure on the inside edge of their feet. Most of this pressure, measured at 14kg/cm^2, is felt by their toes. Only 3kg/cm^2 is applied to their pads, which is similar to the pressure experienced by human feet (based on research conducted by John Hutchinson, Royal Veterinary College).

Following white rhino trails

- White rhinos often follow familiar trails to water holes, especially when water is scarce – drinking mostly in the evening.
- Smooth, polished rubbing posts, used by both black and white rhinos to relieve themselves of ectoparasites and rub off mud, are reliable evidence of their presence.
- They wallow in mud to cool off, then rub themselves on trees, branches and leaves to get rid of external parasites. Evidence of ticks can be found in the drying exfoliated mud.
- White rhinos meander randomly (searching for suitable grazing) and can be challenging to track, but when on the move or marking territory, they will walk with purpose in one general direction, often using game paths.
- Young animals normally graze close to their mother and remain even closer when on the move.
- It can be useful to establish which grass species these animals are feeding on; should you lose the trail, you can focus on areas of their preferred grazing.

MAMMALS ■ Large mammals

- When clear tracks are not visible, trackers must look for other signs, such as bent, damaged or bruised grass and plants, mud clumps, as well as obvious disturbances in the soil.
- Animals' movements can often be inferred from the landscape and the time of day; for example, if following a fresh rhino trail mid-morning, one can assume that the animal is headed for shade in a dry riverbed or dense woodland. Knowing the direction from which the animal has come is also a useful start to determining its intended direction.
- White rhinos will often move between termite mounds in search of nutritious grazing, which makes termite mounds useful beacons for tracking. Bare patches of soil can reveal clues, and should be closely investigated, particularly if the tracking conditions are difficult.
- On hard ground, one may find the odd scuff mark where the animal has slightly dragged its feet, exposing darker soil underneath. Dislodged stones and broken or fractured branches and stumps are also possible evidence of rhinos having passed by.
- Dominant bulls leave urine and territorial scrape marks as they move.
- Sounds of rhinos sighing, snorting, stomping the ground (to rid themselves of biting flies), or the rustle of thorn bushes scraping the tough pachyderms' hide – are all commonly heard when in the vicinity of rhinos.
- Oxpecker birds (genus *Buphagus*), which sit on rhinos to feed on external parasites, may call and fly up in alarm if a human or predator approaches.
- Females with calves are not tolerant of males and will vocalise loudly if an individual gets too close. With their ears folded back, they produce snorting and growling sounds.
- When disturbed, they will raise their ears and turn to face the threat. If bothered, they will mostly avoid confrontation and run in the opposite direction – however, out of confusion and because of their bad eyesight, they may run towards one!
- It is vital to be aware of available cover when tracking rhinos.
- Generally speaking, the white rhino does not display aggression towards people on foot.

Can be confused with ...

- *Confusion between white and **black rhinoceros** tracks is common – the black rhino's track is smaller (by 50–70mm), its outside toes are situated further away from the middle toe, and the profile of its posterior edge shows a less defined indentation. The black rhino's outside toes are significantly smaller.*
  *The posterior edge of the white rhino's track has a distinctive two-lobed indentation – which can be difficult to distinguish in hard substrate. The **black rhino** track shows only one clear lobe on its posterior edge, although there is a slight, indistinct indentation.*
- *White rhinos sometimes drag their bottom lip along the ground, creating a 200mm-wide drag mark. **Hippos** do the same, but less often – and when they do, there's usually evidence in the soil of coarse lower-lip hairs.*

MAMMALS ■ Large mammals

Hippopotamus
Hippopotamus amphibius

The hippopotamus's elongated, barrel-like body weighs 1,500kg and is carried on short, stocky legs. This species' essential habitat requirement is a constant body of water deep enough for full submersion, with good grazing nearby. A taste for crops, combined with a wandering nature, means that hippos have not fared well outside of protected areas in Africa.

Habits

- Hippos require water deep enough for full submersion – a depth of about 1.5m. When at rest, partly submerged in water, the hippo's eyes, ears and nostrils, which are all situated towards the top of its head, remain just above the surface.
- Emerging for a breath of air while resting is an automatic (reflex) action. Adults may remain under water for five to six minutes at a time.
- Water and mud provide protection from biting flies and sunburn.
- Nocturnal, resting in the water during the day, then relocating to their grazing lawns to feed through the night.
- Gregarious, living in groups, or schools, of up to 30, comprising cows with calves, subadults and a single dominant bull.
- Both mating and nursing takes place in the water.
- They regularly sun themselves on riverbanks on warm winter days.
- They have a surprising variety of vocalisations ranging from loud roars and grunts to screams and croaks. They also vocalise in alarm if a predator makes an appearance near the water's edge.
- Yawning – displaying their large tusks – is a show of dominance and can warn of an intention to charge.
- They are potentially very aggressive and dangerous. In spite of their apparently obese frame and short legs, hippos can easily outrun a human.

Hippo droppings deposited on a prominent bush along a game path

MAMMALS ■ Large mammals

Hippo droppings

Scattered hippo droppings on a marula tree – a characteristic sign

Feeding and diet
- Their diet consists mainly of short grass, and they may consume up to 40kg of grass a night, such as *Panicum maximum*, *Urochloa mosambicensis* and *Cynodon dactylon*.
- Occasionally, when there is insufficient grass, they will eat floating aquatic plants.
- Although herbivorous, they may show interest in meat and even gnaw on a carcass (such as may be left by crocodiles).

Droppings
- Hippo bulls scatter their droppings by wagging their tail rapidly from side to side as they defecate. Scattered droppings can be found on prominent bushes and tree trunks next to their paths.
- It is not certain why hippos scatter their droppings. Theories of navigation and territorial marking have been suggested, although hippo bulls are not generally territorial out of the water.
- Females and young hippos may deposit their dung without flicking their tail, creating droppings of 80mm in diameter, which are usually deposited where the animal has rested during the night's feeding.

Hippo tracks

Typical hippo track

MAMMALS ■ Large mammals

Territorial behaviour
- A territorial bull actively defends its stretch of 100–500m of water by aggressively seeing off rivals to its position.
- Fights over territory can be ferocious and noisy, and can inflict serious harm on participants.
- Hippos are not generally territorial out of the water.

About the track
- The hippo track has four distinct toes.
- The front foot toes and main pad are larger than those of the hind foot, the front foot measuring 250mm and hind foot 230mm in length.
- In certain substrates, the two middle toes sometimes 'fuse', making the track resemble that of a rhino (with three toes).
- The heavy toenails push deeper into the sand or mud than the toes; the main pad impression is often indistinct.
- Hippos regularly drag their feet as they walk, leaving short signature scuff marks.
- Left and right feet appear either side of the straddle centre, which creates well-worn paths with a clear 'middelmannetjie' (exposed middle ridge of sand or grass) – called 'hippo highways', unique to hippos.
- At night they can travel up to 30km in search of suitable grass. Hippos use familiar paths to access the water and grazing lawns – paths found both on land and underwater.
- Occasionally, hippos scrape their mouth on the ground, leaving a wide (hairy) drag mark, similar to that of white rhino.
- They regularly drop bits of chewed grass from their mouths as they move.
- Aquatic plants may remain draped over their back for long distances. Dried pieces of stringy black aquatic plant found along a game path may point to the passage of hippos.

Bull hippo tracks in a riverbed

A well-worn hippo path; notice the middle ridge ('middelmannetjie').

MAMMALS ■ Large mammals

Can be confused with ...

- The outside toes are positioned wide of the two middle toes, unlike the two tightly set outside toes of the two species of **rhino**.
- Occasionally, hippos scrape their mouth on the ground, as do **white rhinos**, leaving a wide drag mark. The hippo scrape shows evidence of more coarse, lower-lip hairs.

250mm — Front left foot

230mm — Hind left foot

Hippos in the Sand River at Londolozi

MAMMALS ■ Large mammals

African buffalo
Syncerus caffer

This large, powerful and potentially menacing bovid has short legs, and thick, curving horns that become thicker with age. Buffaloes are dark red to black in colour. Heavily built males weigh up to 800kg. Buffalo face the threat of continuous habitat fragmentation within their range, particularly due to cattle farming, and conflicts with humans exacerbate the issue.

A voracious grazer, this animal requires lots of long grass and plenty of water and shade.

Habits
- Highly gregarious, the basic family unit is made up of related females and their young, collectively forming very large herds of hundreds, sometimes thousands.
- Adult males may form bachelor groups, while old bulls become solitary, moving in small ranges.
- In large herds, adult males are confronted with plenty of competition in their efforts to procreate: intense fights may develop over access to females in oestrus.
- Bigger, older animals enjoy higher social status, as do cows with calves.
- Calves suckle between their mother's back legs while she is on the move.
- Active at night, buffaloes travel long distances in order to feed. During the heat of the day they will lie up in the shade, ruminating.
- They are partial to wallowing in mud to cool down and to rid themselves of ectoparasites.

Feeding and diet
- They graze voraciously wherever they can find the most nutritious grass, and can also feed on dry, moribund grass with little apparent nutritional value. They are also known to browse on mopane leaves.
- Dependent on water, buffaloes drink every day, even twice a day in summer.

Droppings
- Droppings tend to be in one pile, like a large cowpat, but usually darker.
- The consistency and shape of the droppings vary with the seasonal diet. The abundance of nutritious green grass in summer results in looser droppings.

Buffalo droppings can resemble a large cowpat.

MAMMALS ■ Large mammals

African buffalo bull tracks

The hind foot registering directly on top of front foot

About the track
- The average length measured at Londolozi is front foot 122mm and hind foot 126mm (excluding the false hoof impressions) – tracks are slightly longer when false hooves make an impression. The bull's track is broader and more rounded than the cow's more oval-shaped footprint.
- The front foot track is curved and broad, with a small gap often showing between the hooves on the leading edge.
- The leading edge of the cloven hooves is more symmetrically shaped when compared to the asymmetrical, mismatched hoof tips of eland (p. 120).
- The hind track is marginally longer, but narrower than the front foot track, and shows less of a gap between the cloven hooves on the leading edge. The false hooves are positioned further back than those of the front foot, but only make an impression in soft substrate.
- A normal walking gait results in the hind foot registering on top of the front foot.

Following buffalo trails
- Large herds of buffalo can be heard long before they are seen. Sounds of their grunts and other vocalisations are a constant feature of the herd.
- Oxpeckers' churrs and chirping are commonly associated with buffaloes. Starlings and fork-tailed drongos also keep close company, hawking insects flushed out of the grass by the herd. Trackers should therefore listen for bird calls when following buffalo trails.

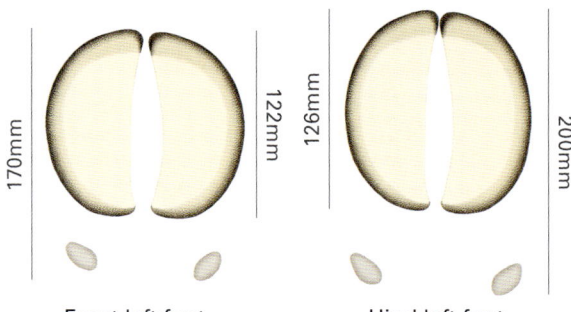

Front left foot　　　　　Hind left foot

MAMMALS ■ Large mammals

Marks where an African buffalo has stripped bark by rubbing its horns on a tree

The normal walking gait of a buffalo bull; notice the register.

- Large herds will leave conspicuous trails of trampled grass and droppings.
- Lone bulls spend much time in and around mud wallows, moving from here to grazing areas and dense thickets in which to lie up during the midday heat. They are best avoided.
- After wallowing, buffaloes leave wet mud on bushes, which is helpful for following their trail.
- They use natural game paths when moving purposefully to water, meandering and feeding.
- Bulls rub their forehead on trees to rid themselves of parasites, often stripping off the bark entirely. Using their head, they also thrash small bushes and break branches – in a combative manner.
- Exceptionally vigilant, particularly in a group, with very good eyesight, sense of smell and hearing. For their safety, trackers should take note of the wind direction.
- In large herds, they are normally calm and peaceful. If surprised, lone bulls can be aggressive, and charge without provocation. One should be very cautious tracking through dense thickets where there are fresh signs of buffalo activity.
- Potential signs of aggression are snorting, with the head held high and tossed.
- Tracks or signs of lions following buffalo herds could signal trouble: buffaloes are well known for showing redirected aggression!

Can be confused with ...

- *The buffalo track can resemble that of the **domestic cow**.*
- *Buffalo tracks can also be confused with **eland**; however, the eland's track is marginally narrower and regularly shows a mismatched (offset) gap between the hoof tips on the leading edge. The buffalo's track is broader, more curved and wider on the leading edge. The hoof edges of the eland are marginally straighter, with a greater difference in width between the larger front and narrower hind feet, whereas the buffalo track width is similar for both feet.*

MAMMALS ■ Large mammals

Giraffe
Giraffa camelopardalis

Giraffe males can reach a height of 5m, making them the tallest terrestrial animal. The scientific name refers to their facial resemblance to a camel teamed with the camouflage of a leopard. Both sexes have hairy, horn-like protuberances on their head, called ossicones, the male's being thicker, with less hair.

The giraffe inhabits savanna woodland areas.

Habits
- Mostly diurnal; gregarious, yet socially aloof; the herd structure changes continuously. Dominant bulls are usually solitary except during mating.
- Constantly on the move, in search of adequate browse.
- Males establish dominance through 'necking' – fighting, using the head and neck as a club-like weapon. These fights may go on for several hours. On rare occasions a male may knock down his rival during a fight.
- Vigilant, with good eyesight; if predators are detected, the giraffe will hold still and stare in the direction of the threat for a long time, occasionally making short blowing sounds.

Feeding and diet
- They browse in the tree canopy, using their tough, rubbery tongue to strip off leaves and flowers in amongst the thorns. Browse lines may form, which are clearly visible on species such as knob thorn (*Senegalia nigrescens*).
- Saliva left on leaves, as well as tracks on the ground below, are sure signs of browsing activity.
- They drink when water is available but also acquire moisture from their food.
- Giraffes are known to chew bones, a behaviour referred to as osteophagia, which enables them to access minerals that may be lacking in their diet, such as calcium and phosphorus.

Droppings
- Droppings are round, dark brown pellets, unusually small, 21–25mm in diameter, tapered at one end and indented on the other.

Giraffe droppings

MAMMALS ■ Large mammals

Giraffe front foot track

Giraffe tracks

Giraffe hind foot track, which is more pointed on the leading edge

- Due to the height from which they fall, droppings are scattered about over a large area. Giraffes defecate while on the move, further spreading their dung.
- Shapeless giraffe droppings clumped together in a blob are common in summer.

About the track

- This large ungulate's track length measures front foot 195mm and hind foot 190mm. Track lengths well over 220mm have been found.
- The front foot is broad and rectangular: the width is relatively constant over the length of the track, meaning the hoof edges are straight.
- The front foot leading edge is wide and blunt, whereas that of the hind foot is more pointed.
- The hooves are perfectly flat underneath, producing a smoothly textured track – which often causes giraffes to lose their footing over wet rocks or slippery terrain.
- Giraffes have an interesting rocking gait: they move both feet (front and hind) on each side simultaneously, followed by the other side, creating the track sequence (in close succession): left hind, left front; then right hind, right front.
- Giraffe tracks are often associated with odd circular marks on the ground (130mm in diameter), showing where the animal has turned around.

MAMMALS ■ Large mammals

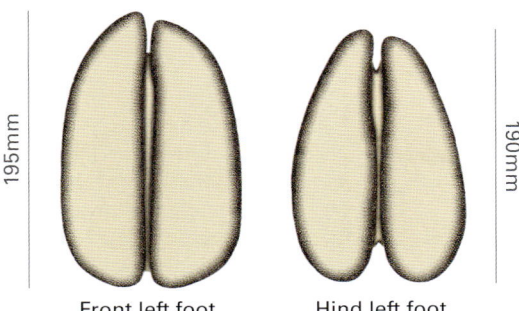

Front left foot — 195mm
Hind left foot — 190mm

- Sounds of breaking branches – more often associated with elephants – can sometimes indicate that giraffes are feeding in a woodland. They will walk over bushes and small trees to scratch their underbelly on the branches and rub their neck against trees.
- Giraffes are very alert around water, where they tend to drink mid-morning, and must spread their front legs wide in order to do so. Tracks showing the spread of the front feet can be found by observant trackers.

Male giraffes 'neck' to establish dominance.

Common eland
Tragelaphus oryx

After the giant eland (which is found further north in Africa), the common eland is the world's second-largest antelope. It stands up to 1.6m in height and can weigh 900kg. Males are darker in colour and considerably bigger than females.

This antelope tolerates a variety of habitats, including semi-desert and woodland savanna.

Habits
- Predominantly browsers, but will also graze during the wet season; largely independent of water.
- Diurnal – active in the early morning and late afternoon – but may also be active nocturnally.
- Gregarious, they are usually seen in small herds. Females are known to form nursery herds, which are joined by subadult males and females. Adult males form bachelor herds.
- Bulls fight to establish dominance yet do not mark or defend territories.

Feeding and diet
- Highly selective mixed feeders, both grazers and browsers. They are partial to mopane (*Colophospermum mopane*), red bushwillow (*Combretum apiculatum*), raisin bush (*Grewia* spp.), and apple-leaf trees (*Philenoptera violacea*).
- They can break off branches with their horns to access the leaves.
- Surviving without water for extended periods, they acquire much of their moisture requirements from the vegetation they eat.

Droppings
- Droppings are relatively elongated pellets measuring 20–25mm in diameter – smaller and with no tapering when compared with those of giraffe.
- Dung can fall in large clumps if the eland's diet has a high moisture content.

Eland droppings

About the track
- Measured at Samara Karoo Reserve: front foot 127mm, hind foot 115mm in length.

MAMMALS ■ Large mammals

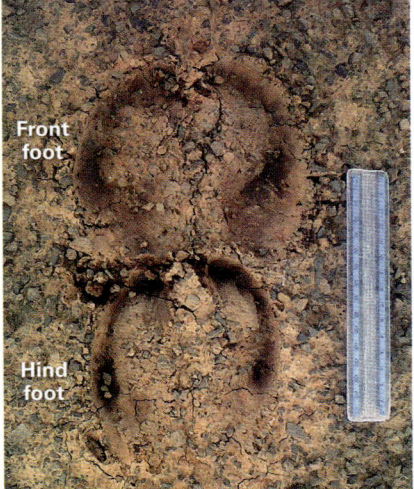

Eland front foot track is significantly broader than the hind foot – this is a diagnostic feature.

Leading edge of both front and hind hooves can be offset.

- The leading edge (hoof tip) of both front and hind tracks, where the cloven hooves meet, can be offset. This asymmetrical shape is seldom seen with buffalo.
- The front foot shows a distinctive gap between the cloven hooves where mud and soil pushes through, forming a ridge.
- The front foot track is wider and more curved than the narrower, less curved hind foot.
- The hind foot is (usually) noticeably narrower than the front foot, when compared with tracks of buffalo, where the widths are similar for front and hind feet.
- The typical gait results in the hind foot registering directly or partially on top of the front foot.

Can be confused with ...

- *This large antelope's track is very similar in appearance to that of a **buffalo** or **domestic cow**. However, the leading edge on the buffalo's front track is symmetrical in shape, whereas the eland's is offset. The buffalo's front foot is broader than the eland's on the leading edge, and the buffalo track is more curved. The presence of false hooves is more common with buffalo.*

Following eland trails

- As these animals graze and browse, their tracks meander, often crossing their own paths several times over a short distance.
- During summer in the Karoo, they move up into the mountains where it is cooler during the day.
- As one approaches eland, one may hear clicking sounds emanating from some individuals. According to research conducted by the Zoological Society of London and the University of Copenhagen, the sound is produced by a tendon in the knee as it moves across a leg bone. It is thought that the clicking sounds indicate the size and dominance of a bull.

MAMMALS ■ Large mammals

Typical eland track

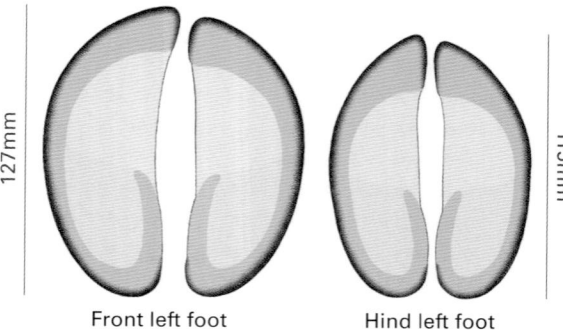

Front left foot — 127mm

Hind left foot — 115mm

Above: *A typical eland gait*
Below: *Bull in woodland*

Cape mountain zebra
Equus zebra zebra

This, the smallest of the zebras, is one of two mountain zebra subspecies, the other being Hartmann's mountain zebra. The Cape mountain zebra does not have the light brown 'shadow' stripes of the Burchell's (or plains) zebra and – unlike Burchell's – its legs are striped down their full length.

It inhabits the more mountainous regions of the Eastern and Western Cape, up to 2,000m above sea level, where it prefers grassland.

Habits
- Diurnal and gregarious; found in groups of four or five mares with their young, and a breeding stallion.
- They prefer grassland, grazing predominantly on the mountain plains in the rainy season and the mountain slopes in the dry season.
- Evidence of fighting (involving biting and kicking), in the form of scuff marks on the ground, is common.
- There is sometimes aggressive social dominance among mares and in bachelor groups.
- They make a high-pitched barking alarm call if predators are detected. Communication between members of the herd using a similar call is common.

Feeding and diet
- They graze in open grassland with access to clean water, usually drinking mid-morning.

Droppings
- Almost black (fresh) to light grey (older), kidney-shaped, coarse droppings – about 40–50mm in diameter.

Evidence of zebras having had a dust bath

The droppings of the Cape mountain zebra are kidney-shaped.

MAMMALS ■ Large mammals

About the track
- Tracks measured at Samara Karoo Reserve are front foot 75mm and hind foot 80mm in length.
- In certain substrates the track shows the 'frog' underneath the hoof – the frog is a triangular-shaped structure of dense tissue, which extends from the posterior edge to a point (the apex) in the middle of the hoof. The frog acts as a shock absorber as the hoof makes contact with the ground.
- The considerably thick hoof edges generally make a clear impression, particularly on hard ground.
- The front track is shorter and broader, while the hind track is longer, narrower and more oval in shape.

The hoof edge generally makes a clear imprint, particularly on hard ground.

Can be confused with ...
- The mountain zebra track is similar in shape and size to that of a **donkey**.
- Although separated by their habitat preference, the mountain zebra could be confused with the **Burchell's (plains) zebra**. However, Burchell's zebra tracks are bigger than those of mountain zebra, but with a marginally thinner hoof edge (hoof wall). It is assumed the thicker hoof edge of the Cape mountain zebra track is an adaptation to the type of mountainous and rocky terrain it inhabits.

Mountain zebra front and hind tracks, indicating where two animals have trodden, one after the other.

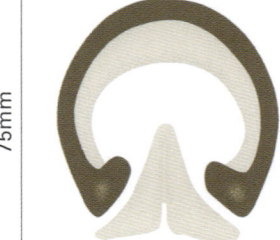

Front left foot

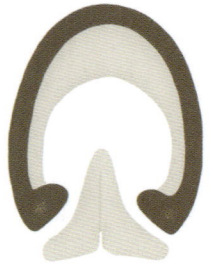

Hind left foot

Burchell's (plains) zebra
Equus quagga burchellii

The most common of the three zebra species in the region. It has characteristic 'shadow' stripes that run between the thicker black stripes. Historically a migratory species, local migrations still take place in large, unfenced reserves, such as in northern Botswana, where zebras migrate on an almost 500km round trip, from Nxai Pan National Park to the Chobe River.

Mainly a grazer, the Burchell's zebra prefers open grassland, scrub and woodland areas.

Habits
- Burchell's zebra is diurnal – active during the early morning and late afternoon.
- Gregarious, they are found in harems of about five mares with their young, and a breeding stallion.
- Stallions fight viciously for control of their mares and to keep bachelors at bay.
- They make a high-pitched barking alarm call if predators are detected, particularly lions. Tracks showing zebra running often indicate where predators have moved the previous evening.
- Burchell's zebras inhabit open grassland with easy access to water.

Burchell's zebra droppings: 40mm in diameter and kidney-shaped

Droppings
- Droppings are green to light brown and grey in colour, and kidney-shaped – about 50–60mm in diameter.

Home range
- Zebras move in home ranges, and stallions do not mark or defend a territory.

*Burchell's zebra hind (**left**) and front (**right**) tracks*

MAMMALS ■ Large mammals

About the track
- Track lengths ranging from 85–110mm have been recorded.
- Preliminary research has shown the average width of the male zebra's hoof to be front foot 85mm and hind foot 75mm. Females measured showed a remarkably similar hoof width; several adult females' hoof widths were greater than those of herd stallions measured.
- If the substrate is soft enough, the triangular-shaped frog underneath the hoof shows in the track.
- The hoof wall (edge) generally makes a clear imprint, particularly on hard ground.

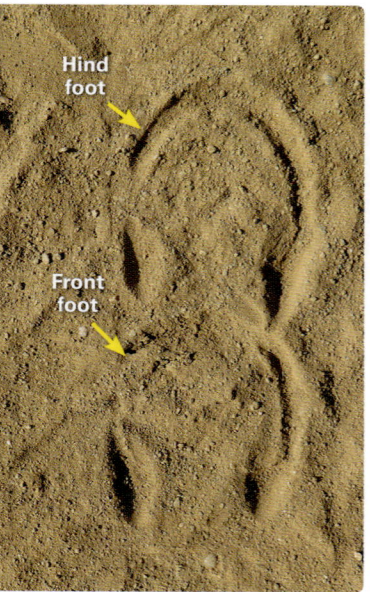

Subtle evidence of a zebra having scraped its muzzle on the ground

Zebra track showing frog impression

Zebras' hind feet typically land ahead of the front feet – known as an overstep.

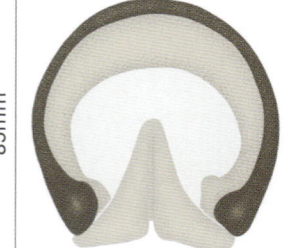

Front left foot

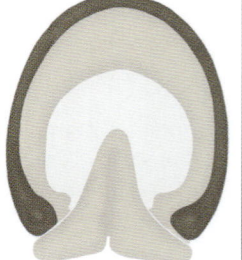

Hind left foot

Can be confused with ...
- The Burchell's zebra's track is similar in shape and appearance to that of the **domestic horse**, except that it's smaller and narrower.
- Although separated by their habitat preference, Burchell's zebra can be confused with the **Cape mountain zebra**. However, Cape mountain zebra tracks are marginally smaller than those of Burchell's zebra, and have a thicker hoof wall (edge) than the tracks of their larger cousins.
- Zebra droppings can be confused with the slightly smaller but similar-looking droppings of **warthogs**.

MAMMALS ■ Large mammals

Bushpig
Potamochoerus larvatus

This cunning but wary pig is usually red-brown in colour with hairy bristles and long white hair running along its back.

Distributed throughout the southeastern parts of southern Africa, it prefers the dense cover of forests and thickets, in the vicinity of water.

Habits
- Predominantly nocturnal. Sensitive to cold weather, they have been known to build a 'nest' during a cold snap. Rest in thick cover, such as in firethorn (*Searsia pyroides*) thickets in the Karoo, and remain alert at all times.
- Monogamous and gregarious, they move in groups of six to eight, with a dominant boar and sow. The main boar will aggressively stand up to intruders.
- They wallow in mud to help regulate body temperature and to protect themselves from biting insects. They are also competent swimmers.
- Potentially dangerous when cornered, they can inflict injury with their sharp lower canines (tusks).
- Their alarm call is a single resonant grunt.

Feeding and diet
- Omnivorous, they feed on bulbs, roots, fruits and other vegetation, but will also eat worms, insect larvae and carrion.
- Bushpigs use the hard upper edge of their snout to unearth bulbs, grass rhizomes and roots, leaving the area with a 'ploughed' look.
- They tend to feed in dense vegetation but will also readily venture into open areas when necessary.

Droppings
- The droppings are loosely formed and break apart easily, revealing the remnants of bulbs and roots.
- Distinctly fibrous, they measure 30–50mm in diameter, and are usually dark brown or black.
- Droppings are deposited randomly as well as in middens.

Notice the hind foot track registering on top of the front foot track. The loosely formed droppings reveal the remnants of bulbs and roots.

MAMMALS ■ Large mammals

Typical bushpig front foot track

Front and hind bushpig tracks

Can be confused with ...

- The bushpig hind foot track is similar to that of the **warthog**, although the hind foot cloven hooves are comparatively broader and more splayed on the leading edge than those of the warthog.

Territorial behaviour

- The bushpig will rub its body and lower canines (tusks) against trees to leave its scent. Scent marks are produced from glands between its hooves (interdigital) and on its face (preorbital).
- Mud and bushpig hair can often be found on tree trunks and fallen trees.

About the track

- A male measured front foot 70mm and hind 60mm in length, and a female front foot 62mm and hind 52mm, without false hooves showing.
- Bushpig tracks are often found in dense vegetation where there is lots of moisture, such as damp forest floors, riverbanks, small wetlands and in thickets at the base of mountains.
- The leading edge of the front foot is significantly wider than that of the hind foot – the front foot cloven hooves often appear to be facing away from each other in a V-shape, and are said to resemble the shape of a mopane tree leaf.
- The false hooves are situated closer to the hooves than those of the warthog, and therefore show more regularly in the track. The false hooves make an impression behind the hooves, usually in line with the outside margin.
- The hind foot typically registers on top of the front foot.
- Bushpigs make regular use of familiar paths.

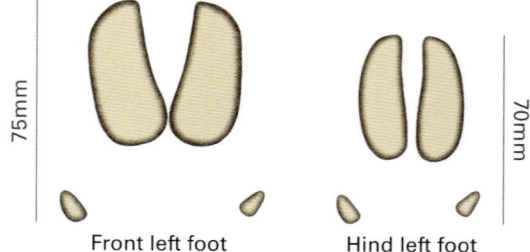

Warthog
Phacochoerus africanus

The warthog belongs to the genus of wild pigs, *Phacochoerus*. Both sexes have two pairs of tusks protruding from the mouth and curving upwards. The lower tusks, which are shorter, become razor sharp through constant grinding against the upper pair. Both sexes also have warts on their face, with the male sporting two prominent sets. The body is covered with sparse hair. Males can weigh up to 100kg.

The warthog prefers open woodland and grassland.

Habits
- Diurnal, but may emerge late in the day during cold weather.
- They occupy large burrows, usually abandoned aardvark dwellings, which they modify by digging with their front feet. Tusk marks at the entrance are a common feature of their burrows.
- They reverse into their burrows so that they may exit at speed, in the event of pursuing predators.
- Although capable of inflicting severe wounds with their tusks, their primary defence is to retreat, and they can run surprisingly fast. Their main predators are lions, leopards, crocodiles and hyaenas.
- Because of their short neck, warthogs will 'kneel' on their forecarpals (wrist bones) to graze short grass, allowing them to leverage their hardened, cartilaginous snout at a better angle for uprooting rhizomes and short grass.
- Warthogs live in groups called sounders, consisting of a mature boar, one or two sows and piglets.
- They wallow in mud to keep cool in the heat and to remove ectoparasites.
- Like the rhino, they use rubbing posts in the form of trees, termite mounds and other surfaces. Occasionally one can find warthog hair on rubbing posts.

Feeding and diet
- Primarily grazers, they also use their snout and tusks to excavate roots and bulbs.
- Omnivorous, their diet comprises roots, tubers, grass, fruits and bark, and occasionally carrion.
- They will consume soil and chew stones – a behaviour called geophagia – to acquire mineral supplements deficient in their diet.
- Warthogs have a relatively inefficient digestive system, and with little subcutaneous fat, they lose condition more rapidly than other ungulates when food is scarce.

MAMMALS ■ Large mammals

Droppings
- Droppings measure 40–50mm in diameter. Dark brown, finely textured droppings are deposited randomly throughout the warthog range.

About the track
- This cloven-hooved track is 45–50mm in length without the false hooves making an impression. False hooves make an impression when the animal steps in wet mud, deep sand, or is running.
- The front foot is broader on the leading edge, appearing box-like in shape.
- There is a gap between the hooves on the leading edge, although it's much smaller than in the bushpig.
- Occasionally the youngsters drag their feet, creating slight drag marks among the tracks.
- Mud spread around may be evidence of warthogs wallowing in the vicinity, which they commonly do in midday heat.
- Because they often 'kneel' while feeding,

Front track showing false hoof impressions

Warthog tracks

Typical warthog tracks

MAMMALS ■ Large mammals

round, 40–50mm-diameter impressions are left in the soil. Parallel lines of 'warthog knee tracks' are made if the animal moves about in this way.
- The normal walking gait reveals the hind foot registering directly or partially on top of the front foot.

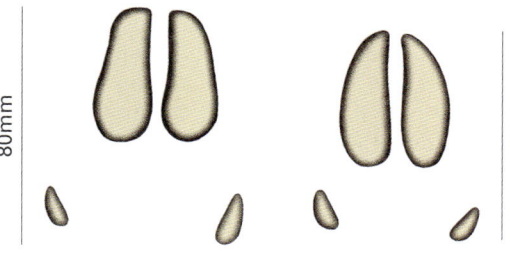

Front left foot   Hind left foot

Hind foot partially registered on front foot

Can be confused with ...

- The cloven hooves are narrower and shorter when compared with those of the **bushpig**; however, the bushpig's hooves show a more pronounced V-shape on the leading edge between the hooves, and its false hooves are situated closer together than those of the warthog.
- Warthog tracks can be confused with those of **nyala**, which are much more pointed.
- Young warthog tracks can be confused with **common duiker** tracks in unclear substrates.
- Interestingly, their tracks are confused with **aardvark** tracks, particularly if the hind track registers on top of the front track, creating an appearance of 'three toes'.
- Warthog droppings are regularly confused with those of the **zebra**, although they are slightly shorter.

Comparison of zebra and warthog droppings

MAMMALS ■ Large mammals

Cape (brown) fur seal
Arctocephalus pusillus pusillus

Classified as an 'eared seal', this semi-aquatic carnivorous mammal has ears with external flaps, large front flippers, and hind flippers that are not connected to the pelvis, equipping this fur seal both with better hearing and greater manoeuvrability, and making it better adapted to terrestrial habitats than the 'true seals' like the walrus and harbour seal.

Found along the southwestern and southern coast of southern Africa, from southern Angola to Gqeberha (Port Elizabeth).

Habits
- Cape fur seals are not known to migrate.
- They can dive up to 400m and can stay under water for seven to 10 minutes.
- Breeding begins in October and cows give birth to a single pup after a gestation period of eight months.

Feeding
- They feed up to 200km offshore on mostly pelagic schooling fish (particularly sardines, anchovies, mackerel, pilchard and hake), squid (*Loligo* spp.) and crustaceans.

Seals are social in the water and highly territorial on land; note the tracks in the sand.

Droppings
- Droppings are blob-like, black in colour and foul-smelling.
- They are found in seal colonies on land.

Territorial behaviour
- Bulls establish and vigorously defend territories on land during the breeding season (between October and January).

About the track
- When moving slowly, they make active use of both front and hind flippers, moving each independently – front, hind, front, hind – to pull the body forwards.
- When moving quickly, the front flippers pull the body forwards powerfully – the back bends to bring the hind flippers forward together – in what can be described as a slow, ungainly and incomplete bounding gait. (See p. 26.)
- When the gait is fast, the body is suspended further off the ground, and most of the drag marks in the trail are produced by the hind quarters and hind flippers.
- Front flippers are broader and leave clear lateral impressions.
- Both front and hind flippers have five digits each.

MAMMALS ■ Antelopes

Black wildebeest
Connochaetes gnou

This southern African native has a dark brown body, a black head and black-fringed, erect mane, and a long white tail. Both male and female adults have horns that curve upwards. They can run at speeds of up to 80km/h.

This antelope belongs to the mammal tribe Alcelaphini and inhabits open Highveld grassland of the central South African plateau.

Habits
- Diurnal, mainly active in the early mornings and late afternoons.
- Social organisation includes territorial males, female herds with calves, and bachelor groups.
- The alarm call is a high-pitched whistle, quite different from the low grunting of its blue cousin, the blue wildebeest.

Feeding and diet
- The black wildebeest is mainly a grazer of grasses such as *Sporobolus*, *Themeda* and *Cynodon*, and will also browse karroid shrubs in the winter months.

Droppings
- Round to oval, dark brown pellets, 10–12mm in diameter; pellets may clump together.

Black wildebeest droppings

Territorial behaviour
- Bulls mark their territory by creating middens – rolling on, scraping and pawing the ground to flatten the grass in a small area, where they also leave droppings and urine.
- Middens are conspicuous, situated in a clearing where the animal will stand, making himself conspicuous to other males.
- Bulls vigorously paw the ground with their front feet to release scent from interdigital glands. They also have preorbital glands, just below their eyes, for rubbing scent onto the ground.
- Bulls go down onto their knees during fighting and when marking territory.

Territorial bull's midden

MAMMALS ■ Antelopes

Above left and right: This large track measurement ranges from 78–93mm in length. Notice the false hooves in the left-hand image.

About the track

- Track measurements range from 78–93mm in length. The false hooves may make an impression, thereby extending the total track length by up to 114mm.
- The cloven hooves, particularly on the front feet, often splay apart on uneven terrain and slippery ground, or while travelling at speed.
- Square and rectangular in shape, the hoof tips are typically blunt on the leading edge.
- The posterior edges of both front and back feet are round in shape, and broad.
- Wildebeest tracks in certain substrates create a feature called a 'step', indicated by the faint grey line on the track illustration. (See p. 38.)
- A walking gait shows the hind foot landing ahead of the front foot (overstep), but it may also register directly on top of the front foot – slower walk.
- The front foot is slightly longer than the hind foot.

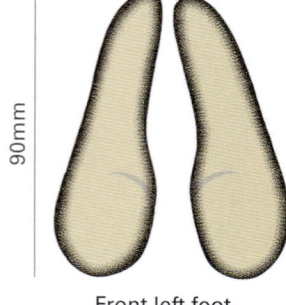

Front left foot

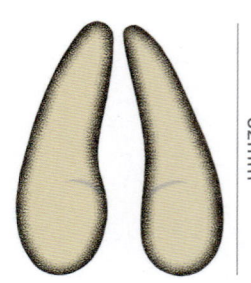

Hind left foot

MAMMALS ■ Antelopes

Blue wildebeest
Connochaetes taurinus

The blue wildebeest is also known as the brindled gnu due to the dark vertical bands over its shoulders. Both sexes have horns that curve upwards and inwards. This antelope belongs to the mammal tribe Alcelaphini and prefers open grassland. In many areas of the greater Kruger National Park, local populations have dwindled as a result of fencing and artificial water holes, which have affected their traditional migratory behaviour.

James Tyrrell

Habits
- These gregarious herbivores occur in herds ranging from 10 to a few thousand, and ultimately 1.2 million in the famous East African migration.
- Diurnal, they graze during the early morning and late afternoon.
- Resident herds with cows and calves move in home ranges close to permanent water.
- Pregnant cows move away from the herd to give birth; the lightly coloured newborn calves are able to move with their mother within half an hour of birth.
- Wildebeest will make an alarm call, a blowing grunt, for lions, leopards and wild dogs. The alarm call produced for lions is more drawn-out than for the other predators.

Feeding and diet
- Grazers, blue wildebeest prefer short grass in open savanna woodland, with access to water.

Far left: *Blue wildebeest droppings deposited during the wet season*
Left: *Wildebeest droppings deposited in a string*

Droppings

- Pellets are slightly tapered at one end and blunt at the other; 14–18mm in diameter, 20mm long.
- Droppings are deposited as individual pellets, in strings of pellets or clumped together.

Territorial midden in the Kalahari

Territorial behaviour

- Dominant bulls hold small, well-demarcated territories in which only they will breed.
- Territorial middens are created during the breeding season, revealing evidence of droppings, hoof scrape marks and rolling.
- Territories are marked by rubbing preorbital glands on the ground, trees and rocks.
- Bulls clash on boundaries, pawing and horning the ground, with tail swishing. When engaging horns, they go onto their knees as they fight.

Blue wildebeest territorial scent-marking on a marula tree

About the track

- Track measurements for blue wildebeest at Londolozi Game Reserve average front foot 102mm and hind foot 95mm. One bull measured front foot 108mm and hind foot 104mm.
- This often rectangular-shaped track has broad cloven hooves, which show a gap on the leading edge (hoof tip).
- The front foot cloven hooves are prone to splaying under certain circumstances, to the extent that they will appear in parallel.
- The hind foot is more pointed and slightly shorter than the front foot.
- Wildebeest tracks in certain substrates give rise to a feature called a 'step' – a ridge feature depicted by a light grey line in the track illustration. (See p. 38.)

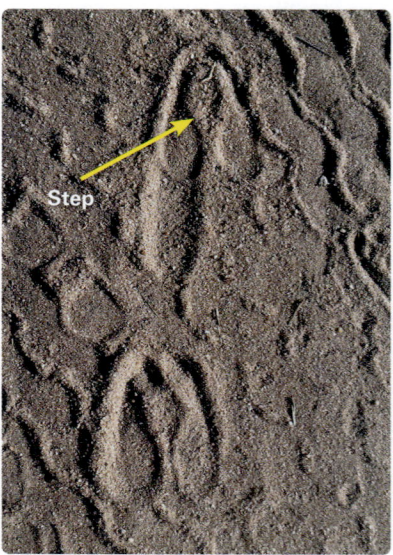

Blue wildebeest tracks showing a clearly defined step

MAMMALS ■ Antelopes

Blue wildebeest bull tracks

Wildebeest front and hind tracks

Occasionally the false hooves of the wildebeest become apparent in soft substrate.

- A typical walking gait shows the hind foot registering ahead of the front foot (overstep). The hind foot seldom registers directly on top of the front foot.
- The posterior edge is wide, and false hooves may be evident if the animal steps in soft substrate.

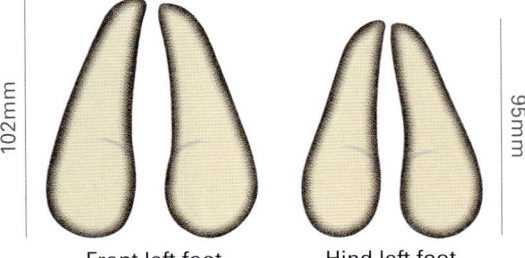

Front left foot — Hind left foot

Can be confused with ...

- *One of the characteristic features is the comparative bluntness of the track on the leading edge. Other antelope tracks of a similar size, such as* **waterbuck**, *are more pointed. The waterbuck's sharper hoof tips tend to show less of a gap between them when compared to wildebeest.*

  The waterbuck's false hooves are comparatively smaller and therefore do not appear as regularly as in the blue wildebeest tracks.

Common waterbuck
Kobus ellipsiprymnus

This robust antelope has a grey-brown body with white underparts, a white collar and a white 'lavatory seat' ring around its rump. Only males have long, ridged horns, which curve inward. The oily waterproofing secretions produced by glands in the skin have an unpleasant, lingering odour.

Never far from permanent water, this antelope prefers grassland with good cover. A subspecies, the defassa waterbuck, is distributed throughout eastern and central Africa, and its range overlaps with the common waterbuck in parts of East Africa.

Habits
- Seldom spend much time in water, but will take refuge there to escape predators. Usually found within 2km of water, and they drink water daily.
- They are both diurnal and nocturnal, but rest in the heat of the day.
- Gregarious, live in herds of up to 30 animals, either in bachelor or nursery herds. Dominant bulls tend to be solitary.
- Females are herded by territorial bulls, and courted before mating.
- Mothers hide newborn calves for three to four weeks before introducing them to the herd.

Feeding and diet
- Mainly a grazer, their diet includes aquatic plants; they may browse when the grass is inadequate.

Droppings
- Irregularly shaped, dark brown pellets, 20mm in diameter. Depending on diet and season, droppings will fall as individual pellets or clumps.

Territorial behaviour
- No distinct territorial marking behaviour has been noted.
- Territorial bulls mark simply with droppings under mature trees, with more dominant individuals occupying territories closer to the water.

*Waterbuck droppings deposited in the wet season (**left**) and in the early dry season (**right**)*

MAMMALS ■ Antelopes

The waterbuck track has straight hoof edges.

Waterbuck front (**bottom**) and hind (**top**) tracks

Hind foot track – notice that it has registered on top of the front foot track.

About the track
- Tracks are typically narrow and pointed, particularly the hind foot.
- A female track at Londolozi Game Reserve measured front foot 80mm and hind foot 75mm. A bull's front foot track was 87mm and hind foot 80mm.
- The front hoof tends to splay if the animal steps on slippery or uneven ground.
- The front foot track can show a slight gap between the hoof tips (leading edge), whereas the hind foot cloven hooves are tighter together.
- In certain substrates these tracks give rise to a feature called a 'step'– a ridge feature depicted by a light grey line in the track illustration. (See p. 38.)
- In thick sand or wet mud, the false hooves may imprint directly behind the posterior edge.
- A typical walking gait shows the hind foot register directly on top of, or just ahead of, the front foot.

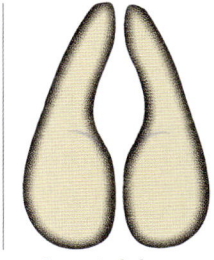

Front left foot — 80mm

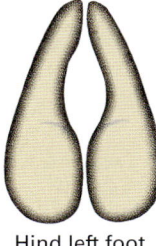

Hind left foot — 75mm

Can be confused with ...
- Can easily be confused with **blue wildebeest** tracks; in both, a prominent mound of soil can form between and near the front of the hooves. However, the wildebeest track is generally 10–20mm longer, broader and more blunt, and the leading edge is broader. The waterbuck's hooves are grouped more tightly together and are more pointed.

MAMMALS ■ Antelopes

Red lechwe
Kobus leche

This antelope is found in marshy, wet grasslands, such as those of the Okavango Delta in northern Botswana. Males weigh up to 110kg and have spiralled horns. The species prefers floodplains and oxbow lakes. They seldom venture further than 3km from water.

Habits
- Active in the early mornings.
- If threatened they run through the water with ease and speed.
- Usually in small groups of four to eight; herds of up to 100 have been recorded.

Feeding and diet
- As grazers, their diet consists of grasses such as Bermuda grass (*Cynodon dactylon*) and sedges.

Droppings
- Droppings are dark brown to black pellets, measuring 15mm in diameter and 15–20mm in length, often clumped together.

Droppings

Territorial behaviour
- Territorial rams occupy small, well-defined territories of 5ha in the breeding season. Lateral displays by males are common.

About the track
- Cloven hooves are prone to splaying, particularly in muddy substrate, sometimes forming a V-shape. Tracks in Khwai, northern Botswana, measured front foot 81mm and hind foot 77mm.
- Hoof tips are typically blunt, yet overall track shape is variable.
- The false hooves sometimes imprint in soft substrate.
- At a walking gait, the hind foot registers behind the front, or in front if the animal speeds up, but seldom directly on top of the front foot.
- The red lechwe regularly drags its hooves.

Tracks

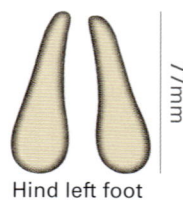

Front left foot — 81mm
Hind left foot — 77mm

Can be confused with ...
- Red lechwe tracks may be confused with similar-sized **waterbuck** tracks, but the red lechwe's cloven hooves are set further apart and are broader on the leading edge.

MAMMALS ■ Antelopes

Greater kudu
Tragelaphus strepsiceros

This large antelope has a grey-tan body with white vertical stripes down its sides. Males weigh up to 300kg, and only they have horns, which are long and spiralled.

They inhabit savanna (knob thorn) woodland and are primarily browsers.

Habits

- Naturally diurnal, but more active at night in certain areas due to constant human persecution.
- Gregarious; in Sabi Sands females and young form small groups of four to 12. Bulls are solitary outside of mating season.
- They are generally shy: when approached they will initially freeze and then bound away, displaying a white undertail.
- If they detect a predator they produce a loud, deep barking alarm call. A kudu found staring into the bush, with its ears facing forward, and alarm-calling, is a reliable sign of a predator – and useful information for trackers.
- Bulls establish dominance through lateral displays; fighting is a last resort, during which they sometimes lock horns.

Evidence of a kudu having horned the ground – behaviour linked to some form of social display

Feeding and diet

- A browser, the kudu feeds on a wide variety of plants and trees, including seedpods, flowers and fruits.
- They may strip bark from trees, and males are known to break small branches with their horns to access the leaves.

Above left and right: *Greater kudu droppings can be scattered as individual pellets or occasionally clumped together to form small piles.*

Droppings

- Medium-sized pellets, occasionally tapered, olive-green to dark brown, measuring 15–20mm in length and 13–15mm in diameter.
- Droppings may fall as individual pellets or form small clumps.

MAMMALS ■ Antelopes

About the track

- This neat, oval (rugby ball-shaped) track is tightly arranged and surprisingly small for such a large animal.
- At Londolozi Game Reserve, a male kudu front track measured 77mm in length and 51mm wide; hind track length was 77mm and 46mm wide. Note: in this case, the extended posterior edge was not making an impression; in certain conditions, it does show, making the track appear longer.
- From a sample of 10 bulls and 10 cows measured, the bulls' tracks were 7.5–11mm longer and 8.5–12mm wider than those of the females.
- A slight gap may show between front foot cloven hooves.
- The leading edge of the front track is more rounded (blunt), whereas the hind track is more pointed.
- The widest point of the kudu track is near the middle, whereas in most other antelope the widest point is near the posterior edge of the track. This is also true for other *Tragelaphus* species such as nyala and bushbuck.
- They walk flat-footed and cautiously, usually placing the hind foot directly on top of the front foot track – a direct register. Co-author and tracker Renias Mhlongo says the kudu track 'irons the ground', referring to the smooth texture it creates in certain substrates.

Can be confused with ...

- *Although similar in shape, the **nyala** track is smaller (15–20mm shorter) than that of the kudu, and regularly shows a larger gap between the cloven hooves, which are more pointed on the leading edge.*

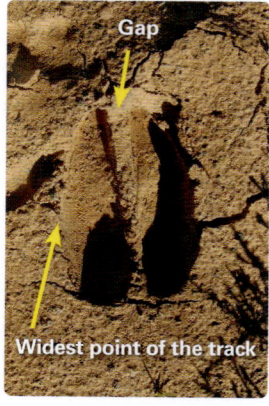

Gap

Widest point of the track

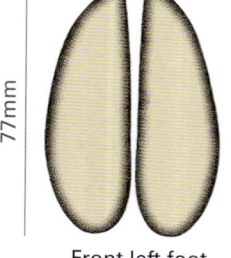

77mm

Front left foot

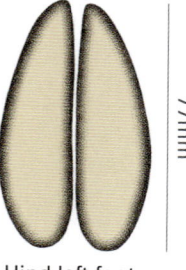

77mm

Hind left foot

Top and middle: *Typical kudu tracks.* **Above:** *Notice that the hind foot has registered directly on top of the front foot.*

MAMMALS ■ Antelopes

Nyala
Tragelaphus angasii

The adult male nyala is grey to dark brown with thin white stripes down its sides, and light brown legs. Its horns sweep backwards and spiral upwards. By contrast, the female is rusty in colour with no horns.

Nyalas inhabit savanna woodland with good cover, including riparian habitats in northeastern South Africa.

Habits
- Nyalas are both diurnal and nocturnal – active at all times of the day except for the hottest hours.
- Gregarious, found in small family groups of females with young. Males are solitary except during breeding.
- Nyalas are usually shy and cautious. They react to the alarm calls of other animals, such as impala, baboon and kudu.
- They become easily habituated to living close to human settlements, such as game lodges.
- Not territorial, occupying overlapping home ranges that are not actively defended.
- Males establish dominance through lateral displays, by standing side by side, stiff legged, with their white mane of hair raised along the back. These demonstrations seldom develop into fights.
- They will also 'horn' the ground, particularly in mud, evidence of which can be found around water.

Feeding and diet
- Nyalas browse in riparian thickets where they eat leaves, flowers and fruits from a variety of plant species. They will also graze on freshly sprouting grass.
- They chew bones (osteophagia) to acquire certain minerals deficient in the diet.
- They have been seen feeding on torchwood fruits (*Balanites maughamii*), which they then regurgitate. These fruits may provide digestive benefit, although the exact reason for this behaviour is unknown.

Top: Nyala female chews a bone to acquire minerals. *Above*: Regurgitated torchwood fruits. *Left*: Nyala droppings

MAMMALS ■ Antelopes

Droppings
- Small to medium-sized pellets, dark brown, measuring 12–14mm in diameter – often scattered.

About the track
- Measured at Londolozi Game Reserve, the average male front foot length is 62mm and hind foot 54mm. The average length of the female front foot is 54mm and hind foot 50mm.

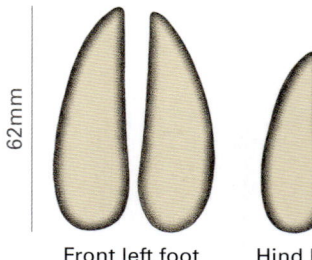

Front left foot   Hind left foot

- A defining characteristic is the pronounced gap between the hooves. On slippery substrate, their hooves may splay to such an extent as to be difficult to identify.
- The gap between the hooves forms a prominent, straight ridge of soil, particularly in moist substrates; in dry, sandy soils the ridge is less prominent.
- The broader front foot is curved on the leading edge; the hind foot is more pointed.
- The widest point of the track is near the middle – in this regard the track is similar to that of kudu and bushbuck.
- The hind foot typically registers partially or directly on top of the front foot.

Far left: There's a prominent gap between front foot hooves.
Centre left: A prominent, straight centre ridge shows in wet sand.
Left: Typical nyala track

Can be confused with …

- The nyala track may be confused with that of the **kudu**, although the kudu track is longer by 15–20mm. The kudu's cloven hooves are grouped much more tightly and their track does not splay. The nyala's hoof tips tend to dig into the ground, whereas the kudu walks more flat-footed.
- Nyala tracks can also be confused with those of the **male impala**, although impala tracks are marginally shorter, much more pointed, and the widest point is at the posterior edge. The prominent hoof edges on the impala's hind foot are often concave in shape whereas the nyala's are convex.
- The **bushbuck** track is similar in shape to the nyala's, but it is smaller, more pointed near the front and does not show much of a gap between the hooves.

MAMMALS ■ Antelopes

Sitatunga
Tragelaphus spekii

This highly specialised, swamp-dwelling antelope prefers dense aquatic vegetation as well as seasonal wetlands, well-vegetated waterways, marshy clearings in forests, riparian thickets and mangrove swamps.

It is found in northern Botswana, Zambia, Tanzania, Kenya and throughout central Africa.

Habits
- Active most times of the day and night.
- They feed alone but will group to form small herds of up to 10 members.
- Excellent swimmers, they will easily take to the water if threatened, almost completely submerging themselves.
- Produce a barking alarm call similar to a bushbuck, but more drawn out, with several barks made in quick succession. Their predators include leopard, lion and crocodile.

Feeding and diet
- In the Linyanti swamp in northern Botswana, sitatunga feed on sprouting reeds (*Phragmites* spp.) and bulrushes (*Typha* spp.) as well as aquatic grasses and plants.

Droppings
- Droppings are black and round to oval, measuring 11mm in diameter and up to 20mm in length.

Territorial behaviour
- Sitatunga are not territorial, but males will engage in threat displays with rivals, such as raising of the front legs or making a barking alarm call.

Female browsing

MAMMALS ■ Antelopes

About the track
- Tracks measure front foot 110mm and hind foot 82mm in length. One individual front track recorded was 145mm in length.
- Diagnostic is the widely-set front cloven hooves – an adaptation that no doubt assists the animal in traversing its swampy environment.
- The hind foot cloven hoof is less splayed and presents two hooves in parallel, with a 20mm gap between them.

Female in favoured wetland habitat

Common (splayed) hoof print of a sitatunga

Can be confused with ...

- Sitatunga tracks may be confused with those of the **red lechwe**, particularly as their ranges overlap. However, the sitatunga's front track is much longer (minimum 30mm) than that of the red lechwe.

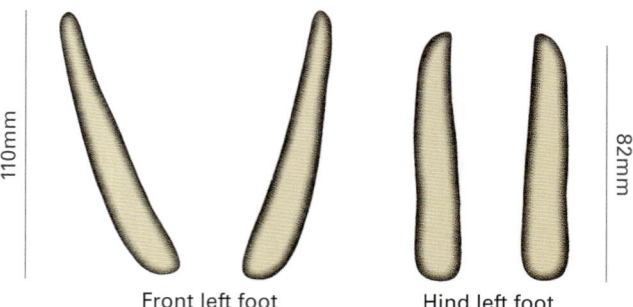

Front left foot · Hind left foot

MAMMALS ■ Antelopes

Bushbuck
Tragelaphus scriptus

This attractive and widespread antelope species is found throughout sub-Saharan Africa. Males are dark brown and females pale brown, both with white spots and stripes on their sides. Only males have horns.

The elusive bushbuck is mainly a browser; it prefers dense cover in woodland and montane or savanna forest, close to permanent water.

Habits
- Bushbuck are nocturnal and diurnal; active at night and in the early mornings and late evenings.
- Generally solitary, but may be found in small female groups or in pairs.
- They are able to survive in agricultural and even in built-up peri-urban environments as long as they have access to dense cover and water.
- Single young are hidden in the undergrowth for several weeks after birth.
- Males rub their head and neck against plants and trees. Male dominance is established using displays, and fights do occasionally occur. Dominant males will persistently chase subordinate males when females are in oestrus.
- Neither male nor female is territorial.
- Not particularly fast runners, they avoid predators by hiding, but are known to show aggression when confronted.
- Their alarm call is a loud bark, similar to that of a dog, and reliably warns of the presence of predators.

Feeding and diet
- Bushbuck browse leaves, flowers and fungi; they also eat grass shoots.
- They will also feed on fruits and flowers dropped by baboons and monkeys, with which they share habitat.

Droppings
- Slightly elongated, small, dark brown, pellets, 15mm in length and 10mm in diameter. Deposited in small piles.

Typical bushbuck droppings, usually deposited in small piles

MAMMALS ■ Antelopes

Bushbuck ram track – notice the offset hooves.

Bushbuck gait; tracks often point outwards.

Typical bushbuck track; one seldom sees the full extent of the track.

The bushbuck's regular gait results in a direct register of the hind foot on top of the front foot.

MAMMALS ■ Antelopes

About the track
- This rugby ball-shaped track is similar in appearance to the tracks of nyala and common duiker. Track measurements taken at Londolozi Game Reserve are front foot 45mm and hind foot 38mm in length.
- As with nyala and kudu, the widest point of the track is near the middle, unlike most other antelope species.
- The hoof tips (on leading edge) of the cloven hooves often show up as being of uneven length and asymmetrical.
- A common feature is that the hoof tips push deeper into the ground – like someone wearing stilettos or walking on tiptoes.
- Bushbuck feet usually land at a slight angle, facing outwards, and twisting as the animal steps – a movement that often results in a slight disturbance or scuffing on the leading edge.
- The bushbuck's regular gait results in the hind foot registering directly on top of the front foot.
- The front foot splays more frequently than the hind foot.

Bushbuck female track

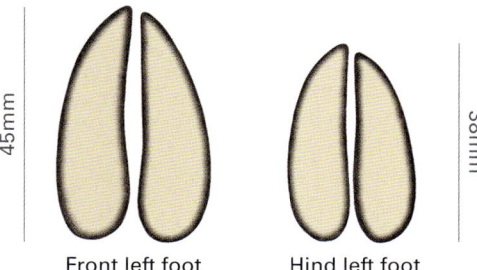

Front left foot   Hind left foot

Can be confused with ...

- *Bushbuck tracks can be confused with those of **common duiker**. However, the duiker's track is marginally shorter, and it walks flat-footed, displaying the full extent of its track more regularly. The duiker's tracks usually face in the direction of travel, as opposed to bushbuck tracks, which regularly land at a slight angle – facing outwards. The duiker's cloven hooves are grouped more tightly together and their track is, overall, more symmetrical than that of the bushbuck. The posterior edge of the duiker track forms a characteristic V-shape, which is not seen with the bushbuck.*
- ***Nyala*** *tracks can also cause confusion with those of bushbuck. However, they are on average 20mm longer, as well as broader, and often show a wider gap between the cloven hooves than bushbuck tracks.*

MAMMALS ■ Antelopes

Common (grey) duiker
Sylvicapra grimmia

Andrea Campbell

The Afrikaans-derived common name 'duiker' refers to the animal's diving bounds as it runs. This small antelope is grey and tan in colour. Only males have horns, which are short and straight.

With the exception of rainforests, it has a wide habitat tolerance but prefers savanna woodland with abundant cover: the presence of bush is essential for its shelter and shade.

Habits
- Common duikers are both diurnal and nocturnal, being active in the early morning and late afternoon and into the night.
- Both sexes are solitary but may be found in male-female pairs when females are in oestrus, or females with single young.

Feeding and diet
- Largely herbivorous, they have a wide diet tolerance, browsing leaves, seedpods, fruits and flowers. Interestingly, they are also known to consume frogs, eggs and carrion.
- They derive some moisture from the vegetation they eat, and they are known to dig and feed on underground bulbs.

Droppings
- Elongated (oval) pellets, tapered on one end, dark brown, measuring 10mm in length and 8mm in diameter.
- Deposited in small piles, sometimes with several piles close together.

Territorial behaviour
- Using preorbital glands below the eyes, territorial duiker males scent-mark on small branches.
- Common duikers occupy territories of 1–3km², and dominant males will drive out rival males.

Droppings vary in shape, from elongated to round, and are dark brown, almost black.

MAMMALS ■ Antelopes

About the track
- The duiker track is well known for its great variety in length and shape. Measurements of 35–40mm were taken, with an average length of 38mm, at Samara Karoo Reserve.
- Duikers generally produce a clean, symmetrical track. Due to the structure of their hooves and their cautious gait, they seldom leave scuff marks and disturbances, except when they're running.
- The cloven hooves are arranged tightly together and rarely splay, unless the animal is moving quickly.

Far left: Elongated duiker track photographed in the Kalahari
Left: Typical duiker track; notice the V-shaped posterior edge.

Above left and right: Common duiker tracks on the left (taken at Samara Karoo Reserve); notice how pointed they are compared to those on the right, which are more rounded (taken at Londolozi Game Reserve).

MAMMALS ■ Antelopes

- The flat-footed duiker tracks face more or less in the direction of travel – unlike the bushbuck track.
- When the duiker runs, it swerves from side to side in a zigzag manner; this causes the outer edge of the hoof to dig into the ground. During a bounding gallop, all four feet land closely grouped. These groupings may be spaced out at a distance of 2–6m, depending on the speed at which the animal is moving.
- The front of the track is typically rounded and broad in shape, and the outer edges of the hooves are curved, although there may be significant variety here. For example, in the Kalahari several duiker tracks found were more elongated, with straighter hoof edges than those seen in Kruger National Park.
- One commonly sees a well-defined V-shape form between the hooves on the posterior edge.
- The typical walking gait shows the hind foot registering directly or partially on top of the front foot.

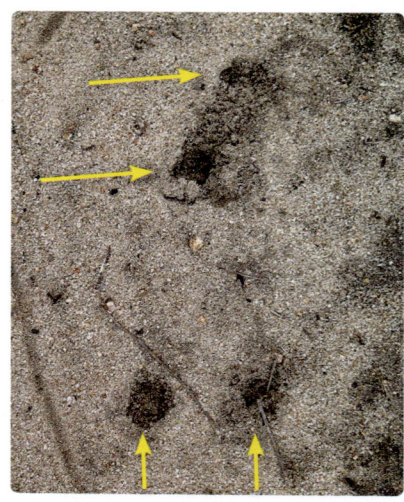

Duiker bounding run

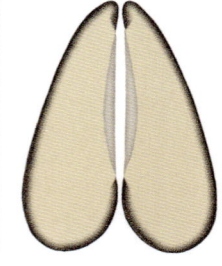 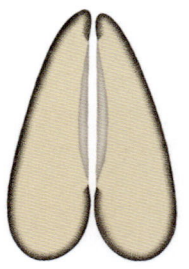

Front left foot   Hind left foot

Can be confused with ...

- The duiker track can be confused with that of the **steenbok**, which is usually narrower and sharper, with generally straighter hoof edges. A ridge created by a marked gap between the steenbok cloven hooves, measuring up to 3mm, also separates it from the duiker, whose cloven hooves are arranged tightly together. In instances of a mix-up, it is usually a variation in the duiker track, not that of the steenbok, that causes confusion.
- The **bushbuck's** hoof tips usually dig into the ground with a slight twist, tending to point more outwards ('duck-footed'), whereas duiker tracks generally face in the direction of travel.

MAMMALS ■ Antelopes

Red duiker
Cephalophus natalensis

Also known as the Natal red duiker, this antelope weighs 10–12kg, which is smaller than the common (grey) duiker.

It prefers dense bush, forests, coastal dune forests and riverine thickets. Its patchy distribution includes northeastern KwaZulu-Natal to southern Mozambique.

Commercial alien afforestation of the Drakensberg foothills, as well as extensive agriculture in the lower-rainfall areas, has resulted in the disappearance of the red duiker from parts of its natural range.

Habits
- Diurnal; active in the early morning and late afternoon.
- Both sexes are solitary, but may be found in male-female pairs when females are in oestrus, or lone females with single young.
- They breed throughout the year.
- Occasionally form small bachelor groups of non-breeding males.
- Seldom seen, with a shy, elusive nature, their preferred habitat is thicket; Phinda Game Reserve in northern KwaZulu-Natal offers good viewing.
- Produce a whistling alarm call if threatened.

Feeding and diet
- Highly selective browsers, their diet consists of fruits, flowers, fallen leaves and stem shoots.
- Red duikers are not dependent on permanent water.

Droppings
- Small and oval-shaped, light brown to black in colour, and measuring 6mm in diameter and 10–14mm in length.

Territorial behaviour
- Although not strictly as territorial as the blue duiker, they use communal middens where they occupy small undefended home ranges (10–15 hectares).

Red duiker droppings at Phinda Game Reserve in KwaZulu-Natal

MAMMALS ■ Antelopes

Red duiker tracks photographed in the Sand Forest at Phinda Game Reserve

About the track
- Track shape remarkably similar to common duiker; measured at Phinda Game Reserve ranged from 28–32mm in length.
- A normal walking gait results in the hind foot registering directly on top of the front foot.
- Tracks are usually found in thickets and established dune and sand forest.

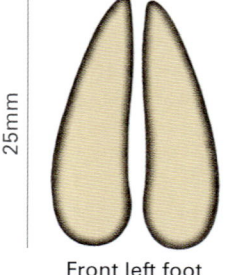 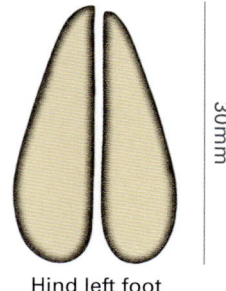

Front left foot   Hind left foot

Can be confused with ...

- The shape of the track strongly resembles that of the **common duiker**, although those measured were 5–8mm shorter than that of the common duiker.
  The red duiker's hoof edges appear to be straighter than the more curved common duiker track. Some red duiker tracks are markedly more pointed than those of the common duiker, although this is not a consistent feature. Red duiker cloven hoof tips (leading edge) are sometimes asymmetrical and of uneven length, whereas the common duiker track is more symmetrical in this regard.
- More research is required to establish the differences between the red and common duikers.

MAMMALS ■ Antelopes

Blue duiker
Philantomba monticola

This secretive and cautious antelope is found in the coastal forests of Kwa-Zulu Natal and the Eastern Cape, and prefers wooded habitats. At a weight of 4.5kg, the blue duiker is the smallest antelope in the southern African subregion.

Habits
- Crepuscular, they are active at dawn and dusk.
- They produce a whistling or sneezing sound as an alarm call and make extensive use of birds and monkeys for security.
- They will follow and pick up discarded bits of fruit dropped by Cape parrots, samango monkeys and baboons.
- A single lamb is born following a gestation period of 207 days; it is not known how long the youngster remains with its mother.

Feeding and diet
- Blue duiker feed on fruits, berries, flowers, leaves and fallen forest litter; they also dig for tubers and roots. They are not dependent on drinking water.

Blue duiker droppings

Droppings
- Droppings are round to oval and black, measuring 4mm in diameter and up to 7mm in length. As with all other duiker species, droppings are deposited in several small piles close to each other.

Territorial behaviour
- The breeding pair maintain fixed territory of 0.75 hectares (1.8 acres) by scent-marking with the preorbital gland, in dense habitat.

Female blue duikers are marginally heavier than males, by about 500g.

MAMMALS ■ Antelopes

Hind foot registering partially on front foot

Blue duiker tracks; notice slight overstep.

About the track
- Tracks measured front foot 26mm and hind foot 23mm in length, however the smallest measured was 18mm in length.
- Hoof edges are typically rounded – evidence of it being a forest and thicket dweller. However, an element common to the duiker species is the great variation found in the track shape between individuals.
- Front foot cloven hooves tend to splay apart.
- At a typical walking gait the hind foot registers directly on top of the front foot – direct register or a small overstep.

Can be confused with ...

- *Blue duiker tracks are similar to **red duiker** but are slightly smaller and rounder. The **suni** track is also remarkably similar and perhaps marginally bigger, however current research data are insufficient to provide definitive differences.*

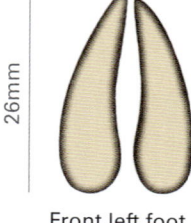

Front left foot

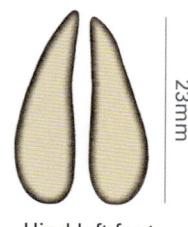

Hind left foot

MAMMALS ■ Antelopes

Gemsbok
Oryx gazella

This large and handsome antelope has a tan-grey body with black and white markings on its face. Both sexes have long, straight horns. Males can weigh up to 300kg.

The gemsbok is exceptionally well adapted to life in arid and desert environments.

Habits
- Gemsbok are particularly active in the cooler hours to avoid the heat.
- Gregarious, can move in herds of hundreds; also found in smaller groups, and males can be solitary.
- Males are territorial but relatively tolerant of other males.
- They prefer open grassland and woodland.

Feeding and diet
- Gemsbok are mostly grazers but may browse more regularly in the winter. They will feed on succulent plants to acquire moisture, and also dig for tubers such as the gemsbok cucumber (*Acanthosicyos naudinianus*) in the dry season.
- Extensive digging may affect the shape of the front foot hooves.

Droppings are usually deposited in small piles. Bulls usually squat when they deposit droppings.

Territorial gemsbok bull's midden – notice the urine, droppings and territorial scrape.

Gemsbok bull's territorial midden consisting of small piles of droppings

155

MAMMALS ■ Antelopes

Droppings
- Bullet-shaped, dark brown, pellets, 15–20mm in length and 10–14mm in diameter – deposited in small piles close to one another.
- In areas where the gemsbok and red hartebeest cohabit, one may see their droppings together.

Territorial behaviour
- Dominant male gemsbok defecate in territorial middens of various sizes, situated throughout the territory and along boundaries.
- Males crouch to defecate, making small piles of droppings, then scrape the ground with their front feet, so activating the interdigital (pedal) scent gland between the hooves.
- Males rub their horns on small bushes, leaving a trail of broken twigs, branches that have bits of bark rubbed off, and leaves that have fallen to the ground.

About the track
- This large antelope track measures front foot 95–115mm and hind foot 90mm (Samara Karoo Reserve).
- The front foot is broader and longer than the hind foot. Both front and hind feet have false hooves, which ordinarily do not make an impression.
- The slightly narrower hind foot tapers into a distinctive sharp point on the leading edge, giving it a triangular appearance.
- The hoof edges on the front foot are slightly convex (bulged and curved) whereas those on the hind foot are straighter.
- The cloven hooves sit closely together, with only a slight gap near the front.
- Gemsbok hind foot tracks seldom register on top of the front foot. The hind foot lands 50–70mm ahead of the front foot (overstep) at a normal walking pace.

Gemsbok front foot track showing the cloven hooves set tightly together. Gemsbok hooves are flat and smooth underneath.

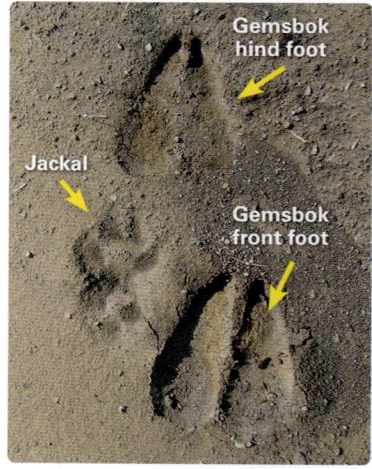

Above: *Gemsbok front and hind tracks; notice the jackal track between the two gemsbok prints.*
Below: *Typical gemsbok tracks*

MAMMALS ■ Antelopes

Gemsbok prefer open grassland and woodland.

Following gemsbok trails

- Thanks to the gemsbok's large hooves and the fact that they prefer to move in open areas and avoid dense cover, following a gemsbok trail is excellent practice for a tracker.
- After rain, gemsbok males spend time reaffirming their territory by moving to each of their territorial marking spots, one at a time.
- In the Karoo, gemsbok will venture into the mountains during the day to seek shade, and return to the open valley at night.

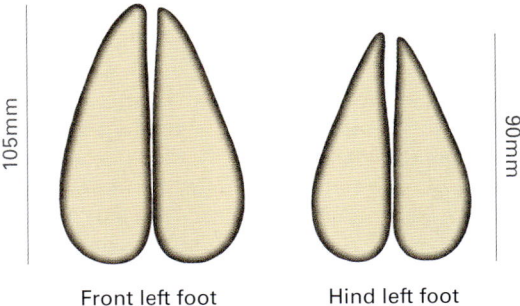

Front left foot   Hind left foot

Can be confused with ...

- Gemsbok tracks can be confused with those of **red hartebeest**, although the hartebeest track is 10–20mm shorter and the hoof edges are straighter. The gemsbok's front foot is broader than that of the hartebeest. The cloven hooves of the hartebeest are situated further apart, forming a larger gap between the tighter hooves than on the gemsbok. The hartebeest tracks are heart-shaped in appearance.

MAMMALS ■ Antelopes

Suni
Neotragus moschatus

This diminutive antelope weighs 4–5kg, and is reddish-brown with white chin, throat and underbelly. Only males have horns, although females are slightly larger. A characteristic feature of the suni is the exceptionally large preorbital glands located beneath its eyes.

Suni prefer dense vegetation and mature forests with low, thick cover. They are found in isolated pockets of northeastern South Africa, including northern KwaZulu-Natal and northern Kruger National Park, and in the coastal dune forests of Mozambique.

Habits
- These secretive antelope are active mainly at night.
- They breed in the summer after which the female gives birth to a single fawn, which remains hidden for a few weeks.
- Pythons and crowned eagles prey on young suni (notably in the sand forests of northern KwaZulu-Natal). The suni defence strategy is to remain completely still if a threat is detected. Their coat provides excellent camouflage in their preferred thicket habitat.

Feeding and diet
- Suni browse on fallen leaves, flowers and fruits.

Droppings
- Droppings measure 5mm in diameter and 7–10mm in length.

Territorial behaviour
- Males are territorial and scent-mark using preorbital glands situated below the eye, as well as interdigital (pedal) glands between the hooves. They use scent-marking, rather than latrines, to define their territory.

MAMMALS ■ Antelopes

A slightly pointed variation of the suni track

Suni hind foot registering on top of the front foot track

About the track
- This tiny antelope track measures 20–22mm in length.
- The hoof edges are relatively curved, although a more pointed variation of the track also exists.
- The track is rounded on the leading edge (hoof tip), which is accentuated if the animal steps in deep sand.
- The normal walking gait results in the hind foot registering directly on top of the front foot.

Can be confused with ...

- *The rounded suni track is substantially smaller than that of the **red duiker**, with which it regularly shares habitat.*

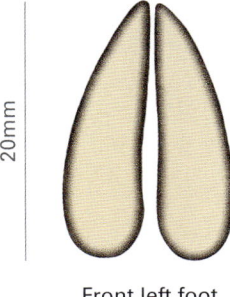

Front left foot

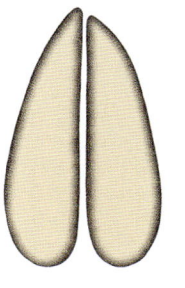

Hind left foot

MAMMALS ■ Antelopes

Oribi
Ourebia ourebi

This uncommon and inquisitive little antelope's distribution is scattered about southern, eastern and central Africa. The species is usually seen in adult pairs, or mother and youngster. They prefer open grasslands and floodplains, with a combination of short and tall grass, and are partial to recently burnt areas.

Habits
- Known to make local seasonal movements if food supply dwindles. They are water dependent.
- A single young is born between October and December, and hidden in long grass for the first three to four months.
- Oribi produce a snorting whistle as an alarm call.

Feeding and diet
- As exclusive grazers, their diet consists of grasses such as red grass (*Themeda triandra*) and giant spear grass (*Trachypogon spicatus*).

Droppings
- Droppings are round and slightly tapered on one end, dark brown, 6mm in diameter and 11mm in length.

Territorial behaviour
- Territorial males scent-mark grass stems with a preorbital gland beneath the eye, leaving a little blob of secretion.
- Make use of middens to mark territory.

About the track
- Tracks measured front foot 40mm and hind foot 42mm in length, with the smallest measure being 35mm for the hind foot.
- The hoof tips are typically sharp with straight outer hoof edges and a pronounced gap between the cloven hooves.

Oribi droppings

MAMMALS ■ Antelopes

Hind on top of front foot; direct register

Oribi tracks in wet sand; notice the gap between the cloven hooves.

- Front and hind tracks are similar in shape and size, however some hind foot tracks occasionally measure longer and are slightly rounded on the leading edge.
- At a typical walking gait the hind foot registers on top of the front foot – direct register. They move carefully and leave remarkably few scuff marks as they move.

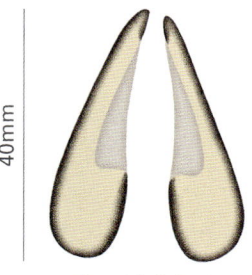

40mm

Front left foot

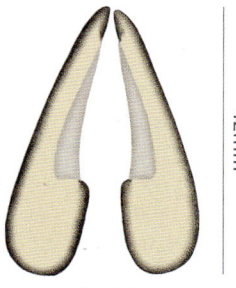

42mm

Hind left foot

Can be confused with ...

- The oribi and **steenbok** tracks can look similar, however the steenbok track is sharper on the leading edge, while the **duiker's** track is far more rounded on the leading edge.

MAMMALS ■ Antelopes

Sharpe's grysbok
Raphicerus sharpei

Weighing only 7kg, this secretive little antelope is reddish-brown with silver streaks. Only the males have horns.
They prefer relatively thick bush, mountain slopes and rocky areas. Distribution is limited to the very northeastern corner of South Africa, as well as Zimbabwe and southern Mozambique.

Habits
- These antelopes are solitary and predominantly nocturnal.
- A single lamb is born during the summer months after a gestation period of 200 days.
- Exceptionally shy, it tends to crouch and slink away into the undergrowth when disturbed.

Feeding and diet
- Grysbok are predominantly browsers but are also known to graze, feeding on young leaves, the shoots of small plants, seedpods and flowers.

Droppings
- Oval, slightly elongated pellets vary from light brown to dark in colour, measuring 5–6mm in diameter and 9–14mm in length.

Territorial behaviour
- Sharpe's grysbok is territorial and deposits its droppings in a midden.

About the track
- Tracks measured in the northern Kruger National Park are front foot 25mm and hind foot 26mm in length.
- The cloven hooves are positioned tightly together, sharp and pointed on the leading edge.
- The usual walking gait shows the hind foot register on top of the front foot.
- Tracks can be found on rocky slopes and hilly areas as well as in mopane and sandy areas with enough cover.

Sharpe's grysbok tracks

Can be confused with ...
- *Tracks are ±12mm shorter than both* **common duiker** *and* **steenbok**.

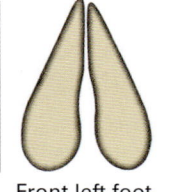
Front left foot

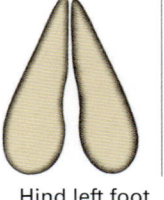
Hind left foot

Cape grysbok
Raphicerus melanotis

This diminutive antelope has an attractive reddish coat flecked in white. Males have short, sharp, straight horns and weigh about 10kg. It is endemic to the Western Cape region of South Africa.

Habits
- Mostly active at night, usually found solitarily, except mothers and young.
- Prefers thick scrub bush, thickets along sand dunes and dense cover along the lower levels of rocky hills.
- A single lamb is born during the summer months after a six-month gestation period.

Feeding and diet
- Predominantly browsers, favouring dune guarrie (*Euclea racemosa*) as well as targeting fruits in vineyards and orchards of the Cape. They are not dependent on water.

Droppings
- Droppings are oval and dark brown, measuring 6mm in diameter and 2mm in length.

Territorial behaviour
- Males are territorial and make use of a well-developed preorbital gland to scent-mark. They also make extensive use of communal middens. Males are particularly aggressive with rival males.

About the track
- Tracks measured front foot 32mm and hind foot 34mm in length; the smallest hind foot measured is 25mm in length.
- Front foot hoof edges are typically straight, but a rounder variation is also found. Hoof tips are usually pointed and sharp.

Cape grysbok droppings; the species also uses communal middens.

MAMMALS ■ Antelopes

Cape grysbok tracks; notice the hind foot registers directly on the front foot.

Typical track in wet sand

- In some tracks there is a small gap between the cloven hooves.
- At a typical walking gait the hind foot registers directly on top of the front foot – direct register.

Can be confused with ...

- The Cape grysbok track can be confused with the **common duiker** and **steenbok**, both of which have longer tracks measuring 38–40mm in length. The steenbok track is narrower and usually gives rise to a prominent step. The duiker track is broader, particularly on the leading edge.

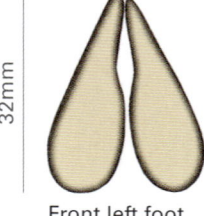

Front left foot

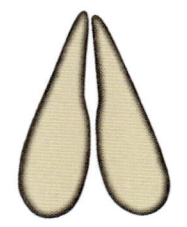

Hind left foot

MAMMALS ■ Antelopes

Steenbok
Raphicerus campestris

This highly territorial little antelope has a red-brown body, white underparts and very large ears. An adult weighs 10–12kg. Only males have horns, which are widely spaced and straight.

The steenbok inhabits open grassland and woodland that has some cover.

Habits
- Diurnal, active during the early morning and late afternoon – but become nocturnal in areas where they are subjected to persistent human persecution.
- Although monogamous, both sexes are solitary, reuniting with their habitual partners when the female is in oestrus.
- They are largely independent of water.
- Exceptionally vigilant and quick – steenbok kills are seldom seen at Londolozi or Samara game reserves; cheetah, thanks to its speed, is the predator that most successfully preys on steenbok.

Feeding and diet
- They browse on small plants including forbs, leaves and fruits, and may dig for bulbs.

Droppings
- Pellet shape is variable – rounded, oval or elongate. Droppings are light to dark brown and measure 6mm in diameter and 10–12mm in length.

Striking hoof marks show where the steenbok covered its droppings. In this instance the droppings were uncovered for the photograph.

MAMMALS ■ Antelopes

See the distinctive ridge of soil between the cloven hooves. Notice the slight concave shape of the hind foot track on top of the front foot track.

A steenbok front foot track

Tracks of a running steenbok

- The steenbok is the only antelope that buries its droppings. It prepares a space in the ground with its front hooves, then urinates, defecates and finally covers up the droppings. Theories for this behaviour range from the antelope's taking care not to attract predators, territorial marking behaviour to keeping the droppings moist and scent-bearing. The last theory seems most plausible.

Territorial behaviour

- Both males and females occupy territories of 1–2km².
- They defend these well-defined and overlapping territories, each of which has resting places, territorial middens and preferred feeding places.
- Interdigital (pedal) glands between their hooves and preorbital glands beneath the eyes are used to mark territory.

About the track

- The steenbok track is 40mm in length; the cloven hooves are narrow and distinctively sharp and pointed.
- Characteristic of the track is the central ridge of soil that pushes between the cloven hooves.

MAMMALS ■ Antelopes

- Recorded track measurements range from 35–44mm in length; steenbok tracks measured at Samara Karoo Reserve were comparatively smaller in width and length than those at Londolozi Game Reserve. The type of terrain and substrate, as well as extensive digging by steenbok in the Karoo (affecting the shape of the hooves), could account for the track size differences.
- Steenbok tracks seen in certain substrates give rise to a feature called a 'step' – a ridge feature depicted by the light grey line in the track illustration.
- Steenbok tracks will splay when the animal is running.
- A typical walking gait shows the hind foot registering on top of the front foot.
- The hind foot hoof edges are slightly concave in shape when compared with those of the front foot.

Steenbok front and hind foot tracks

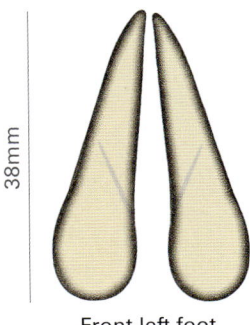

Front left foot   Hind left foot

Can be confused with ...

- *Steenbok tracks, particularly when this antelope is running and the hooves are splayed, can be confused with those of the **common duiker**, although the duiker's hooves are often broader, as well as more rounded and blunt on the leading edge.*
  The duiker also displays a different running (diving) movement. The cloven hooves of the duiker sit tightly together whereas there is a distinctive ridge between those of the steenbok.

MAMMALS ■ Antelopes

Springbok
Antidorcas marsupialis

This striking antelope – and national symbol of South Africa – gets its name from its exceptional ability to leap. Springbok were once numerous in the Karoo – migrating herds numbered over a million animals and could extend over several kilometres.

They are not dependent on water and prefer open dry grassland and scrubland, including the Kalahari.

Habits
- Diurnal; mainly active during the early morning and late afternoon.
- Gregarious, they live in mixed herds and bachelor groups, with solitary males joining the herd during the rut (mating season).
- Small herds in the dry season may congregate into much larger groups in areas where rain has fallen.
- Springbok engage in 'stotting' or 'pronking' to display their physical agility and power, presumably in an attempt to dissuade ambitious predators, and possibly when they are excited. Arching its back, the animal jumps high into the air with its legs held stiffly, appearing to bounce back on all four legs before rebounding. At the same time, the white hair along its spine is raised (called 'piloerection'), and the hair under the tail stands up in a fan shape.

Feeding and diet
- Predominantly grazers in the wet season, during the dry season they browse on shoots and leaves of karroid shrubs and succulents. Also known to dig up roots and tubers in the dry season.
- They can subsist without water for long periods, acquiring moisture from succulent plants.

Droppings
- Dark brown and pellet-shaped, sometimes tapered on one end, measuring 8mm in diameter and 12mm in length.

Territorial behaviour
- Territorial males remain in their territories throughout the year. They actively herd females during the breeding season, and may fight to defend their territory.

Fresh male springbok droppings usually scatter. Females mostly deposit droppings in small piles. Notice the sharp ends of the individual pellets.

MAMMALS ■ Antelopes

- Dominant males ritualistically mark their territories by urinating close to the ground with their hind legs widespread, then squatting to deposit droppings on the spot and finally scraping the ground with their front hooves.
- They use preorbital glands beneath the eyes to scent-mark branches.

About the track
- Track measurements taken at Samara Karoo Reserve are front foot 50mm and hind foot 54mm.
- This heart-shaped track has relatively sharp hoof tips but a broad posterior edge.
- The hoof edges are straight or slightly concave, particularly on the hind foot track. The hind foot is longer, narrower and sharper.
- A slight gap may appear between the hoof tips on the hind foot.
- Springbok tracks seen in certain substrates give rise to a feature called a 'step' – a ridge feature depicted by the light grey in the track illustration.
- The typical gait results in the hind foot overstepping – landing ahead of the front foot.

Springbok tracks are relatively sharp on the leading edge and broad on the posterior edge.

Clear tracks in the Karoo

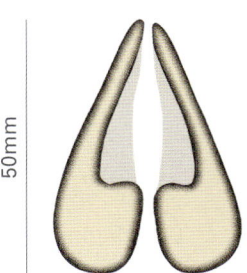

Front left foot   Hind left foot

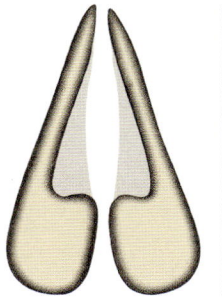

Can be confused with ...

- *Springbok tracks can be confused with those of **impala**, although the impala track is broader and less pointed on the leading edge. The hoof edges show more prominently in impala tracks. The springbok track is marginally longer than the impala's.*

MAMMALS ■ Antelopes

Impala
Aepyceros melampus

This common and fleet-footed antelope is a rich red-brown colour on the upper part of its body and lighter-coloured on its sides and legs. Adult rams are 60kg and females 40kg in weight. Male impala have horns that are ridged on the lower part and smooth up to the sharp tips.

The impala prefers areas of mixed woodland and the ecotones between different habitat types. It usually moves within easy reach of water.

Habits
- Diurnal and gregarious, they are found in breeding herds of females, youngsters and adult males. Herds of over 100 animals are common during the wet season when food is plentiful.
- During the short rutting (or breeding) season in May and June, dominant males will establish territories and begin mating.
- During the rut, territorial males advertise their status with astonishingly loud growling or coughing sounds, some of which are similar to their snorting alarm call.
- Successful breeding males are usually those that hold territory with abundant food, water and cover.
- Impala are exceptionally vigilant and all their senses are well developed.
- If a predator is detected, they advance towards it, stare and make an alarm call. Their alarm call is an intense 'blow', which sounds like an intense nasal exhalation.

Feeding and diet
- Mixed feeders, with the ability to both browse and graze – they feed on leaves, flowers, fruits and pods, switching predominantly to grass in summer.
- In the Sabi Sands they show a preference for *Senegalia*, *Combretum* and *Ziziphus* in the dry winter.
- Although generally sedentary, they cover larger distances during the dry season in search of adequate browse.

An alert male impala

MAMMALS ■ Antelopes

Impala droppings

Urine and droppings of a two-month-old female impala lamb

Droppings
- Pellets are round, oval or elongated, measuring 8–10mm in diameter and 15–20mm in length.
- They vary from black to surprisingly light brown in colour in the winter.
- Droppings are deposited in middens during the rutting season, or randomly throughout their territory.

Territorial behaviour
- Males defend their territories vigorously. Fighting becomes intense as they chase off challengers.
- During the rutting season the males will thrash small bushes with their horns, often stripping off some of the bark in the process. Male impala will even horn wet mud, as do nyala.

Male impala droppings deposited in a territorial midden

171

MAMMALS ■ Antelopes

An impala hind foot track

Tracks of a large herd of impala

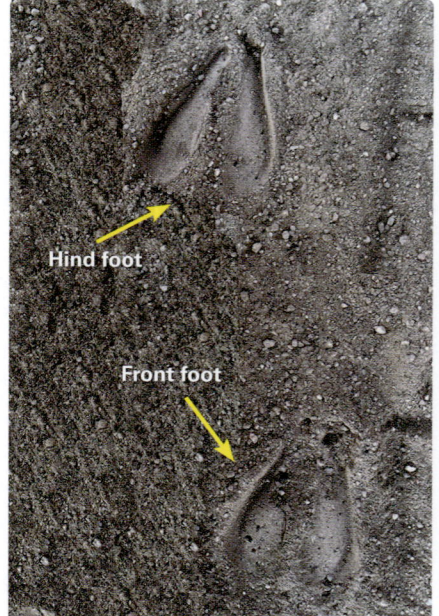

Clear impala front and hind tracks. Notice the concave edges of the hind foot.

Impala front foot track. Notice the prominent hoof edge – a feature that gives rise to the name 'rim walker'.

MAMMALS ■ Antelopes

About the track

- Front and hind tracks measure roughly the same length. Female track lengths range from 42–46mm, and male 46–51mm in length. Male tracks measured were slightly broader than those of females, although more research is required in this field.
- The track is triangular – showing a wide posterior edge with a sharp hoof tip on the leading edge, particularly on the hind foot.
- The cloven hooves are prone to splaying if the animal moves quickly or walks on slippery terrain.
- The hind foot is more pointed, and the hoof edges are slightly concave in shape near the leading edge.

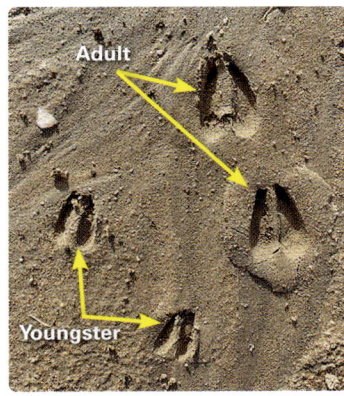

Multiple impala tracks usually seen

- On hard ground, the hoof edges may show up distinctly in the track. For this reason, some have described the impala as a 'rim walker'.
- Impala tracks seen in certain substrates give rise to a feature called a 'step' – a ridge feature depicted by the light grey in the track illustration.
- The normal gait results in the hind foot registering 60–80mm ahead of the front foot. As the animal's pace increases, its hind foot will land up to 120mm ahead of its front foot.
- Impala commonly drag their hind feet, creating short drag marks in among the tracks.

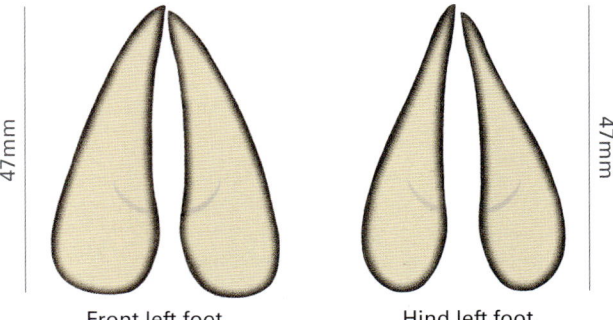

Front left foot   Hind left foot

Can be confused with ...

- Impala tracks can be confused with those of **nyala** in areas where the two species coexist. However, the nyala track shows a larger gap between the cloven hooves, is rounder and broader at the leading edge, and does not show a 'step'. The impala track is widest at the posterior edge whereas the nyala's is widest near the middle of the track.

Red hartebeest
Alcelaphus buselaphus caama

This antelope has a rusty red-brown-coloured body with black legs and a black face. It has high humped shoulders, a sloping back and a long head on an upright neck. Both males and females have horns.

The red hartebeest is found in open grassland savanna, including semi-desert, in southern Africa.

Habits
- Diurnal, most active during the early morning, late afternoon and all day when it is cool.
- Gregarious, living in small herds of up to 20, but sometimes in much larger groups.
- They are mostly grazers, but will switch to browsing Karoo scrub when grass is in short supply.

Droppings
- Droppings are slightly elongated, round on one side and flat on the other, dark brown, measuring 10–12mm in diameter and 15–22mm in length.
- Dung is dropped both in middens and randomly throughout their territory.

Territorial behaviour
- In areas where red hartebeest and gemsbok share ranges, their territorial droppings may be seen together.
- The male red hartebeest defecates in middens along territorial boundaries and makes use of preorbital glands situated below the eyes to scent-mark on trees and on the ground.

About the track
- Measurements taken at Samara Karoo Reserve Karoo were front track 87mm and hind track 80mm.
- The track is triangular (or heart-shaped) and symmetrical.
- Both front and hind tracks show a slight oval-shaped gap between the hooves. This is very prominent in firm mud where tracks imprint clearly.
- Red hartebeest tracks seen in certain substrates give rise to a feature called a 'step' – a ridge feature depicted by the light grey in the track illustration.

Red hartebeest droppings

MAMMALS ■ Antelopes

Red hartebeest front and hind feet tracks

Typical red hartebeest front foot track. If you look carefully you will notice the oval-shaped, raised area between the hooves.

Red hartebeest trail; notice the hind foot does not register on top of the front foot.

- The hooves will splay evenly in muddy conditions.
- At a normal walking gait, the hind track registers ahead of the front track.

Following red hartebeest trails

- Makes use of the same paths repeatedly. After rain, it reaffirms its territorial boundaries and dominance by marking in territorial middens.
- Evidence of territorial battles is common; scuff marks and even their knee marks on the ground can be found.
- This animal readily scratches its body and rubs its face on trees, such as the shepherd's tree (*Boscia oleoides*) in the Karoo. It tends to use the same trees repeatedly, and evidence of hair and mud can often be found on them.
- The red hartebeest is also prone to horning mud as part of its territorial or social display.

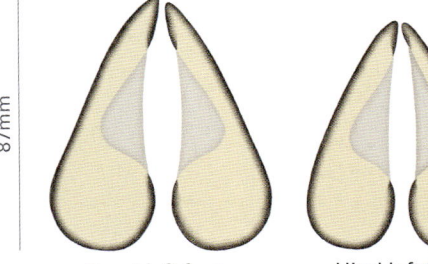

Front left foot   Hind left foot

Can be confused with ...

- **Gemsbok** tracks are larger than the red hartebeest's, and their tracks usually have less of a gap between the hooves, which are broader. The hartebeest track's posterior edge is usually broader than that of the gemsbok.

MAMMALS ■ Antelopes

Lichtenstein's hartebeest
Alcelaphus lichtensteinii

This large, red-brown species has a lighter belly, humped shoulders, a sloping back and ridged horns. Adults weigh up to 175kg. Its range used to include Kruger National Park, but is now limited to central and northern Mozambique, Zambia and Tanzania. As a savanna species, it prefers the ecotone of open woodland and vleis or floodplain grassland.

Habits
- Gregarious and territorial, they form small herds of no more than 10 individuals.
- Female gives birth to a single calf after a gestation of eight months. She does not attempt to conceal it while she grazes or drinks.
- Dominant bulls are alert and usually run at the back of the herd when fleeing.
- Vigilant and inquisitive animals, they produce a 'sneeze–snort' alarm call.
- Almost exclusively grazers of *Panicum*, *Digitaria* and *Echinochloa* species.

Territorial behaviour
- Bulls are highly territorial and maintain territories throughout the year.
- They horn and stomp the ground.
- Create small middens, not extensive.

About the track
- Front 90mm and hind 85mm in length; reasonably blunt on the leading edge.
- Hoof edge is usually prominent; there is a substantial gap between the cloven hooves.
- The typical walking gait is a small overstep.

Can be confused with ...
- Lichtenstein's track is 10–15mm shorter than that of the **blue wildebeest** and its cloven hooves are proportionately narrower than the wildebeest's.
- The **waterbuck's** track is marginally narrower, with cloven hooves tighter together and straighter hoof edges than the Lichtenstein's.

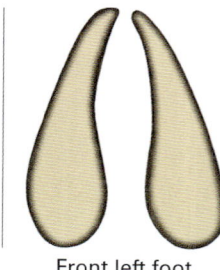
Front left foot (90mm)

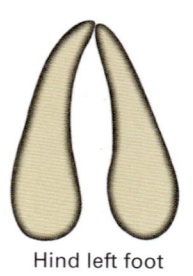
Hind left foot (85mm)

Above left: Front foot is more curved. **Above right:** Hind foot is more pointed.

MAMMALS ■ Antelopes

Klipspringer
Oreotragus oreotragus

The klipspringer's body colour ranges from yellow-brown to grey-brown, with a white underbelly. Females are larger than males; only the male has horns. The Afrikaans common name means 'rock jumper' and refers to this antelope's ability to move between the rocks, its chosen habitat. Hollow, coarse hairs may assist in cushioning the body against falls and they offer insulation against extreme temperatures.

Habits
- Monogamous, found in pairs, and sometimes in small family groups with young.
- Male and female pairs occupy permanent territories.
- When threatened, the pair will freeze and make loud whistling alarm calls in duet.
- Exceptionally vigilant; if disturbed, they will move to higher ground.
- This sure-footed animal jumps and bounces in among the rocks with an unusually stiff but effective gait.

Feeding and diet
- They are selective yet adaptable browsers of plants, shrubs and succulents, including berries and flowers.
- Occasionally they will leave their rocky habitat to graze on nearby flat ground, and are partial to newly sprouted grass on burnt areas.

Droppings
- Droppings are usually tapered at one end; they measure 7mm in diameter and 15mm in length.
- Deposited in middens throughout their territory.

Droppings may be found in middens throughout the klipspringer's territory.

MAMMALS ■ Antelopes

Territorial behaviour
- Klipspringers defend territory with visual displays by the dominant male, as well as scent-marking and depositing droppings in middens.
- Both sexes scent-mark, using the preorbital glands beneath their eyes to deposit little blobs of oily black secretions on twigs and branches.

About the track
- The unique track resembles a 'gemstone suspended on an earring' or a 'raindrop' – with the leading edge of the hoof being rounded and the posterior edge more pointed. Front and hind tracks are a similar size and shape, measuring 20mm long, on average.
- The narrow soles and rounded hooves assist the animal to keep its footing among rocks, crevices and uneven terrain. Light grey-coloured, curved lines in the track drawing depict the soles.
- Walks on the very tips of its shortened hooves, like a ballerina. Only the front half (20mm) of the hoof makes contact with the substrate.

A klipspringer scent mark

Klipspringer track

This animal stands on the tips of its hooves and can fit all four feet into a very small area.

MAMMALS ■ Antelopes

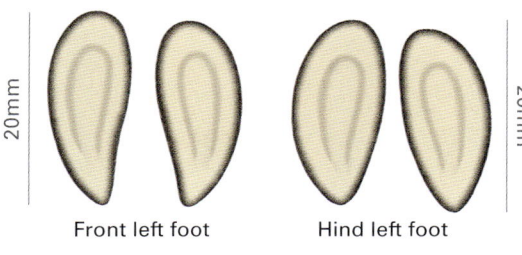

Front left foot   Hind left foot

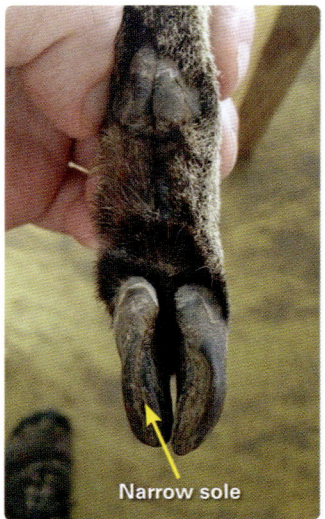

Klipspringer hoof; only the front half (20mm) makes contact with the ground.

- The outside edges of the hooves are significantly more curved than the inside edges.
- If seen in dry sand, the tracks appear as two indistinct 'holes' situated next to each other.
- Although the klipspringer's habitat includes koppies, mountain edges and rocky outcrops (where tracks are difficult to see), tracks are left when it descends to drink water or when it moves between territories or koppies.
- Will venture into riverbeds adjacent to rocky territories to drink from water holes in the dongas, or from holes where elephants have dug for water.
- At Londolozi Game Reserve, klipspringers – particularly the males – have been seen to cover large distances, leaving tracks far away from any mountain or koppies. One individual was seen on the reserve's soccer field!

Klipspringer trail

Can be confused with ...

- *Klipspringer tracks can be confused with those of **baby warthogs**, but, there's a larger gap between the cloven hooves of the klipspringer than between those of the warthog.*

MAMMALS ■ Antelopes

Puku
Kobus vardonii

A sturdy, medium-sized antelope, sandy brown in colour with a slightly lighter brown underbelly. Males have ridged, backward-curved horns of 50cm. It prefers wet grasslands and floodplains in Tanzania, Zambia and northern Botswana. Numbers have dwindled outside protected areas.

Habits
- Gregarious; in small herds, constantly fluctuating in number.
- Males are territorial although territories are not permanently maintained, lasting from a few days to a couple of months.
- Crepuscular, active in the early morning and late afternoon.
- Puku produce a shrill whistle sound as an alarm call.

Feeding and diet
- Predominantly a grazer, heavily reliant on permanent water; research shows 88% of their diet comes from grasses.

Droppings
- Round and dark brown, sometimes clumped together; measuring 10mm in diameter and 15mm in length.

Clear track

Territorial behaviour
- Territorial males are not prone to fighting, but will use various displays to dissuade rivals, like tail-wagging and horning grass.

About the track
- Tracks of one adult measured front foot 65mm and hind foot 60mm in length, with a range of 55–70mm being recorded.
- Front foot hoof edges are slightly convex (bulging slightly outwards), whereas the hind hoof edge is straighter.
- There is a substantial gap between the cloven hooves, which widens when the animal walks on a slippery substrate.
- At a typical walking gait the hind foot registers behind the front foot – understep.

Front and hind tracks

Can be confused with ...
- Similar to the **waterbuck** but slightly shorter (up to 10mm) and without a step.

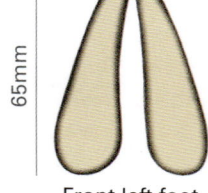

Front left foot   Hind left foot

MAMMALS ■ Antelopes

Mountain reedbuck
Redunca fulvorufula

This antelope's body is brown-grey with a white belly and a bushy tail. Its coat is thick and woolly. Only males have horns.

It prefers a mountainous habitat with grassy slopes, bushes and trees. Males occupy their territories year-round.

Habits
- Active in the early mornings, late afternoons and at night. When resting, they lie in a tight group.
- Gregarious, found in groups of three to eight, sometimes more, depending on the season.
- Form groups that may consist of a territorial male, subadults and females with young.
- Mature males chase younger males from the herd at nine to 15 months. Usually only one adult ram in a family group.
- Alarms with a high-pitched whistle.

Feeding and diet
- The mountain reedbuck is a selective grazer.
- It descends from the mountain slopes at night to feed and drink, and stays longer when grazing is poor in winter.

Droppings
- Droppings are found in clusters of rectangular pellets, and measure 7mm in diameter and 5–8mm in length.
- Pellets may be clumped together.

About the track
- Tracks measured in the Karoo showed a length of 48mm (up to 54mm) for both the front and hind feet.

Droppings are found in clusters of rectangular pellets, and measure 7mm in diameter.

MAMMALS ■ Antelopes

- The mountain reedbuck track is relatively blunt on the leading edge, particularly on the front foot. However, a narrower, more pointed variation is also commonly seen.
- The hind foot is more pointed than the front.
- Their tracks are seldom seen due to their preference for mountains, hills and rocky habitat.
- A normal walking gait shows the hind foot registering on or just ahead of the front foot.

The mountain reedbuck hoof tips are relatively blunt.

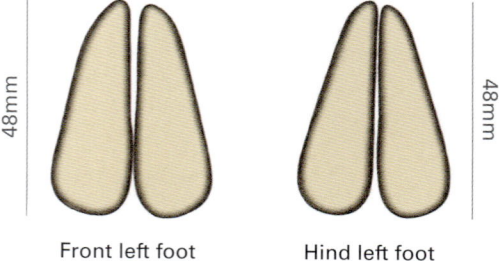

Front left foot   Hind left foot

A typical herd of mountain reedbuck

MAMMALS ■ Antelopes

Southern reedbuck
Redunca arundinum

A medium-sized antelope with a woolly-looking coat that ranges from light to greyish brown. Southern reedbuck measure an average of 85cm at the shoulder and only males have horns.

Found in vleis, reed beds and tall grass, where water is in regular supply, its patchy distribution is limited to southern Africa, including northeastern South Africa, Zimbabwe, Zambia and Malawi. They avoid flat, open veld.

Habits
- Occur singly, in pairs or in small family groups; they never form large herds.
- Young are born any time of the year, with a peak during the summer months.
- Tend to use fixed game trails to access water, and are exceptionally vigilant while drinking.

Feeding and diet
- As exclusive grazers, their diet consists of grasses such as yellow thatching grass (*Hyperthelia dissoluta*), giant spear grass (*Trachypogon spicatus*) and a common water reed (*Phragmites communis*).

Droppings
- Round to oval, dark brown to black, measuring 8mm in diameter and 20mm in length.

Southern reedbuck droppings

Territorial behaviour
- Territorial males demonstrate their status through a stiff-legged rocking canter, sometimes making a whistling call; males also defecate and urinate to show dominance.

About the track
- Tracks of both front and hind feet measured 62mm in length.
- The hoof tips are typically sharp; the track is similar to but more elongated than that of the impala. Hoof edges can be concave in shape.
- Variations show a more blunt version – with outer edges being more rounded.
- Southern reedbuck tracks seen in certain substrates give rise to a feature called a 'step' – a ridge feature depicted by the light grey line in the track illustration.

MAMMALS ■ Antelopes

Typical southern reedbuck track

Blunt, rounded version of reedbuck track

Tracks splaying apart in wet sand

- Cloven hooves are set apart showing a gap of 4–7mm, and may splay as much as 20mm apart in slippery or soft substrate.
- False hooves may show if the southern reedbuck steps in soft substrate.
- At a walking gait the hind foot registers ahead of the front foot (overstep).

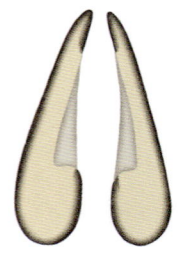

Front left foot

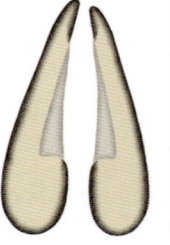

Hind left foot

Can be confused with ...

- The southern reedbuck track is about 10mm longer and sharper than that of the **impala**, with which it can be confused. The reedbuck's cloven hooves can show a marked central ridge (gap) that is not usually seen in impala tracks.

Grey rhebok
Pelea capreolus

Also known as the Vaal ribbok or common rhebok, these antelope are grey-brown in colour with a white underside. They are easily recognisable by the white under their tail, which they hold up when they bound away, usually towards the top of a slope. They have a relatively long neck and long ears. The male has straight horns. In winter they grow a woolly grey coat that insulates them from the cold.

They inhabit rocky hills and mountainous areas with grassy plains, where they are often found grazing in small groups.

Habits
- Rhebok are both nocturnal and diurnal but will rest during the midday heat.
- Females are gregarious, forming groups of up to 12, while territorial males are solitary. Young and non-territorial males form bachelor herds.
- Rhebok react quickly and can produce a powerful leap. They are efficient at staying out of reach of predators such as leopard and cheetah.
- They produce a snorting alarm call if they detect danger.

Feeding and diet
- Exclusively grazers, they are not dependent on water to survive, deriving most of their moisture through grazing.

Territorial behaviour
- Males take on females only when they have established a permanent territory, which they defend vigorously.
- Males are highly territorial, using aggressive lateral displays – feet stamping and snorting – to reinforce territorial dominance.

Droppings
- Droppings are black, and measure 6–8mm in diameter and 10–15mm in length.

About the track
- The track measures 45mm in length and is distinctively narrow, with often just the hoof edges showing.
- The leading edge of the tracks is sharp and pointed.
- Grey rhebok tracks seen in certain substrates give rise to a feature called a 'step' – a ridge feature depicted by the light grey line in the track illustration.

Grey rhebok droppings

MAMMALS ■ Antelopes

Rhebok front foot track

Rhebok hind foot track

- The hind track may register on top of or ahead of the front track.
- Due to the rocky habitat in which the grey rhebok lives, its tracks are not easily found.

The track is distinctively narrow, often with just the hoof edges showing.

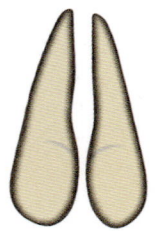

45mm | 45mm

Front left foot | Hind left foot

Can be confused with ...

- Although similar in length, the grey rhebok track is distinctively narrower than that of the **mountain reedbuck**.

Grey rhebok on a mountain slope in the Karoo

Blesbok

Damaliscus pygargus phillipsi

This antelope is endemic to southern Africa. Brown with a white belly, it has a prominent white blaze on the face. Although the sexes are very similar, males are 10kg heavier and have thicker horns.

It occurs naturally in grasslands in the central and eastern areas of southern Africa.

Habits

- Diurnal – active in the early mornings and late evenings, particularly when the weather is cool and overcast.
- Herds of females and calves are found with a male in attendance during the breeding season.
- Bachelor groups are common.

Feeding and diet

- They are predominantly selective grazers of short grass where water is permanent.

Droppings

- Elongated pellets are dark in colour: 15–20mm long with 10mm diameter.

Territorial behaviour

- Territorial males deposit droppings in middens, on which they will lie.
- They scent-mark by using preorbital glands as well as interdigital (pedal) glands between the hooves.
- Territorial males use lateral displays – foot-stamping and holding their heads high with hind legs apart and front legs straight – to warn off rivals.

Blesbok droppings

About the track

- The front track measures 67mm and hind track 63mm in length. The front foot length and width measurements are very similar.
- Both front and hind tracks are broad, particularly at the posterior edge of the front track.
- The outside edges of the hooves are straighter, rather than curved.

MAMMALS ■ Antelopes

- The blesbok's typical walking gait shows the hind foot landing ahead of the front foot (overstep). The hind foot seldom registers directly on top of the front foot.
- Blesbok tracks seen in certain substrates give rise to a feature called a 'step' – a ridge feature depicted by the light grey line in the track illustration.

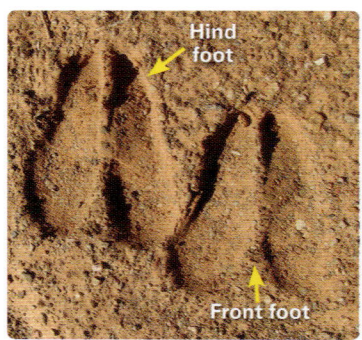

Above: Blesbok tracks
Right: Blesbok trail

Adult and subadult blesbok

Blesbok track; notice the step.

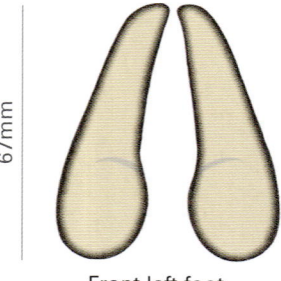

Front left foot
67mm

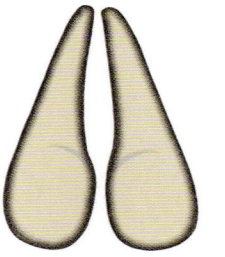

Hind left foot
63mm

Can be confused with ...

- The blesbok is one of two subspecies of *Damaliscus pygargus*; the other is the **bontebok** (*D. pygargus pygargus*). The bontebok has darker brown colouration on its flanks, head and upper legs. Horns are black (blesbok horns typically have a yellow-brown hue on the front). The bontebok is mostly confined to protected areas and is considered Endangered.

Roan antelope
Hippotragus equinus

This large antelope is fawn in colour, with a black-and-white masked face. Both sexes have horns that are relatively short and scimitar-shaped. Males may weigh up to 270kg.

Roan antelope prefer open woodland and grassland savanna with medium-height grass, and easy access to water. Disease, overgrazing and general habitat degradation have caused this antelope to disappear from most of its original range; it is now considered Endangered.

Habits
- Gregarious, females and young form nursery herds of up to 25 individuals, while males form bachelor groups.
- In Kruger National Park, dominant roan bulls defend a herd of females, yet are not strictly territorial in their behaviour.
- Bulls will thrash branches as part of their dominance display.
- Females hide newborn calves for the first six to eight weeks before introducing them to the herd.

Feeding and diet
- These antelope are predominantly grazers of tall grass, although they switch to browsing leaves in the winter.

Droppings
- Rounded dark brown to black droppings, uniform in shape, measure 14mm in diameter and 18–22mm in length.

About the track
- An individual cow's track measured in northern Botswana was front foot 105mm and hind foot 95mm. A single bull at Tswalu in the Kalahari measured front foot 130mm and hind foot 110mm.
- The cloven hooves are broad.
- The front foot cloven hooves may splay apart slightly, but the hind foot hooves are usually grouped tightly together.

Roan antelope droppings

MAMMALS ■ Antelopes

Roan antelope tracks

- Roan antelope tracks seen in certain substrates give rise to a feature called a 'step'– a ridge feature depicted by the light grey line in the track illustration.
- A normal walking gait results in the hind foot registering on or just ahead of the front foot (an overstep).

Roan antelope front and hind tracks

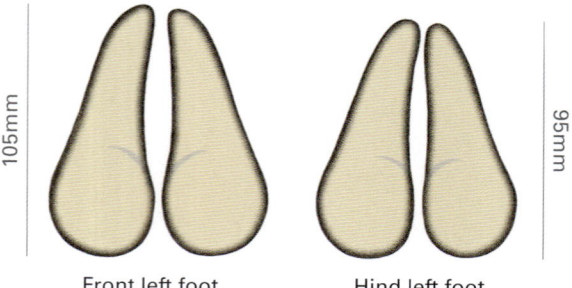

Front left foot   Hind left foot

Can be confused with ...

- The roan antelope track can be confused with the **blue wildebeest** track; however, it is more pointed (with sharper hoof tips) and the two hooves are situated tighter together than the wildebeest's. The blue wildebeest track is slightly shorter than that of the roan.

MAMMALS ■ Antelopes

Sable antelope
Hippotragus niger

This regal antelope has a compact, robust build, characterised by a thick neck and long, ringed, scimitar-shaped horns that arch backwards. Females and juveniles remain rich chestnut to dark brown in colour, but males turn black after three to five years.

Sable antelope prefer savanna woodland and grassland.

Habits
- Well known for showing aggression towards predators; using their large, scimitar-shaped horns, they are often able to defend themselves.
- Gregarious and found in herds of 20–30 females, their young and a dominant bull.
- Bulls are occasionally solitary; mostly they form small bachelor groups of eight to 12 members.
- One or more females take the lead in finding food and water, and warning against predators. The alarm call is a loud, horse-like snort.
- They are dependent on adequate cover and availability of water.

Feeding and diet
- Sable graze medium to tall grasses and will also browse during the winter.

Droppings
- Round or oval in shape, dark brown, 20mm in length and 15mm in diameter.

About the track:
- The track is usually very pointed on the leading edge, although a more blunt and rounded variation is also found.
- The posterior edge is rounded but not broad; the track is relatively narrow compared to those of many other similar-sized antelope species.
- Front track measures 100mm, hind is 95mm in length. One individual measured 105mm for both front and hind tracks.

Sable antelope droppings

MAMMALS ■ Antelopes

Sable antelope front track; note the unusually pointed leading edge.

The sable antelope outer hoof edge is often concave in shape.

- The hoof edge is often concave.
- The gap between the two cloven hooves is small, although the hoof does splay under certain conditions, such as in mud or if the animal is moving quickly.
- The sharp groove created by the hard rim of the hoof edge is characteristic.
- Sable antelope tracks in certain substrates give rise to a feature called a 'step' – a ridge feature depicted by the light grey line in the track illustration.
- It is important to note that there is tremendous variation in sable tracks.
- The typical walking gait is an overstep.

Sable bull tracks

Can be confused with ...

- The sable track may be confused with the slightly larger and more blunt **roan antelope** track.
  The roan antelope seldom shows a marked hoof edge (hoof rim), which is commonly seen with the sable. The roan's cloven hooves are also broader than those of the sable.

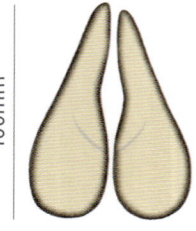

Front left foot

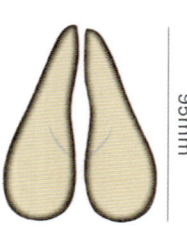

Hind left foot

100mm · 95mm

Tsessebe
Damaliscus lunatus

This reddish-tan-coloured antelope is similar in appearance to the hartebeest, yet slightly smaller. Both sexes have horns.

It prefers open grassland and the transition with woodland, where there is access to water. Historically it was distributed widely, from Senegal southwards to South Africa; however, its natural range has been steadily and extensively reduced.

Habits
- Gregarious, tsessebe form small groups of six to 10 females with youngsters and a dominant bull. Subordinate males form bachelor herds.
- Cows give birth to a single calf, which may remain in hiding for several months.
- Tsessebe make regular use of familiar game paths leading to water or favoured grazing areas.
- Reputed to be the fastest-running antelope in Africa, reaching speeds of up to 83km/h.

Feeding and diet
- They feed on tall grass almost exclusively, as well as grass that has freshly sprouted after a fire.
- They are dependent on access to water and will move if water resources dry up.

Droppings
- Elongated dark brown pellets measuring 13mm in diameter and 22–30mm in length.

Territorial behaviour
- Dominant bulls are territorial. They scent-mark grass stems with the preorbital glands beneath their eyes, as well as paw the ground with their front feet, releasing scent from interdigital (pedal) glands between the hooves.
- The dominant bulls make use of elevated areas, such as termite mounds, to advertise their presence and scent-mark territory.

Tsessebe droppings

MAMMALS ■ Antelopes

About the track
- This uncommon antelope's front track measures 90–95mm and hind track 80–82mm in length. One bull's front track measured 97mm and hind track 87mm.
- The front track is broad at the posterior edge, and shows a significant gap between the cloven hooves.
- The hind track is narrower and much more pointed than the front.
- A grooved impression created by the hard rim of the hoof edge is often noticeable.
- Tsessebe tracks seen in certain substrates give rise to a feature called a 'step' – a ridge feature depicted by the light grey line in the track illustration.
- The tsessebe's cloven hooves are prone to splaying apart.
- A normal walking gait results in the hind foot overstepping – registering ahead of the front foot.

Tsessebe front and hind foot tracks

Tsessebe hind foot track

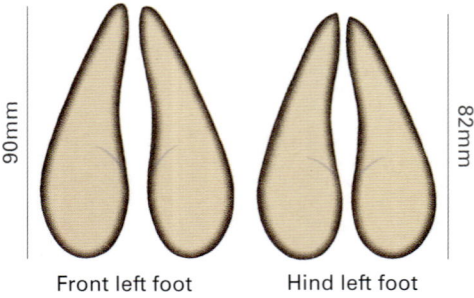

Front left foot   Hind left foot

Can be confused with ...

- Tsessebe tracks can be confused with those of the **red hartebeest** and **sable antelope**. The tsessebe track is 10–18mm shorter but marginally broader than that of the sable antelope. The red hartebeest track is slightly broader on the posterior edge than that of the tsessebe.

MAMMALS ■ Small mammals

Aardvark (antbear)
Orycteropus afer

The aardvark has a thin coat of light-coloured hair over pink-grey skin, with long, pointed ears and a thick tail. It has sturdy legs and feet with long, robust claws. It eats predominantly termites in summer and ants in winter, which it extracts with its long, sticky tongue. Its Afrikaans name comes from its pig-like snout with slit nostrils.

The aardvark prefers grassland, bushveld and desert habitats throughout the region.

Habits
- Nocturnal, but may be active during the day in winter and in times of drought.
- Solitary, though pairs may be seen during the mating season, and females with young.
- Trackers followed an aardvark's winding trail for four hours (over 5km), noting several visits to previously dug termite colonies. They were finally led to the animal's burrow, where it was safely ensconced.
- Aardvarks have acute hearing but poor eyesight.

Burrow
- Capable of digging very rapidly, making large, 'permanent' tunnelled burrows with several entrances; adults and their young shelter in these refuges.
- Burrows can be 5–8m in depth, with a number of smaller cavities and compartments leading away from the main chamber.
- Also dig less extensive temporary burrows in which the family will stay for short periods.
- Fresh tracks from the night before, as well as the presence of flies on the upper inner wall of the entrance, can indicate

The presence of flies on the inner wall of the burrow may indicate an aardvark in residence.

MAMMALS ■ Small mammals

aardvark in residence. They will shift deeper into the burrow if disturbed.
- Other animals such as African wild dogs, hyaenas, honey badgers, warthogs, snakes and certain bird species inhabit their disused burrows.

Feeding and diet
- Their diet comprises formicid ants and termites. Conspicuous diggings in termite mounds may suggest that termites are preferred; however, field research suggests otherwise. Aardvarks appear to target more termites in the summer, and ants in the winter.
- They make small exploratory digs to investigate possible food sources.
- Presumably for moisture, they also feed on aardvark cucumber (*Cucumis humifructus*), a plant that bears its melon-like fruits underground.

Droppings
- Droppings are usually buried under the excavated soil as the aardvark digs, and measure 21mm in diameter and 50mm in length.
- They consist mainly of compressed sand, and termite and ant carapaces and fragments.

Territorial behaviour
- Aardvarks scent-mark their home range with an anal gland, but do not defend a territory.

About the track
- Aardvark track lengths are front foot 75–85mm, hind foot 90–110mm.
- Diagnostic are the three long toes and robust claw marks. Aardvarks meander about, making exploratory digs for food and investigating many old diggings, eventually coming to rest in one of their burrows.

Aardvarks excavate along the way as they forage.

Aardvark droppings are rarely seen in the open.

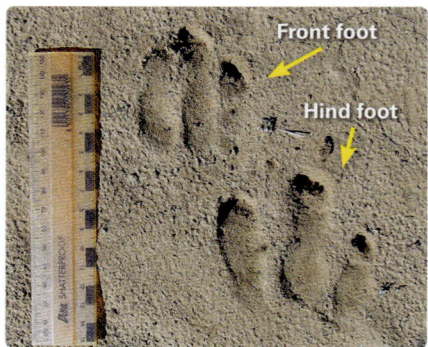
Aardvark tracks

MAMMALS ■ Small mammals

- The track is particularly distinctive, showing three long toes with thick claws on both the front and hind feet. In soft substrate, one may see claw marks indicating the presence of claw number 5 of the front feet and claws number 1 and 5 of the hind feet.
- Aardvarks walk on their toes, with the main pad leaving no impression.
- The larger hind foot track shows toes that are more splayed than those of the tightly arranged front foot digits.
- Most commonly, the hind foot lands just behind the front foot, indicating a normal walking gait. However, the partial registration of the hind foot on top of the front foot is also seen.
- The tail plays an important anchoring function, enabling the animal to grip the ground and remain stable as it digs. Thick tail impressions are left after digging.

Can be confused with ...

- *Aardvark tracks can be confused with those of **warthog**, **bushpig** and **medium-sized antelope** such as **nyala** if the full extent of the track is not clearly seen.*
- *Occasionally, when two hoof prints of an **antelope** are registered together, it gives the false impression of an aardvark's three toes.*

Aardvark trail showing direct register

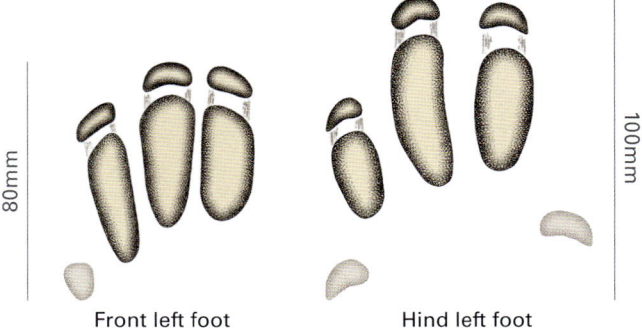

Front left foot　　　Hind left foot

MAMMALS ■ Small mammals

Temminck's pangolin
Manis temminckii

Africa is home to four species of pangolin, although only the Temminck's pangolin occurs in southern Africa. This scaly anteater's body is covered with sharp, overlapping, plate-like scales.

It prefers savanna woodland and sandveld, including the Kalahari.

It is the most trafficked animal in the world; an estimated 195,000 pangolins were trafficked for their scales in 2019 alone. Critically Endangered.

Habits
- Pangolins are nocturnal and solitary.
- They are active predominantly at night but also during daylight hours.
- The young ride on their mother's back and at the base of her tail.
- Pangolins defend themselves by curling up into a tight, armoured ball. Should they be captured, they will thrash their tail. The scales' edges are sharp and can easily cut human skin.
- They can emit a noxious-smelling acid from their anal glands.

Burrow
- They occupy abandoned aardvark and springhare burrows and rest in thick, low vegetation.

Feeding and diet
- Diet includes formicid ants and termites.
- Pangolins locate ant nests by smell, dig them open and eat the ants using their long sticky tongue to penetrate deep into narrow holes.
- Constantly digs shallow exploratory scrapes from which to establish the presence of ants or termites.

Droppings
- Vary from dark brown to black in colour; 20mm in diameter and 30–55mm in length.

Pangolin droppings – foul-smelling – are deposited in the open or under their diggings in the soil.

MAMMALS ■ Small mammals

About the track

- The pangolin uses bipedal movement (moves predominantly on its hind feet), seldom putting its front feet down.
- The triangular-shaped hind foot is padded, with five toes, and measures 50mm in length.
- Both front and hind feet have five toes, although the front toes number 1 and 5 are reduced, leaving three middle toes with long curved claws that are well adapted for digging.
- The front foot track reveals the upper surfaces of the three middle claws, which curl right under the foot.
- Occasionally it drags its tail, leaving a sign and scuff marks.

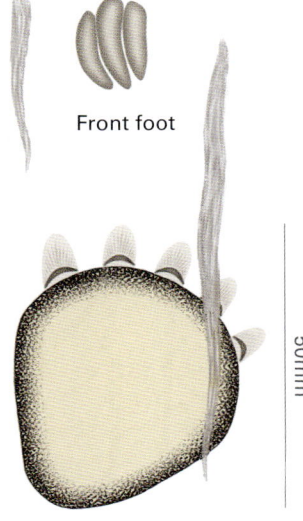

Front foot

50mm

Hind foot

Pangolin trail

199

African civet
Civettictis civetta

This small to medium-sized animal has a grey coat with black blotches on the body, and black and white stripes on the neck and tail. The black bands around its eyes make it resemble a racoon. It has disproportionately large hindquarters and erect hair along its back.

It inhabits savanna woodland with tall grass and thickets, and needs to be near permanent water.

Habits
- Primarily nocturnal, civets' most active period is two to three hours after sunset until the early hours of the following morning.
- They rest in dense vegetation or in holes in termite mounds, and have been known to climb trees.
- Although generally solitary, they may be seen in small family groups.
- Occasionally fall prey to large predators like leopards.

Feeding and diet
- Omnivores; they feed on berries, millipedes, reptiles and small rodents.

Droppings
- Surprisingly large droppings are mostly dark brown in colour. They measure an average of 33mm in diameter and 150mm in length.
- The civet's droppings often show a characteristic plug of tightly folded dry grass at one end.
- Droppings contain fruits, grass, seed and insect fragments and millipede remains.
- Droppings are often deposited in extensive and characteristically scented latrines called civetries, usually adjacent to game paths and roads.

Territorial behaviour
- Civets mark tree stumps, small harvester termite mounds and rocks with a black, gel-like secretion from their anal gland.

African civet droppings containing jackalberry seeds
(*Diospyros mespiliformis*)

MAMMALS ■ Small mammals

About the track

- Diagnostic is the very round front foot. Tracks measure front foot 53mm and hind foot 55mm.
- Although civets are not part of the cat family, their tracks appear very cat-like.
- They have five toes on each foot, although only four show on both.
- Claws do make an impression but are not a given feature of the track.
- Front foot toes are tightly situated against the main pad.
- The hind track's two middle toes are oval in shape, main pad is narrower, particularly on the leading edge – causing confusion with the jackal track.
- The main pad posterior edge may appear asymmetrical.
- The civet's typical gait results in the hind foot registering partially or fully on top of the front foot.

Can be confused with ...

- *The civet's hind foot track can be confused with that of the **jackal**. However, the gap between the toes and main pad of the jackal is bigger than in the civet; jackal claws are longer and the outside toes on both front and hind feet are significantly more oval in shape than the civet's, which are distinctively round.*
- *Civet tracks are frequently confused with those of **leopard cubs**, particularly in an area where a female leopard is known to be denning with cubs, or if the tracks are found in a sandy riverbed that leopards frequent. However, although leopard cub tracks are of a similar size, they are narrower, with a bigger gap between the toes and the main pad; they don't show claw marks unless the cub is moving quickly; the leopard's toes are more oval in shape when compared with a similar-sized civet track, and their toes splay more when the cub is running, jumping and playing.*

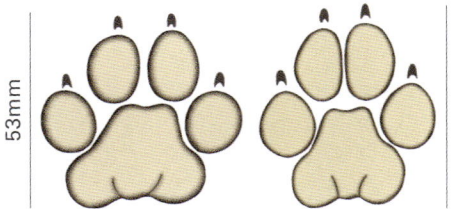

53mm | Front left foot   Hind left foot | 55mm

Below: Civet hind foot track registering on top of front foot
Centre: Civet front foot and hind foot tracks
Right: African civet territorial markings on a tree

MAMMALS ■ Small mammals

Large spotted and small spotted genets
Genetta tigrina and *G. genetta*

Large spotted genet

These genets are short-legged with an elongated body and a white-ringed tail about the same length as the head and body combined. The large spotted has a black-tipped tail, and the small spotted a white tip. There can be much variation in the colour of the bands and spots.

Efficient hunters of rodents, small mammals and birds, both genet species prefer areas with abundant water and cover, including savanna grassland and vlei areas.

Habits
- Both solitary and nocturnal.
- During the day, they rest in holes in trees, hollow logs and under exposed tree roots.
- Both are exceptional predators, often killing prey well above their own body weight.

Feeding and diet
- They prey on small rodents, birds, reptiles, insects, spiders and scorpions.
- They are also known to go after domestic chickens with great efficiency.

Droppings
- Dark-coloured, sometimes twisted, droppings are usually deposited in latrines.
- They are 12–16mm in diameter and 150mm in length. Evidence of hair is common in the droppings.

Territorial behaviour
- Scent-mark with secretions from an anal gland – this is known as olfactory communication. Markings have a distinct smell of 'burnt popcorn' and are similar to those of leopards.

Large spotted genet droppings

MAMMALS — Small mammals

Above left and right: Tracks show four toes on both front and hind feet. They actually have five toes, but toe number 1 seldom makes an impression.

About the track

- Track measurements at Londolozi are front foot 27mm and hind foot 30mm. It is presumed that tracks of the two species are remarkably similar.
- A diagnostic feature are the round little toes, which suggest the track of a small cat (which it is not).
- Tracks typically show four toes on both feet, as toe number 1 and claw seldom make an impression.
- Claw marks show if the animal runs, jumps, or if it ventures into mud.
- The front feet are slightly shorter but toes are more splayed than on the hind feet.
- The hind foot main pad is marginally longer than that on the front foot. The two middle toes on the hind foot are typically more oval when compared with the two middle toes of the front foot.
- Occasionally, a small oval impression is seen behind the main pad – this is a proximal pad showing in the track and usually appears when the genet ventures into mud.
- Relative to the overall size of the track, the main pad is large, and is a distinguishing feature.

Large spotted genet's hind and front tracks. Note the rarely seen impressions made by toe 1 and its claw, and by the proximal pad of the front foot.

MAMMALS ■ Small mammals

- The main pad has two distinct outer lobes on the posterior edge of both front and hind feet.
- Tracks showing the genet running, jumping and skidding are common – indicating a possible attempted kill or an interaction with another genet.
- The normal walking gait shows the hind foot register on top of the front foot.

Can be confused with ...

- *The genet track can be confused with that of the **African wild cat** – however, the wild cat track is longer by 10mm. The wild cat's main pad is broad on the leading edge and has three distinct lobes on the posterior edge, and its toes are oval in shape, as opposed to the genet's round toes.*
- *The **slender mongoose** track is also confused with that of the genet; however, mongoose's toes are smaller and usually show claw marks.*
- *There is currently no published information regarding the differences between large and small spotted genet tracks.*

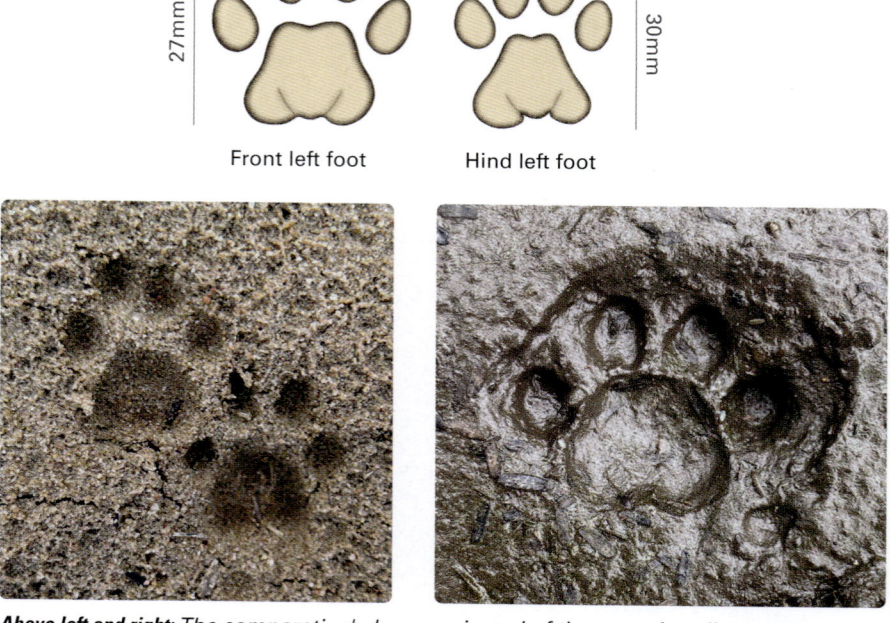

Front left foot   Hind left foot

27mm   30mm

Above left and right: *The comparatively large main pad of the genet is a diagnostic feature of the track.*

Striped polecat (zorilla)
Ictonyx striatus

This easily recognisable little carnivore has a black body with white stripes running from its head, along its back to its tail. It produces a vile-smelling secretion as a defence against predators.

It is found in open savanna country in most of sub-Saharan Africa, excluding the Congo basin and West Africa.

Habits
- Nocturnal and generally solitary, but they may be found in pairs or family groups.
- They avoid predators by emitting foul-smelling secretions – which can be sprayed at attackers – from their anal glands. They also feign death or climb trees when threatened.

Burrow
- Dig their own burrows, leaving a small, narrow entrance, just big enough for this little animal to gain entry.
- Tend to stay in the same burrow for longer than is customary for similar-sized burrowing animals.

Feeding and diet
- Proficient diggers, they create many small, shallow holes in search of food. These can be confused with holes dug by the suricate, although they are generally stand-alone holes, as opposed to the multiple diggings of the gregarious suricate.
- Polecats eat mainly insects, but also mice, reptiles, birds, spiders and scorpions.

Droppings
- Fresh droppings are black but turn grey over time; measured a diameter of 11mm and length 70–80mm.

Striped polecat dropping

MAMMALS ■ Small mammals

- They deposit droppings in or near holes that they have dug.
- Usually deposit a single, long, twisted-looking dropping.

About the track
- The polecat has five oval toes on both front and hind feet – a typical and diagnostic feature of the track.
- Measured at Samara Karoo Reserve, the length of the front track was 38mm, and the hind foot track 29mm.
- Another characteristic feature is the low positioning of toe number 1 and its claw – in line with the main pad.
- On hard substrates, toes number 1 and 5 do not always make a clear impression.
- The front foot claws are exceptionally long – almost double the length of those on the hind foot – and they usually show clearly.
- The hind foot may register behind, on top of, or in front of the front foot.
- Faint tail drag marks can sometimes be seen partially obscuring the tracks.

Above and below: The diagnostic features of the track are the five toes and exceptionally long claws. Toe 1 is positioned unexpectedly far back (see track drawing).

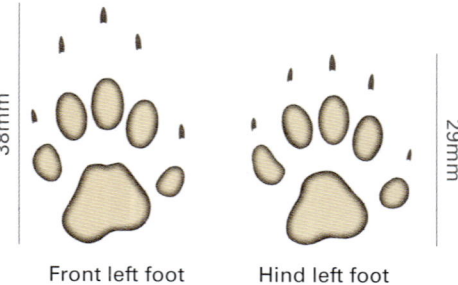

Front left foot   Hind left foot

Can be confused with ...

- The polecat track can be confused with that of the **ground squirrel**, although its toes are broader and its front claws are longer than those of the squirrel.

Southern African hedgehog
Atelerix frontalis

This unmistakeable, spiny little creature is found throughout southern Africa, specifically in Botswana, Malawi, Namibia, South Africa and Zimbabwe.

They occupy a wide variety of habitats, from suburban gardens to grassland and scrub bush, in semi-arid and subtemperate regions, as long as there is good ground cover. They are not present in the Kruger National Park.

Habits
- Solitary and shy, found singly or in pairs.
- Nocturnal, spends daylight hours curled up in a ball in a thicket or hole in the ground.
- Hedgehogs enter torpor, a period of inactivity during the winter months, although the timing and duration is not well understood.
- The alarm call is a high-pitched scream, and when threatened they will roll into a ball and depend on their sharp spines for protection.
- A litter of four blind young are born in the summer months after a gestation of 35 days.

Feeding and diet
- Omnivorous; it consumes invertebrates (beetles, grasshoppers, termites, millipedes, slugs, etc.) as the bulk of its diet, as well as vegetable matter.

Droppings
- Droppings are dark brown rectangular tubes, often containing insect fragments, 8mm in diameter and 20mm in length.

Territorial behaviour
- These hedgehogs are not territorial but do occupy a home range which is not actively marked or defended.

About the track
- Track measures front foot 16mm and hind foot 14mm in length; however, getting an accurate measurement may prove challenging.
- Although both front and hind feet have five round toes, toe number 1 and its claw on the front foot seldom make a clear impression.
- Both front and hind feet have short claws.
- A characteristic feature is regular dragging of the hind foot's toes and claws – with the drag mark often obliterating the front foot track.

MAMMALS ■ Small mammals

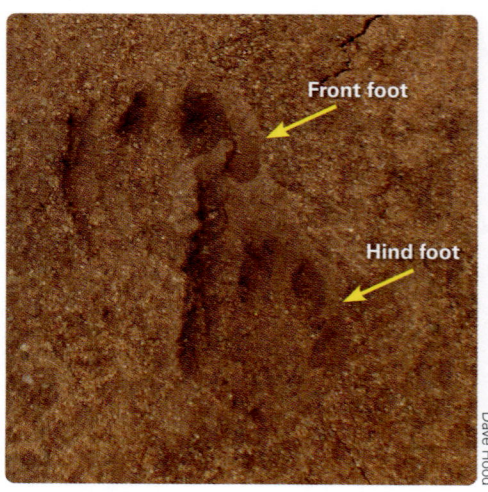

Hedgehog tracks

Typical gait; notice subtle hind foot drag marks.

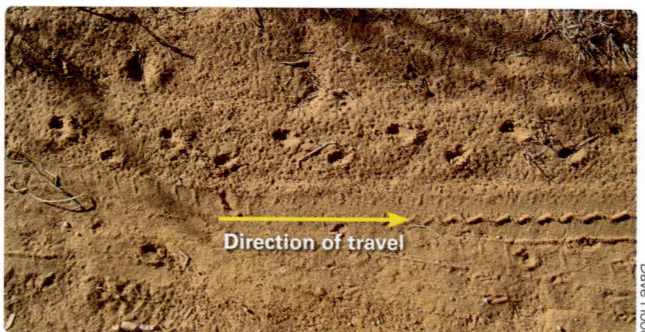

Gait showing wide straddle

Drag mark

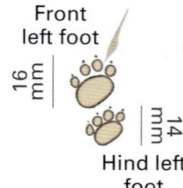

Front left foot

16 mm

14 mm

Hind left foot

- The typical walking gait shows the hind foot registering just behind or partially on top of the front foot track. Hind feet usually register at an angle facing outwards.
- Another diagnostic feature is the noticeably wide straddle (distance between left and right tracks).

Can be confused with …

- Hedgehog tracks may be confused with those of the **yellow mongoose**, although the mongoose has much longer claws.

MAMMALS ■ Small mammals

Banded mongoose
Mungos mungo

This is a small, sturdy animal with a long tail. It is light brown and white to grey, with black bands from mid-back to the base of the tail.

The banded mongoose inhabits South Africa's eastern grassland and woodland savannas.

Habits
- Diurnal, emerging at sunrise and retiring at sunset.
- Gregarious and intensely social, they live in a group of up to 30 animals.
- They are exceptionally vocal; members of the group maintain constant contact by twittering as they go about their foraging.

Burrow
- The group utilises abandoned burrows in termite mounds, or any crevice where they will fit, and they change burrow residences regularly.

Feeding and diet
- They forage together, with each individual finding its own food by continuously scratching, digging and overturning small logs to winkle out prey. They break open eggs by forcing them against a rock or log.
- Insectivores, but will also eat mice, birds' eggs, small fruits and small reptiles.
- Frequently dig in elephant and rhino droppings in search of insects such as beetles and millipedes.

Droppings
- Droppings are 15mm in diameter and 100mm in length, and are much larger than those of the dwarf mongoose.
- Droppings vary from light brown to very dark in colour, and usually show fragments of their insectivorous diet.
- They deposit droppings in latrines as well as randomly throughout their range.

Territorial behaviour
- Using an anal gland, they scent-mark frequently on logs and stones as well as on other members of the pack.

Banded mongoose droppings contain mostly insect fragments.

MAMMALS ■ Small mammals

Tracks of a bounding banded mongoose

Banded mongoose tracks in wet mud

About the track
- The front foot length is 39mm when measured without the proximal pad and toe number 1 showing. The length including proximal pad is 50–55mm. The hind foot measures 32mm in length.
- This mongoose has five toes on both front and hind feet. However, toe number 1, its claw and the proximal pad of the front foot will only show if the animal moves slowly over soft, fine substrate. In the hind foot track, these features normally do not make an impression.
- The long claws on the front foot are a characteristic feature of the track; they show very clearly in most substrates and often draw attention to this track.
- The toes and claws on the front foot may appear as continuous connected digits, but closer examination should reveal their individual detail.
- During a normal walking gait the hind foot registers behind (or occasionally on top of) the front foot. They also bound.
- Solitary tracks are unusual; up to 20 sets are common. They usually retrace their steps to and from their burrows.

Can be confused with ...
- A banded mongoose track may be confused with that of a **slender mongoose** (14mm smaller) or of a **white-tailed mongoose** (10–20mm bigger, without claws showing).

Front left foot

Hind left foot

Dwarf mongoose
Helogale parvula

This smallest of the mongooses is also Africa's smallest carnivore. Its fur is light to dark brown and it has a large pointed head, small ears, a long tail and short limbs.

It inhabits both woodland and grassland savanna that is dry and open, including rocky areas, and is independent of water.

Habits
- Diurnal and highly gregarious, they live in groups of up to 30 animals.
- Females dominate males in each age group.
- There is a strict hierarchy among same-sex animals within the group, which is headed by a dominant pair.
- All group members co-operate in rearing the young and guarding the group from predators.
- Sentries (usually subordinate males) are constantly on watch during foraging, and communicate detailed information about predators with a variety of high-pitched, hissed alarm calls.
- Potential threats are eagles, ground hornbills, snakes, marabou storks, honey badgers, black-backed jackals and even leopards, as well as the slender mongoose.
- These animals share an interesting symbiotic relationship with yellow-billed hornbills: the birds feed on insects escaping from the foraging mongooses. In return, the mongooses take advantage of the vigilant hornbill's alarm calls for predators. So established is the relationship that hornbills often gather in the early morning on a termite mound where the mongooses are in residence to wake them up!

Burrow
- Den in abandoned termite mounds and rocky crevices.
- The group makes regular moves from one abode to another, particularly in areas with abundant termitaria.

Feeding and diet
- Their diet consists of insects (mainly beetle larvae and termites, but also grasshoppers and crickets), spiders, scorpions, lizards, snakes, small birds and rodents.

Droppings are long tubes, light to dark brown in colour.

MAMMALS ■ Small mammals

- They are independent of water.
- Little diggings of a few centimetres in width, made in search of food, are often associated with dwarf mongoose tracks.

Droppings
- Larger than expected, have the appearance of long tubes with blunt ends, dark brown in colour, 10mm in diameter and 50mm in length.
- Latrines may be found on the eastern edges of termite mounds, where the mongooses bask in the morning sun – behaviour that is more common in the winter months.

Territorial behaviour
- They scent-mark with anal and cheek glands.
- The group defends its territory and sometimes engages with other groups in territorial fights, but these seldom lead to injury or death.

About the track
- Track lengths measured at Londolozi Game Reserve are front foot 31mm and hind foot 25mm – the smallest of the mongooses in Kruger area.
- Although they have five toes on both front and hind feet, in most cases only four toes make an impression.
- Evidence of all five toes and proximal pad will show only if the animal is moving slowly in perfect substrate.
- Both feet have long, thin, sharp claws used for digging, the front's claws being longer than the hind.

Evidence of a dwarf mongoose having dug up recently emerged winged termites (alates); notice the discarded wings.

Two front tracks of a bounding dwarf mongoose

MAMMALS ■ Small mammals

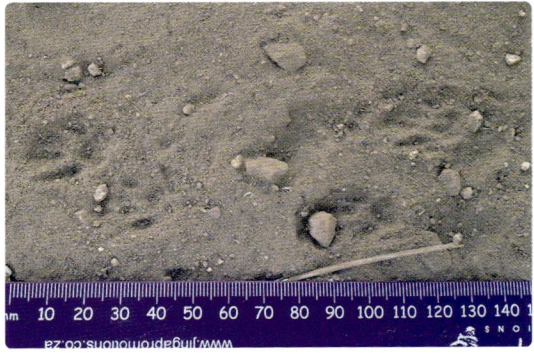

Left and above: *Dwarf mongoose track sequences: the diminutive size and evidence of long claws are helpful in identifying this species' tracks correctly.*

- Occasionally the front foot toes and claws appear as one long, single digit, without a gap between them (similar to a banded mongoose in this regard).
- The main pad is asymmetrical on the posterior edge.
- Generally, tracks of several dwarf mongooses are seen together, where they have run, skidded, bounded and jumped, making it difficult to distinguish details. Tail drag marks are sometimes evident.
- The hind tracks usually do not register on top of the front ones.

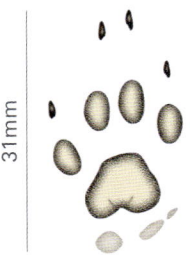

31mm · Front left foot   25mm · Hind left foot

Can be confused with ...

- *The bounding gait of the dwarf mongoose is very similar to that of the **African tree squirrel**, the difference being in the position of the front feet: when bounding, the mongoose places its front feet one behind the other, whereas the squirrel's front feet land next to each other, or one partially on top of the other.*

  Another similarity is in their track size. The dwarf mongoose shows four forward-facing toes on front and hind feet, whereas the squirrel usually shows five clear toes on the hind feet. The squirrel's hind foot track has three middle toes that are grouped tightly together, and its main pad is square with tread-like patterns underneath, while the mongoose has a traditionally shaped main pad. The squirrel's claws are shorter than those of the dwarf mongoose.

MAMMALS ■ Small mammals

Meller's mongoose
Rhynchogale melleri

The seldom-seen Meller's mongoose is light brown to grey-brown with a black, brown or white tip to its tail.

It prefers open savanna woodland and grassland, wherever termites can be found.

Mark Lautenbach

Habits
- These mongooses are nocturnal and solitary.
- They may have up to four young.

Feeding and diet
- They eat mainly termites, but will take other insects too.

About the track
- Measured at Londolozi Game Reserve, the front foot is 30mm and hind foot 37mm in length. This rare mongoose has five toes on both front and hind feet, but toe number 1 and its claw do not show in the track.
- The track reflects only four toes on all feet.
- The track shows distinct claw marks.
- The front foot is shorter than the hind foot and shows a characteristic gap between the two middle toes.

Above and below: *Meller's mongoose tracks*

Front foot: notice gap between middle toes

Hind foot: longer, with middle toes grouped more tightly together

MAMMALS ■ Small mammals

- The hind foot also shows a marked gap between the toes and the main pad, although this gap is not always very prominent when seen in the field.
- This mongoose has relatively large toes and a substantial main pad, the posterior edge of which is symmetrical in shape.
- Tracks found at Londolozi have usually been within 500m of the Sand River.

Can be confused with ...

- *Although seldom seen, the track (main pad in particular) shares features with that of the **large spotted genet**.*
- *This track can also be confused with a **young white-tailed mongoose** track, especially the toe shape and claw marks.*

Front left foot   Hind left foot

Most Meller's mongoose sightings and track records have been in the vicinity of the Sand River in the Sabi Sand Nature Reserve, Kruger National Park.

Slender mongoose
Galerella sanguinea

This small, slim mongoose is yellow, red or dark brown in colour.

It can live almost anywhere as long as there is good cover. It prefers open areas with trees, logs, holes in the ground and rocks. Found in many regions, from arid to well-watered, but this species is not normally found in the Karoo.

Habits
- Diurnal, but inactive in cold, cloudy weather.
- Found singly or in pairs moving.
- They are known to climb trees when hunting or when disturbed.
- If threatened they have been known to raise their fur, making themselves look bigger.
- They characteristically move along the edges of roads and open clearings. Their tracks can often be found along natural game paths where the grass is long or the vegetation is thick. If startled, they will immediately take cover in the adjacent vegetation.
- They regularly venture into mud at the edges of water holes or small pans.

Slender mongoose on fallen log

Feeding and diet
- An opportunistic omnivore, the slender mongoose is primarily carnivorous.
- Insects make up the bulk of its diet, but lizards, rodents, snakes, birds, amphibians and fruits are taken when the opportunity presents.

Droppings
- One or two thin, dark brown cylindrical tubes, measuring 12mm in diameter and 30–40mm in length.

Droppings are dark brown (almost black), comprising one or two thin, cylindrical tubes.

MAMMALS ■ Small mammals

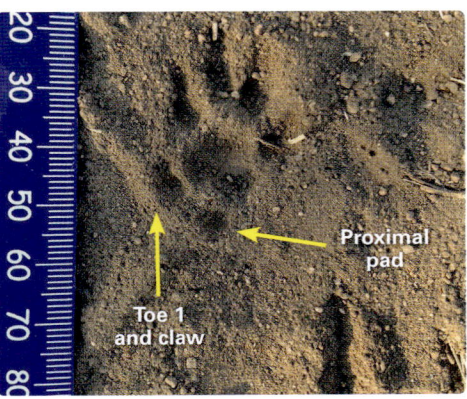

The front foot showing toe number 1, its claw and proximal pad

Slender mongoose hind foot track

About the track

- Track lengths measured at Londolozi are front foot 36mm and hind foot 28mm.
- Five toes on both front and hind feet, although only four toes show clearly in the track.
- The front foot proximal pad, toe number 1 and its claw are occasionally visible in the track, but don't show if the mongoose is moving quickly.

The bounding gait of a slender mongoose – note the direction of travel.

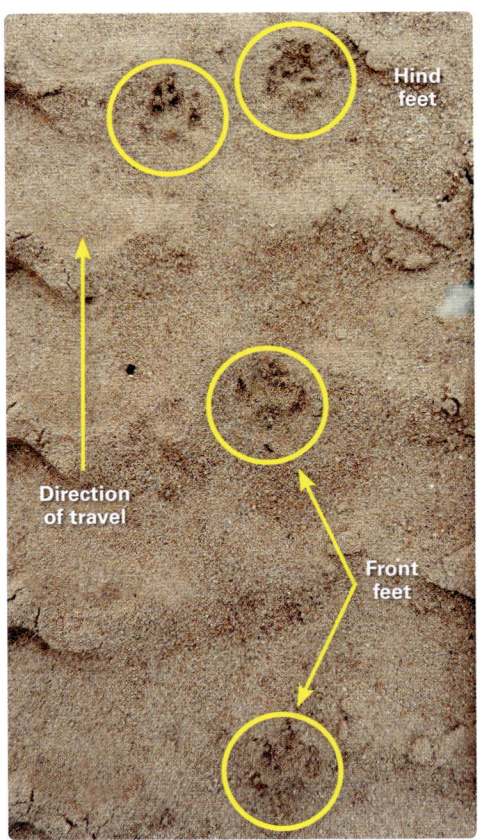

217

MAMMALS ■ Small mammals

- The front foot toes are oval in shape and more splayed than those of the hind foot.
- The hind foot toes are grouped more closely together. Toe number 1 is positioned higher up on the foot and so does not make an impression, and the claw shows infrequently.
- Sharp claw marks are evident on both front and hind feet, and can be seen in most types of substrate.
- The posterior edge of the front foot main pad is asymmetrical, with one lobe extending lower than the other.
- A normal walking gait results in the hind foot landing in front of the front foot, or occasionally on top of it.
- When moving quickly, this mongoose will bound, leaving a track pattern similar to that of hares.

Slender mongoose tracks in wet sand

Can be confused with ...

- *The slender mongoose track can be confused with that of the **genet**, although the genet has a significantly larger main pad. The genet's toes are round, whereas the mongoose's are oval-shaped. The genet seldom shows claw marks unless it is moving quickly.*
- *This mongoose's track can also be confused with that of an **African tree squirrel**. However, the squirrel shows five hind foot toes with the three middle toes grouped tightly together – the mongoose's toes are more evenly distributed; the shape of the squirrel's main pad is different from that of the slender mongoose. (See page 257.)*

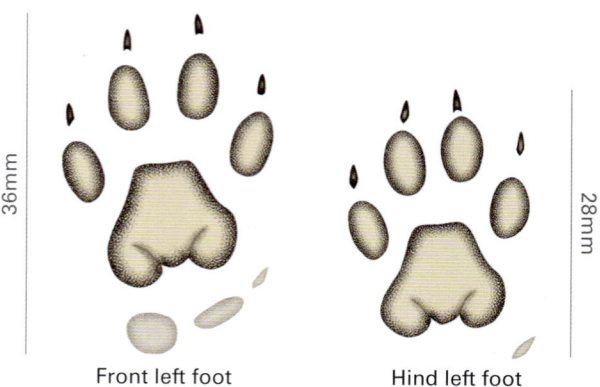

Front left foot — 36mm
Hind left foot — 28mm

Small grey mongoose
Galerella pulverulenta

Also called the Cape grey mongoose, this little animal is speckled grey with dark grey legs and a dark-tipped tail. Small and exceptionally light, it weighs barely 1kg.

It has a wide habitat tolerance but prefers fynbos, Karoo semi-desert scrub, thicket and forest.

Habits
- Diurnal; in summer they rest during the hottest part of the day.
- Solitary, but may be found in pairs or in small family groups.
- Mainly terrestrial, they will climb trees when hunting or when threatened.

Burrow
- They prefer areas with an abundance of thickets that provide dense cover and will shelter under rocks or old tree stumps that have holes in them.
- Den entrances are small and dens extend straight downwards into the ground.
- These mongooses tend to reside in the same burrow for extended periods.
- They generally do not make use of other mongoose or suricate burrows.

Feeding and diet
- They hunt small rodents, which they stalk and kill with a bite to the head.
- They also eat insects, fruit, carrion, rats, mice, reptiles, and small ground birds and their eggs.

Droppings
- Droppings are dark in colour and similar in size to those of the suricate – 11mm in diameter.
- They deposit droppings at burrow entrances where their urine may give off a strong smell of ammonia.

About the track
- Without toe number 1 and proximal pad showing, track measurements are front foot 28mm and hind foot 26mm, taken at Samara Karoo Reserve.
- It has five toes on both front and hind feet. However, the track shows four toes on each foot, with toe number 1 and its claw seldom making an impression.

Typical small grey mongoose dropping, deposited randomly throughout range

MAMMALS ■ Small mammals

Small grey mongoose tracks

Front left foot   Hind left foot

Tracks showing bounding mongoose gait

- Several mongoose species (including this one) venture into muddy (slippery) substrate in pans and wetlands to scavenge insects stuck in the mud, which results in the toes of both front and hind feet splaying as the animals attempt to steady themselves.
- Their claws are sharp, with those on the front foot being longer.
- A normal walking gait results in the hind track registering partially on top of the front one.
- The front foot main pad's leading edge is wide – a square, 'box-like' shape. This is particularly evident in the field.

Can be confused with ...

- The small grey mongoose track can be confused with that of the slightly larger **yellow mongoose**, which has longer, thicker claws and significantly larger (oval) toes, compared with the smaller, round toes of the small grey mongoose.
- Although its track is similar in length, the **suricate** has much longer claws on its front feet; its toes are grouped more closely together, and are larger and more elongated in shape. Overall, the suricate track is larger and does not produce a register gait like mongooses do.

MAMMALS ■ Small mammals

Water mongoose
Atilax paludinosus

This large water or marsh mongoose has a dark brown undercoat and guard hair, which is long and coarse. It has short, blunt claws for digging. The water mongoose readily paddles and is a good – if reluctant – swimmer.

It prefers aquatic habitats such as rivers, streams, reed beds, vleis, swamps and dams, and rests on patches of grass and floating vegetation.

Habits
- Nocturnal and crepuscular (active at twilight).
- Solitary or move about in mating pairs; females care for their young.
- Territorial, scent-mark on roots and rocks using an anal gland, which leaves a black gel-like substance that lightens as it ages.

Feeding and diet
- Voracious carnivores, they will consume whatever prey they can overpower, and are also known to scavenge.
- Feed on frogs, crabs, fish, insects, freshwater mussels and some vegetation.
- They hunt and forage near the water's edge and feed on a nearby bank. Crab fragments are evidence of their activity.

Droppings
- Cylindrical droppings are 50–100mm in length, and 17–20mm in diameter – smaller than those of the Cape clawless otter.
- They make use of latrines near the water's edge, where crab carapaces and fragments of other small aquatic animals and hair can be found in their droppings. Unlike otters, they do not completely demolish the crab carapaces.

Above: *Typical water mongoose aquatic habitat; notice the droppings.* **Right:** *Droppings contain shell fragments.*

MAMMALS ■ Small mammals

Toe 1 and claw of front foot

Hind foot

Above: Water mongoose trail in wet mud
Right: Water mongoose tracks. The long, splayed toes are typical of an animal that lives in a predominantly aquatic environment.

About the track

- Track lengths measured at Samara Karoo Reserve are front foot 46mm and hind foot 52mm (lengths measured without toe number 1 and proximal pad showing, which is typical).
- Short, thick claws are situated close to the toes.
- The toes are long, broad, splayed digits – typical of an animal that lives in a predominantly aquatic environment. The front foot toes tend to splay more than those of the hind foot. Interestingly, the water mongoose has no webbing between its toes.
- Although both front and hind feet have five toes, toe number 1 and its claw are not always clearly visible in the track.
- The proximal pad makes an impression only if the animal moves particularly slowly over soft substrate. However, in such conditions, the front foot's toe number 1 and its claw do show.

MAMMALS ■ Small mammals

- Without toe number 1 and proximal pad showing, the front foot appears shorter than the hind foot.
- The front foot main pad posterior edge has two distinct outer lobes, the outside lobe extending significantly lower than the inside one – asymmetrical in its form.
- A commonly used gait shows the hind foot registering on top of the front foot, although a variety of gaits have been noted.
- The water mongoose will move up and down riverbanks over long distances, even in areas where little water is evident. At Samara Karoo Reserve (a semi-arid region) water mongooses occur in large numbers.

Water mongoose tracks in mud

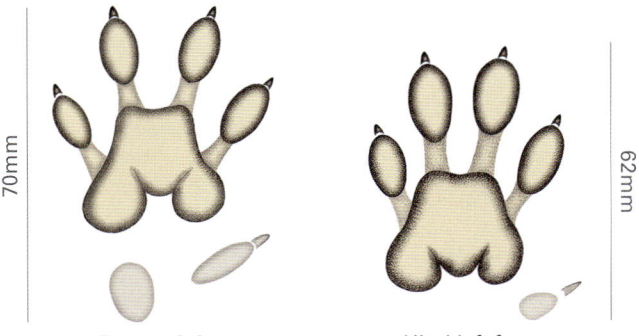

Front left foot   Hind left foot

70mm   62mm

Can be confused with ...

- *Water mongoose tracks can be confused with those of the **white-tailed mongoose**, although the white-tailed has shorter toes, which are situated more tightly together than the water mongoose's, and its claws are longer. A large toe number 1 and claw will not show in the white-tailed mongoose track.*

MAMMALS ■ Small mammals

White-tailed mongoose
Ichneumia albicauda

This large mongoose is grey-brown in colour, has long legs and a bright white bushy tail.
It prefers savanna woodland with abundant water.

Habits
- These mongooses are nocturnal and mainly solitary, but are also found in pairs or family groups.
- Territorial; scent-mark territory with their anal gland.

Burrow
- They do not dig their own burrow, instead making use of holes in termite mounds excavated by other animals, such as aardvarks.

Feeding and diet
- Insectivorous, but they will also eat small rodents, birds, reptiles, amphibians and fruits.
- They are known to raid chicken enclosures.
- Proficient diggers, they use their strong front-feet claws for digging up burrowing insects, beetles and insect larvae.

Droppings
- Droppings measure 12–16mm in diameter and contain insect fragments, fruits and even leaves.
- They deposit their droppings in latrines as well as randomly throughout their territory.

Droppings may contain buffalo thorn (Ziziphus mucronata) *berries and leaves.*

About the track
- Track measurements taken at Londolozi Game Reserve are front foot 52mm and hind foot 51mm.
- This large mongoose has five toes on both front and hind feet, yet only four toes generally show in the track. Toe number 1 is seldom seen – although the claw on toe number 1 of the front foot may make an impression in soft, fine soils.
- It has long, clearly evident claws on both front and hind feet.

White-tailed mongoose typical track

MAMMALS ■ Small mammals

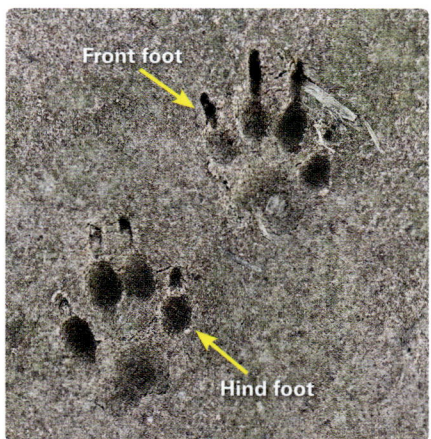

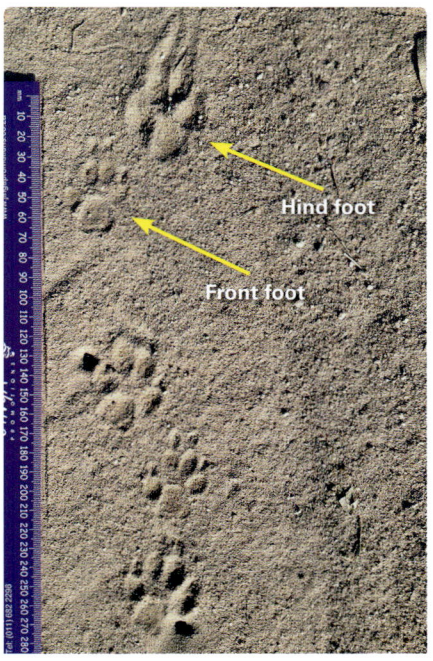

Above and right: White-tailed mongoose front and hind tracks **(above)** and track sequence **(right)**

- The toes are arranged in a semicircle (arc). The two middle toes are situated close to one another – particularly on the hind foot.
- The front foot main pad's posterior edge is asymmetrical, the outside lobe extending lower than the inner one.
- The hind foot main pad is typically square on the leading edge.
- This mongoose occasionally – and very lightly – drags the hind foot claws along the ground.
- The typical gait shows the hind foot registering behind (and occasionally ahead) of the front foot. No direct register has been recorded.

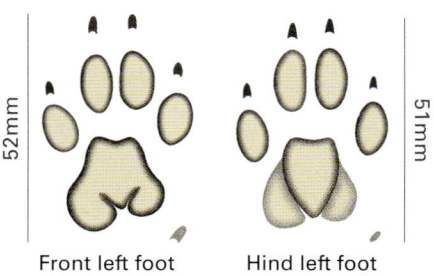

Front left foot   Hind left foot

52mm   51mm

Can be confused with ...

- The white-tailed mongoose tracks can be confused with those of the **jackal**. However, the jackal has significantly larger toes and the length of its track (front and hind) is 5–8mm longer than that of the mongoose; its middle toes tend to lie in parallel, as do the two outside toes, whereas the mongoose's toes are arranged in a semicircle (arc). The jackal's main pad is symmetrical in shape at the posterior edge, while the mongoose's is slightly asymmetrical.
- The white-tailed can be confused with the **water mongoose**, although the water has shorter claws and longer, splayed toes.

225

Yellow mongoose
Cynictis penicillata

This mongoose's colour varies from tawny-grey to yellow. It has a long, white-tipped tail in the southern regions; in the northern regions it is greyer, with a shorter tail.

It lives in open sandy country, savanna and vlei areas, but is not found in forests.

Habits
- Diurnal, but switch to nocturnal behaviour in certain places.
- Usually found alone, but may occur in pairs and in family groups with two or three young.
- Pairs of yellow mongooses, and family parties of up to five individuals, may den in an underground burrow with single or multiple entrances.
- Predators include birds of prey, jackals and snakes.

Burrow
- Warren entrances are small and extend straight back into the ground. Entrance holes (160mm in diameter) are smaller than those of the springhare and ground squirrel.
- Yellow mongooses create a latrine close to the burrow entrance, which may give off a strong smell of ammonia.
- Tend to keep the same burrow for long periods of time, which they occasionally share with suricates and ground squirrels.

Feeding and diet
- They dig small, shallow holes in search of food.
- Mostly insectivorous, although they also take mice, small birds, reptiles, frogs, scorpions and millipedes.

Droppings
- The droppings are dark in colour and usually contain insect fragments.
- Cylindrical, 11–15mm in diameter – which is larger than the suricate's droppings.

Entrance to a yellow mongoose warren

MAMMALS ■ Small mammals

Territorial behaviour
- The yellow mongoose scent-marks and deposits droppings in territorial latrines close to its burrow entrances.
- Males scent-mark daily, usually in the early morning, to reaffirm territory and dominance.

About the track
- Track lengths measured at Samara Karoo Reserve are front foot 29mm and hind foot 27mm.
- The track shows four toes on its front and hind feet. Although the front foot has five toes, its toe number 1 and claw seldom show in the track.

Yellow mongoose droppings at a latrine

- The size and shape of the toes is similar for front and hind feet. However, the front foot outside toes are situated somewhat further apart than on the hind foot.
- The toes are oval and elongated in shape.
- The main pad is large and prominent, and makes a clear impression.
- Typically no proximal pad shows in the track, but this feature has been recorded.

Near-perfect front and hind tracks

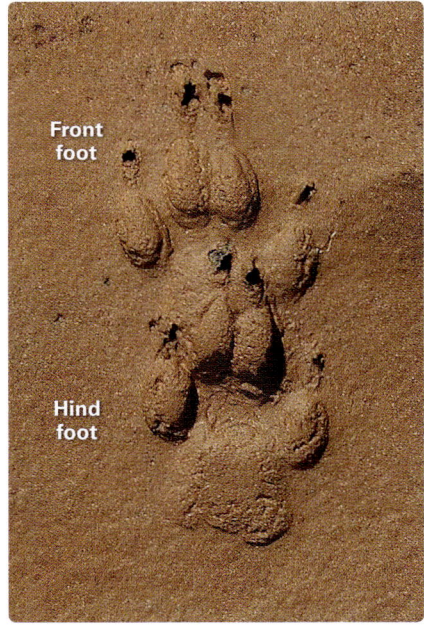

Typical yellow mongoose tracks

MAMMALS ■ Small mammals

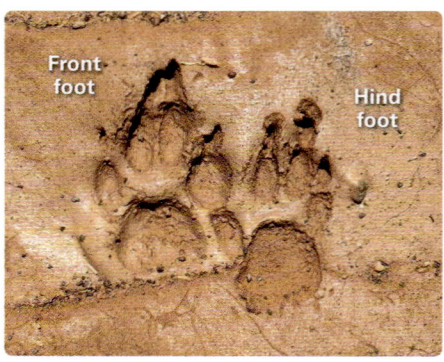

Front and hind tracks

Yellow mongoose in the Kalahari

- The yellow mongoose has a substantial set of claws on front and hind feet (those on the front are slightly longer) although they are not as long as those of the suricate.
- The typical gait results in the hind foot registering partially or completely on top of the front track.

Front left foot   Hind left foot

Can be confused with ...

- *The yellow mongoose track can be confused with that of the* **suricate** *– which has much longer claws on the front than on the hind feet, while the claws of the yellow mongoose are more even in length on both front and hind feet.*

  The posterior edge of the suricate's main pad is less symmetrical in shape – with one of the lobes extending lower than the other; whereas that of the mongoose is more symmetrical.

  An important difference is that in a normal walking gait the suricate's hind track seldom registers on top of the front track.

Selous' mongoose
Paracynictis selousi

Selous' mongoose has a pointed muzzle and small ears. This seldom-seen and poorly known mongoose is tawny to grey in colour; the lower parts of the legs are dark brown to black. The tail has a broad white tip.

This mongoose prefers open scrubveld and woodland, including floodplains, and is largely independent of water.

Habits
- Selous' mongoose is nocturnal.
- Solitary, but they are sometimes seen with young.
- If threatened, this mongoose tends to retreat into a hole.

Burrow
- These mongooses dig their own deep burrow, which has several entrances.

Feeding and diet
- Their diet includes insects, lizards, small snakes and rodents.

About the track
- Tracks measured in southeastern Botswana (Tuli Circle) are front track 32mm and hind track 37mm in length.
- The track shows four toes with sharp claws – similar to the white-tailed mongoose.
- The hind track shows a marked gap between the toes and the main pad, and the toes are marginally narrower than those on the front track.
- The front foot main pad is proportionately large, and is a characteristic feature.
- Occasionally one sees evidence of tail drag marks in perfect substrate.
- A normal walking gait usually shows the hind foot registering on top of the front foot.

Selous' mongoose hind foot track

MAMMALS ■ Small mammals

Above left and right: Selous' mongoose tracks; notice the subtle evidence of the tail dragging over the tracks. Selous' tracks are 10–15mm shorter than those of the white-tailed mongoose.

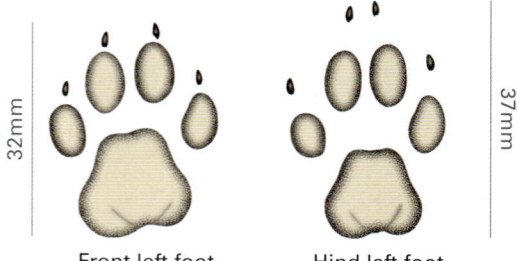

Front left foot   Hind left foot

Can be confused with ...

- The track can be confused with that of the larger **white-tailed mongoose**, whose track is 10mm longer and 5mm broader, and its toes and claws are also bigger. The posterior edge of the **Selous' mongoose's** main pad is more symmetrical in shape than the white-tailed's.

Large grey mongoose
Herpestes ichneumon

The large grey mongoose has an elongated body and a long tail with a black tip. It is speckled grey with a darker-hued head, black legs and long hair around the hindquarters.

It inhabits riverine thickets, reedbeds, wetlands and densely wooded savanna – habitat that is never too far from water.

Habits
- Diurnal, it frequently hunts in muddy pans with shallow water, and is a capable swimmer.
- They move about singly or in pairs, and occasionally in family groups.

Large grey mongoose dropping in latrine

Feeding and diet
- Powerful diggers, they forage for beetles among dead trees.
- They also eat fish, frogs, birds, reptiles, snakes and insects.

Droppings
- Droppings are grey to dark brown in colour and measure 15mm in diameter – deposited in latrines.

Territorial behaviour
- These mongooses make use of their well-developed anal glands to delineate their territory, usually some 3km^2.
- They also make extensive use of latrines to mark their territory.

About the track
- The front track measures 60mm, including the proximal pad, although this shows only if the animal is moving slowly; the hind track is 50mm in length (closer to 40–45mm without proximal parts showing).
- Track shows four toes and claws on both front and hind feet, although five toes may show on the front track if toe number 1 and its claw make an impression in a perfect substrate.

MAMMALS ■ Small mammals

Large grey mongoose front and hind foot tracks

Large grey mongoose tracks, Samara Karoo Reserve

- The front foot's toe number 1 and its claw, which are situated well behind the main pad, show more regularly; toe number 1 on the hind foot does not make an impression, but its claw may leave a slight mark.
- The oval-shaped toes are relatively splayed and the claws are long and substantial.
- Evidence of several individuals' tracks along the same game path is commonplace.

Front left foot   Hind left foot

Can be confused with ...

- The large grey mongoose track may be confused with that of the **white-tailed mongoose**, although the large grey is up to 10mm longer and its toes are far more splayed.
- It may also be confused with the track of the larger **water mongoose**; however, the water mongoose's claws are much shorter and track length about 10mm longer than that of its large grey cousin.

Suricate (meerkat)
Suricata suricatta

The suricate, also known as the meerkat, is a small, silvery brown mongoose with dark brown bands on its back, dark rings around its eyes and a tapering tail. Its hindquarters are stockier than the forequarters and it has a broad head and pointed muzzle.

It inhabits arid open areas with little vegetation.

Habits
- Strictly diurnal and gregarious, they live in groups of up to 40 members.
- One of the group is constantly on sentry duty, and will make an alarm call if it detects a threat. The group responds quickly by scurrying under bushes or down a burrow. Predators include large raptors, martial eagles and jackals. Interestingly, fork-tailed drongos have been seen to mimic suricate alarm calls in order to steal the food once the suricates scurry off in fear!
- They are prodigious diggers; when foraging, they constantly sniff the ground, dig, and turn over stones in their quest for insects.

Burrow
- Multiple burrow entrances are small and measure 120mm in diameter.
- Suricates move frequently from one burrow residence to another; they may share burrows with yellow mongooses and ground squirrels.
- The burrow is cleaned each morning.

Feeding and diet
- Feed mainly on insects, as well as scorpions, millipedes and reptiles.
- Very active diggers, suricates create many shallow, conical excavations as they forage in search of subterranean food.
- Feeding activity begins at first light, with a break at midday, and continues until the group reaches their night's residence in the late afternoon.

A typical suricate excavation, made in the quest for food

MAMMALS ■ Small mammals

A typical suricate burrow with several entrances

Droppings
- Droppings are dark tubes 11mm in diameter and 50mm in length.
- They deposit their droppings close to burrows in latrines, as well as in little holes dug while foraging.

Territorial behaviour
- Territory is marked predominantly with latrines. Dominant males scent-mark by rubbing their anal glands on the ground or on rocks and bushes.
- To bond, members of the group may smear saliva on each other.

Suricates commonly deposit droppings on top of diggings – here on a trapdoor spider's hole.

About the track
- The suricate has four toes, with claws, on both front and hind feet; track length measured 32mm for both feet.
- A diagnostic feature is the front foot's exceptionally long claws (much longer on the front foot) that leave prominent marks, even on firm substrate.
- The size of the hind foot, when measured without the claws, is longer and wider than the front foot.

MAMMALS ■ Small mammals

Above left, centre and right: *Suricate tracks; notice the offset, sloped main pad of the hind foot as well as the strikingly long claw marks of the front foot.*

- The posterior edge of the main pad is asymmetrical, with one lobe extending lower than the other. This characteristic feature is especially true of the hind foot.
- Typically the hind foot does not register on the front foot – landing either behind or ahead, depending on speed.
- As suricates live in groups, trackers will generally see several individuals' trails. That said, trackers must familiarise themselves with the size, shape and features of the track instead of relying on seeing it in a group. A track indicating a lone suricate is possible!

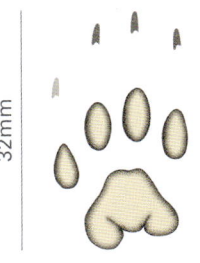 

Front left foot   Hind left foot

Can be confused with ...

- *The suricate track is regularly confused with that of the **yellow mongoose**, particularly if the suricate is seen singly. However, the mongoose has shorter claws and its main pad is more symmetrical in shape.*

Cape clawless otter
Aonyx capensis

The Cape clawless otter has thick, smooth fur, chestnut-brown in colour, with white facial markings down to the throat and chest. Paws are webbed, with five fingers and insignificant little claws on three of the hind feet toes.

This amphibious animal is widely found, from open coastal plains to semi-arid regions and densely forested areas. It may move large distances between water sources.

Habits
- Cape clawless otters are most active during the early morning and late afternoon.
- Solitary, but sometimes pairs or family groups are seen.

Burrow
- They construct burrows in riverbanks under dense vegetation or rocks, close to the water's edge.

Feeding and diet
- They feed on freshwater crabs and mussels, fish, frogs and worms – prey for which they dive before swimming ashore to eat it.
- Fragmented crab or mussel shells and fish scales indicate possible otter activity.

Cape clawless otters build burrows in banks near the water.

Droppings
- Tapered cylinders measure 22–28mm in diameter and 30–50mm in length, and contain mostly crab shell fragments.
- These otters deposit their dung in latrines in open ground.
- They also produce small quantities of dung, called 'spraint', consisting of fish scales, bones and other fragments bound together with a black, jelly-like secretion produced by the anal gland.

Territorial behaviour
- Territories are marked using a pair of glands under the tail that secrete a scent.

Dropping showing shell fragments

MAMMALS ■ Small mammals

About the track

- Tracks measured at Londolozi Game Reserve showed hind foot length 118mm and front foot 110mm. Partial tracks are common.
- The otter has five toes on both front and hind feet, which usually mark clearly in the track.
- Three hind feet toes have claws, but no claw marks are visible in the tracks – unlike the claws visible in tracks of the spotted-necked otter.
- Both the main and proximal pads appear in soft substrate; the proximal pad is often obscured and not easily discernible.
- Designed for swimming, the hind feet are larger than the front feet, the toes are larger and more splayed, and are webbed, although webbing cannot be seen in the track.
- Their typical loping gait makes the following track pattern: front foot – then front foot and hind foot half-registered – then hind foot (a 1–2–1 pattern). Otters may also produce a side lope, where the animal partially turns its body as it moves, so the track pattern shows a diagonal line of four tracks that repeats with each stride.
- Otters move over large distances, often following dry riverbeds to new water sources.

Trail showing a typical otter loping gait; notice the 1–2–1 track pattern.

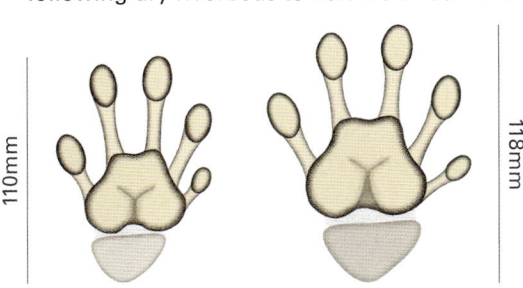

Front left foot   Hind left foot

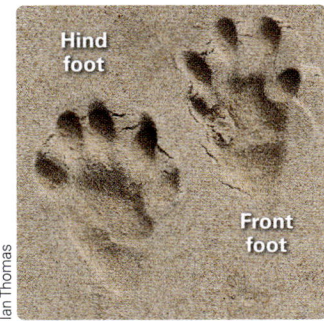

Otter tracks

Can be confused with ...

- A **water mongoose** feeding in the same areas as otters can make identification more difficult; however, the mongoose usually leaves larger shell fragments than the otter.
- Trackers occasionally confuse otter tracks with those of the **leopard** – particularly in riverbeds where tracks are obscured and where trackers expect to find leopards!
- Otter tracks can also be confused with those of **vervet monkeys**.

Honey badger
Mellivora capensis

This formidable animal has a characteristic silver back. It is a powerful digger with knife-like claws and is well known for being courageous and aggressive. Family of the weasel and polecat (Mustelidae), it is not a true badger, and instead belongs to the genus *Mellivora*, which is derived from the Latin 'mel' for honey, and 'voro' meaning devour.

It can live almost anywhere, except in dune desert.

Habits
- The honey badger is generally diurnal but nocturnal in areas where it feels threatened.
- Found singly or in family groups comprising a mother and her young. Mothers give birth to one or two young that remain in the burrow for up to three months.
- Although shy, it fears few in the face of a direct threat. It has been known to put up a fierce fight even when defending itself against lions.

Feeding and diet
- A powerful digger, it uses its strong front legs and sharp claws for excavating deep holes to catch hibernating snakes and other food items such as scorpions, dung beetle larvae, mice, bulbs and lizards. It is also fond of honey and the larvae of mocca bees (genus *Trigona*).
- A tenacious honey badger was once seen to climb a tree and feed on the remains of a leopard's kill at Londolozi.

Droppings
- Cylindrical with blunt ends, and dark in colour, droppings measure 15–20mm in diameter and 60–80mm in length.
- They contain bits of hair, feathers, insects and seeds.

About the track
- Measurements taken at Londolozi Game Reserve showed hind foot length 80–93mm; main pad width 50mm; and front foot length 108–112mm.

Evidence of a honey badger digging out a hibernating puff adder

Fresh droppings – often confused with leopard or wild dog droppings

Above left and right: Honey badger tracks
Right: Honeycomb and larvae of the mocca bee (genus *Trigona*), dug up and eaten by a honey badger

- Feet have five toes, although toe number 1 and its claw occasionally do not make an impression.
- The front foot claws are exceptionally long (20–25mm), and the middle three claws usually show clearly.
- A diagnostic feature is the three tightly grouped middle toes on the hind foot.
- The main pad is large and unsegemented – a feature often confused with a leopard.
- A single proximal pad makes an impression behind the main pad, although it can be difficult to distinguish in hard substrate.
- The front feet often land facing slightly inwards (pigeon-toed), whereas the hind feet land facing the direction of travel, or even at an angle, facing outwards.
- Tracks indicating a pair of honey badgers are common.

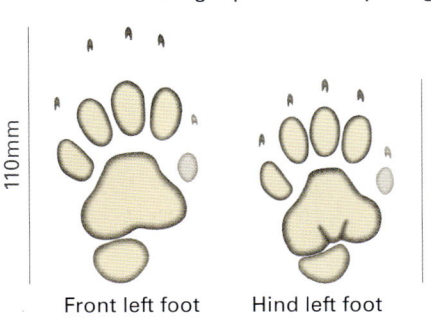

Can be confused with …

- The large sausage-shaped toes are substantially bigger than the **porcupine's** smaller, round toes.
- The large main pad can make it possible to confuse the badger with a **leopard** in unclear substrates.

MAMMALS ■ Small mammals

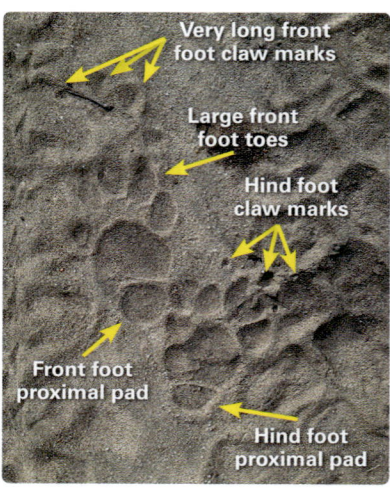

Notice the difference in the angle of approach from front to hind foot.

A faster walk; notice that the hind foot lands ahead of the front foot.

GENERIC DIFFERENCES BETWEEN HONEY BADGER AND PORCUPINE TRACKS

	HONEY BADGER	PORCUPINE
Toes	Five toes on both front and hind feet; occasionally toe 1 does not show	Front foot usually shows four toes; occasionally the hind foot shows five toes
Toe shape	Large and oval in shape (sausage-like); middle toes grouped tightly together	Smaller and rounder in shape; toes more splayed in their positioning
Claws	Very long and thick, particularly on the front foot – up to 20mm long	Short, stubby claws
Main pad	One large unsegmented main pad	Main pad is segmented into three separate pads indicated by faint ridges
Proximal pads	One proximal pad on both front and hind feet	In most cases, two proximal pads show on both front and hind feet
Gait / other	Hind foot lands behind front foot, front feet land facing inwards slightly; occasionally hind foot will register on top of front foot	Hind foot registers on top of, or just behind, the front foot; quill drag marks sometimes evident
Track length	80–110mm	70–80mm

Rock hyrax (dassie)
Procavia capensis

This animal varies from light to dark brown in colour, with short ears and a short tail. It has a patch of long black hair in the centre of its back. Its limbs are short and sturdy and the pads on its feet give it traction on steep and smooth rock surfaces.

The rock hyrax generally inhabits rocky outcrops, cliffs and boulders with sufficient vegetation.

Habits
- Crepuscular: they are most active at dawn and dusk, although their activity pattern varies with season and climate.
- Gregarious, living in 'herds' that vary in size, from 10–80 animals.
- The most common alarm call is high-pitched and shrill, but they use at least 20 different vocal signals, or 'songs', which give important biological information such as the singer's size, age, social status, condition and hormonal state.
- They make use of sentries: one or more individuals take up position at a vantage point and make alarm calls in the form of sharp barks to warn of predators. Their primary predator is the Verreaux's eagle.

Den
- Rock hyrax make use of natural crevices in the rocks or boulders.

Feeding and diet
- They are both grazers of grasses (*Eragrostis*, *Cynodon*) and browsers of shrubs.
- They will climb trees to strip off and eat bark from the branches.
- In the southern Kruger National Park, rock hyrax browse on buffalo thorn (*Ziziphus mucronata*) and *Combretum* species.
- They feed twice daily for about 30 minutes, eating exceptionally quickly.
- They descend from their rocky abode to drink in the mornings and evenings in areas where water is available.

Droppings
- Pellets are dark brown and resemble those of a small antelope; measuring 7–10mm in diameter.
- The rock hyrax urinates and defecates in latrines, which may become very large. White urine stains formed by crystallised calcium carbonate are a common feature alongside latrines.

Rock hyrax droppings

MAMMALS ■ Small mammals

Territorial behaviour
- Unique to hyraxes is the dorsal scent gland on their back that secretes an odour used for social communication and territorial marking.

About the track
- The large hind foot has three distinct toes and is 48mm in length. The front foot has four toes and measures 37mm.
- The long main sole pad is a characteristic feature – large, soft, segmented pads that are kept moist by glandular secretions.
- Their soles have a rubbery texture that assists with gripping and climbing on rocks that are often slippery.
- Segmentation of the front foot main pad can be seen in soft substrate.
- Interestingly, the front feet are plantigrade (walking flat-footed), and the hind feet semi-digitigrade (walking on toes).
- The hind foot has a grooming claw on the inner toe, although this does not always make a clear impression.
- The hind tracks usually imprint more clearly than the front tracks.
- Tracks can be found on roads or paths adjacent to rocky outcrops and koppies.
- This animal produces a bounding gait similar to that of hares and other rodents.

Rock hyrax latrine with droppings and urine stains on rock

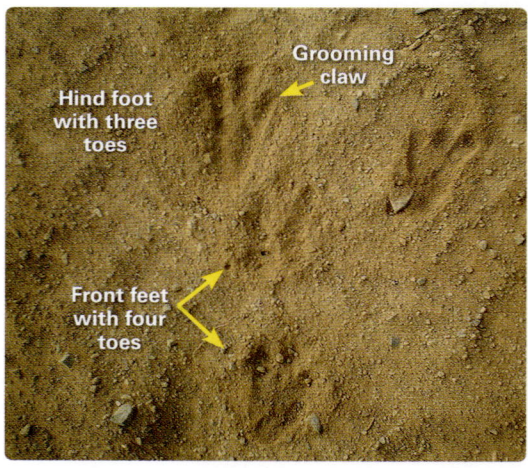

Tracks of a bounding rock hyrax

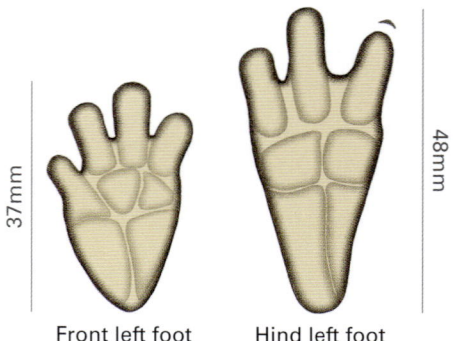

Front left foot — Hind left foot

Chacma baboon
Papio ursinus

This large primate is dark brown to grey, with black feet, although colours may vary from area to area. It has very large canines, a long nose and an arched tail. Males are larger than females.

The chacma baboon tolerates a wide range of habitats, including savanna, mountainous areas and the edges of forests all over southern Africa.

Habits
- Diurnal and gregarious, they may live in groups of up to 100.
- Female ranking within the troop is inherited through the mother and remains fixed; male ranking is often in flux, as the dominant male can be replaced.
- At night baboons sleep in tall evergreen trees or on secluded rocky outcrops; they remain alert.
- They bark loud alarm calls when they detect a predator – particularly a lion or leopard. While calling loudly, they climb to the tops of trees and stare intently at the threat. Alarm calls can be confused with domestic conflict within the troop.

Feeding and diet
- Omnivorous, they eat grasses, seeds, roots, bulbs, leaves, flowers and wild fruits; insects, spiders and scorpions.
- They dig in the soil in search of food, sometimes over large areas, turning over logs and rocks and stripping vegetation as they go.
- They also scavenge and may systematically hunt and kill small mammals, such as impala fawns, during the lambing season.

Droppings
- Cylindrical and variable in shape, varying from light or dark brown to dark green; measuring 35–50mm in diameter, from coarsely grainy to finely textured.

About the track
- Adult baboon tracks measured at Londolozi are front foot 70–80mm, hind foot 140–155mm, although measurements vary depending on the sex and age of the individual.

Baboon droppings

MAMMALS ■ Primates

Baboon front and hind tracks; notice the broad heel of the hind foot.

Baboon front and hind feet tracks

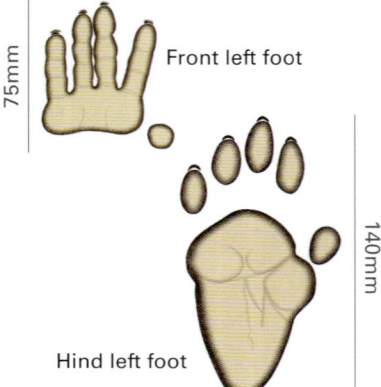

- Very human-like, particularly the hind foot, on which the 'big toe' is characteristic.
- Both front and hind feet have five digits, with opposing thumbs. The thumb on the front foot (or hand) opposes the index finger more widely, and does not always make a clear impression in the track.
- The hind foot is double the length of the front one, and its heel is broad and rounded.
- Diagnostic is the large, circular-shaped big toe joint on the hind foot (located between main pad and toe itself).
- The front foot is short with long, thick digits and short nails, positioned tightly together and parallel.
- In soft substrate, human-like fingerprints (or creases) can be seen in the track.
- Tail drag marks become evident only if the baboon sits down.
- The typical normal walking gait shows the hind foot registering just behind the front one (on the same side), known as an 'understep'.

Can be confused with ...

- Diggings in soil are similar to, but shallower than those of **bushpigs**.
- The baboon's hind foot heel is broad and rounded, whereas the **vervet monkey's** is much narrower and more pointed (V-shaped).

An adult baboon's hind foot is 40–50mm longer than that of the vervet monkey. The digits on the hand are usually parallel and grouped tightly together, whereas the vervet monkey's digits tend to splay out. Monkeys grip the soil as they move, creating little mounds of sand, but baboons walk flat-footed. Unlike baboons, vervet monkeys may drag their tails on the ground while on the move. Young baboon tracks may be confused with those of adult monkeys.

MAMMALS ■ Primates

Vervet monkey
Chlorocebus pygerythrus

The widely distributed vervet monkey weighs 4–5kg and has a black face and long tail. The male has a prominent blue scrotum and red penis.

This species inhabits mainly savanna woodland and is found all over East and southern Africa.

Habits
- Diurnal, active in the day and retiring to treed roosts at night.
- Gregarious, they live in troops of up to 40 members in which there is a clear order of dominance. Aggressive displays are used to threaten other (subordinate) individuals.
- They use a variety of alarm calls to distinguish a range of predators, including leopards, snakes and eagles. While alarm calling they will usually stare intently at the predator. Judging by the intensity of their alarms, crowned eagles appear to be their most feared predators.

Feeding and diet
- Omnivores, they prefer a vegetable diet of fruits, flowers, leaves and seeds, but that includes insects.

Droppings
- Droppings are cylindrical and vary substantially in size and shape; diameter is 15–25mm and length 50–100mm.
- Colour also varies (depending on diet) from dark green to brown, becoming darker with age.
- They may contain berries, seeds and insect fragments.

Vervet monkey scat

About the track
- Measurements taken at Londolozi Game Reserve are front foot 55–70mm, hind foot 80–93mm, depending on the age of the animal.
- Both front and hind feet have five digits, with an opposing thumb or big toe.
- Front foot digits are longer and tend to splay more than on the hind foot, particularly when the animal is moving quickly.

Vervet monkey front left hand track

MAMMALS ■ Primates

Vervet monkey front and hind feet tracks

Hind foot track; notice the long narrow heel compared to that of the baboon.

Track of vervet monkey dragging its tail

- The front foot opposing thumb is positioned at just less than 70 degrees to the other digits.
- The hind foot digits are shorter and are grouped tightly together – but will splay when the monkey moves quickly or changes direction.
- The hind foot heel (posterior edge) is narrow and pointed (V-shaped) compared with the broad heel of a baboon track.
- A normal walking gait shows the hind foot placed next to the front foot.
- Tail drag marks are common, resulting both from walking and sitting.
- Due to monkeys' varied movements, playfulness and gait, their tracks can present as exceedingly obscure.

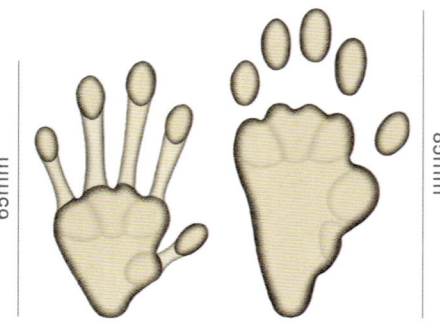

Front left foot   Hind left foot

Can be confused with ...

- The vervet monkey track can easily be confused with that of a **young baboon**. Monkeys' digits tend to splay more often. The baboon's heel is wider and bolder than that of the monkey. The monkey tends to create little mounds of soil in the track at the base of its digits as it grasps the ground, whereas the baboon walks flat-footed.

Southern lesser bushbaby
Galago moholi

The southern lesser bushbaby weighs 150g and is light grey to brown in colour. It has large eyes surrounded by dark markings, ears that are large and mobile, and a long tail.

It inhabits woodland savanna with *Senegalia* and *Vachellia* (acacia) trees, riverine bush and the fringes of forests.

Habits
- Nocturnal, although they often become active before the sun sets during the winter months.
- Arboreal, and agile climbers, able to leap long distances (3–5m) from branch to branch. Will descend from the trees intermittently to feed on the ground but are far more arboreal than their thick-tailed cousin.
- During the day they rest communally in holes in trees, or in dense foliage higher up.
- They give a range of calls, including a loud chattering when alarmed, a plaintive defensive call, and one to announce territory occupied.

Feeding and diet
- They eat both insects and gum from *Senegalia* and *Vachellia* (acacia) trees, an important source of food during the winter when insects are scarce – insects are detected by sight and sound, and the bushbabies catch them with their hands.
- All their water requirements are met by the moisture in their food.

Droppings
- Unsegmented and irregular-shaped, elongated cylindrical droppings are light to dark brown in colour, 5mm in diameter and 15mm in length. Insect fragments are usually evident.

Territorial behaviour
- Male ranges overlap territories of females with young.
- Territorial, they scent-mark with chest gland secretions and urine, which they transfer to their hands and feet and deposit on tree branches as they move through their range.
- Males will urinate on females to mark them.

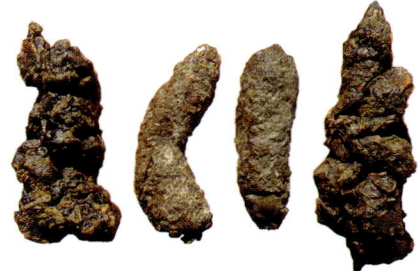

Lesser bushbaby droppings

MAMMALS ■ Primates

Above left and right: Souther lesser bushbaby hind feet tracks, which measure 25mm in length; tracks are rarely seen.

About the track
- The hind track measures 25–30mm in length.
- When they descend from the trees, lesser bushbabies generally hop bipedally (on their hind feet). Seldom do they move quadrupedally (on all fours).
- Diagnostic is the unusually large opposing 'big toe' on the hind foot (used for climbing); it makes a clear impression in the track.
- Both front and hind feet have five digits. The digits and palms of the hands and soles of the feet are cushioned with subcutaneous tissue that enables this bushbaby to move quickly through rough and often thorny branches.
- Left and right hind feet tracks register closely alongside one another as the animal hops over the ground.

Can be confused with ...
- *Tracks may be confused with those of a **young vervet monkey**.*
- *They may also be confused with the **thick-tailed bushbaby's**; however, these are up to 30mm larger, and both the front and hind tracks of thick-tailed bushbabies usually make an impression, whereas the lesser mostly shows just the hind feet tracks.*

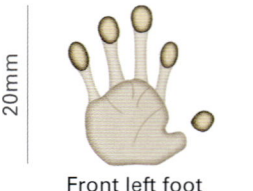

Front left foot

Hind left foot

MAMMALS ■ Primates

Thick-tailed bushbaby
Otolemur crassicaudatus

This primate is silver-grey to dark brown in colour. It has strong hind legs and a long, fluffy tail, which gives it balance in its arboreal environment. Its large, forward-facing eyes provide good night vision, and big, rounded ears enable acute hearing.

The thick-tailed bushbaby inhabits forest, thicket and savanna woodland.

Habits
- Nocturnal and arboreal, they are agile climbers that can leap from branch to branch over long distances. In mid-flight they tuck in their arms, legs and delicate ears to slip through dense foliage.
- Their bat-like ears allow them to locate insects in the dark with exceptional accuracy.
- Gregarious; they live in groups of several adults and their young.
- They forage, sometimes over fairly long distances, either singly or in groups.
- In the day they shelter in leafy nests amidst thick foliage high up in mature trees. Females with young build well-defined nests using leaves and small branches.
- Social interaction includes grooming, play fights and following-play.

Feeding and diet
- Groups of thick-tailed bushbabies are attracted to trees with plenty of ripe fruit, as well as *Vachellia* (acacia) gum.
- They also feed on insects, small birds and reptiles.

Droppings
- The unsegmented droppings are light brown in colour, measuring 15mm in diameter and 50mm in length. They may contain seeds and insect fragments.

Thick-tailed bushbaby droppings

Territorial behaviour
- Fixed overlapping ranges, which they mark with glands on their chest, lip, chin and with ano-genital secretion and urine.
- They scent-mark by rubbing their chest glands and anus on tree branches. Male scent-marking intensifies if intruders are detected.
- Communication is by vocalising and by marking their paths with urine.
- The thick-tailed bushbaby's call sounds rather like that of a crying human baby, hence its name.

MAMMALS ■ Primates

About the track
- The hind foot track is 55mm and front foot 35mm in length; this often-confusing track has five digits on both front and hind feet.
- These bushbabies spend more time on the ground than their lesser cousin – the lesser galago – leaving more opportunity to observe their tracks.
- The hind foot has a large opposing 'big toe', which assists with grabbing and holding branches.
- This disproportionately large hind foot digit makes a clear impression in the track, although its position varies considerably.
- Toenails are present, except on toe number 2 on the hind foot, which bears a grooming claw, although none of the claws make impressions in their track.
- This species commonly walks on all four limbs (quadrupedal movement), but may also hop bipedally on its hind legs.
- The typical gait shows the hind foot register partially on top of the front foot, making interpretation of the front and hind tracks more difficult.

Can be confused with ...
- Thick-tailed bushbaby tracks may be confused with those of **vervet monkey**, although the monkey's thumb is not as large. The vervet monkey's hind foot does not register on top of its front foot.
- **Lesser bushbaby** tracks are much smaller (up to 30mm), and these little animals move around bipedally, so do not often show their front feet tracks.

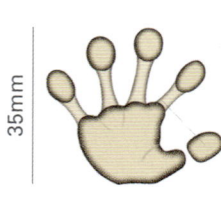
Front left foot

Hind left foot

Above and right: Bushbaby tracks

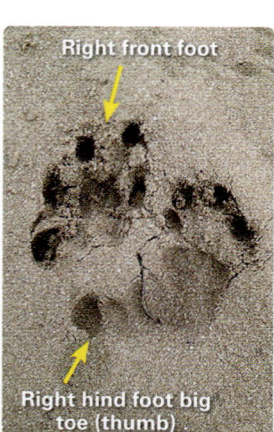

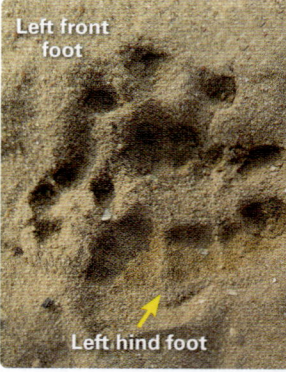
Above: Notice how the large 'big toe' digit has changed position – see track illustration to compare.

MAMMALS ■ Hares & rodents

Cape hare
Lepus capensis

The Cape hare (of the order Lagomorpha, not a rodent) has a light brown-grey body with white-and-ochre-coloured underparts. The female is larger than the male, which is somewhat unusual among mammals.

It inhabits grassland, bushveld and semi-desert biomes in the region's southwest.

Habits
- Nocturnal, but also active in the early morning and late afternoon when it is cool and overcast.
- Both sexes are solitary but male and female may be seen together during mating season, and females with young.
- Females in oestrus may be accompanied by several males at a time.
- They will run for hundreds of metres when pursued by a predator, and suddenly swerve off to the side when the pursuer gets too close.

Burrow/Den
- These hares lie up in small 'forms' (natural depressions in the ground) under cover of long grass or small bushes.
- They also make use of burrows dug by other species, to take refuge from predators.

Feeding and diet
- Primarily grazers, they prefer short green grass but browse on the leaves, stems and flowers of small shrubs when grass is scarce.
- Small groups of Cape hares may be found on patches of good grazing.

Droppings
- Round or oval-shaped pellets, light brown or pale, measure 10mm in length and are deposited singly or in small piles throughout the range.
- Hares produce two kinds of dung: a faecal pellet made of indigestible fibre and waste (not normally re-ingested), and a caecotrope or caecal dropping (dark in colour and covered with mucus), which is digestible fibre that has been processed in the caecum and is re-ingested by the hare to absorb more nutrients – a process called 'caecotrophy'. This pellet is seldom seen as it is ingested directly from the anus.

Cape hare droppings are pale, oval-shaped pellets in small heaps.

MAMMALS ■ Hares & rodents

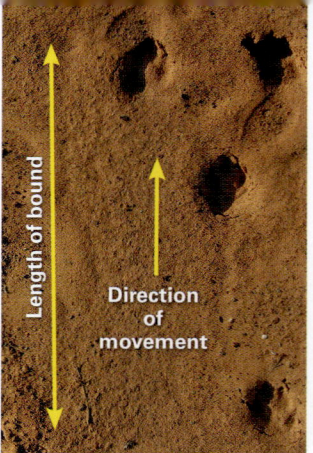

Left: A Cape hare track. Claw marks are often seen if the animal accelerates or changes direction suddenly.

Right: Typical hare bounding gait: hind feet are at the top and front feet in the middle and at the bottom.

About the track
- Characteristic is the copious hair beneath its feet and between its toes, usually obliterating details of its claws and toes.
- Tracks are mostly seen as 'smudges' in the soil, often showing up in the typical hare track pattern or gait. (See p. 27 for illustration.)
- A hare moves with a bounding gait, which creates a specific pattern. First, one of the front feet is placed on the ground. Then the other front foot lands directly in front of the first foot. After that, the two hind feet come around and land ahead of the front feet, next to each other but a few centimetres apart. The distance the hare jumps in each bound depends on how fast it is moving.
- If the hare sits up on its hocks, evidence of this posture may show in the hind feet tracks, as its two hind feet impressions lengthen and imprint in full.
- If the animal accelerates or changes direction suddenly, its claws, particularly those of the hind feet, leave marks. Regularly preyed on by jackals and caracals, hares sometimes leave evidence of claw marks and skidding in their attempt to escape.
- In mud, details of the toes and claws may be clearly seen.

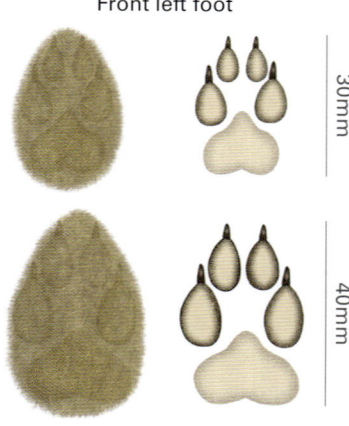

Can be confused with ...
- Track is very similar in appearance to that of the **scrub hare**. Even though the Cape hare is marginally lighter than the scrub hare, its hind foot track appears to be slightly larger, and its toes bigger.
- The Cape hare dropping is marginally smaller than that of the scrub hare.
- In the Karoo, where the two species occur together, it is noted that the scrub hare inhabits the comparatively denser scrubland areas while the Cape hare prefers terrain that is more open.

MAMMALS ■ Hares & rodents

Scrub hare
Lepus saxatilis

The scrub hare (also of the order Lagomorpha) has a grey body with black speckles, pure white underparts, and very long ears. It has long, strong hind legs and large hind feet with much hair between the pads.

This animal prefers open savanna woodland with grass and scrub.

Habits
- Nocturnal, but also active in the early morning and late afternoon.
- Solitary but male and female may be seen together during mating season, and females are accompanied by their young.
- Females in oestrus may be accompanied by several males.

Burrow/Den
- They lie up in small 'forms' (natural depressions in the ground) under cover of long grass or small bushes, sometimes leaving impressions in the soil.
- They do not usually make use of other animals' burrows or holes.

Feeding and diet
- A grazer, it prefers short green grass, but also feeds on leaves, rhizomes, roots and small stems of shrubs and herbs when grass is scarce.

Droppings
- The oval-shaped pellets, pale green to yellow, are dropped in small heaps.
- Measuring 12mm in length, the droppings are slightly larger than Cape hare droppings.
- Hares produce two kinds of dung: a faecal pellet made of indigestible fibre and waste (not normally re-ingested); and a caecotrope or caecal dropping (dark in colour and covered with mucus), which is digestible fibre that has been processed in the caecum and is re-ingested by the hare to absorb more nutrients – a process called 'caecotrophy'. This pellet is seldom seen as it is ingested directly from the anus.

About the track
- Characteristic is the copious hair beneath its feet and between its toes, usually obliterating details of its claws and toes.
- Tracks are mostly seen as 'smudges' in the soil, but are often arranged in the typical hare track pattern or gait.

Scrub hare droppings

MAMMALS — Hares & rodents

The urine of hares and rabbits sometimes dries white, caused by excess calcium in the diet.

Typical hare tracks on dry sand

Scrub hare bounding sequence

In mud, details of the track can be seen more clearly because the animal sinks in slightly. In this case, the hare's track can resemble that of a jackal.

- This hare moves with a bounding gait, which creates a specific pattern. First, one of the front feet is placed on the ground. Then the other front foot lands directly in front of the first. After that, the two hind feet come around and land ahead of the front feet, next to each other but a few centimetres apart. The distance the hare jumps in each bound depends on how fast it is moving.
- The hind feet are slightly larger than the front feet.
- If the hare sits up on its hocks, one may see evidence of this posture as its two hind feet impressions lengthen and imprint in full.
- If the hare accelerates or changes direction quickly, its claws may imprint in the substrate.
- Details may be clearer in mud, where the animal's toes, claws and main pad sink in slightly.

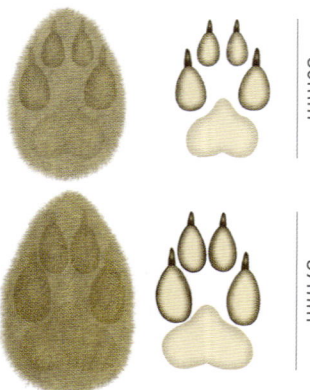

Front left foot

Hind left foot

30mm

37mm

Can be confused with ...

- Although very similar in appearance, the scrub hare hind foot track is smaller than that of the **Cape hare**.
- In the Karoo, where the two species occur together, it is noted that the scrub hare inhabits the comparatively denser scrubland areas, while the Cape hare prefers more open terrain.
- Individual scrub hare footprints may be confused with those of **small antelope** such as the **common duiker**.

MAMMALS — Hares & rodents

South African ground squirrel
Xerus inauris

As its name implies, the ground squirrel lives on the ground rather than in trees. It inhabits arid areas with open spaces in South Africa, Botswana and Namibia.

Habits
- Diurnal; it does not emerge during rain or dust storms.
- Gregarious, they live in groups of up to 30 females and their young.
- Males are resident temporarily for mating purposes and then move on.
- Dominant males show aggression towards other males, often chasing them.
- They are able to rise up on their hind legs and stand fully erect, and remain comfortably so for long periods, to scan for predators.
- Extremely alert, they alarm by flicking their tail and issuing a high-pitched whistle.
- Predators include large raptors and small carnivores.

Burrow/Den
- Avid diggers, these squirrels excavate their own burrows, but also share those of suricates and yellow mongooses.
- They may share burrows with other squirrels (20 or more), using several entrances, measuring 100–160mm in diameter.
- The mounds of excavated sand around the entrance are characteristic.

Feeding and diet
- They eat leaves, flowers, fruits and seeds, as well as termites and other insects.
- They dig for underground bulbs and tubers.
- In the Karoo, these squirrels feed on the berries of the shepherd's tree (*Boscia albitrunca*).

Droppings
- Their nondescript droppings are small (5–7mm in diameter), elongated, light brown pellets, usually rounded on one side and tapered on the other, deposited either in piles or spread out.

Territorial behaviour
- Home ranges vary in size according to food availability, where the animal scent-marks with urine.

Typical squirrel burrow with mounds of sand around its entrance

Ground squirrel droppings

Above left and right: The three middle toes on the hind foot are usually conspicuous. Notice the large gap between the toes and main pad of the hind foot – this is typical.

About the track

- Track lengths measured at Samara Karoo Reserve show front foot 32mm and hind foot 40mm when the squirrel is walking. When it's sitting up, the hind foot to the hock makes an impression, increasing the length to 60–70mm.
- The ground squirrel track typically shows four toes on the front foot and five toes on the hind.
- The three middle toes on the hind foot often group together. Toes can be surprisingly broad.
- Claws well adapted for digging always show, and measure up to 10mm over the curve.
- Front foot main pad is asymmetrical on the posterior edge, with the outside lobe extending further back than that on the inside.
- Evidence may be seen of its bushy tail having brushed over the squirrel's tracks.
- Depending on its gait, the squirrel's hind foot may register on top of the front foot or ahead of it.

Hind feet register ahead of the front feet, indicating a fast walk.

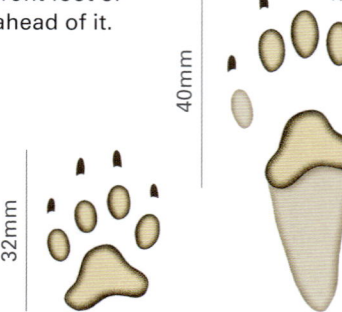

Front left foot   Hind left foot

Can be confused with ...

- The squirrel track may be confused with that of the **suricate**, and **slender**, **yellow** or **small grey mongoose** in areas where these species share a range; however, the squirrel has five toes on its hind feet, and the shape of the hind foot main pad is significantly different from that of these other small mammals.
- Although the **striped polecat** also has five toes on each foot, these toes are significantly larger than the squirrel's.

MAMMALS ■ Hares & rodents

African tree squirrel
Paraxerus cepapi

African tree squirrels are predominantly arboreal. They prefer woodland habitats, such as mopane woodlands, because the availability of natural holes in trees is essential to their breeding success.

Habits
- Diurnal, they are most active during early morning and late afternoon.
- They are found singly or in pairs or small family groups.
- Vocalising, grooming, urinating and scent-marking using an anal gland all play an important role in social cohesiveness, as well as to mark territory.
- They have excellent hearing and eyesight, and are extremely agile in trees.
- Vociferous and watchful, they make a vocal 'tsirr, tsirr, tsirr' cry, and a high-pitched whistling alarm, while flicking their tail. Predators include eagles, snakes and leopards. Trackers can interpret much from squirrels' vocalisations, as the cadence, pitch and tone of a call indicate particulars about the predator threat.

Burrow/Den
- They create a nest of leaves in a natural cavity, or claim a nest made by barbets or woodpeckers, in a tree.

Feeding and diet
- The tree squirrel feeds on a wide variety of vegetable matter, such as flowers, leaves, grass, plants and fruits, and also insects.

Droppings
- Slightly elongated, cylindrical pellets, light brown, have a diameter of 5–7mm and a length of 13mm.
- Bits of vegetation are usually evident in the droppings.

Territorial behaviour
- Territory is marked by urination or anal gland secretions, and is defended by males and females.
- Individual tree squirrel nests are aggressively defended against other squirrel intruders. Males may show battle scars, such as torn ears and a damaged tail, as evidence of their territorial behaviour.

Typical tree squirrel nest, packed with green leaves

Kevin Murray

Tree squirrel droppings

MAMMALS ■ Hares & rodents

A bounding tree squirrel

Tracks of a bounding squirrel

*Comparison of bounding gaits of slender mongoose (**right**) and African tree squirrel (**far right**)*

About the track

- Front foot measures 23mm and hind foot 27mm, unless the squirrel is sitting up on its hocks, balancing on its tail, in which case the hind foot may cast a print of up to 45mm in length.
- Has four toes on front foot and five on the hind foot, with indistinct claw marks.
- The main pad is not a conventional triangular shape; it often appears to have no particular shape or form and can be difficult to distinguish. Characteristic features are bulges and grooves under the main pad, giving the impression of a tread-like texture, which assists with grip for climbing trees.
- The outside toes of both front and hind feet are situated wide and lower down; the toes are very flexible, so their positions appear to change.
- Their common bounding gait shows two front feet landing next to each other (or partially on top of each other); then the hind feet swing around and land ahead of the front feet, parallel to but apart from each other. (See p. 27 for illustration of gait.)

Can be confused with ...

- The main pad is a less conventional shape than those of other, similar-sized small mammals, for example the **dwarf or slender mongoose**.
  The squirrel's toes are more elongated than those of the dwarf mongoose, and its claws are shorter. The squirrel feeds alone, leaving a single set of tracks, whereas mongooses, being gregarious, leave several sets of tracks.

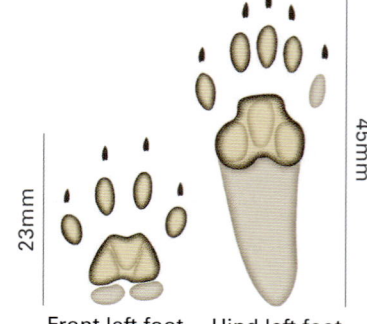

Front left foot   Hind left foot

Greater cane rat
Thryonomys swinderianus

The greater cane rat, weighing up to 10kg, is a heavily built rodent.

It prefers marshy areas and is found along banks of rivers and lakes. As the name implies, the cane rat is partial to sugar cane plantations, where it is regarded as a pest.

Habits
- Nocturnal, they live in small groups that are led by a single male.
- If threatened, cane rats grunt (or hiss) and run towards water or thicket. In the Sabi Sands Game Reserve they are preyed on by leopards and other smaller carnivores.
- Individuals may live for up to four years.

Burrow/Den
- They make nests from grass above the ground, or excavate shallow underground burrows.

Feeding and diet
- Feed mainly on aquatic grasses found in dense thickets along riverbanks and near marshes.
- They cut grass with their upper incisors, often producing a teeth-chattering sound.
- Although they prefer green fodder, they can survive on dry grasses thanks to the presence of digestive microbes in their hindgut.
- Sometimes evidence remains of cut grass or reed stems (which the cane rat discards) left in little piles in areas where they are active.

Droppings
- Rectangular and slightly elongated light brown pellets, 10–14mm in diameter; they possess a diagnostic groove along the length of the pellet.

About the track
- Front foot track is 40mm in length and hind foot 50mm in length.
- Tracks show four toes on both front and hind feet; although the front has five toes, toe 1 is reduced.
- Should the animal move over perfect substrate, both front and hind feet tracks show all four toes and their claws. However, it is common for only three toes to make a clear impression.

Cane rat droppings

MAMMALS ■ Hares & rodents

Cane rat hind feet tracks

Cane rat track, showing a faint outline of the main pad

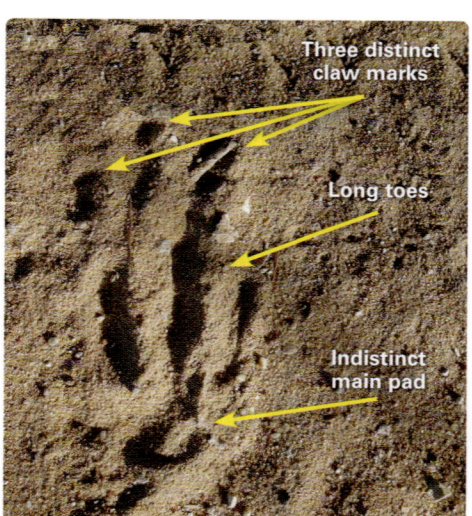

Cane rat track

- The main pad is not always clearly defined; however, the hind foot has a larger extended main pad.
- The cane rat's distinctive long, thick claws give its track the appearance of a table fork being pressed into the soil.
- Cane rats create well-worn paths of 80–100mm in width (called 'runs'), in grassy areas and vleis, which they use regularly.

Can be confused with ...

- The greater cane rat track may be confused with that of the **banded mongoose**, which shows four clearly marking toes and claws, as opposed to the cane rat, which regularly shows only three clearly marking toes and claws. Confusion is caused by the similarly sized long claw marks that are evident in both these species' tracks.

Front left foot   Hind left foot

MAMMALS ■ Hares & rodents

Cape porcupine
Hystrix africaeaustralis

The porcupine is Africa's largest rodent. Its upper body is covered with long spines and shorter sharp quills. The rest of the body is covered with short, coarse black hair with white patches on the sides of the neck.

It is found in most habitat types throughout the subregion.

Habits
- Nocturnal and monogamous; both parents participate in raising the young.
- When threatened, they will raise their quills and, if necessary, reverse into the threat, sacrificing quills in the process. Quills strewn about over a small area may indicate the scene of a confrontation.

Burrow
- It may live singly or in a group in a burrow, usually taken over from aardvark.
- It will also rest in rock crevices and caves.

A burrow used by a porcupine

Feeding
- Herbivorous, mostly digs for its food, preferring certain bulbs and plant roots. Its diggings are typically narrow and usually expose the root it has fed on at the bottom of the hole.
- It also feeds on bark from the lower reaches of tree trunks, such as tamboti trees (*Spirostachys africana*) in the southern Kruger National Park.
- It will occasionally gnaw on bones (osteophagia), presumably to add minerals to its diet. Bones and bone fragments can often be found in its burrows.

Evidence of a porcupine having fed on tamboti bark (Spirostachys africana)

MAMMALS ■ Hares & rodents

Droppings
- Dark, fibrous tubes measure 16–23mm in diameter.
- Sometimes clumped together, often connected.
- Droppings are deposited randomly, and occasionally in a midden.

Territorial behaviour
- Porcupines maintain a core territory within a broader non-exclusive home range.
- Both males and females scent-mark by rubbing their anal (perineal) scent gland on the ground, particularly on rocks, and even on small plants.

About the track
- The track measures 70–80mm in both Samara (in the Karoo) and Londolozi (near the southern Kruger National Park) game reserves.
- The main pad is segmented and there are a further two proximal pads located directly behind the main pad. Main pad is separated into three segments, indicated by grey lines in the illustration and ridges in the track.
- Identifying the two proximal pads is key to interpreting this track correctly.
- The toes are typically round in shape, particularly on the front foot.
- Although both front and hind feet have five toes, only four toes and claws may show clearly, toe number 1 does not always make an impression. In loose sand the toe prints can be very indistinct.

Porcupine droppings

Porcupine scent-mark on a rock; notice the quill marks below the rock.

Notice the two clearly evident proximal pads of the hind foot.

Typical porcupine tracks

Evidence of feeding; notice how the root has been exposed.

MAMMALS ■ Hares & rodents

GENERIC DIFFERENCES BETWEEN PORCUPINE AND HONEY BADGER TRACKS

	PORCUPINE	HONEY BADGER
Toes	Front foot usually shows four toes; occasionally the hind foot shows five toes	Five toes on both front and hind feet; occasionally toe 1 does not show
Toe shape	Smaller and rounder in shape; toes more splayed in their positioning	Large and oval in shape (sausage-like); middle toes grouped tightly together
Claws	Short, stubby claws	Very long and thick, particularly on the front foot – up to 20mm long
Main pad	Main pad is segmented into three separate pads indicated by faint ridges	One large unsegmented main pad
Proximal pads	In most cases, two proximal pads show on both front and hind feet	One proximal pad on both front and hind feet
Gait / other	Hind foot registers on top of, or just behind, the front foot; quill drag marks sometimes evident	Hind foot lands behind front foot, front feet land facing inwards slightly; occasionally hind foot will register on top of front foot
Track length	70–80mm	80–110mm

- Certain individual porcupines have unusually long front foot claws.
- Faint evidence of dragging quill marks, or finding the quills themselves, is common but not guaranteed.
- At a normal walking gait the hind foot registers on top of the front foot.

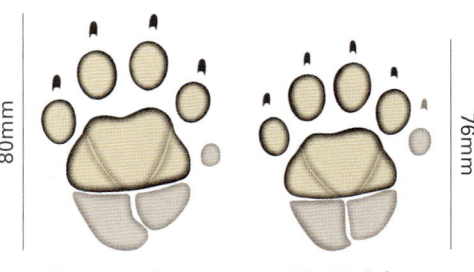

Front left foot   Hind left foot

Can be confused with ...

- *Porcupine tracks can be confused with those of the **honey badger** where these two animals share a range; however, the badger has larger, sausage-shaped toes, very long claws on its front feet, a single (unsegmented) main pad and a single proximal pad on each foot. The honey badger's three middle toes are grouped together tightly (particularly on the hind foot) whereas the porcupine's toes are more evenly spread.*

MAMMALS ■ Hares & rodents

Springhare
Pedetes capensis

A true rodent (unlike the other two hares), this medium-sized animal has large hind feet with sharp claws and a long, black-tipped tail. It has long ears and large eyes, which enable it to see better at night.

It prefers dry, sparsely vegetated areas where compacted sand is available for digging burrows.

Habits
- Strictly nocturnal, springhares come out to feed at night unless the weather is cold or wet.
- They use a bipedal hop, like a kangaroo, and when moving fast make long bounds of 2–4m.
- Predators include caracal, leopard and jackal.
- Young are suckled inside the burrow until about half-grown. This extra parental care boosts the survival rate of their offspring, which is usually very low for rodents.

Burrow
- Springhares occupy burrows singly, with up to 20 individual burrows located in close proximity to each other.
- The burrow is very long with several interconnected entrances, which the springhare plugs with soil when it is in residence.

A typical springhare burrow

Feeding and diet
- They eat mainly short grass and the fresh leaves of small shrubs; also seeds.
- They dig shallow, half-moon-shaped holes in order to access and feed on underground stems and rhizomes.
- In winter they browse on plants such as black thorn (*Senegalia mellifera*), nipping off buds at a slight angle.

Springhare feeding sign – twig nipped off at an angle

MAMMALS ■ Hares & rodents

Droppings are rectangular in shape and pale in colour.

Droppings
- Droppings are pale in colour, distinctively flat and rectangular in shape, and measure 13–18mm in diameter.

About the track
- The hind foot track measures 45mm in length, but 75mm if the springhare sits up on its hocks. The front foot measures 35mm in length (measured with toes and main pad).
- Although the springhare has four toes on the hind foot and five toes on the front foot, one mostly sees tracks of just the three distinctive toes and claws of the hind feet.
- It steadies itself with its long tail, which occasionally makes an impression in soft substrate.
- The indistinct front foot track with its five claws is seldom seen, only showing if the animal stops to feed close to the ground in perfectly soft substrate.
- The springhare hops bipedally, propelling itself forward with its strong, explosive hind legs. The hind tracks usually land side by side.
- The average distance of a single hop is 1.1m, measured in the Karoo.

Springhare hind feet tracks

Front feet

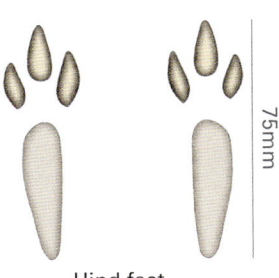

Hind feet

Left: Tracks of a hopping springhare
Top: A rare photo of springhare front feet tracks
Above: Typical springhare hind feet tracks

MAMMALS ■ Hares & rodents

Small rodents, gerbils, sengis and shrews
Muridae (murids), Gerbillinae (gerbils), Macroscelidea (sengis), Soricidae (shrews)

Woodland mouse

Characteristic features of rodents are the pointed snout, small, rounded ears, and a long, naked (almost hairless) tail. This diverse group of mammals (all order Rodentia) is highly adaptable; they inhabit a wide variety of habitat types – from agricultural lands, natural forests and aquatic environments to developed urban areas.

Habits
- Some rodents are nocturnal, others are diurnal; there is great variation in their habits.
- Most rodents, particularly gerbils and sengis, constantly use familiar paths to enter and leave their burrows.

Evidence of a rodent having dust-bathed; notice the tail drag mark.

Burrow/Den
- Rodent burrows have a small entrance hole just big enough to accommodate the particular resident rodent; the entrance is usually concealed by grass.

Feeding and diet
- A rodent's diet consists of grasses, seeds, plants, small reptiles, birds' eggs and insects.

Droppings
- Rodent droppings are typically very small, narrow, oval-shaped black pellets, 4–8mm in length.

Signs that a murid has been digging marula kernels

About the tracks
Mice and rats (murids)
- **Mouse and rat** tracks show four toes on the front and five on the hind feet, the feet being 10mm in length, but this varies from species to species.
- The broad hind feet show three forward-facing middle toes and two widely set outside toes.
- Toe and claw marks can be seen clearly in certain substrates.
- Tail drag marks are a common feature of small rodent tracks.
- Mice and rats may walk, run or bound on their hind legs, depending on the species.

Hind feet

Front feet

Mouse tracks

MAMMALS ■ Hares & rodents

Above left and right: Tracks of bounding murids

Gerbils, sengis and shrews

- **Gerbil** tracks show four toes on the front foot and five on the hind foot. Gerbils are known for their bounding gait, similar to that of hares and squirrels.
- The four-toed **sengi** (previously known as an elephant shrew) track shows four toes on both front and hind feet. Although the front foot has five toes, toe number 1 seldom leaves an impression as it is positioned higher up on the foot. **Sengis** make use of well-worn paths along which they hop continually. In a bipedal hop, only the hind feet make an impression.
- A **shrew** track is significantly smaller than tracks of the rat and mouse. It has five toes on both front and hind feet and its hind foot has a long, narrow posterior edge that may show if the animal sits up.

Murid tracks

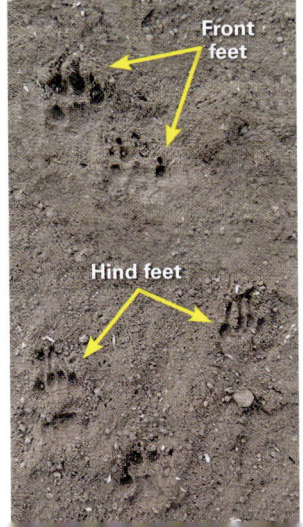

Above: A gerbil's burrow
Right: Four-toed sengi tracks; notice the difference in shape between the front and hind tracks. Tracks measure 10mm in length.

Frogs and toads
Order Anura

Southern foam nest frog

There are 178 known species of frogs in southern Africa, represented in 13 families. All frogs – including toads, which constitute one of the 13 frog families – belong to the order Anura. Two of the common features of members of this order are that adults lose their tail through metamorphosis, and most have the ability to vocalise for breeding purposes (with Rose's mountain toadlet an exception).

Frogs generally inhabit areas near water, but toads and rain, tree and sand frogs have a wider habitat tolerance and so are common in southern Africa, inhabiting both aquatic areas and drier places away from water.

SOME GENERIC DIFFERENCES BETWEEN FROGS AND TOADS

FROGS (ORDER ANURA)	TOADS (FAMILY BUFONIDAE)
Aquatic – live near water	Less aquatic – require water only during breeding
Smooth, moist skin	Dry, rough, leathery skin
Narrow body	Wide body
Strong, mostly long legs for jumping and swimming (many with short legs)	Short hind legs for walking or taking short hops
Tend to lay eggs in clusters	Tend to lay eggs in long chains
Not known for being particularly poisonous (banded rubber frog is toxic)	Parotoid glands behind eyes that secrete poison
Round eyes, which may appear to bulge	Rugby ball-shaped eyes, with less bulging

Feeding and diet
- All members of order Anura feed on insects, spiders, small fish, worms, algae, snails and even – in the case of the African bullfrog – small rodents and birds, reptiles and other amphibians.

Painted reed frog

■ AMPHIBIANS & REPTILES

Track information

The great diversity of amphibians in southern Africa has resulted in a very shallow knowledge of their individual tracks and signs. With the exception of two or three common species, no published material exists that accurately separates the tracks of different frog species.

Should one positively identify a frog making tracks, these should be photographed, drawn and accurately measured, and can be submitted to the Animal Demography Unit (ADU), a recognised research unit based at the University of Cape Town.

Eastern olive toads mating encircled by chain of eggs

Guttural toad droppings are 10mm in diameter and 35–50mm in length.

Frog tadpoles

Tracks of a hopping toad

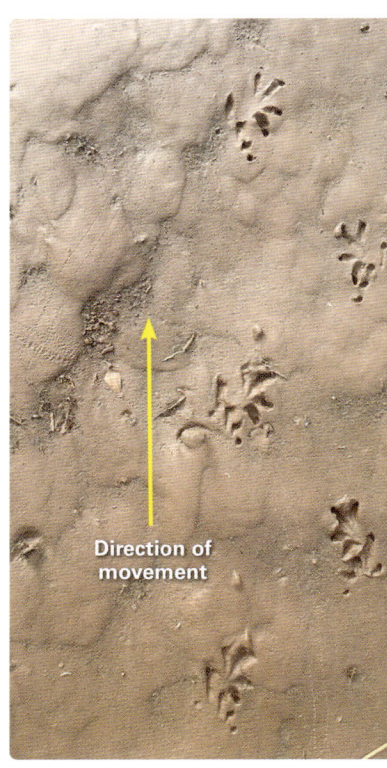

Tracks of a walking giant bullfrog

AMPHIBIANS & REPTILES

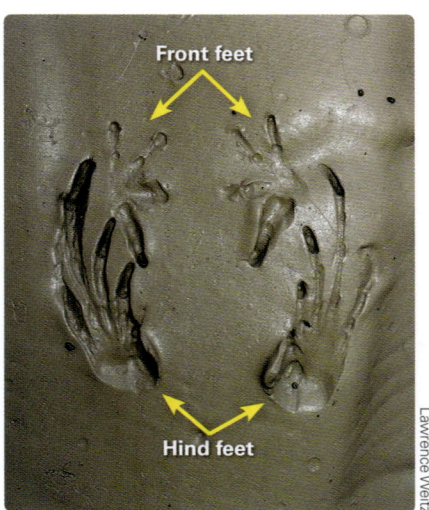

Hopping toad tracks; the front feet position changes with a change in the toad's speed of movement.

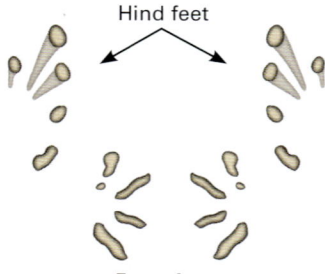

- Frog and toad track patterns can help determine whether the creature has been walking or hopping. During a hopping gait one may even see evidence of the belly making an impression on the ground.
- In addition to hopping, certain frog species – such as the bushveld rain frog, bubbling kassina, banded rubber frog and African bullfrog – make regular use of a walking gait.
- Frog tracks are commonly found around water, especially on wet mud adjacent to water holes and rivers. Toad tracks may be found far from water, sometimes along dusty roads.
- Local frogs and toads have five toes on the hind foot and four on the front foot.
- African bullfrog tracks – the largest in the region – measure 30mm in length.
- Several frog species have rounded terminal disks on their fingers or toes. Most toads do not have terminal disks at all on their fingers and toes.
- Certain frog species have toes with hard claws and webbing between the toes.
- Some frogs have webbing between the toes.
- Most active during the rainy season.

Interesting frog facts

- The **southern foam nest frog** (Chiromantis xerampelina) *creates a white nest of foam in which to lay its eggs, in trees above water.*
- The **giant bullfrog** (Pyxicephalus adspersus) *is the largest frog in southern Africa, weighing up to 1.4kg. It is regarded as Near Threatened on the Red Data List. This bullfrog aestivates during the dry months, and can remain cocooned underground for several years if dry conditions persist.*
- The **common platanna** (Xenopus laevis) *is an almost completely aquatic frog. Seldom does one find its tracks on dry land. It feeds on a wide variety of food and indulges in cannibalism. During periods of drought this species may aestivate under the mud.*

■ AMPHIBIANS & REPTILES

Lizards, skinks and geckos
Order Squamata and suborder Lacertilia

Common rough-scaled lizard

Southern Africa is home to 287 species of lizards in four genera; these include 63 species of skink and 88 species of gecko. This adaptable, diverse group of reptiles is built for speed and agility, with species having elongated, slender bodies, well-developed legs and long toes. Predominantly insectivorous, these reptiles typically use a sit-and-wait or stalking approach when hunting for prey. Many have developed excellent camouflage abilities, which help them to avoid predators and ambush prey. Like many other reptiles, they often engage in basking behaviour.

All are terrestrial and inhabit a wide range of sandy, rocky, broken ground, grass clumps, and trees in grasslands, savannas, deserts and scrublands. The coral rag skink is the only semi-aquatic species, found only in KwaZulu-Natal. Some geckos climb smooth surfaces using tiny, branched structures (setae) on their toes, which help maximise contact with the surface. This allows Van der Waal's forces to come into play, enabling geckos to stick to walls and ceilings.

Habits
- Some species are diurnal and others nocturnal.
- Hunting modus operandi of these reptiles is to sit and wait for their insect prey to move close enough before the predator dashes out from under cover and pounces on the unsuspecting prey.

Burrow
- They shelter in small burrows dug beneath a flat rock, a dense bush or in a termite mound. Many are legless and fossorial, burrowing through soft sand, and leaving snake-like tracks at night when they move on the surface.
- Gecko burrows are cleaned out daily.

Feeding and diet
- Mostly insectivorous, lizards, skinks and geckos also feed on other small invertebrates, and occasionally plant material, and even other reptiles and rodents.

Droppings
- Similar to bird droppings; they contain (white) uric acid.

Unidentified lizard trail in the Kalahari

AMPHIBIANS & REPTILES

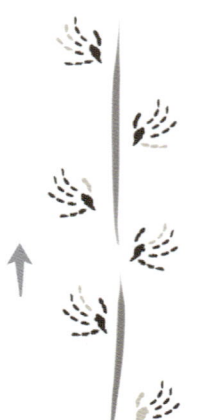

Lizard track with tail drag marks

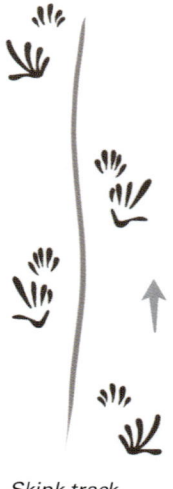

Skink track

Evidence of a Kalahari ground gecko having cleaned its burrow

Skink trail

House gecko showing five toes on each foot

About the track
- Most **lizards** have five digits on both front and hind feet. Some species raise their front legs and/or their tail off the ground when moving at speed.
- **Skink** trails show the hind foot registering directly behind the front. Some skinks, like the giant legless skink (*Acontias plumbeus*), have no legs, and may seem to 'swim' through sand.
- **Geckos** have five thick toes on front and hind feet.
- At speed, the hind feet register on top of the front feet, with the trail showing evenly spaced track impressions diagonally across from each other.
- Tracks are often indistinct, but may show a continuous or intermittent tail drag mark, with impressions of the feet on either side.

■ AMPHIBIANS & REPTILES

Flap-necked chameleon
Chamaeleo dilepis

Flap-necked chameleon

Fresh dropping showing both components – insect fragments and urates

Dropping with insect fragments visible

Chameleons (family Chamaeleonidae) are a highly specialised group of lizards, with over 150 species described around the world and 24 species in southern Africa. Depending on their mood, sexual status and the external temperature, they can change their colour by dispersing and contracting pigment cells in the skin. The flap-necked chameleon is a common arboreal species native to southern Africa.

Habits
- All southern African chameleons are diurnal.
- Tolerates a wide variety of habitats, such as forests, wooded savanna grasslands and domestic gardens.
- The adult female digs a hole and lays 10–40 eggs, which take 12 months to hatch.
- When stressed or threatened, their body darkens, and they may hiss, puff up their throat and body, and open their mouth.

Feeding and diet
- Predominantly insects, caught with their long tongue (double their body length), which they can project with exceptional speed and accuracy. They have been recorded eating small vertebrates including bats and other chameleons.

Droppings
- Cylindrical droppings have two parts; a dark component containing insect fragments, and a white, yellow or even orange component, which is the urates (a form of uric acid, also in bird droppings).
- They are 5–8mm in diameter and up to 30mm in length.

Territorial behaviour
- Flap-necked chameleons are territorial, and males make use of various displays to ward off intruders.

About the track
- On each foot the toes are fused into two opposing pairs. The claws are sharp.
- The front foot has three toes on the inside and two on the outside, making five in total.

AMPHIBIANS & REPTILES ■

- The hind foot is the opposite with three toes on the outside and two on the inside.
- Distance between left and right pair of fused toes on each foot is 20mm.
- If the chameleon is walking undisturbed, tracks may exhibit the full underside detail of the foot, revealing tiny lines of scales, and claw marks. However, if it walks quickly, tracks usually do not reveal detail of the foot underside.
- On hard ground one may only see evidence of the claws.
- A typical walking gait shows the hind foot register directly behind the front foot, with a relatively wide straddle.

Front right foot
Hind right foot

This chameleon's track sequence shows pairing of front and hind feet.

Hind foot lands behind front foot.

Typical chameleon trail

20mm

Left front and hind feet paired together

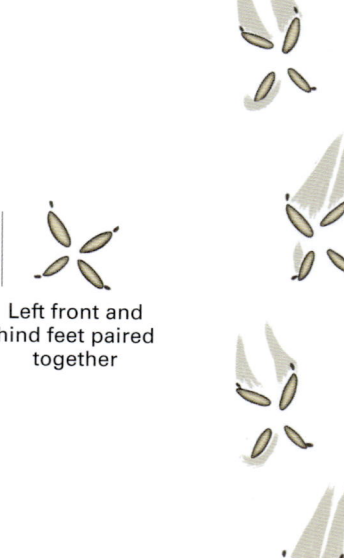

■ AMPHIBIANS & REPTILES

Rock monitor
Varanus albigularis

The rock monitor is the heaviest lizard in Africa. It has a long neck, powerful tail, and strong, stocky legs with long, sharp claws. The head has a bulbous snout, and the long tail is cylindrical at the base and flattens towards the tip. The body is dark grey-brown with pale yellow markings. Rock monitors are among the largest lizards in Africa and can grow to lengths of over 1.5m.

The rock monitor is found throughout the savanna and semi-desert regions of southern Africa, including the Western Cape.

Habits
- Solitary. In winter they go into a state of torpor; they are less active but may still bask on warmer days.
- When defending itself it adopts a side-on posture and lashes out with its tail. It will also bite and hold on tenaciously.
- The female usually digs a hole in soft, moist soil where she lays up to 50 eggs in midsummer.

Burrow/Den
- It takes refuge in tunnels that it digs under rocky overhangs, or in disused animal burrows, or in holes in trees or cracks in rocks.

A rock monitor's burrow

Feeding and diet
- The rock monitor feeds on invertebrates such as millipedes, grasshoppers and land snails, also reptiles, birds, eggs and snakes.
- It will kill and eat any small mammal that it can swallow whole, and has been known to scavenge carrion.

Droppings
- Droppings are relatively shapeless. They vary in colour from light to dark brown, and measure 18–22mm in diameter.

Rock monitor droppings

AMPHIBIANS & REPTILES ■

About the track
- Track measurements may vary considerably, given the wide variation of body size. (An individual rock monitor of 1m in length made a track with front foot 60mm and hind foot 80mm.)
- Track shows five toes with long claws on both front and hind feet.
- The undersides of the toes have many tiny horizontal layers of scales that are diagnostic.
- A diagnostic feature on the hind foot is the prominent outside toe situated at almost 70 degrees to the other toes.
- Long claws make clear impressions, even in hard substrate where the track is not easily distinguishable.
- The normal walking gait shows the hind foot registering on or slightly behind the front foot.
- Occasionally a lateral tail drag mark partially obliterates the track, making it difficult to identify.

Can be confused with ...
- The rock monitor's track is very similar to that of the **water monitor**. The rock monitor has a shorter tail than its cousin, and as a result one can expect greater lateral tail drag marks than those of the water monitor – often obliterating the tracks.
  Photographs of a captive rock monitor's toes revealed they were slightly broader than those of a water monitor of similar size, although this distinguishing feature may be difficult to interpret in the field.
- The tiny horizontal layers of scales under its feet as well as a different number of toes separate it from a **young crocodile**.

Tracks at Samara Karoo Reserve; notice the diagnostic horizontal scale marks.

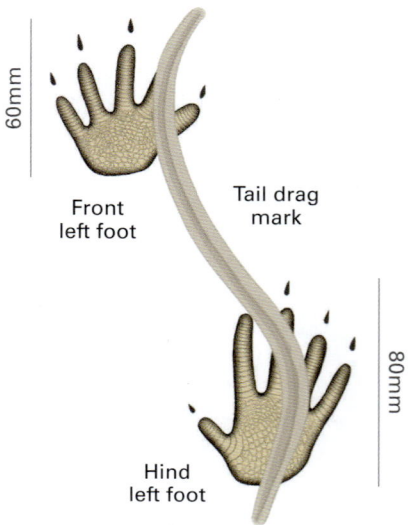

■ AMPHIBIANS & REPTILES

Water (Nile) monitor
Varanus niloticus

This large, intelligent lizard has a dark, green-grey body with yellow and white patches. It occupies habitats near permanent water.

Habits
- Its short, powerful legs and strong claws are used for digging and climbing.
- An excellent swimmer, the water monitor folds its legs under its body and uses its tail to propel itself through the water like a crocodile.
- The water monitor is able to stay underwater for up to 30 minutes.
- It can run fast over a short distance and usually heads for water when threatened.
- This big lizard is often found in trees and, if threatened, will hurl itself into water from a considerable height.

Feeding and diet
- Feeds on crabs, mussels, frogs, fish and birds; also reptiles including snakes, crocodile and terrapin eggs, and bird eggs.
- A cunning, common predator of crocodile eggs, it often uses teamwork to steal eggs; one may distract the mother crocodile while other monitors move in to dig up the nest.

About the track
- Track sizes for an individual of 1.15m in length are front foot 50mm and hind foot 70mm.
- Track shows five toes with very long claws on both front and hind feet.
- Unlike the crocodile, its toes show many tiny horizontal layers of scales.
- A diagnostic feature on the hind foot is the prominent outside toe situated at almost 70 degrees to the rest of the toes.
- Its long claws make clear impressions even when the substrate is hard and the track not easily distinguishable.
- At a normal walking gait the front foot registers 5–20mm in front of the hind foot.

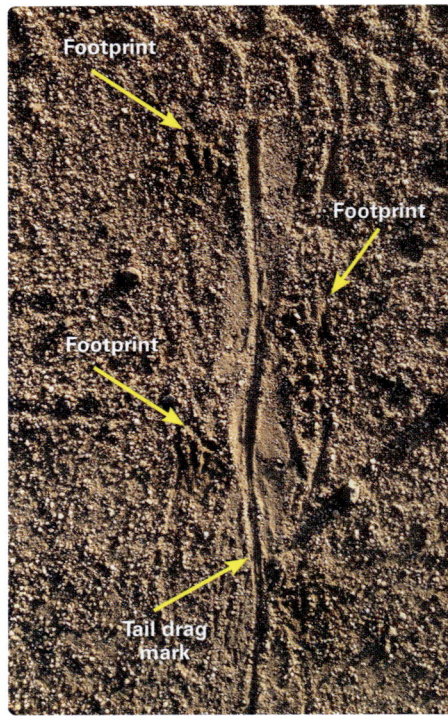

Water monitor tracks; notice the straight tail drag mark.

AMPHIBIANS & REPTILES

Tracks after a rainstorm

Water monitor front and hind feet tracks

- The water monitor drags its long tail along the ground, usually leaving a clear and relatively straight drag mark.
- Water monitor tracks are associated with watercourses, dams and wetlands, and their tracks are often found in muddy areas close to riverbanks. However, they may also venture far from the water's edge.

Tracks showing a faint tail mark

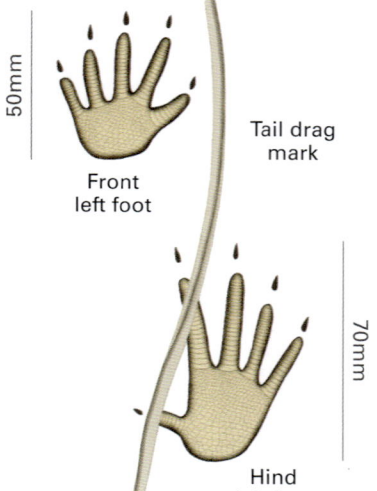

Can be confused with ...

- Its track is very similar to that of the **rock monitor**. However, the water monitor's toes are slightly narrower and its claws are slightly longer; its tail is longer, and the tail drag mark is relatively straight.
- The toes of very young water monitors can be confused with those of **aquatic bird** tracks in the mud.
- Tracks may be confused with those of a **young crocodile**.

■ AMPHIBIANS & REPTILES

Snakes
Suborder Serpentes

Puff adder

There are over 170 species of snake in southern Africa. The snake is an elongated, legless, carnivorous reptile. Depending on the species, a snake's length can vary from 100mm to more than 5m. Snakes' skin is covered in scales, and their textures, colours and patterns vary widely. They are found in a wide range of habitats, from deserts to tropical rainforests.

Habits
- Snakes periodically shed their entire outer layer of skin in a process called ecdysis, leaving behind the moulted skin, sometimes in a single piece.
- Being ectothermic, snakes are sensitive to extreme temperatures, and many species are less active during cold periods of winter.

Feeding and diet
- Their diet includes insects, eggs, birds, amphibians, lizards and other snakes – even mammals (mostly small).

Puff adder dropping measuring 80mm in length and 30–40mm in diameter

Snake locomotion

Snakes make use of five forms of locomotion, of which the following are the two most common.

- ***Terrestrial lateral undulation*** *(serpentine movement), which is the most common form of terrestrial locomotion, used by species such as mambas, cobras and the boomslang. In this form, waves moving along the body push against contact (push) points on the ground, such as stones and uneven surfaces. These objects generate a reaction force, which creates forward thrust. The speed of snake movement depends on the number of contact points, with an optimum number of seven contact points along the snake's length.*
- ***Rectilinear locomotion****, which describes how thick-bodied or heavy snakes such as the puff adder and the python move. In this form, belly muscles move the broad ventral scales and aided by its own weight, the snake grips any coarseness on the ground with the back edges of the scales. These muscle contractions draw the snake forwards.*

AMPHIBIANS & REPTILES ■

About the track

- Snake tracks are represented by either one of the two forms of locomotion described in the box on the previous page.
- Diagnostic of the puff adder's rectilinear locomotion is a noticeable narrow tail drag mark in the middle of the trail (not always continuous) made by the tail tip.
- Serpentine locomotion produces a wavy or zigzag pattern; such tracks are left by cobras, mambas and many other snakes, including young puff adders or those that are moving quickly or are agitated.
- To establish a snake's direction, look for clues left by little stones, pebbles, leaves or twigs that have been dislodged as the snake has moved forwards. On softer sands, the body will push up small mounds of sand at the back of each bend in the track.
- When climbing slopes or slight inclines, to maintain their grip and momentum, all snakes (including puff adders) will employ a more intensive serpentine form of movement with increased frequency of undulations. Conversely, the undulations in the trail will greatly decrease or even disappear if the snake slides downhill, helping determine the direction in which the snake is moving.

Left: Puff adder trail in the Karoo – the rectilinear form of movement is typically slow. **Right:** Puff adder moving in a rectilinear fashion **Below:** Puff adder track drawing; notice the narrow tail drag in the middle of the trail.

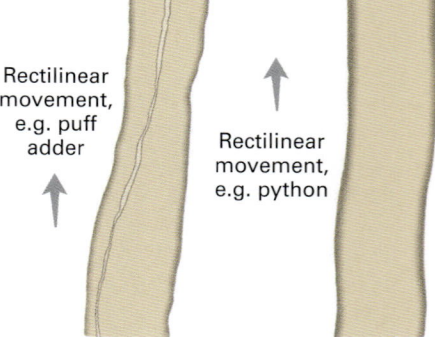

Rectilinear movement, e.g. puff adder

Rectilinear movement, e.g. python

AMPHIBIANS & REPTILES

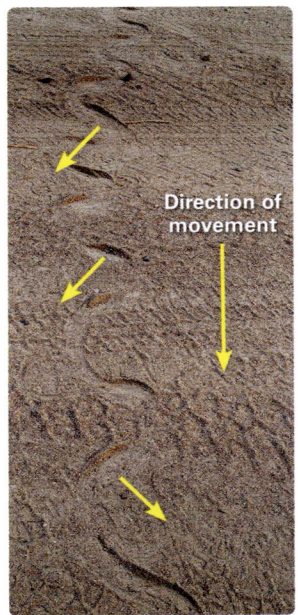
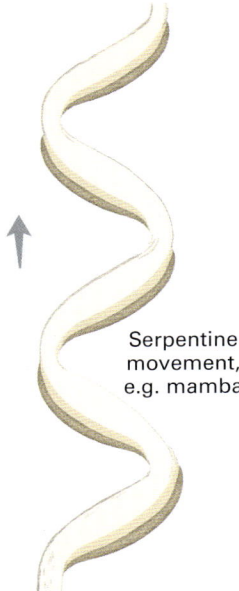

Serpentine movement, e.g. mamba

Far left and left: Terrestrial lateral locomotion, showing direction of movement; this is a quicker form of movement used by snakes such as cobras, mambas and even pythons and puff adders, if they are in a hurry. *Above:* Shield-nose snake, which moves using lateral undulation

Puff adder – *Bitis arietans*

Puff adders are common throughout southern Africa, except in deserts, dense forests or on mountain tops. The puff adder's colour is variable – yellows, oranges, browns and greys – with a regular chevron pattern extending down the back and a yellowish-white underside with scattered dark blotches. There are two dark patches on its head, one on the crown and the other above the snout, separated by a light line between the eyes. On the sides of the head are two oblique bars.

The puff adder is responsible for many snakebite fatalities in Africa because of its sluggishness on the ground, quick striking ability and highly toxic venom. The venom itself is known to be 'cytotoxic' which creates severe swelling and cell destruction or 'necrosis'.

If disturbed, this snake will hiss loudly and adopt a tightly coiled defensive position with the front part of its body held in a tight S-shape. It may strike suddenly and quickly before returning immediately to the defensive position, ready to strike again. During a strike, the force of the impact is so strong and the fangs so long that it is said that prey may be killed by the physical trauma alone.

The puff adder is a live-bearing snake; the eggs are carried within the mother during incubation and the young snakes hatch from the eggs before they emerge from the mother. This adaptation allows viviparous snakes to avoid predation of their eggs before they hatch.

Nile crocodile
Crocodylus niloticus

The Nile crocodile has short legs and a long, scaly, powerful tail. The crocodile's nostrils, eyes and ears are situated on the top of its head, enabling it to see while the rest of the body remains concealed under water.

Habits
- They are most active at night.
- More hunting activity takes place in the summer months; in winter crocodiles are less energetic and may not hunt for extended periods.
- The female lays up to 75 eggs on dry ground close to the water. She will select a nest site in a warm, sunny area and will usually stay close to the nest to deter predators such as water monitors. When the eggs hatch she carries the hatchlings to the water in her mouth, and stays close to them for an extended period.

Feeding and diet
- Nile crocodiles prey on fish, amphibians, birds and mammals; they also scavenge. Diet varies according to size and age of crocodile and the availability of prey in the environment.
- They are capable of using their speed and the power of their large jaws to grab, hold and drown large prey like wildebeest and zebra.

Old crocodile droppings

Droppings
- They defecate both in the water and on land. Fresh dung is light green and turns white as it dries. It is very finely textured, similar to plaster of Paris.
- Unsegmented; 50–120mm long and 30–50mm in diameter; droppings are often flattened by the tail.
- Dried (white) droppings look similar to those of the hyaena but are more finely textured.

Territorial behaviour
- Male crocodiles patrol and defend territories along a stretch of riverbank and body of water. Courtship displays include head-slaps on the water, snapping their jaws and occasionally vocalising (bellowing).

Fresh crocodile droppings, flattened by the body and tail

AMPHIBIANS & REPTILES

Note tail drag mark in this trail

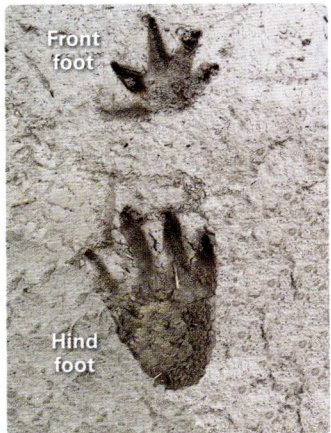

Nile crocodile tracks

About the track
- The crocodile track shows five thick, splayed toes on the front foot – a defining feature of the track – and four toes on the hind foot.
- Adult's front foot (80–100mm) is much shorter than the hind foot (200–250mm); the front foot has no webbing, but the hind foot is webbed.
- The claws are thick and usually make clear imprints in the track; only the three inside toes on both front and hind feet have claws.
- The hind foot has a wide, rounded 'heel', which reveals the scale pattern underneath in clear substrates.
- Research by W.R. Thomson (1964) shows the hind foot length multiplied by 12 gives the mean average overall length of the crocodile.
- Marks of the tail being dragged are common; they occasionally partially obliterate the tracks.
- At a walking gait, the hind foot registers just behind the front foot.
- Crocodile tracks are found close to rivers and dams, although they do also move long distances overland, often along roads or natural game paths.

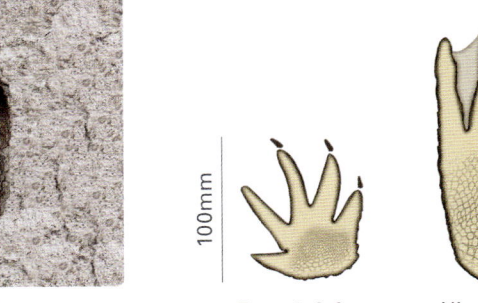

Front left foot   Hind left foot

Can be confused with ...

- A young crocodile track can be confused with that of a **monitor lizard**. However, the monitor has five toes on both front and hind feet, whereas the crocodile has only four toes on the hind foot. Also, unlike the crocodile, the monitor lizard's hind foot outside toe is positioned at a greater angle (70 degrees) from the rest of the toes, and the lizard's toes are longer and narrower. Also, no webbing on hind feet of monitor lizard.

Tortoises
Family Testudinidae

Leopard tortoise

Temporary cover utilised by a tortoise in the Karoo

Tortoise droppings can vary from light brown to black in colour.

Southern Africa is home to 14 tortoise species and two subspecies. All have protective bony shells covered with layers of scutes (scales). Males have a longer tail than females, and a concave-shaped plastron (underside), facilitating mounting the female.

Habits
- Tortoises prefer moderate temperatures, and are most active at 25–30° C. They generally drink water at midday in winter, and in the early morning in summer.
- Mating is very vocal, with loud groans and grunts. The female digs a hole in soft sand and lays five to 20 eggs in the depression.
- Predators such as lion, leopard, hyaena, jackal, ground hornbill and monitor lizards will prey on both tortoise hatchlings and adults.

Droppings
- Tortoise droppings are very coarse and consist of grass, sedges and other plant material, including insect fragments in the case of the hinge-backed tortoise.
- Leopard tortoise droppings measure up to 30–40mm in diameter and 70–90mm in length.

Common southern African tortoise species

Southern Africa is home to 14 tortoise species, of which two of the most common are:

- The **African leopard tortoise** (Stigmochelys pardalis), *which is known for its attractive markings. It prefers semi-arid, thorny environments and savanna grassland. In extreme weather it seeks protection in abandoned jackal and aardvark burrows. The leopard tortoise is herbivorous and grazes mostly on grasses, while also showing a preference for succulent plants.*
- **Speke's hinge-backed tortoise** (Kinixys spekii), *a small, light brown tortoise. It has a hinge on the back of its shell which, when closed, can protect its hind legs and tail from predators. An omnivore, it feeds on twigs, roots, leaves, fruits, millipedes, earthworms, snails, tadpoles and other small invertebrates.*

■ AMPHIBIANS & REPTILES

About the track
- Tracks show five claws on the front foot and four on the hind.
- The scale pattern under their feet occasionally reveals itself, particularly with larger individuals.
- They partially drag their hind feet along the ground as they move, leaving little scuff marks.
- The front foot faces inwards while the hind foot is turned outwards, unlike the track of the terrapin.
- The width of the straddle depends on the size of the tortoise. In soft sand, parallel 'tramlines' are unmistakable.
- The normal walking gait shows the hind foot registering partially on top of the front foot.
- Tortoises will venture into mud to access water, so one should be aware of the differences – and possible confusion – between tortoise and terrapin tracks.
- Leopard tortoises grow very large in certain areas, such as the Eastern Cape Karoo, and can weigh up to 40kg, thereby producing very large footprints.

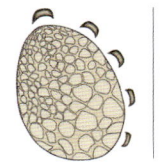
Front left foot

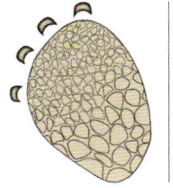
Hind left foot

Tortoise tracks in mud

Leopard tortoise tracks showing scale marks

Leopard tortoise tracks showing feet drag marks in the sand

Can be confused with ...

- The tortoise has five claws on the front foot and four on the hind foot, whereas the **terrapin** has five claws on both the front and hind feet. It's important to count the claw marks carefully to differentiate their tracks.
  A tortoise's front foot faces inwards and the hind foot outwards, which is markedly different from terrapins: the terrapin's front foot claws face in the direction of travel, and on the hind foot, three claws face forwards and two face partially outwards.

Terrapins
Family Pelomedusidae

Marsh terrapin basking in the sun

A total of nine terrapin species belonging to three groups (marsh, hinged and soft-shelled) occur in southern Africa. The marsh (African helmeted) terrapin is the most common. Males are larger than females. This reptile is semi-aquatic, living in rivers, lakes and marshes.

Habits
- The marsh terrapin folds its neck sideways to retract its head under the shell, leaving one eye still visible.
- The marsh terrapin's eyes and nostrils are situated forward on the head, allowing it to breathe and see while the rest of its body remains submerged.
- They have musk glands from which they can emit a foul-smelling fluid to repel predators.
- This terrapin will aestivate in drying mud during periods of drought.

Feeding and diet
- The marsh terrapin is omnivorous, eating almost anything, including insects, crustaceans, fish, earthworms, snails and ticks – off buffalo and rhino that come to wallow in the water.
- Terrapins have been known to capture and drown much larger prey such as doves that come to drink at the water's edge.
- They also eat carrion, gripping and tearing the flesh using their long, sharp claws.

About the track
- The terrapin has five long claws on both front and hind feet – a feature that separates it from the tortoise.
- The terrapin's front feet claws face in the direction of travel. On the hind foot, three claws face forwards and two face partially outwards – another point of difference with the tortoise, particularly if tracks are found in an aquatic environment.
- The front foot claws are arranged in a semicircle or arc.

Typical terrapin tracks

■ AMPHIBIANS & REPTILES

Above and below: Terrapin tracks

- The terrapin does not drag its feet as much as the tortoise does, except in thick mud where it may sink in slightly.
- The feet are slightly webbed, although the webbing cannot be seen in the tracks.
- It is common to see only the claw marks making an impression in mud, and particularly so in the case of very young terrapins.
- Scale marks beneath the feet are seldom seen in terrapin tracks, unlike in those of the tortoise.
- The normal walking gait shows the hind foot registering directly behind the front foot.
- Large numbers of young terrapins' claw marks can be found in mud near water, indicating where they have been active. Check for points of difference to make sure they are not tortoise tracks.

Front left foot

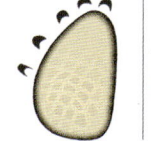

Hind left foot

Can be confused with ...

- The terrapin has five claws on both front and hind feet, whereas the **tortoise** has only four on the hind foot. It's important to count the claw marks carefully to differentiate their tracks.

  A tortoise's front foot faces inwards and the hind foot outwards, whereas the terrapin's front foot claws face in the direction of travel, and on the hind foot, three claws face forwards and two face partially outwards.

  The terrapin drags its feet less than does the tortoise, and its tracks seldom show scale marks, which tortoise tracks tend to do.

AMPHIBIANS & REPTILES ■

Sea turtles
Superfamily Chelonioidea

Baby turtle tracks

Loggerhead (70–100cm) and leatherback (160–180cm, can reach 290cm) turtles are the only two species that breed and lay their eggs in southern African waters. The northeastern coastline of KwaZulu-Natal (Kosi Bay) is the epicentre for turtle breeding.

Habits
- Sea turtles mate in the water near offshore nesting sites.
- The female uses her back flippers to dig a nest in the sand. She lays up to 100 eggs, which incubate in the warm sand for 60 days.
- Newly hatched baby sea turtles emerge from nests and travel from the shore to the water.

Feeding
- The leatherback feeds mostly on jellyfish. The loggerhead is omnivorous and has greater variety in its diet.

About the track
- The turtle drags itself, bit by bit, predominantly using its large front flippers – with the hind ones providing little assistance in locomotion.
- The plastron (underside of the shell) drags along the sand.
- Mounds of sand are pushed up on either edge of the trail by the front flippers.
- From a distance the trail resembles that of a one-wheeled tractor driving along the beach.

Loggerhead sea turtle

Leatherback sea turtle

Loggerhead sea turtle tracks

Leatherback turtle tracks

■ BIRDS

African penguin
Spheniscus demersus

The African penguin is listed as Endangered due to a 70% decline in numbers over the last 30 years, attributed to depleted breeding habitat, predation, oil spills, disease and the impact of commercial fishing on food resources. Monogamous and colonial, it feeds mostly on pelagic fish such as anchovies, pilchards, horse mackerel and herring. The African penguin is a southern African coastal resident.

Track and other signs
- Track measures 85mm in length, with three webbed, forward-facing toes and no hind toe.
- A large, triangular metatarsal pad is a prominent feature of the track.
- All toes have substantial claws, which usually make an impression in the track.
- There is a wide straddle between the left and right feet.
- Droppings take the form of a long squirt of white faeces.

Penguin trails show a wide straddle.

African penguin tracks

African penguin trails on the beach

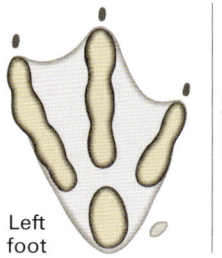

Left foot

85mm

BIRDS

Kelp gull
Larus dominicanus

Kelp gulls form large colonies on islands where monogamous pairs breed. They feed in the open ocean, as well as in lagoons and along the shores, on crustaceans such as mussels, snails, insects and crabs, as well as frogs, fish and cuttlefish. A common resident of the southern African coastline.

Track and other signs
- Track measures 65–70mm in length, with three webbed, forward-facing toes (palmate foot structure).
- Hind toe does not usually make an impression.
- Claw marks are clear.

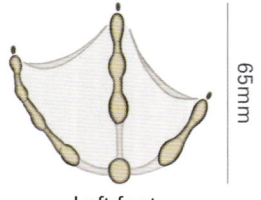
Left foot
65mm

Kelp gull track

African (black) oystercatcher
Haematopus moquini

The African or black oystercatcher feeds primarily on limpets, as well as mussels, worms and aquatic insects. This striking, Near-Threatened resident bird (10,000 individuals at most) is locally common along mixed sand–rock shorelines of southern Africa.

Track and other signs
- Track is 55mm, with three broad, blunt, short, forward-facing toes and no hind toe.
- Claws usually make an impression.
- Toe number 2 is substantially shorter than the outer toe.

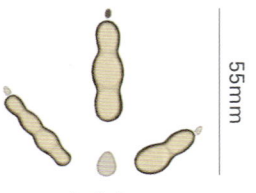
Left foot
55mm

Oystercatcher right foot track; notice the shorter inner toe.

White-breasted cormorant
Phalacrocorax lucidus

This cormorant feeds on fish, crabs and frogs. A mostly fresh-water resident, it is found throughout southern Africa, including along the coastline, but not in the arid regions of the Northern Cape, Namibia and Botswana. It breeds in colonies.

Track and other signs
- Track measures 130mm in length. All four toes are connected by webbing (totipalmate).
- All four toes are prominent in the track, with the outer toe (toe number 4) being the longest.
- It takes short steps and regularly drags its feet.
- This unusual bird track bears a close resemblance to the **larger pelican's** footprint.
- It is assumed that the substantially smaller **reed cormorant's** track is shorter.

Left foot — 130mm

White-breasted cormorant trail down the beach

Track in sand

African spoonbill
Platalea alba

This gregarious and common local resident with a spoon-shaped bill constructs a nest on a stick platform lined with leaves, in reedbeds or trees overhanging water. The spoonbill may make unusual migratory movements in search of adequate water. It prefers shallow aquatic environments, swamps and marshes, where it hunts for small fish and aquatic insects.

Track and other signs
- Track is 150mm long, with one individual spoonbill's track measuring 160mm long by 150mm wide. Track shows three strong, forward-facing toes and an angled hind toe (hallux).
- Claw marks usually make an appearance in the track.
- Feet are slightly webbed, although this does not necessarily show in the track.
- The metatarsal pad does not always make an impression in the track.

The track is similar in shape to that of most storks.

BIRDS

Greater flamingo
Phoenicopterus roseus

The greater flamingo is a locally common resident but highly nomadic, moving in response to localised rains. It prefers shallow saline water bodies such as salt pans, lakes, mudflats and lagoons, and feeds on aquatic insects such as shrimps and fly larvae, as well as algae.

Track and other signs

- Track measures 120mm in length, much larger than that of the **lesser flamingo** (*Phoenicopterus minor*), which is 90mm in length. The middle toe is characteristically long. The hind toe (hallux) rarely makes a clear impression. Webbing is usually evident, typical of a bird with three forward-facing webbed toes (palmate).
- A characteristic sign associated with flamingos is the 'tramway' of feeding tracks as the bird moves along, stomping its feet to flush out aquatic insects.
- It nests communally; nest is a cone-shaped mound of mud on the ground.
- Tracks of hundreds of flamingos are common; they often congregate with their smaller cousin, the **lesser flamingo**.

Greater flamingo and nest

Typical lengthy stride of the flamingo

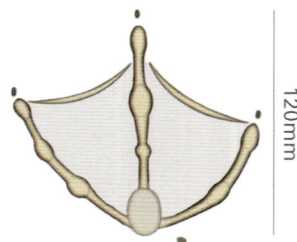

Left foot

120mm

Tracks of several flamingos

BIRDS

Great white pelican
Pelecanus onocrotalus

A locally fairly common resident, the great white pelican is sedentary or nomadic, depending on food resources. It is a monogamous but highly social species. They form large flocks and are excellent gliders. These pelicans prefer shallow estuaries, lakes and pans where they feed in small groups in an effort to corral fish and shrimps. They will kill other birds' chicks and are known to scavenge.

Track and other signs
- The great white pelican's very large track measures 230mm in length.
- All four toes are connected by webbing (totipalmate foot structure).
- It waddles with feet facing inwards slightly (pigeon-toed).
- It nests colonially; nest is a shallow scrape on the ground, lined with grass, twigs and feathers.
- Similar in shape and structure to a **cormorant** track, but is 50mm longer than that of the cormorant.

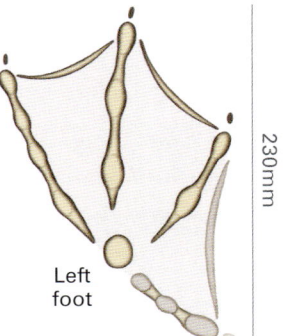

Left foot

230mm

A squadron of great white pelicans

Typical track

Measurement showing 230mm extent of track

293

BIRDS

Black-headed heron
Ardea melanocephala

This large bird is common throughout southern Africa. Unlike the slightly larger grey heron, it hunts less often around water, preferring open dry grassland.

Track and other signs
- Track measures 130mm – smaller than that of the **grey heron**.
- Track shows three forward-facing toes and a hind toe (hallux) that extends straight back from an off-centre position behind the metatarsal pad – diagnostic of a heron track.
- The offset hind toe is also evident in other herons.

Black-headed heron track

Green-backed heron
Butorides striata

Also known as the striated heron, this small heron inhabits well-wooded wetlands such as rivers, dams and pans. It hunts along the water's edge, moving with a crouched posture.

Track and other signs
- Track measures 70–75mm in length; usually found on muddy banks along rivers and dams.
- Slight webbing between the toes may show in perfect substrate.
- The offset hind toe is characteristic of the heron family.
- This heron treads remarkably lightly so that its tracks are not always clearly defined.

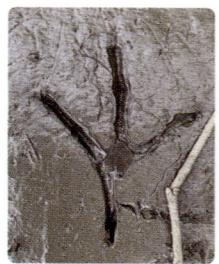

Far left and left: Green-backed heron tracks

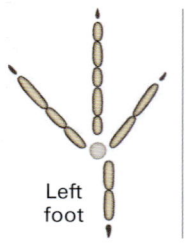

Left foot

75mm

Grey heron
Ardea cinerea

These grey-and-white waterbirds stand up to 1m tall. They build a nest of sticks and reeds in heronries, situated in trees close to water or reedbeds.

Track and other signs
- Track measures 150–160mm in length. It shows three forward-facing toes and a hind toe that extends straight back from an off-centre position behind the metatarsal pad – also evident in other herons.
- Grey heron tracks are usually found close to watercourses and small pans.

Grey heron track in mud

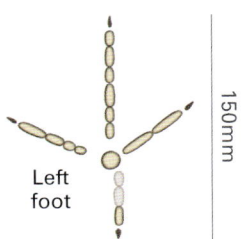

Left foot — 150mm

Goliath heron
Ardea goliath

This, the world's largest heron, is three times the weight of the grey heron. An uncommon resident, it prefers rivers, lakes and dams where it often hunts in relatively deep water, feeding on large fish, frogs and reptiles.

Goliath heron track in sand

Track and other signs
- These very large tracks measure 220mm in length and 190mm wide.
- Track shows three forward-facing toes and a hind toe (hallux) that extends straight back from an off-centre position behind the metatarsal pad.
- Tracks are usually found along riverbanks and around dams.

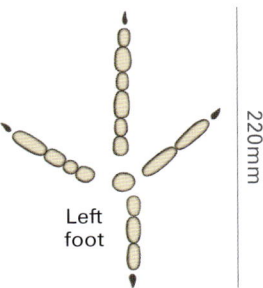

Left foot — 220mm

BIRDS

Western cattle egret
Bubulcus ibis

This smallest member of the egret family found in southern Africa is common throughout the region. It prefers open grassland and farmlands, as well as coastal open areas.

Western cattle egret tracks

Track and other signs
- Track measures 110mm in length. It shows three slender, forward-facing toes and a hind toe that extends straight back from an offset position.
- The toes are slender compared to those of similar-sized **herons**.
- Claw marks are usually evident in the track.
- The metatarsal pad does not show in the track; in soft substrate, the inside toe and hind toe form one continuous feature, as in the **little egret** track.
- As these birds typically feed in small groups, one may see tracks of several individuals together.

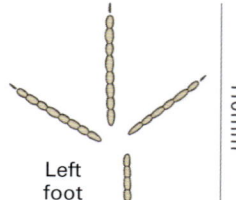

Left foot — 110mm

Little egret
Egretta garzetta

Joe Grosel

This pure white egret inhabits areas with permanent shallow water such as dams, lakes, estuaries and along the coast, where it hunts fish as well as aquatic insects.

Little egret track

Track and other signs
- Track measures 118mm in length. It shows three forward-facing toes and a hind toe that extends straight back from an offset position. The track of the **great egret** (*Ardea alba*) is 170mm long.
- Toes are slender compared to those of similar-sized **herons**.
- Claw marks are usually clearly evident.
- The metatarsal pad does not show in the track; in soft substrate, the inside toe extends through to the hind toe as one continuous feature.
- Typically feeds alone, but large groups gather at rich food sources.

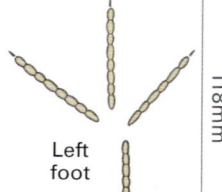

Left foot — 118mm

BIRDS

White stork
Ciconia ciconia

These large migratory birds are highly gregarious, with extensive flocks circling at great heights. They frequent large open grasslands, including agricultural lands and areas that were recently burnt.

White stork track

Track and other signs
- Track measures 140mm long and 130mm wide, slightly larger than that of the **woolly-necked stork**. It shows three sturdy forward-facing toes and one angled hind toe (hallux).
- Many sets of tracks can be found when storks congregate.

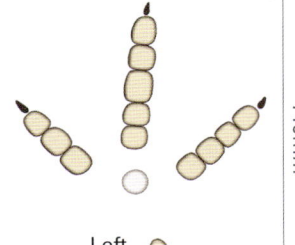

Left foot

140mm

Black stork
Ciconia nigra

This widespread but uncommon stork is a wader and active near rivers, vleis and pans. Its diet includes frogs, fish, snails and aquatic insects.

Track and other signs
- Typical stork track measures 150mm long and 125mm wide.
- Track shows three long, forward-facing toes and a short hind toe (hallux) situated at a slight angle.
- Tracks are often found around pools of water in dry riverbeds.

Black stork track

BIRDS

Saddle-billed stork
Ephippiorhynchus senegalensis

These huge water birds are found at the edges of dams, pans and rivers. They are usually seen in pairs.

Track and other signs
- This is the second largest of all the stork tracks, 180mm in length.
- Track shows three long, forward-facing toes with claws, and one short, angled hind toe (hallux).
- The metatarsal pad does not always make an impression.
- Tracks are found along riverbanks or around pans and dams.

Notice the stride length.

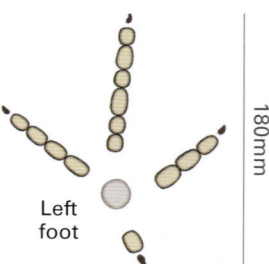

Left: Saddle-billed stork track

Left foot — 180mm

Marabou stork
Leptoptilos crumeniferus

This enormous scavenging bird's wingspan can reach 3m. It is found in the northern and eastern regions, more commonly in protected wildlife reserves and anywhere carrion is available. It prefers semi-arid habitats.

Track and other signs
- This is the largest of all stork tracks; 210–230mm at Londolozi. Track is much larger than that of the **saddle-billed stork**.
- Track shows three long, thick, forward-facing toes with claws. The thick hind toe (hallux) and its claw sit at an angle, but often appear to extend straight back.
- The metatarsal pad usually makes an impression.
- Occasionally, evidence of slight webbing between the toes is visible.

Metatarsal pad

The metatarsal pad is noticeable.

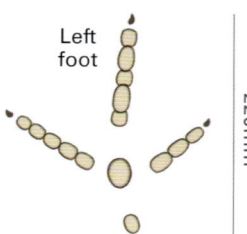

Left foot — 220mm

BIRDS

Woolly-necked stork
Ciconia episcopus

Woolly-necked stork track

One of the smallest of the stork species in southern Africa, common around dams and pans in the southern Kruger National Park during the summer months. It usually moves around singly, constantly probing for food.

Track and other signs
- Track is 120–130mm long and 100–110mm wide, with three long, forward-facing toes with claws.
- Metatarsal pad is usually evident in the track.

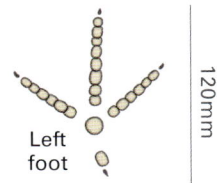

Left foot / 120mm

Pied avocet
Recurvirostra avosetta

The pied avocet is a locally common resident. This monogamous bird nests on exposed mud in a rudimentary scrape close to the water. It prefers shallow inland saline water bodies, floodplains, marshes and temporary wetlands, and feeds on crustaceans, insect larvae and small fish.

This pied avocet track clearly shows the partial webbing.

Track and other signs
- Track length measures 45mm. It shows three forward-facing toes and no hind toe.
- Avocet feet have partial webbing between the toes (semipalmate) – a feature which seldom makes an impression.
- The avocet uses its curved beak to find food in the mud using an action called beak scything. Tracks may be associated with arc shapes in the substrate.

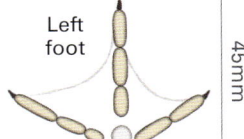

Left foot / 45mm

Pied avocet track in the Karoo

BIRDS

African sacred ibis
Threskiornis aethiopicus

This bird is found all over southern Africa. It occurs in marshy wetlands and mud flats, both inland and on the coast.

Track and other signs
- Track is 130mm in length. It shows three forward-facing toes and one angled hind toe.
- Tracks may be associated with holes in the mud made by the beak probing as it searches for food.
- Tracks are regularly found on the edges of wetlands and along the coastline.

Sacred ibis track in sand

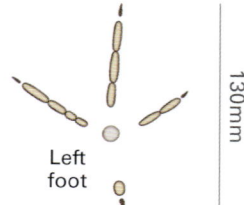

Left foot

130mm

Hadeda ibis
Bostrychia hagedash

This glossy bird feeds on the ground, probing for insects, worms, frogs and spiders. A common urban resident, it prefers open grassland, muddy flats, agricultural pasture and suburban lawns.

Track and other signs
- Track is 120–130mm in length, with three forward-facing toes and one hind toe, which is at a slight angle behind the metatarsal pad.
- **Hamerkop** tracks are 20mm shorter, show slight webbing, and the hind toe extends backwards at less of an angle.
- Tracks are found on the edges of muddy pans. They may be associated with feet drag marks and holes in the mud made by the beak probing for food.

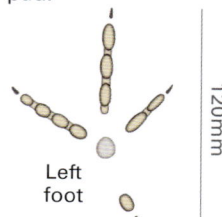

Left foot

120mm

Clear hadeda tracks in mud

BIRDS

White-faced whistling duck
Dendrocygna viduata

White-faced whistling duck tracks

This highly gregarious species gathers in flocks to rest on banks of pans and floodplains in the northeastern parts of the region. A nomadic yet common resident.

Track and other signs
- This webbed track measures 65–75mm (if the hind toe is present).
- Occasionally one may see evidence of the hind toe in wet mud.
- Several tracks may be found together.
- Tracks are usually found around small water holes, pans and dams.

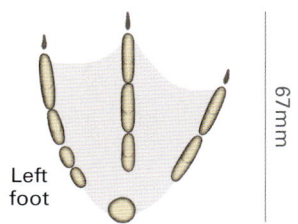

Left foot — 67mm

Yellow-billed duck
Anas undulata

This duck prefers freshwater habitats and large open lakes and dams. It is a common resident throughout southern Africa.

Track and other signs
- Track measures 65mm, which is shorter than that of the **Egyptian goose**. Track shows typically webbed feet, although this is not always obvious in the track.
- Outer toes characteristically slightly inward curved.
- The hind toe (hallux) seldom makes an impression in the track.
- Tracks of pairs of yellow-billed ducks are commonly found during mating season in summer.
- This duck performs the greatest variety of courtship displays of any African duck – probably due to its drab appearance.

Yellow-billed duck tracks

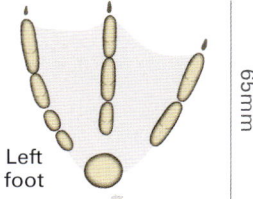

Left foot — 65mm

BIRDS

Spur-winged goose
Plectropterus gambensis

Africa's largest waterfowl, these geese have long legs for wading and long necks for feeding underwater. They occur around pans, dams and floodplains.

Track and other signs

- Track measures 140mm in length, significantly larger than that of the **Egyptian goose**. Female tracks appear smaller (140–145mm) and male tracks are 175mm including the hind toe (hallux). The hind toe is seldom seen, but its claw is sometimes evident in mud.
- This goose has typically webbed feet, which cannot always be seen in the track. In mud, evidence of webbing may be seen on the leading edge of the track.
- Outer toes of its webbed feet are characteristically slightly inward curved.
- The front toes have claws, usually present in the track.

Spurwing on nest

Male spurwing

Female spurwing

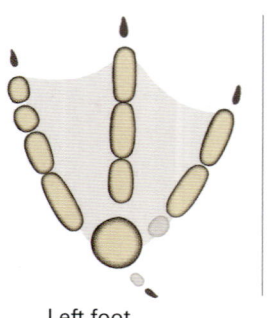
Left foot

140mm

Near-perfect track of spur-winged goose

Spur-winged goose track in dry sand; notice webbing.

■ BIRDS

Egyptian goose
Alopochen aegyptiaca

A member of the ducks and geese family, this herbivore is particularly partial to foraging in agricultural lands.

Track and other signs
- Tracks are 110mm in length and show webbing, which includes the hind toe (hallux). The total length is closer to 90mm without the hind toe, which is seldom seen (the claw may show in mud). The front toes have claws that are usually evident.
- Outer toes are characteristically slightly inward curved.
- Tracks are commonly found around floodplains, dams and pans where water is not flowing strongly.

Egyptian goose track; notice subtle evidence of hind toe (hallux) claw.

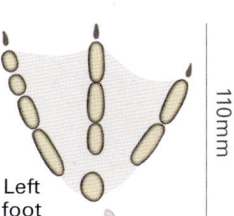

Left foot

110mm

Red-knobbed coot
Fulica cristata

Coot on its floating nest

The red-knobbed coot is a distinctive waterbird found in southern Africa. It has a black body, white bill, and bright red knobs on its forehead. Known for its aggressive territorial behaviour, this coot vigorously defends its nesting area from intruders by engaging in aggressive displays and vocalisations. It builds a floating nest made of vegetation.

Track and other signs
- Track length is 150mm. It has noticeable bulges along the toe length. It features lobed toes with broad, flat, paddle-like structures (lobate).
- The track should reveal a hind toe (hallux).
- Track is similar-looking to that of **grebes**, but larger.

Foot has lobate characteristics.

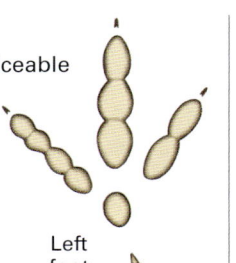

Left foot

150mm

BIRDS

Grebes
Podiceps and *Tachybaptus*

Great crested grebe

Little grebe

Little grebe nest

A little grebe's lobate foot

There are three species of grebe in southern Africa. All three are excellent divers, capable of staying submerged for extended periods to catch prey. The great crested is known for its elaborate courtship displays and diving abilities. The black-necked displays a striking black neck during the breeding season and prefers freshwater habitats. The little grebe (or dabchick) is the smallest and has a rusty-coloured neck and golden eye.

Grebes can be found in mostly freshwater habitats. They feed on small fish and aquatic insects.

Track and other signs

- Grebes predominantly inhabit aquatic environments. As a result, physical footprints are rarely encountered. Consequently, precise measurements of their track sizes are not readily accessible.
- A grebe's foot is uniquely adapted to its semi-aquatic lifestyle. Feet are partially lobed (lobate), with each toe ending in a broad, flat, paddle-like structure (unlike duck feet, which are typically webbed or palmate). The webbing on a grebe foot extends along the toes, aiding in swimming and diving, and giving efficient propulsion and stability in the water.
- It is unclear whether the short hind toe (hallux) makes any impression.
- Floating nests are built from small sticks and vegetation.

Black-necked grebe nest

Great crested grebe nest

BIRDS

Black crake
Amaurornis flavirostra

This common waterbird feeds on crustaceans, tadpoles, small frogs, worms, small fish and aquatic plants, as well as on ectoparasites on the backs of hippos. It inhabits mostly perennial wetlands with moderate vegetation cover.

Black crake tracks, underwater

Track and other signs
- Track measures 70–75mm, which is much smaller than that of the **African jacana**.
- Track shows three long, thin, forward-facing toes and an angled hind toe. Claw marks are usually evident.
- Tracks can be found in shallow water and on muddy banks adjacent to water.

Black crake tracks in mud

African jacana
Actophilornis africanus

The jacana's very long toes and claws enable it to walk on floating vegetation on quiet waters and pans with floating aquatic plants, where it catches insects such as dragonfly nymphs.

African jacana track in mud, underwater

Track and other signs
- Track is surprisingly large – much larger than the **black crake's** – with long, slender toes and sharp claws; it measures 150–160mm in length.
- Track shows three forward-facing toes and one long hind toe.
- Tracks can be found at water edges as well as in the shallows.

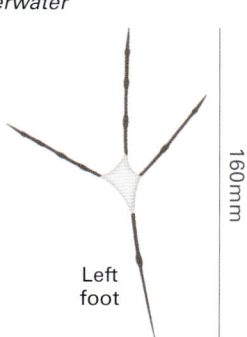

Left foot

Blacksmith lapwing (plover)
Vanellus armatus

Pairs or family groups of these ground birds inhabit grasslands close to fresh water, where they feed on invertebrates.

Track and other signs
- Track is 35mm long and 40mm wide, with three slender, forward-facing toes. Webbing between toes number 3 and 4 may make an impression.
- Characteristic is the wide angle at which the outside toes are situated in relation to the middle toe.
- The **crowned lapwing's** tracks are shorter (32mm) and its outside toes are not as widely set as the blacksmith's. The **African wattled lapwing's** tracks are longer and wider.
- Tracks are found around the edges of water holes and on grass verges near water.

Blacksmith lapwing tracks in wet mud

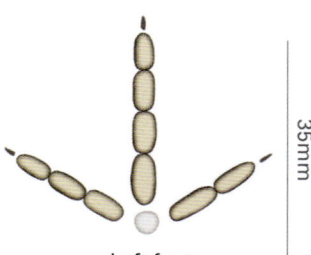

Left foot — 35mm

Crowned lapwing (plover)
Vanellus coronatus

This ground bird eats insects and larvae. It prefers short, dry grassland. Large flocks arrive when good rainfall occurs.

Track and other signs
- Track is 32mm long and 25mm wide, with three forward-facing toes; claws make slight impressions.
- Can be confused with track of the **blacksmith lapwing**, which is 35mm long, with the outside toes wider of the middle toe.
- Also similar to the smaller **Senegal lapwing's** track, which is 28mm long; one bird's stride length measured 150mm – significantly longer than the Senegal lapwing's.
- The track is similar in length to that of the **bronze-winged courser**.

Crowned lapwing track

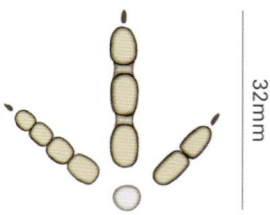

Left foot — 32mm

■ BIRDS

African wattled lapwing
Vanellus senegallus

African wattled lapwing track

Preferring open areas, damp floodplains and agricultural lands, this bird feeds on beetles, grasshoppers, termites and grass seeds. A relatively common resident throughout northeastern South Africa and Zimbabwe.

Track and other signs

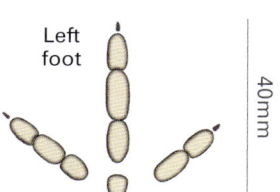

Left foot — 40mm

- Track measures 40mm long and wide, which is slightly longer and wider than that of the **blacksmith lapwing**.
- Track shows three relatively splayed, forward-facing toes. The hind toe (hallux) is situated high up on the back of the leg, and has not been seen to make an impression on the ground.

Senegal lapwing
Vanellus lugubris

Senegal lapwing track

This intra-African migrant is a ground bird, preferring short, grazed grass and burnt veld in particular, where it forages for insects and grass seeds. It is found in the extreme eastern areas of southern Africa.

Track and other signs

- Track measures 28mm long and 30mm wide, and shows three forward-facing toes, the outer two of which are almost symmetrically arranged. Claw marks are not easily visible.
- Stride lengths of 80mm can help separate this from other similar-sized ground birds.
- Tracks are slightly smaller (by 4mm) than those of the **crowned lapwing**.
- These gregarious birds live in groups of two to eight; they usually leave multiple tracks.

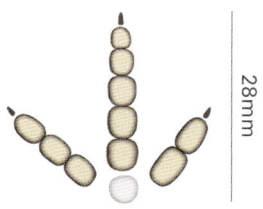

Left foot — 28mm

BIRDS

Bronze-winged (and double-banded) courser
Rhinoptilus chalcopterus and *R. africanus*

These nocturnal and crepuscular birds are the largest of the 'plover-like' coursers. Found in the extreme north and east of the region, they prefer open, broad-leaved woodlands and thornveld.

Track and other signs
- Track measures 32mm long and 22mm wide, similar in length to the **crowned lapwing**, but the inside toe is shorter and closer to the middle toe, making it relatively asymmetrical. One individual double-banded courser track measured 35mm in length.
- When viewed up close, the track's sharp little claws are visible, situated close to the toes.
- The stride length of one **bronze-winged** was measured at 190mm.
- Tracks are often found on roads and in clearings.

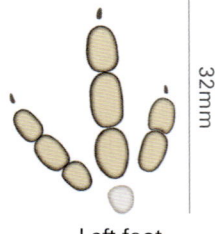

Left foot

Top right: Track sequence. **Right:** The inside toe is shorter and closer to the middle toe.

Black-winged stilt
Himantopus himantopus

This locally nomadic wader is usually seen in pairs or groups. It is a common resident in most of southern Africa, preferring pans, dams and slow-flowing rivers, where it may be seen striding about, picking insects off the surface.

Track and other signs
- Track measures 38mm. It may show webbing between the middle and outside toes.
- This non-passerine's outside toes are set quite wide of the middle toe.
- Track is very similar to that of the **blacksmith lapwing**, but the stilt's stride length is probably longer than that of the lapwing.

Black-winged stilt track

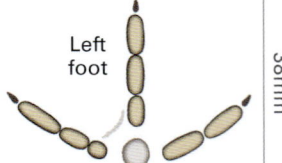

Left foot

■ BIRDS

Three-banded plover
Charadrius tricollaris

This plover, although terrestrial, feeds on aquatic insects and their larvae. It is monogamous and makes nests on the ground, close to water.

A common wading resident, the three-banded plover prefers freshwater lakes, dams and pans throughout southern Africa, with the exception of southwestern Botswana.

Tracks; notice the slightly inward-facing feet.

Track and other signs
- This tiny track is 23mm in length and 20mm wide, with slender toes. No hind toe (hallux) is present.
- The outside toe (toe number 4) is marginally longer than toe number 2. Toe number 4 also sits closer to the middle toe, giving this track an asymmetrical appearance.
- Residual webbing between toes number 2 and 3 may be seen in soft, perfect substrate.
- The bird walks pigeon-toed, with its feet facing inwards.
- It leaves little probe marks from its beak feeding in the mud.

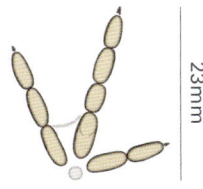

Left foot

White-fronted plover
Charadrius marginatus

This little shorebird is a common resident of the southern African coastline. It feeds on insects and worms, and inhabits sandy beaches, dunes, mudflats and the shores of rivers and lakes in much of sub-Saharan Africa.

Track and other signs
- Track measures 22mm in length. It has three forward-facing toes and no hind toe (hallux).
- It strides about beaches, with each stride measuring 50–70mm in length.
- The metatarsal pad is not commonly seen in the track.

A trail of tracks on the beach

White-fronted plover tracks

BIRDS

Spotted thick-knee (dikkop)
Burhinus capensis

This nocturnal bird inhabits open savanna grassland and semi-desert, including stony hills, and disturbed habitats. It forages on the ground, mainly for insects.

Track and other signs
- Track measures 42–45mm long and 25mm wide, with three sturdy, forward-facing toes and no hind toe (hallux).
- The canoe-shaped toes are grouped more tightly than those of the **water thick-knee**. Claw marks are usually evident.
- The spotted thick-knee's metatarsal pad is not always clearly visible in the track.

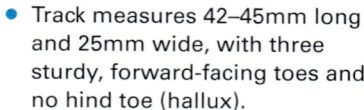

Spotted thick-knee tracks in the Karoo

Water thick-knee (dikkop)
Burhinus vermiculatus

This common ground bird is crepuscular and nocturnal. It prefers areas near freshwater wetlands, rivers and dams. Hunts for crabs, frogs and aquatic insects, and often leaves behind discarded fragments from its meals.

Track and other signs
- Track measures 42mm, with three forward-facing toes and no hind toe (hallux).
- Toes are more splayed than those of the spotted thick-knee – to a width of 35mm.
- The metatarsal pad may show as a dot, but isn't always clearly visible.
- Evidence of webbing may be visible between the middle and outside toes.

Water thick-knee track

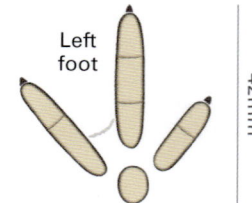

■ BIRDS

Kori bustard
Ardeotis kori

The world's heaviest flying bird, although it is essentially a ground bird. An omnivore, its diet includes large insects, small rodents, reptiles, seeds and bulbs. It prefers dry, open grassland and is common in the Karoo.

Kori bustard track

Track and other signs
- Track length is 90–110mm, with a stride length from 100–180mm.
- Track shows three thick, forward-facing toes with substantial claw marks.
- The oval-shaped metatarsal pad is large and characteristic.
- The middle toe shows two distinctive segments; the outer toes are unsegmented.
- The kori bustard track is 10–20mm longer than that of the **Ludwig's bustard**; it can also be mistaken for that of the **secretarybird**.

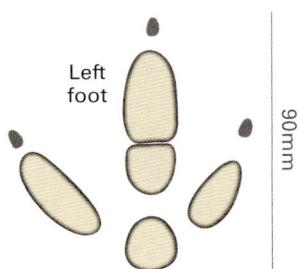

Left foot / 90mm

Ludwig's bustard
Neotis ludwigii

This large bird of the plains strides about singly or in larger groups. It avoids detection by freezing and remaining motionless. A common resident of the semi-desert Karoo, it feeds on berries, lucerne, locusts, crickets and caterpillars.

Ludwig's bustard track

Track and other signs
- Track measures 70–75mm, which is smaller than that of the **kori bustard**.
- The metatarsal pad is rounder and shorter than that of the kori bustard.
- Claws do not always make a clear impression.

BIRDS

Black-bellied bustard
Lissotis melanogaster

Also known as the black-bellied korhaan, this ground bird's preferred habitats include broad-leaved woodland and tall open grassland.

Notice the slight drag mark created by the black-bellied bustard's middle toe.

Track and other signs
- Track measures 50mm and shows three forward-facing toes.
- The middle toe has three segments that are not always clearly visible.
- A large metatarsal pad is prominent.
- These birds regularly drag their feet ever so slightly.
- Although similar in shape, the track is 10mm longer than that of the **red-crested korhaan**.

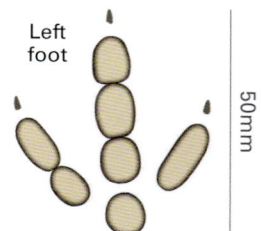

Southern black korhaan
Afrotis afra

Male korhaans utter their raucous calls from an open patch or mound, particularly in the breeding season. These solitary ground birds may be found in grassland, open thorny savanna or semi-desert habitats.

Track and other signs
- Track measures 50mm in length and shows three forward-facing toes.
- Claw marks are evident in the track.
- Differences between the tracks of southern and **northern korhaans** are unknown; the two species are very similar in most respects.

Southern black korhaan track

Red-crested korhaan
Lophotis ruficrista

Males of this small, solitary korhaan species display by flying straight up into the air, folding their wings, and then tumbling to the ground before gliding to land. They feed on insects and seeds found in dry woodland savanna.

Red-crested korhaan tracks

Track and other signs
- Track is 42mm in length and shows three forward-facing toes. The middle toe has three segments.
- All the korhaan species tend to drag their feet slightly.
- The **spotted thick-knee** track is similar, but the korhaan's toes, particularly the middle toe, are broader (and more bulging), and the impression made by the metatarsal pad is larger.
- The **black-bellied korhaan** track is 10mm longer.

Red-crested korhaan track

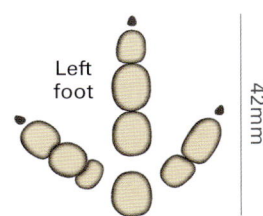

Blue crane
Anthropoides paradiseus

South Africa's national bird, the blue crane eats mainly grasses and sedges but also takes insects, frogs, lizards and snakes. It inhabits open grassland, the Karoo and wetland habitats.

A rare showing of a blue crane's hind claw

Track and other signs
- Track is 100–115mm in length, with wide-set thick toes and claw marks that usually show clearly.
- Seldom do the hind toe (hallux) and its claw make an impression as they sit relatively high up on the leg.
- Similar, but slightly larger, is the track of the Critically Endangered **wattled crane**, measuring 160mm in length.
- The blue crane track can be found in grassland habitats, where this large bird occurs either in pairs or in large flocks.

Blue crane track

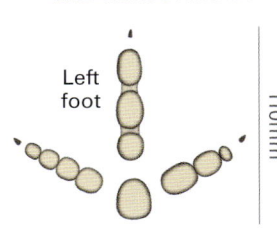

Francolins and spurfowls
Family Phasianidae

Natal spurfowl

Known as game birds, these birds regularly take dust baths in dry sand or soil, and mostly move about in small groups of four or five. They nest on the ground but roost in trees. Found in a variety of habitats that offer both cover and open grassy patches, these birds feed on insects, grass seeds and other vegetable material. They have loud territorial calls, and will alarm at their many predators, such as eagles, snakes, mongooses and leopards.

Track and other signs
- Track lengths vary: the **Swainson's spurfowl** track is 70mm long; the **Natal spurfowl** track measures 65mm (see track illustration and photograph); the **coqui francolin** track is 42mm; and the **crested francolin** is 55mm in length.
- Francolins and spurfowls have three forward-facing toes and a hind toe (hallux) situated at an angle behind the foot.
- Males have a single metatarsal spur situated high on the leg, above the hind toe; it does not make an impression in the track.
- Francolin and spurfowl droppings can be grey to dark green and cylindrical, or black and shapeless.

Crested francolin

Swainson's spurfowl

Natal spurfowl track

Crested francolin tracks

Francolin dropping

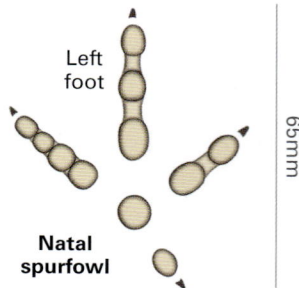
Natal spurfowl

■ BIRDS

Quails
Family Phasianidae

There are three species in southern Africa, the common, harlequin and blue quail. Omnivorous, they feed mainly on insects, snails and worms, also seeds, green shoots and leaves. These small ground birds prefer habitat with thick ground cover in grasslands, floodplains and open savanna. They migrate southwards in the rainy season.

Track and other signs
- Track measures 30mm in length, with three forward-facing toes and a hind toe (hallux).
- The hind toe makes a prominent impression.
- Quails take small steps; their trails are similar to a **dove's**, but smaller.

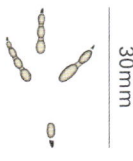

Left foot | 30mm

Common quail trail in the Kalahari

Common (kurrichane) buttonquail
Turnix sylvaticus

These small solitary ground birds are omnivorous, feeding on insects, seeds, green shoots and leaves. They prefer open savanna woodland habitats and scrub bush with reasonable ground cover. Trackers have not yet established if there is a clear pattern of regular seasonal movement in southern Africa, but it is a known summer visitor to Kruger National Park, and a resident in Hluhluwe–Umfolozi in KwaZulu-Natal.

Buttonquail foot

Track and other signs
- Track measures 22mm in length, with three forward-facing toes and no hind toe (hallux). (**Buttonquails** do not have a hind toe.)
- The buttonquail walks pigeon-toed, with the feet facing inwards.
- It takes small steps, creating trails similar to a **dove's**, but smaller and without a hind toe.
- Also similar to **double-banded sandgrouse** tracks, but the sandgrouse's metatarsal pad is much larger and the toes are thicker.

Buttonquail tracks

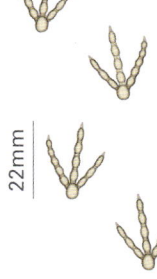

315

BIRDS

Crested guineafowl
Guttera pucherani

This bird produces a noisy 'clucking' call, particularly when threatened. It feeds on seeds, fruits, shoots and insects.

A common resident, it inhabits the extreme eastern and northeastern regions, preferring riparian thickets, dense woodlands and coastal and sand forests.

Crested guineafowl track

Track and other signs
- Tracks measured in northern KwaZulu-Natal are 85–90mm in length, slightly smaller than those of the **helmeted guineafowl**.
- Track shows three forward-facing toes and a hind toe (hallux) situated at an angle.
- The crested's outside toes may be slightly wider apart than those of its helmeted cousin.

Helmeted guineafowl
Numida meleagris

Occurs in large flocks during winter, roosting in trees and nesting on the ground in thickets. It forages terrestrially, moving slowly as it scratches for food. It produces a high-pitched alarm call when predators are detected. Its wide habitat tolerance includes woodland, grassland, agricultural lands and thornveld.

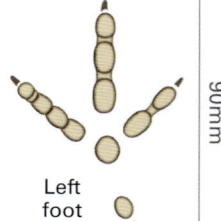

Left foot

90mm

Track and other signs
- Tracks are large, 90–95mm in length, but closer to 70mm without the hind toe (hallux) showing.
- The hind toe sits at an oblique angle, making it difficult to see in some substrates.
- Long claws for scratching and digging are usually evident in the tracks.
- Tracks can be confused with those of the larger **hadeda ibis**, but are 30mm shorter.
- Flocks of these birds give rise to multiple tracks.

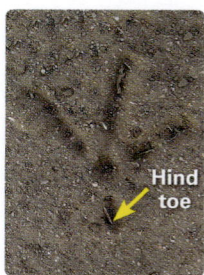

The hind toe may be difficult to see in certain substrates.

Left: Helmeted guineafowl track sequence; notice the slight drag marks of its feet.

■ BIRDS

Common ostrich
Struthio camelus

This is the largest bird on Earth, reaching 2m in height. Ostriches prefer grassy plains and semi-desert areas and are found in pairs or groups sometimes comprising hundreds of individuals. They lay 10–20 eggs in a 'scrape' in the sand. Ostriches eat herbs, grasses, seeds, flowers, succulents and *Senegalia* and *Vachellia* pods.

Track and other signs
- An adult's track is 164–185mm in length. It is a distinctive, two-toed (didactyl) track, showing a large inside toe with claw, and a smaller outer toe.
- Evidence of dust bathing can be seen in open patches of soil, sometimes with feathers.
- Nest sites can be up to 3m in diameter, round, with a slightly raised rim. Given that they are communal birds, more than one female may make use of a single nest.
- Droppings are large and contain both solid and liquid components, showing splattered white uric acid.

Ostrich droppings contain both solid and liquid components; however, in this particular example the liquid has dried.

Ostrich track, right foot

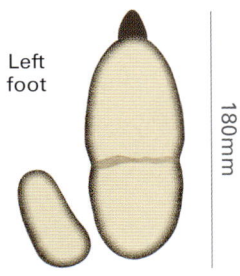

Left foot

180mm

Ostrich nest

317

Secretarybird
Sagittarius serpentarius

In effect terrestrial eagles, these large raptors make a guttural croaking while doing aerial displays. They are monogamous; pairs stride through open grassy habitats, scanning the ground for prey – anything they can overpower using their feet, including snakes, rodents, insects and small mammals.

They build a large, shallow nest, usually on a low, flat-topped acacia (*Senegalia*) tree.

Track and other signs
- Track measures 130mm in length, with hind toe.
- It typically shows three strong, forward-facing toes; the hind toe is seldom clearly visible, but occasionally leaves an impression of the claw in soft substrate or when the bird is running.
- The inside toe shows two segments (or lobes); the outside toe shows three.
- Claw marks are usually evident.
- Without the hind toe, the impression resembles that of a ground bird, such as a **kori bustard**.
- Like **owls**, secretarybirds regurgitate pellets, which measure 50–80mm in length and 25mm in width. An accumulation of pellets can be found under their nests.

Above: A typically large and shallow secretarybird nest, built in an acacia tree

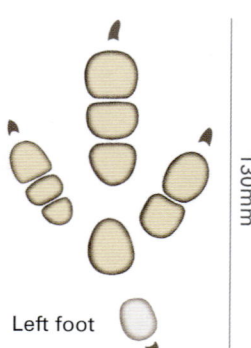

Far left: Secretarybird left foot track. **Left:** Track showing claw

BIRDS

Vultures
Family Accipitridae

White-backed vultures

Vultures defecate on the ground and in trees.

Most vultures are ungainly on the ground, yet their broad wings enable them to soar high in thermal currents. They may cover up to 150km a day in search of food; acute vision enables them to locate carcasses kilometres below. They reuse their large nests of sticks in the tops of trees or on cliff ledges year after year. Found throughout southern Africa, but more commonly seen in or near protected areas, preferring savanna woodland and bushveld.

Track and other signs
- Track lengths vary: the largest is the **Cape vulture's** at 220mm; the **lappet-faced vulture's** is 200mm; the **white-backed vulture's** is 190mm; and the smaller **hooded vulture's** is 180mm.
- Tracks are typically curved, with strong, segmented toes showing claw marks.
- Tracks can be found near a freshly killed carcass or near water, where the vultures bathe after feeding.
- During frenetic feeding, vultures shed feathers. They defecate on the ground and in trees surrounding the carcass.
- **White-backed vultures** regurgitate hair-filled pellets, which can be found below their nests.

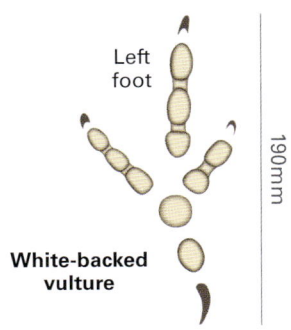

Left foot

190mm

White-backed vulture

Hooded vulture track in mud

White-backed vulture track

BIRDS

Eagles
Family Accipitridae

African fish eagle

Among the most spectacular birds of prey, eagles are categorised into smaller groups such as fish eagles, snake eagles and true eagles – not all related. Southern Africa is home to 26 species of eagle, some of which are migratory, arriving in early summer.

Track and other signs
- Track lengths vary: the track illustration shows a **crowned eagle** track, 250mm (from the tip of the middle toe's talon to the talon on the hind toe). The **martial eagle** track measures 270mm in length, the **African fish eagle's** track 190mm, the **tawny eagle's** track 175mm, the **bateleur** 130mm and the **African hawk eagle** 120mm.
- All eagle species have strong, muscular, well-segmented, bulging toes, with significantly large talons that indicate their exceptional muscular strength.
- In most cases, the track is relatively straight, especially the middle toe (toe number 3).
- Eagle tracks are unlike those of **vultures**, which are curved, have shorter claws, and have the outside toes set closer to the middle toe than, for instance, the fish eagle.

Eagle track

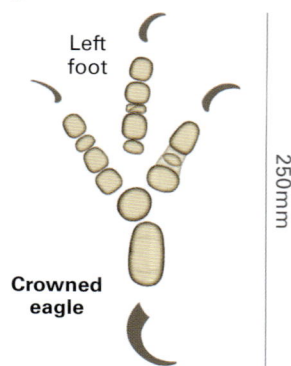

African fish eagle track

■ BIRDS

Hamerkop
Scopus umbretta

This common resident throughout southern Africa prefers the edges of dams, rivers, pools and vleis, where it targets aquatic prey. These birds make a huge nest that is sometimes also used by other animals.

Track and other signs
- Tracks are 80mm in length and show three forward-facing toes and a hind toe (hallux).
- There is characteristic evidence of partial webbing between the toes (semipalmate).
- Tracks can be confused with those of the **hadeda**, which are 30mm larger. The hadeda hind toe is at a greater angle than that of the hamerkop.

Hamerkop track

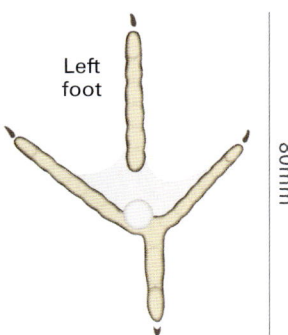

An impressive domed hamerkop nest

Notice that the webbing is not apparent in these tracks on beach sand.

BIRDS

Double-banded sandgrouse
Pterocles bicinctus

These pigeon-sized birds are found mainly in pairs and small groups, often at water holes, where they drink at dawn and dusk. They prefer short trampled grass, and feed mainly on seeds. Found in the northeast of the region, they frequent open savanna woodland.

Track and other signs
- Track is 30mm in length and shows three relatively broad, forward-facing toes. The hind toe (hallux) will make an impression in soft substrate.
- The broad, triangular-shaped metatarsal pad usually shows clearly in the track.
- The sandgrouse shuffles along using short strides, so that the tracks register partially on top of each other, and can cause confusion with the **dove** species.
- Tracks are usually found on roads where these birds move, usually in pairs.

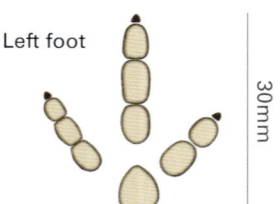

Left foot — 30mm

Above and right: Double-banded sandgrouse tracks

■ BIRDS

Doves
Family Columbidae

Cape turtle dove

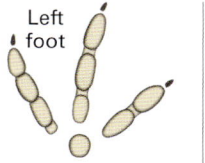
Left foot

Cape turtle

Doves represent a diverse group of birds in southern Africa, with around 10 distinct species. They share common traits such as a dependence on surface water, a daily need for drinking, and foraging habits in open areas for seeds, fruits and insects. Known for their distinctive calls, which can vary among species. They exhibit adaptability to various habitats, including woodlands, semi-desert scrublands, alien tree plantations and urban parks.

Track and other signs

- Track lengths vary for different dove species: the **red-eyed dove** track is 60mm long; the **African mourning dove's** is 55mm; **Cape turtle dove** track 45mm; **emerald-spotted** and **laughing dove** tracks are 40mm; **Namaqua dove's** 30mm.
- The middle toe curves inwards, making a pigeon-toed gait, common to all doves.
- Doves typically shuffle as they feed, creating a characteristic meandering trail.
- Tracks can be found meandering along roads and at water holes, where the birds drink mid-morning and late afternoon.

Above: Cape turtle dove tracks in mud; notice the curved shape of the tracks.
Right: Emerald-spotted dove tracks show that the bird shuffled along on its short legs.

BIRDS

Grey go-away-bird
Corythaixoides concolor

Also known as the grey loerie, this passerine is a lumbering flier, yet is nimble through tree branches. It eats mainly fruits, flowers, leaves and insects, and is dependent on drinking daily. Inhabits dry thornveld and savanna woodland. Often found in small parties.

Track and other signs
- Track measures 70mm in length.
- The outside toes curve downwards slightly – more so than those of the **francolin**.
- The species is partial to dust bathing, usually in the late afternoon.
- It will alarm at predators such as raptors and leopards, but has a more intensive, higher-pitched alarm call for owls and eagles.
- Flowers, bits of fruit and regurgitated seeds can be found beneath trees where this bird feeds.

Foot of grey go-away-bird

Grey go-away-bird tracks

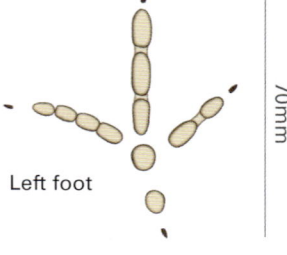
Left foot

Evidence of a grey go-away-bird having taken a dust bath

BIRDS

Burchell's coucal
Centropus superciliosus

Coucals are zygodactyls, with two toes facing forwards and two facing backwards. Voracious feeders, they eat anything they can overpower, including snails, insects, rodents, chameleons, snakes, frogs, lizards, other birds' eggs and nestlings. Prefer riparian thickets on riverbanks along the coastline and in the northeastern region.

Track and other signs
- Track measures 70–80mm in length.
- It resembles the letter 'X'.
- The toes are strong with long sharp claws, particularly on the hind toes.
- Tracks may be seen where the bird has run across a sandy riverbed or between thickets, or around muddy pans.

Left: Burchell's coucal tracks in riverbed
Above: This zygodactylous bird produces a track resembling the letter 'X'.
Above right: Burchell's coucal feet

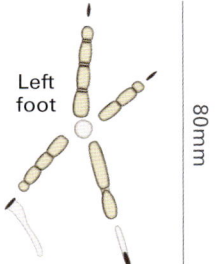

BIRDS

Verreaux's eagle-owl
Bubo lacteus

This large owl has powerful zygodactylous feet and large talons, enabling it to catch sizeable prey, including guineafowl, genets and hares. It roosts in dense evergreen trees, usually along riverbanks and dongas, leaving traces of its meals, such as regurgitated pellets containing bone fragments, rodent skulls and feathers, beneath favoured perches. Pairs give distinctive grunting territorial and contact calls in the evenings and at dawn. Inhabit woodland, savanna and tree-lined watercourses.

Track and other signs

- Track measures 125mm in length. It shows two forward-facing and two backward-facing toes. Its fishing cousin, **Pel's fishing owl**, has a remarkably similar track measuring 120mm in length.
- The toes are thick and strong, and form a shape resembling the letter 'K', which faces outwards, indicating a left or right foot.
- The leading edge of the track shows the two longest toes, with the biggest claws.
- Although seldom seen, Verreaux's eagle-owl tracks can be found on roads, sandy riverbanks or around small water holes.

Left foot — 125mm

Far left and left: Verreaux's eagle-owl tracks, left and right feet respectively

BIRDS

Spotted eagle-owl
Bubo africanus

This eagle-owl takes a wide range of prey, including insects, ground squirrels, birds, bats, rodents, frogs and snakes. This bird roosts in trees, usually along riverbanks and dongas, and regurgitated pellets found below its perches or nesting sites contain bone fragments, rodent skeletons, hair and feathers. It nests in holes in trees or on the ground in dense thickets. The call is a characteristic, deep 'hoo-huuu'. Widespread in southern Africa, it tolerates a range of habitats.

Track and other signs

- Track measures 85mm in length. It shows two forward-facing and two backward-facing toes.
- The strong toes form a shape resembling the letter 'K' facing outwards, indicating a left or right foot.
- The leading edge of the track shows the two longest toes with the longest claws.
- Tracks can be found on roads, sandy riverbanks or around water holes.
- This is the most regularly seen owl track in the southern Kruger National Park.

Regurgitated spotted eagle-owl pellet

Spotted eagle-owl right foot track in sand

Spotted eagle-owl tracks

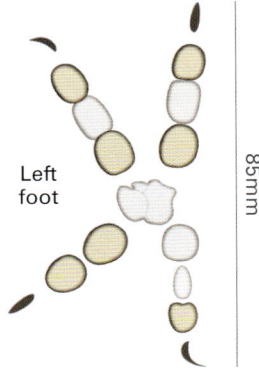

Left foot

Nightjars
Family Caprimulgidae

Fiery-necked nightjar

Southern Africa is home to seven nightjar species, of which the fiery-necked, square-tailed and freckled nightjars are common residents. These crepuscular birds feed on flying insects. They nest informally on the ground, flying up at the last moment if disturbed.

Track and other signs
- Track measures 30mm in length and is slightly curved.
- This seldom-seen track shows three forward-facing toes and a hind toe.
- The middle toe on each foot has a serrated ('pectinate') claw for preening, but this does not show in the track.
- Nightjars hunt on the ground, changing position regularly within a confined area to detect insect silhouettes against any available light, leaving tracks facing in many directions in a small area.

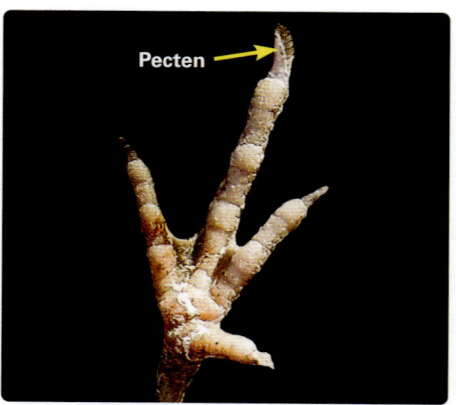
The grooming comb is called a pecten.

This nightjar has changed position a few times.

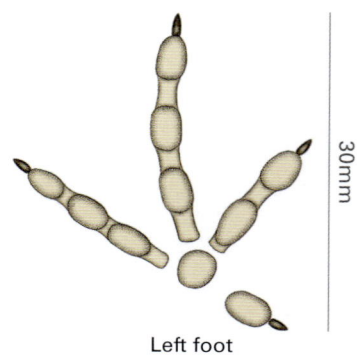
Left foot

■ BIRDS

Swallows and martins
Family Hirundinidae

Wire-tailed swallow

Swallows and martins are passerines, with three forward-facing toes and a hind toe (hallux). Eleven species are found in southern Africa, some migratory, but most breed in the region during summer. Many construct nests using mud collected from the edges of dams and pans. They feed aerially over waterways, grassland and in open woodland.

Track and other signs
- Tracks of the **greater-striped swallow** measure 20mm in length. (It is assumed that track sizes will differ between species, although this level of detail is not yet available.)
- In some swallow and martin species, the forward-facing toes are grouped more tightly (as shown in the illustration), while in others they are more splayed.
- Tracks are often difficult to distinguish, being small and faint.
- Signs of swallows and martins can be found in glazed mud, where they collect mud for their nests.

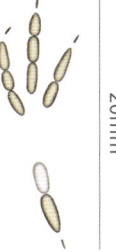

Left foot

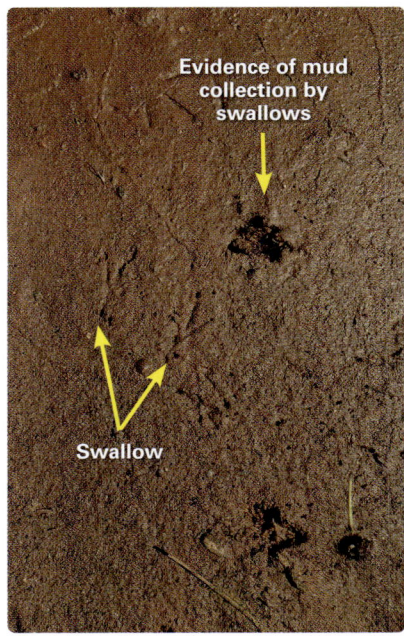

Above: A rock martin in a mud 'cup' nest, unlike most other swallows and martins, which build an enclosed mud nest with an entrance tunnel
Right: Swallow tracks and evidence of mud collection for nest material

329

BIRDS

Great spotted cuckoo
Clamator glandarius

This cuckoo is a brood parasite; its primary hosts are crows and the pied starling. It is a fairly common summer migrant to southern Africa, preferring open savanna (acacia) woodland, where it feeds on caterpillars, as well as beetles, ants, crickets and small lizards.

Track and other signs
- This cuckoo's track measures 55mm and resembles the letter 'X'.
- As with all zygodactyls' feet, the hind toe (hallux) and toe number 4 face backwards, while toes number 2 and 3 face forwards.
- It walks and hops, and is partial to sunbathing, and bathing in small ponds.
- The track is similar to that of the **Burchell's coucal**, but smaller by 20–30mm.

Toes 2 and 3 face forwards.

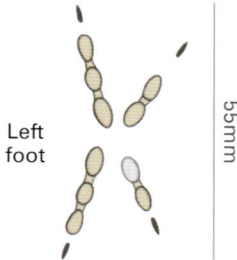

Zygodactyl track resembling the letter 'X'

BIRDS

Mousebirds
Family Coliidae

White-backed mousebird sunning itself; notice the unusual toe positions.

This interesting family of fruit eaters occurs only in Africa. Three of the six species are found in southern Africa, namely the speckled, red-faced and white-backed mousebirds. All have a partial 'mousey' colouration, hence the common name. They are usually found in small flocks.

Track and other signs
- Track measures 30mm in length and up to 43mm with the lower leg imprint showing (shown in illustration).
- Mousebird toes are highly versatile: they can rotate from the anisodactyl position (three toes forward, one toe back) to a pamprodactyl position, where all four toes face forwards. This adaptation allows them to hang from branches as they feed or sun themselves, even when sleeping.
- When a mousebird crouches, the lower leg bone makes an imprint in the track, giving the impression of a fifth toe.
- Mousebirds walk, run and hop, with tail drag marks usually conspicuous in the trail.
- The **speckled mousebird** tends to pivot further forward and stay lower to the ground than the **white-backed**, causing its tracks to be obscured by its body. It also tends to hop more than it walks.
- The **white-backed mousebird** leaves a clearer trail, with less disturbance caused by the body and tail drag.
- Mousebirds are partial to dust bathing.

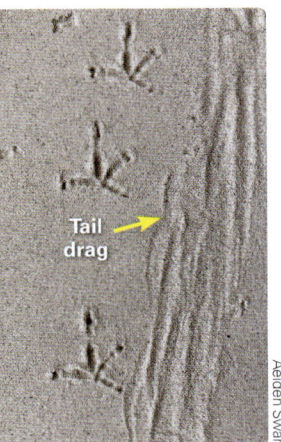

Above: Clear track of white-backed mousebird with tail drag
Right: Track showing lower leg imprint

Speckled mousebird foot showing a semi-pamprodactyl position

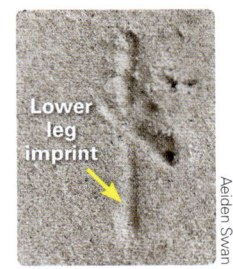

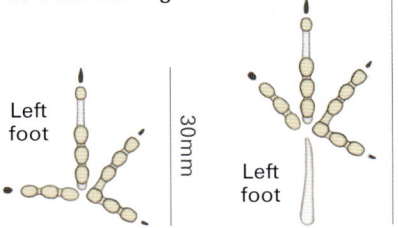

Above left: White-backed mousebird track – walking. **Above right**: Speckled or red-faced mousebird track showing lower leg impression

BIRDS

Southern ground hornbill
Bucorvus leadbeateri

Ground hornbill kills a black mamba.

Ground hornbill nest in a hole in a jackalberry tree (*Diospyros mespiliformis*)

These turkey-sized ground birds live in family groups of about five – usually a dominant pair with additional females and young. They walk slowly, closely inspecting the ground for signs of prey and taking anything they can dispatch with their strong bill and swallow, including reptiles, frogs, snails, insects and small mammals. Their booming call is often mistaken for that of a lion. They require woodland and grassland with large trees for roosting and nesting.

Track and other signs

- Track measures 150–165mm in length.
- This bird walks on its toe tips, so the metatarsal pad does not make an impression. Front and hind toe (hallux) are separated by 50mm, to the extent that one may not link the two features as being from the same track.
- Two of the three forward-facing toes are grouped more closely together, dividing the toes into two segments; the hind toe has only one segment.
- Claw marks usually show clearly in the track.

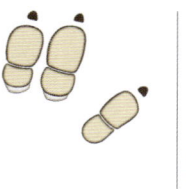

Left foot

150mm

Right: Ground-hornbill track; note space between the front and hind toes.

■ BIRDS

Southern yellow-billed hornbill
Tockus leucomelas

This monogamous hornbill has a wide-ranging, omnivorous diet consisting of termites, ants, beetles, frogs, small rodents, seeds and fruits. It prefers acacia and broad-leaved savanna woodland. Red-billed hornbills spend more time foraging on the ground than their slightly larger yellow-billed cousins.

Track and other signs
- Track measures 60mm in length. The claws are long and usually make a clear impression.
- Track shows three forward-facing toes and a hind toe. Toes number 3 and 4 are partially fused (syndactyl). The toes are grouped so tightly, they may appear indistinguishable.
- Research suggests that tracks of the **yellow-** and **red-billed hornbill** are of a similar length.
- Common gaits observed are walking, running or hopping.
- Evidence is common of this hornbill taking dust baths in dry sand, and collecting mud for nesting material.
- This bird forages in the droppings of large mammals, such as elephant, tossing and scattering faecal material in search of insects and undigested seeds.

Tracks of the yellow-billed hornbill running; notice the tightly arranged front toes.

A typical nest in a natural cavity; notice how the ground below is covered in droppings.

Tracks of a hopping hornbill

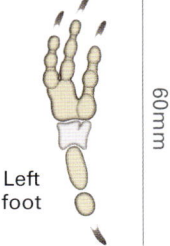

Left foot — 60mm

BIRDS

Red-billed oxpecker
Buphagus erythrorhynchus

These slender, starling-sized birds are integrally dependent on large ungulates from which they obtain their food in the form of ticks, blood-sucking flies, lice and other ectoparasites. They nest in tree holes, which they line with hair plucked from host animals, particularly kudu. Vigilant birds, they will fly up and alarm if predators (including humans) approach their host.

Track and other signs
- Track is 40mm in length. It shows three thickish, forward-facing toes grouped relatively tightly together, and a hind toe. The middle toe is much longer than the two outer toes.
- Claws are surprisingly long and sharp, presumably assisting the oxpecker with clinging to moving bovids. Tracks curve slightly inwards, and toe number 4 (the outer toe on the extreme left in the illustration) has the adaptive flexibility to swivel outwards and backwards, giving the impression that the feet are zygodactyl rather than anisodactyl.
- Tracks are found at pans and dams, and are often associated with evidence of ungulates having visited the area recently.

- The red-billed oxpecker will take a dust bath in suitable, fine-textured soil.
- This bird's call can be helpful to a tracker, indicating the presence of animals such as impala, kudu, giraffe, buffalo and rhino – all of which oxpeckers use as hosts.

Left and below: Oxpeckers are regularly transported to the water's edge when their host mammals come down to drink.

Red-billed oxpecker tracks

Left foot

40mm

334

BIRDS

African pied and Cape wagtails
Motacilla aguimp and *M. capensis*

African pied wagtail

Cape wagtail

African pied wagtail tracks

These are two wagtail species found in southern Africa. The African pied sports contrasting black and white plumage, and a long, wagging tail. It frequents wetlands, rivers and urban areas, skilfully catching insects in mid-air and often perching on rooftops. It usually constructs a cup-shaped nest over water.

The Cape wagtail has more subdued grey and white colouration with a distinctive long, dark tail. Highly adaptable, it prefers grasslands, gardens, and water edges, expertly foraging for small invertebrates. It makes a well-constructed cup nest of grass, twigs and plant fibres.

The 'tail-wagging' helps with stability and acts as a signal for communication with other members of their species.

Track and other signs
- Track measures 28mm long. It shows three forward-facing toes, with a slightly curved middle toe, and a hind toe (hallux).
- Track is similar to a **dove's** track but shorter, with longer strides.
- **African pied** tracks are found close to water, along riverbanks and the coast.
- **Cape wagtail** tracks are found in open areas, grasslands and gardens.

Cape wagtail nestlings, 13 days old

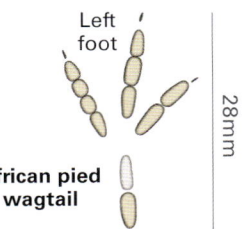

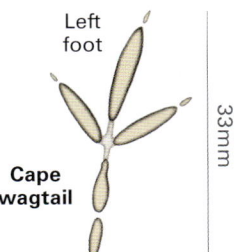

335

BIRDS

African hoopoe
Upupa africana

The African hoopoe is a bird known for its distinctive appearance. Its crest can be raised or lowered at will. Seen singly or in pairs, it probes the ground for insects, larvae, earthworms and other large invertebrates. The hoopoe hops backwards as it forages, making it easier to catch prey.

It is a cavity nester, making nests in tree hollows, crevices, or even abandoned termite mounds. The African hoopoe inhabits woodland savanna, preferring short grass clearings in which to feed.

Tracks show hoopoe walking, then a hop; notice the beetle trail over the bird's track.

Track and other signs
- Track is 40mm in length.
- It is remarkably similar in size and shape to a **dove's** curved track, but the hoopoe track is marginally straighter.
- The hoopoe shuffles along somewhat like a dove; however, its feet register one on either side of the central straddle line. By contrast, dove tracks register one in front of the other.
- Tracks are found in open woodland with short grass, usually in pairs.

African hoopoe tracks; notice tracks registering on either side of the straddle.

Hoopoe feeding chick a tiny caterpillar

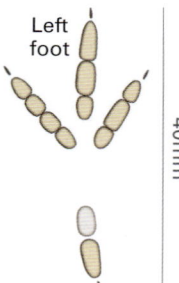

■ BIRDS

Crows and ravens
Family Corvidae

Pied crow

Cape crow

House crow

White-necked raven

Crows are intelligent birds and also accomplished flyers, known to catch small birds in mid-flight. Omnivorous, they eat fruits, seeds, insects and small reptiles, but are best known as scavengers. They are a common resident throughout southern Africa, other than in parts of the Kalahari.

One of three commonly seen species of crow and raven, the pied crow is found in pairs or large flocks in a wide range of habitats, including urban areas.

Track and other signs
- Track lengths vary: the largest is made by the **white-necked raven**, 110–120mm in length; the **Cape crow's** is 90mm; the **pied crow's** 75mm (similar to the **house crow's**).
- Members of this large anisodactyl family have three forward-facing toes and one hind toe (hallux).
- Toes number 2 and 3 (and hind toe) are curved slightly towards the inside – a generic form true for crows and ravens.
- This passerine's tracks show well-developed, muscular toes, all with substantial claws.
- Crows walk and hop; they often drag their feet as they walk, creating drag marks.

Pied crow track

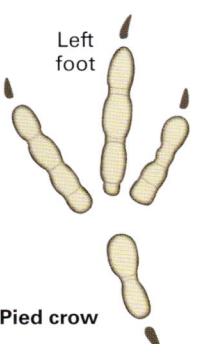

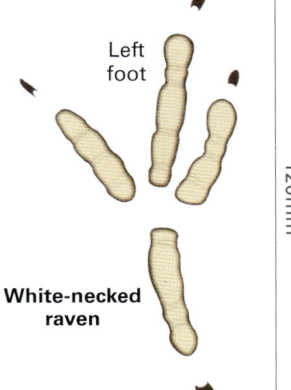

337

BIRDS

Red-winged starling
Onychognathus morio

This starling's natural habitat is rocky hills and cliffs, but it will venture into most habitats in search of food – fruit such as figs and berries, as well as insects, small reptiles, ticks off cattle, and even millipedes. They form strong pair bonds and are highly territorial, actively defending their nesting sites against intruders.

Red-winged starling tracks

Track and other signs
- Track measures 55mm in length.
- A diagnostic feature of the starling track is the elongated hind toe (hallux).
- The track shows long claws.

Left foot

Burchell's starling
Lamprotornis australis

Largest of the 14 starling species in southern Africa, Burchell's starlings are medium-sized passerines, usually found in pairs, occasionally in groups, and sometimes in large flocks in the winter. They search for insects on the ground. They are cavity nesters, usually nesting in large trees. They inhabit open thornveld and broad-leaved woodland.

Burchell's starling track

Track and other signs
- This track measures 60mm in length.
- The elongated, mostly straight, hind toe (hallux) is diagnostic, which is true for most starling species.
- Starlings tend to run along the ground when feeding.
- Tracks of the **Cape glossy starling** are 55mm in length and those of the **greater blue-eared** 50mm, while the **Meves's starling** track is similar to **Burchell's** (60mm).

Left foot

■ BIRDS

Red-billed quelea
Quelea quelea

A small passerine, the red-billed quelea is reputed to be the world's most populous wild bird, with numbers in sub-Saharan Africa in the billions. During the breeding season, males get a black throat and face surrounded by red, yellow or buff. They breed in large colonies in dense acacia stands during midsummer.

Left foot

Track and other signs
- Track measures 30mm in length.
- This track shows three tightly set front toes and a hind toe (hallux).
- Quelea walk and hop; the hopping gait is shown in the bird's track.

Red-billed quelea hopping tracks

Bushveld pipit
Anthus caffer

This sparrow-sized passerine is found in small, scattered flocks or in pairs. The species is often located by its 'bzeeet' contact calls. They occasionally also call in duet. Pipits are insectivorous. They inhabit savanna woodland and thornveld, and prefer areas with short, dry grass.

Bushveld pipit track; notice unusually long hallux.

Track and other signs
- Track length is 50mm.
- The diagnostic feature is the elongated hind toe (hallux), which appears longer than it really is.
- The bushveld pipit walks or runs along the ground, with characteristic long strides. The 70–90mm strides are much longer than those of most similar-sized birds.

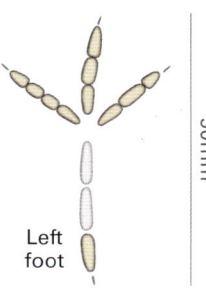

Left foot

INSECTS & OTHER INVERTEBRATES

Antlion
Family Myrmeleontidae

*Antlion adult
(Myrmeleon obscurus)*

Strictly speaking, the term 'antlion' applies to the larval form of the members of this family. The adults are sometimes called 'antlion lacewings' and are recognisable by their long, clubbed antennae. As with all insects, they have six legs.

The antlion larva eats mainly ants. It creates a small, funnel-like pit in soft sand. When an ant or other small insect steps inside the rim of the pit, it will slip and fall to the bottom, whereupon the predatory antlion captures and consumes it with the help of its large mandibles.

Track and other signs

- Meandering antlion trails are produced as the larvae move backwards through the sand in search of a suitable substrate in which to build a trap.
- Most activity begins in the early evening, as the temperature cools, or early morning. Evidence of antlion activity over another animal's track can be helpful to a tracker trying to interpret the freshness of the track.
- Antlion trails are often associated with their traps – small, tapered pits, 10–30mm in diameter.
- Pit traps are usually constructed in locations best shielded from rain, often found under the eaves of human dwellings.
- Antlions regularly demolish and reconstruct their pits in new locations in an effort to find better hunting grounds.

Above left: Dead ant in an antlion trap
Centre: Antlion in its larval stage, in its pit trap
Right: An antlion larva trail and pit trap; notice from the sequence of the trail that the larva has vacated the trap.

■ INSECTS & OTHER INVERTEBRATES

Ants
Family Formicidae

Matabele ant with termite kill

Ants are found all over the globe and are related to wasps and bees. They are easily identified by their elbowed antennae and the segmented, node-like structure that forms their slender waist.

Ants live in nests that may be underground, in ground-level mounds or in trees.

Track and other signs
- Ants can be identified through their trails, their nest entrances and through the collections of discarded vegetation such as seed chaff.
- The light, shallow trails are 10–40mm in width and smooth.
- Raised, roughly circular entrances, varying in shape and size, are constructed of soil to protect the nest from rainwater.
- Harvester ants (*Messor capensis*) discard seed husks around the entrance of the colony.

Ant trail after rain

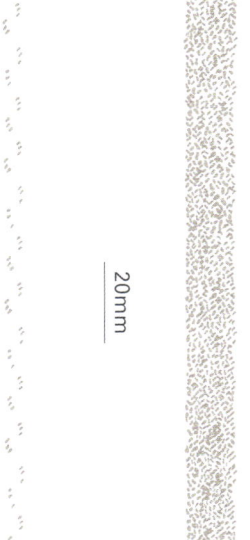

Above left: Collection of discarded seed husks of the snowbush (Eriocephalus ericoides)
Above right: Circular raised entrances to a colony of ants, presumed to be a species of Pheidole

Above left: A single ant's trail
Above right: The trail left by multiple ants

Matabele ant tracks (subfamily Ponerinae)

INSECTS & OTHER INVERTEBRATES

Beetles
Order Coleoptera

Dung beetles
(Scarabaeidae family)

This order of insects is the largest and most diverse in the entire animal kingdom.

Beetles grow and develop through metamorphosis, from egg, larva and pupa into an adult. Beetles vary in size from very small to large. They have a hard, sclerotised body, three pairs of legs attached to the thorax, and mouthparts that are adapted for chewing. Although not all beetles fly, they usually have two pairs of wings. The forewings are modified into hardened covers called elytra; when the insect is at rest, the hind wings are folded under and protected by the elytra.

Track and other signs

- Beetle tracks show three footprints on either side of the body. A generic sequence for a toktokkie (tenebrionid) beetle's trail appears as follows: the middle feet face outwards at a slight angle in the direction of movement, and imprint most visibly; the front feet make much smaller impressions, facing inwards at a 45-degree angle (they are not always easily detectable); the hind foot faces backwards.

Dung beetle trail

Toktokkie beetle trail

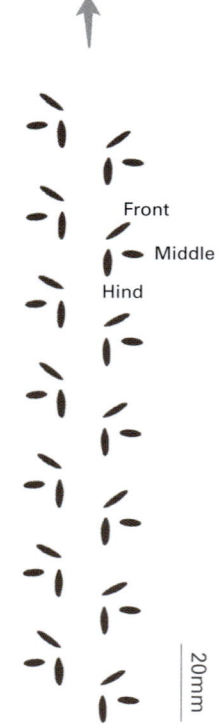

Tenebrionid beetle trail

342

INSECTS & OTHER INVERTEBRATES

- The three footprints are clustered relatively close to each other.
- The distinctive dung beetle (family Scarabaeidae) trail is slightly different from that of the typical tenebrionid beetle: its track sequence shows two parallel lines (hind and middle feet) and curved 'half-moon' impressions (front feet) in the middle of the trail.
- The dung beetle produces a different-looking trail when rolling a dung ball.
- Tracks vary according to the particular species of beetle.

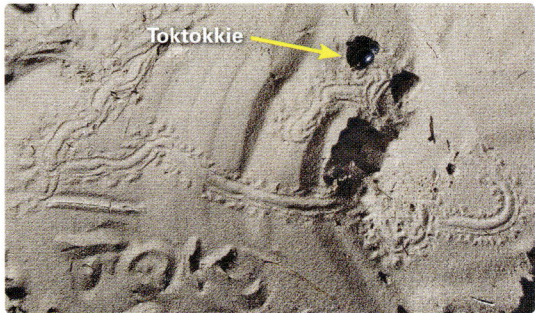

Toktokkie beetle and its trail

Ground beetle trail

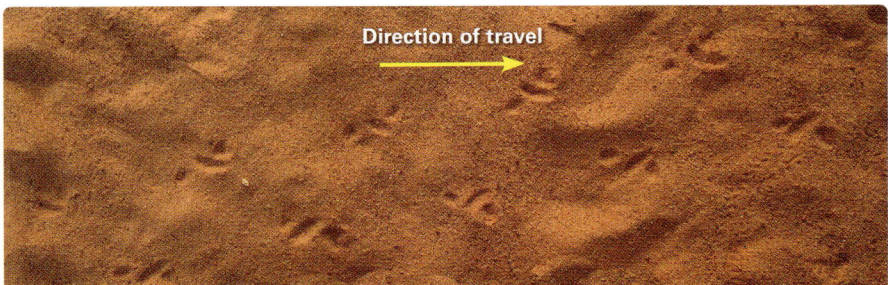

Ground beetle trail (family Carabidae)

Fork-horned rhino beetle (Cyphonistes vallatus) *tracks*

INSECTS & OTHER INVERTEBRATES

Caterpillars
Order Lepidoptera

Caterpillar of Cape hawk moth (Theretra capensis)

Caterpillars are the larval stage of members of the order Lepidoptera (butterflies and moths). Most are herbivorous, although some species are insectivorous.

Track and other signs
- Caterpillar tracks vary significantly in size, according to the insect's body width.
- The trail resembles a railway line, with two repeating parallel dots representing its footprints along the trail.
- Droppings (or frass) may be found beneath trees they inhabit, such as marula and mopane trees.
- Processionary caterpillars (family Thaumetopoeidae) move about in long columns of well over 100 individuals, following in single file, head to tail, believed to be a defence against predators.

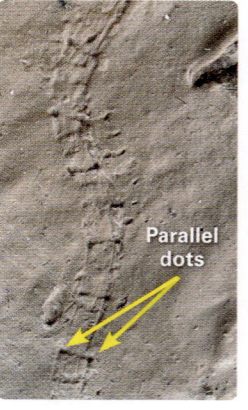

Above left and centre: Caterpillar trails
Above right and far right: Processionary caterpillars on the move
Below: Processionary caterpillars leave a thin trail of silk.

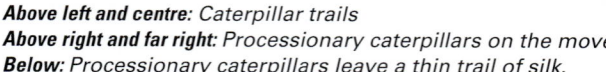
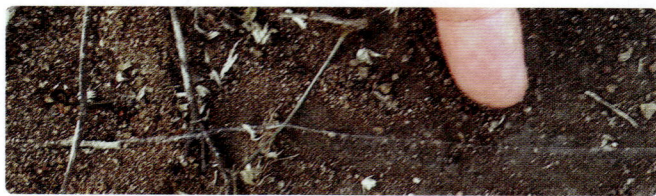

■ INSECTS & OTHER INVERTEBRATES

Butterflies
Order Lepidoptera

African monarch butterflies

Butterflies have large, often brightly coloured wings, and a conspicuous, fluttering flight.
   Certain species of butterfly, such as the brown-veined white *Belenois aurota*, will migrate over great distances. They are important pollinators of many trees and other plants.

Track and other signs
- Occasionally, in very soft, fine substrate, there are signs of a butterfly having taken off from a particular spot.
- Although butterflies have six legs, the front pair is often tucked up under the body, meaning only four footprints show.

Left: Only four legs of a butterfly showing in very fine substrate; this particular track measured 14mm in length.

Corn cricket
Family Bradyporidae

Corn or armoured ground cricket

These large, heavily armoured crickets are flightless. They defend themselves against predators by squirting haemolymph (insect blood) from their body. When deprived of protein and salt they can become cannibalistic.

Track and other signs
- Generic track sequence, in the direction of movement: a hind footprint facing backwards; a middle footprint facing outwards at a 45-degree angle; and an inner front footprint facing inwards at a 45-degree angle.
- The footprints are surprisingly large.
- Tracks may vary from species to species.

Left: Armoured ground (corn) cricket track sequence

INSECTS & OTHER INVERTEBRATES

Grasshoppers
Order Orthoptera

Foam grasshopper (Pyrgomorphidae family)

Grasshoppers have a pair of pincers or mandibles (jaws) used to cut and tear off food, and a pair of antennae. They eat grass, leaves and cereal crops, but many are omnivorous – and many species, in turn, are edible.

Track and other signs

- A feature of the trail of larger grasshoppers is that the hind footprint is slightly separated from the front and middle tracks. Also, the hind foot usually lands parallel to the abdomen drag mark (more so than with beetles), although this is not always the case.
- Smaller grasshoppers leave trails that can be difficult to interpret.
- When a grasshopper hops, it creates a smaller, star-shaped pattern, showing evidence of its six feet. Evidence of its hopping can be obscure in certain substrates.

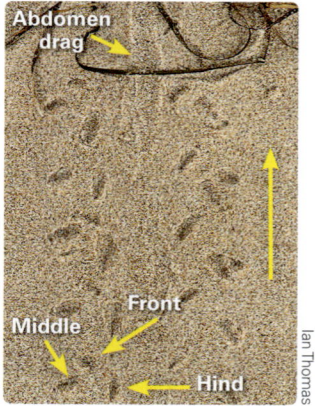

Grasshopper track sequence

Left: Notice the star-shaped impressions left by the hopping grasshopper. **Below**: These tracks are made by a walking shieldback grasshopper (Pamphagidae).

■ INSECTS & OTHER INVERTEBRATES

Wasps
Families Vespidae, Sphecidae and Mutillidae

Mud-dauber wasp collecting mud

Several genera such as the potter wasps and mud-dauber wasps construct their nests from mud. These nests can be situated on the ground, in trees, among rocks and under building eaves.

The Mutillidae family consists of more than 3,000 species of 'velvet ant' worldwide; the females of these wasps are wingless.

Track and other signs
- Scrapings measure 6–10mm in width.
- Evidence of little scrapings dug by wasps can sometimes be found at water holes, where they have collected mud as a building material.
- Velvet ants also create tiny diggings (or scrapings) – presumably in search of food – as they move over dry sand.

Evidence of wasps having collected mud at a water hole can be seen by the little scrapings.

Ticks
Order Ixodida

Male bont tick (Amblyomma hebraeum)

There are two families of ticks that are important in southern Africa: soft ticks (Argasidae) and hard ticks (Ixodidae). The latter is a much larger group.

Track and other signs
- Trails produced by ticks usually show signs of the abdomen having been dragged and evidence of their short legs.
- Trails are often associated with bovid tracks.

Tick trail

INSECTS & OTHER INVERTEBRATES

Spiders
Class Arachnida

Spiders are eight-legged and have silk glands for spinning their webs and wrapping up prey items. Certain species use silk to reinforce their burrows.

Track and other signs
- Spider footprints are represented by faint lines or dots, which can be seen only in perfectly soft substrate.
- The entrance to tunnels of trapdoor spiders can sometimes be seen.

Rain spider (Palystes superciliosus) *nest*

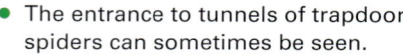

Orb-web spider (Nephila *species*)

Above left and right: *The trapdoor spider constructs a tunnel with a hinged lid, which gets flung open when prey arrives.*

A spider track sequence in soft substrate

Above: *A fast-moving spider's track sequence*

348

■ INSECTS & OTHER INVERTEBRATES

White lady spiders
Genus *Leucorchestris*

Evidence of a white lady 'dancing'

Also known as the white lady dancer, this nocturnal spider is found in desert and semi-desert in the Northern Cape, Kalahari and Namibia. It communicates by tapping its front legs on the ground. Feeds mainly on other arthropods, small insects, and geckos.

Track and other signs
- Performs a 'dance' when threatened.
- Circular patterns are evidence of a white lady 'sand drumming' to communicate threat.

Buckspoor spiders
Genus *Seothyra*

The shed skin of a buckspoor spider

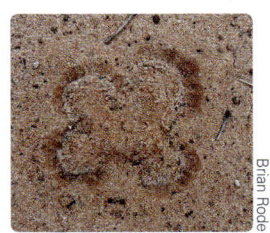

This spider's trap resembles an antelope's track. The male hunts by running down prey; the female remains in her burrow, beneath her trapdoor, which is an almost-invisible sheet of silk. She uses a line of silk to detect vibrations, then darts out and overpowers her prey.

Track and other signs
- The web shows two, three or four curved depressions on the ground that resemble an antelope's track.
- The C-shaped depression is created from sticky silk camouflaged with sand.
- One particular trap measured 75 x 37mm.

Top right and middle: *Buckspoor spider traps; notice the silk web on the edges.* ***Right:*** *Buckspoor spider trap 'track'*

INSECTS & OTHER INVERTEBRATES

Scorpions
Order Scorpiones

Scorpionidae species

Ian Thomas

The two most commonly encountered scorpion families are the Buthidae, with their slender pedipalps and thick tails, and the Scorpionidae, which have large pincers and a relatively small tail and sting. The former have powerful venom that can kill or paralyse prey, while the latter capture and subdue prey with their large pedipalps. Scorpions have eight legs.

Scorpions are generally burrowing (they excavate an oval-shaped burrow), rock-dwelling or arboreal (living under tree bark).

Track and other signs
- Track shows four footprints on either side; however, it is common to see only three as the tiny feet register so close to each other.
- Footprints are not always clearly visible.
- Some scorpions such as the rough burrowing scorpion (*Opistophthalmus glabrifrons*) feed on millipedes and discard segments outside their burrow.
- Their oval-shaped burrows can sometimes be seen.

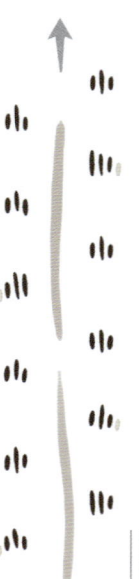

Above: *This burrow of a rough burrowing scorpion shows evidence of its millipede diet.*
Right: *Scorpion tail drag marks*

20mm

350

■ INSECTS & OTHER INVERTEBRATES

Millipedes
Family Spirostreptidae

Millipedes are common in southern Africa, with over 350 species identified. They move with great purpose and, when disturbed, will twist vigorously or roll into a spiral. They feed mostly on dead or decaying plant material.

Track and other signs
- The trail shows two tiny parallel tramlines resembling a railway track – in mud, one can almost see the individual footprints.
- Millipedes also produce little burrows with entrances allowing for the shape and size of their body.

Left: A millipede and its trail
Far right: A millipede trail in mud; note the inidividual footfalls.

Earthworms
Subclass Oligochaeta

Earthworm

Earthworms are thin, tube-shaped, segmented worms commonly found living in soil. Burrowing earthworms will emerge after a substantial rainstorm, leaving random trails.

Track and other signs
- Trails found are mostly during or after rainfall. Earthworm trails (or paths) show irregular routes, either twisting or moving in a straight line.
- Earthworms also produce muddy droppings called casts.

Left: Earthworm trail in the Karoo
Right: Earthworm casting; undigested material deposited by the worm

351

INSECTS & OTHER INVERTEBRATES

Snails and slugs
Class Gastropoda

Giant land snail

The name 'snail' used in the most general sense includes not only land snails but also thousands of species of sea and freshwater snails. Snail-like animals that lack a shell into which they can retract are usually called slugs.

In Sabi Sands the giant African land snail (*Archachatina marginata*) is common, along with several herbivorous slug species (family Veronicellidae).

Track and other signs
- Both slugs and snails leave behind trails of mucus (or slime) as they move along.
- The slug produces a continuous mucus trail, whereas the snail produces an intermittent trail.
- Larger snails, such as the giant land snail, create a wider mucus trail than others.
- Both snails and slugs are common in southern African suburban gardens, and their trails can often be found on house walls.

Plough snail (Bullia digitalis) *on the Cape south coast*

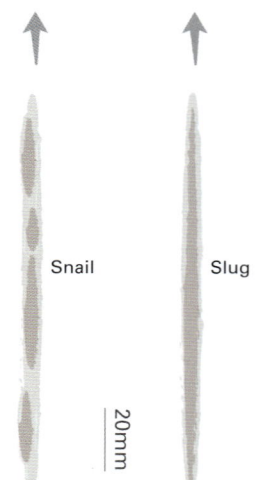

Snail   Slug

20mm

Left: *A slug produces a continuous mucus trail.*
Below: *The snail's mucus trail is intermittent.*

■ INSECTS & OTHER INVERTEBRATES

Crabs
Order Decapoda

Freshwater crab

Crabs have four pairs of legs and are covered with a thick, calcified exoskeleton, forming a hard crust that gives Crustacea their scientific name. Southern Africa is home to 19 species of freshwater crab (family Potamonautidae) and several semi-terrestrial, sea-dwelling crabs (family Ocypodidae), which are found in rivers, streams, vleis, beaches and on land. Crabs create burrows in muddy, sandy or marshy substrate.

Track and other signs

- Both freshwater and sea crabs produce trails that show several seemingly randomly placed little incisions (or nicks) in the mud as they move sideways. If one looks carefully, evidence of all eight legs may be identified.
- Tracks may be seen a long way from water.
- There is often discarded mud surrounding a crab's burrow entrance, which has been shovelled out from inside.

Crabs produce a unique trail that shows series of little incisions as they move sideways. Depending on the speed of the crab, slightly different track sequences are produced.

Theory for trackers

Activities and mindsets for successful tracking

Top wildlife trackers follow trails and find animals with greater consistency than their amateur tracker counterparts. The animals they track are wild and their behaviour is unpredictable; the environment in which they operate is constantly changing. Consequently, track information is usually incomplete. Therefore the process of tracking requires a particular combination of mindsets.

It is worth keeping in mind that tracking may be considered as a potent metaphor for pursuing *anything* in life. To explore this idea further, readers may visit: **www.trackingsuccess.tv**

We have identified five interrelated activities to manage when trailing an animal, which go hand in hand with specific mindsets or qualities that the tracker should master. Take note that these activities do not necessarily happen in a linear way – they often occur concurrently.

1 Find the track To successfully find the track, you must correctly identify the intended species' track, and you should possess the knowledge to determine the track's age.

Sound technical knowledge of identifying, ageing and interpreting tracks is crucial. Trackers must invest time finding the right track (ideally the freshest) of the species they intend to trail. An early mistake can have far-reaching consequences. The tracker must focus on areas of greatest opportunity –

Lead Tracker Tsundzukani Hlungwane interprets a genet track.

THEORY FOR TRACKERS

Lion and impala tracks on top of the track of an African elephant

preferably habitats where the (targeted) species occurs and locations where the substrate is conducive to tracking, if the choice exists.
- **HOW** Go early. Get active. Be observant, detailed and analytical. Think critically and carefully evaluate every track with patience. Consider exploring other tracks before making a decision about which track to follow.
- **DOMINANT MINDSET Discernment**

2 Follow the track Create a clear story by following the set of tracks and collecting and organising important information from the trail, so you can understand the animal's behaviour.

This phase requires an emphasis on the accumulation of relevant evidence. As the trail is followed, so the nature of the substrate causes the evidence (track impressions) to change. The challenge is to know what to look for and what to ignore. It is necessary to 'cut through the clutter' in order to recognise only the essential details. This requires constant questioning. To make sense of the trail the tracker must rigorously gather the physical evidence to develop a theory of the animal's intention. Other animals' signs may help or hinder the process. Following the track is usually the primary activity of the trailing process.

- **HOW** Systematically follow the trail of (sometimes obscure) evidence. Zoom in and zoom out; be aware of all signs; and maintain momentum. To start, go slowly. Let the terrain and substrate determine the appropriate speed.
- **DOMINANT MINDSET Curiosity**

3 Regain a lost trail Losing track is an inevitable part of the trailing process. To get back on track, you must confront the facts and review any assumptions you have made without bias – and make the necessary adjustments.

There are multiple reasons for losing track, some of the common ones are: loss of concentration, hard or difficult substrate, radical change in the animal's behaviour, and other animals having trampled the trail.

There are two simple methods for regaining a lost trail:
1. Go back to the last confirmed track and follow the trail again with extra care, observing the detail.
2. Alternatively, stop; review your original hypothesis, and attempt to predict where the animal has gone. (This is a more advanced and speculative approach.)
- **HOW** Remain calm and focused. Stay positive. Take into account the animal's origin and its probable direction of travel. If necessary, return to the last track seen in the trail. Be extra vigilant and observe all the details. Pick up the trail and follow it again, slowly, until it becomes clearer.
- **DOMINANT MINDSET Honesty** (followed closely by **courage** – to accept that one is lost)

4 Close the gap At some point in the trail, you must engage in creative thinking, so that you can speed up, maintain forward momentum and close the gap on the animal. To accurately anticipate the animal's movement, you must combine all the evidence collected thus far and assimilate it holistically. Reflect on all the information together; notice how each piece fits with others to develop a comprehensive understanding of the animal's behaviour. The tracking process is effectively a chain of constant mini predictions. Closing the gap in this manner involves an informed yet simultaneously speculative pursuit.

Trackers must integrate the track evidence gathered with the influence of the physical landscape to form a mental picture of what the animal is doing.

- **HOW** Constantly note the detail collected along the trail, and how this relates to the bigger picture. Put yourself in the skin of the animal and ask youself: 'Considering what I know so far, what would I do if I was this animal?' Below are three questions to help you gain clarity:
  1. What is the track evidence saying?
  2. How is the landscape influencing the animal's movement?
  3. What is the animal doing?

The answers to these questions give valuable insight, enabling you as the tracker to form a logical theory of the animal's activity. The questions can be summarised in the following 'tracking formula':

> **Evidence** (track detail, etc)
> **+ Landscape's significance**
> **+ Animal's behaviour**
> **= Animal's possible whereabouts**

- **DOMINANT MINDSET Imagination and creativity**

5 Encounter the animal This is the moment when the animal is found. If your tracking effort is successful, you will encounter the animal. The goal is to find the animal without causing any disturbance, as this can lead to a risky or unwanted confrontation. Ideally, you should be able to observe the animal without it being aware of your presence. Respectful encounters increase your chances of future tracking success. Adopting a mindset that prioritises safety, trust, and appreciation for the process often leads to safer encounters, and improved relationships with the animals.

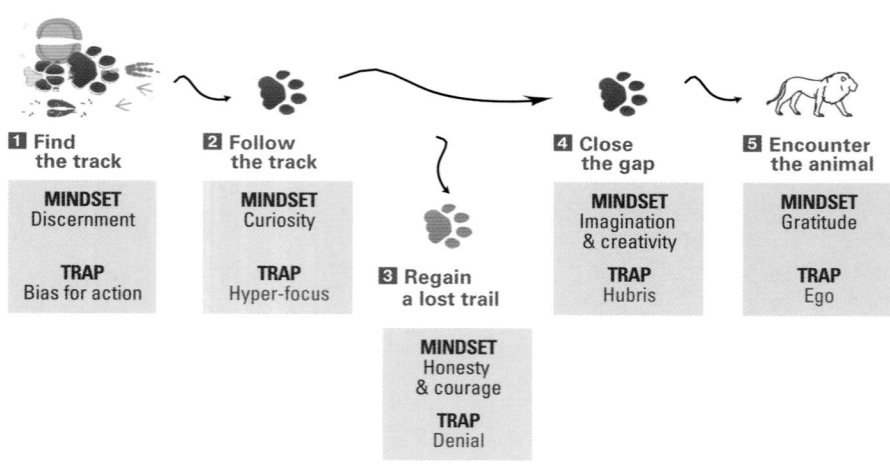

The pathway to tracking success

THEORY FOR TRACKERS

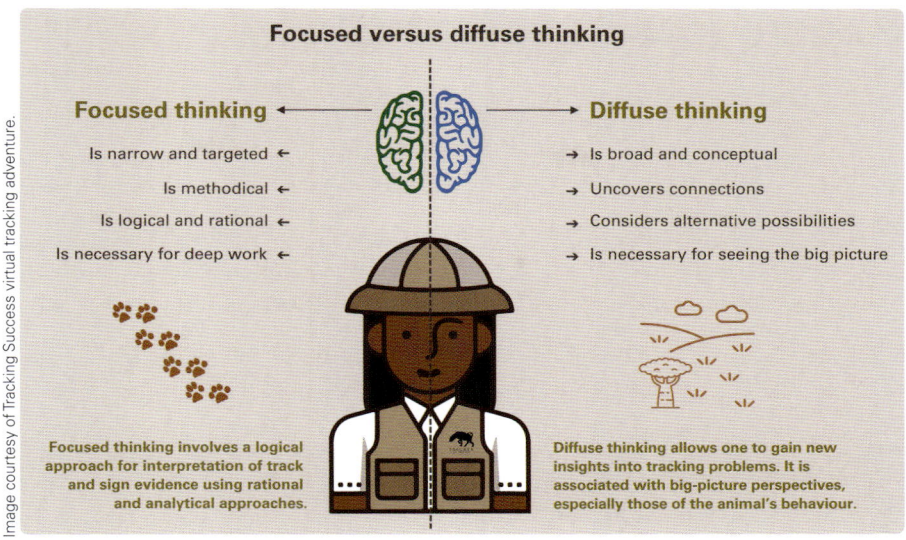

Trackers apply both modes of thinking.

- **HOW** Go safely, be compassionate, stop often and be vigilant. Remember to listen, and to enjoy the experience. Don't be cavalier, it's not worth it.
- **DOMINANT MINDSET** Gratitude

Focused versus diffuse thinking

To track effectively in difficult conditions trackers must closely examine the evidence (tracks) **and** consider how this information relates to the animal's behaviour. Consequently, animal trackers rely on a combination of 'focused' and 'diffuse' thinking. The expert tracker seamlessly transitions between intense concentration on specific details and broad awareness of the environment, in a process that is similar to solving a complex puzzle; the tracker is both searching for the puzzle pieces and trying to complete the picture on the puzzle box. This constant shifting of attention enables trackers to build a picture of what the animal is doing.

Using 'focused' thinking the tracker zooms in on critical clues left by the animal, such as footprints, a displaced stone, broken branches, an alarm call or scat. Trackers draw from their knowledge (and experience) and technical competence to interpret the evidence accurately.

Using diffuse thinking the tracker zooms out, temporarily stepping back from the fine details of the trail, and expanding awareness of the broader surroundings. The tracker adopts a more relaxed and open mindset, taking in the interconnectedness of the ecosystem. This broader perspective helps the tracker to anticipate the animal's behaviour, its choice of route, and how water, food, cover or other animals may influence its movement.

By blending these thinking modes, expert trackers can stay attuned in a dynamic, potentially dangerous environment. The ability to switch between focus and diffuse modes ultimately enhances problem-solving capabilities, and overall tracking proficiency.

ANIMAL TRACK COMPARISONS

Animal track comparisons

Scan to download these pages

These animal tracks have been grouped in tables because they are the ones most often confused in the field, based on the similarity of their track morphology and the animals' shared habitat.

The terms below are used frequently in the descriptions given:
- **straddle** – distance between left and right feet, measured from outside edges
- **register** – when the hind foot lands partially or directly on top of the front foot track
- **variable gait** – refers to when an animal uses a variety of gaits, including understep, register or overstep
- **symmetrical** – refers to when left and right features of the track are equal
- **asymmetrical** – refers to when left and right features of the track are unequal
- **negative space** – the space between toes, and/or main pad and toes
- **central ridge** – the space between the cloven hooves that leaves a prominent ridge of soil

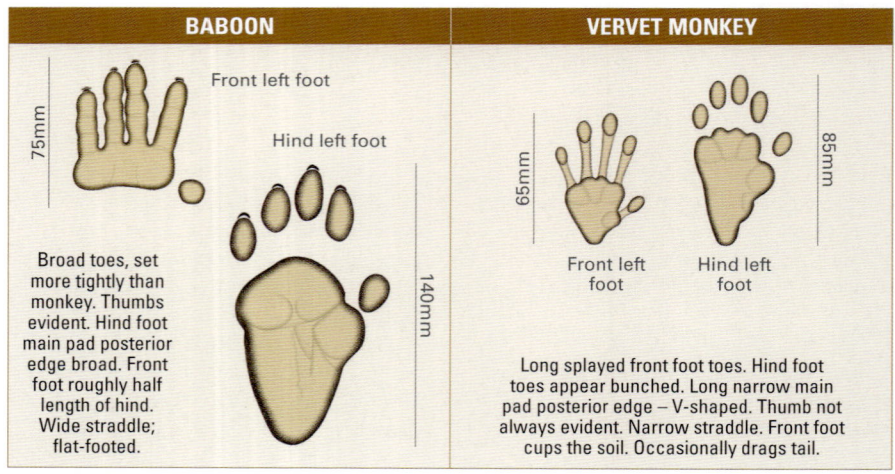

BABOON	VERVET MONKEY
Front left foot / Hind left foot — 75mm / 140mm	Front left foot / Hind left foot — 65mm / 85mm
Broad toes, set more tightly than monkey. Thumbs evident. Hind foot main pad posterior edge broad. Front foot roughly half length of hind. Wide straddle; flat-footed.	Long splayed front foot toes. Hind foot toes appear bunched. Long narrow main pad posterior edge – V-shaped. Thumb not always evident. Narrow straddle. Front foot cups the soil. Occasionally drags tail.

A chacma baboon shows its underfoot.

Vervet monkeys often leave obscure tracks.

ANIMAL TRACK COMPARISONS

SMALL GREY MONGOOSE

Front left foot — 36mm
Hind left foot — 32mm

Longish thin claws and small oval toes. Very small, close to 3cm without proximal pad showing. Main pad asymmetrical. Variable gait.

YELLOW MONGOOSE

Front left foot — 29mm
Hind left foot — 27mm

Surprisingly large toes. Toe 1 seldom shows. Negative space between toes and main pad. Variable gait. Track more symmetrical than suricate.

SURICATE

Front left foot — 32mm
Hind left foot — 32mm

Very long claws. Hind foot main pad is large. Hind foot markedly larger than front. Main pad asymmetrical. No register.

GROUND SQUIRREL

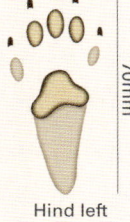

Front left foot — 32mm / 40mm
Hind left foot — 70mm

Large toes with broad claws. Hind foot: three middle toes are prominent, and significant negative space between toes and main pad. Proximal pads show occasionally. Variable gait, including bound.

CIVET

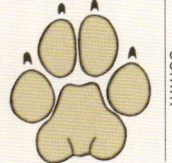

Front left foot — 53mm
Hind left foot — 55mm

Round track. Claws not always evident. Very little negative space. Often register. Hind track similar to jackal's.

BLACK-BACKED JACKAL

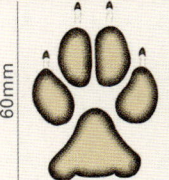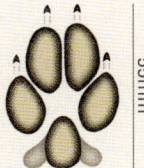

Front left foot — 60mm
Hind left foot — 55mm

Symmetrical track. Large toes with claws. Middle and outer toes sit in parallel. Triangular-shaped main pad. Variable gait.

WHITE-TAILED MONGOOSE

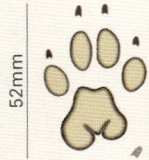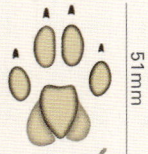

Front left foot — 52mm
Hind left foot — 51mm

Oval toes arranged in arc. Box-shaped hind main pad. Asymmetrical front main pad. Toe 1's claw shows occasionally. Tracks don't register. Toes smaller than jackal.

WATER MONGOOSE

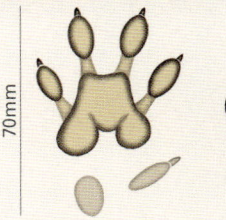

Front left foot — 70mm
Hind left foot — 62mm

Long splayed toes with short claws. Asymmetrical front main pad. Large front proximal pad and toe 1 show occasionally. Variable gait, seldom register.

ANIMAL TRACK COMPARISONS

BAT-EARED FOX

Front left foot — 46mm
Hind left foot — 42mm

Front foot oval toes quite splayed. Very long front foot claws. Underfoot hair often obscures track. Main pad not always visible. Variable gait. Don't usually register.

CAPE FOX

Front left foot — 47mm
Hind left foot — 42mm

Symmetrical track. Oval toes. Long claws. Main pad often unclear due to hair under foot. Variable gait. Often oversteps.

AARDWOLF

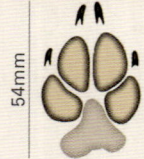 

Front left foot — 54mm
Hind right foot — 45mm

Asymmetrical track. Kidney-shaped outer toes set tightly together. Substantial claws. Main pad often appears small or unclear. Typical hyaena gait: smaller hind feet register close to opposite side's front foot.

SCRUB HARE

Front left foot — 30mm
Hind left foot — 37mm

Underfoot hair obscures detail – resembling smudges on the ground. Toes reveal in mud. Main pad not visible. Typical hare gait.

BANDED MONGOOSE

Front left foot — 50mm
Hind left foot — 32mm

Very long claws resembling elongated toes. Main pad asymmetrical. Toe 1 shows when moving slowly. Highly gregarious – they move in groups.

SLENDER MONGOOSE

Front left foot — 36mm
Hind left foot — 28mm

Slightly splayed oval toes with sharp claws. Outer toes widely set. Proximal pad and toe 1 show when moving slowly. Moves along edges of roads, singly. Often bounds.

DWARF MONGOOSE

Front left foot — 31mm
Hind left foot — 25mm

Looks like miniature banded mongoose. Very small. Long claws. Highly gregarious. Often bounds. Don't usually register.

GENET

Front left foot — 27mm
Hind left foot — 30mm

Round toes. No claws. Large, substantial main pad with two large outer lobes. Proximal pad shows occasionally. Variable gait.

TREE SQUIRREL

Front left foot — 23mm
Hind left foot — 45mm

Hind foot five toes with three middle toes closely set. Main pad shows tread-like features. Variable gait, including bound. Often confused with slender mongoose.

MELLER'S MONGOOSE

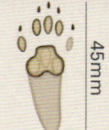 

Front left foot — 30mm
Hind left foot — 37mm

Large main pad. Claws evident. Front foot middle toes separated. Significant negative space. Similar to genet or small white-tailed mongoose.

The honey badger is a prodigious digger.   *A Cape porcupine digs for roots.*

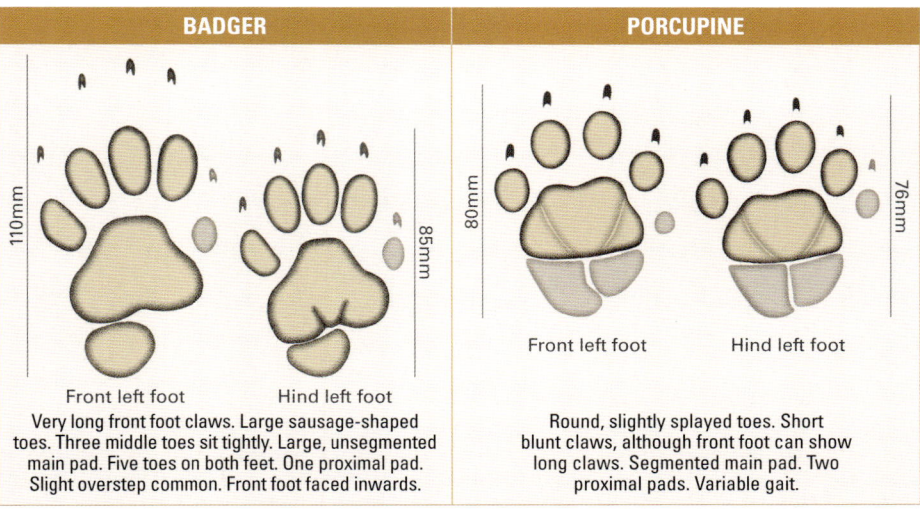

BADGER

Front left foot — 110mm
Hind left foot — 85mm

Very long front foot claws. Large sausage-shaped toes. Three middle toes sit tightly. Large, unsegmented main pad. Five toes on both feet. One proximal pad. Slight overstep common. Front foot faced inwards.

PORCUPINE

Front left foot — 80mm
Hind left foot — 76mm

Round, slightly splayed toes. Short blunt claws, although front foot can show long claws. Segmented main pad. Two proximal pads. Variable gait.

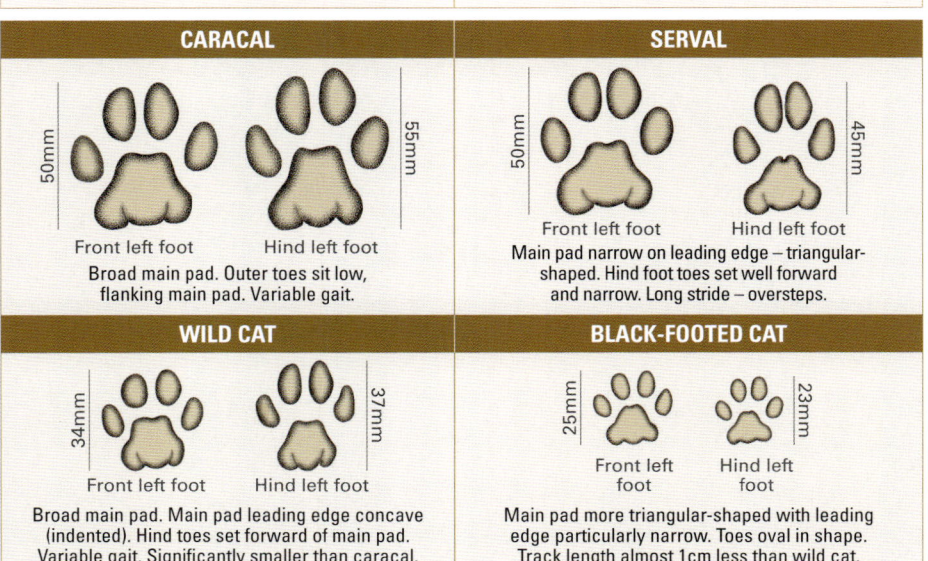

CARACAL

Front left foot — 50mm
Hind left foot — 55mm

Broad main pad. Outer toes sit low, flanking main pad. Variable gait.

SERVAL

Front left foot — 50mm
Hind left foot — 45mm

Main pad narrow on leading edge – triangular-shaped. Hind foot toes set well forward and narrow. Long stride – oversteps.

WILD CAT

Front left foot — 34mm
Hind left foot — 37mm

Broad main pad. Main pad leading edge concave (indented). Hind toes set forward of main pad. Variable gait. Significantly smaller than caracal.

BLACK-FOOTED CAT

Front left foot — 25mm
Hind left foot — 23mm

Main pad more triangular-shaped with leading edge particularly narrow. Toes oval in shape. Track length almost 1cm less than wild cat.

ANIMAL TRACK COMPARISONS

CHEETAH

Front left foot — 95mm
Hind left foot — 105mm

Oval toes. Claws usually evident. Angular main pad shows clear ridges on posterior edge – leading edge is square. Three posterior lobes of main pad distinctive. Significant negative space in hind foot. Hind foot longer and appears slender. Typically oversteps.

SPOTTED HYAENA

Front left foot — 106mm
Hind right foot — 101mm

Kidney-shaped outer toes arranged tightly. Main pad distinctly asymmetrical. Little negative space. Typical hyaena gait: hind feet register close to opposite side's front foot. Hind foot lands at a slight angle, facing outwards.

BROWN HYAENA

Front left foot — 97mm
Hind right foot — 78mm

Kidney-shaped outer toes arranged tightly. Main pad distinctly asymmetrical. Longer claws. Hair around track. Very little negative space. Hind much smaller than front. Typical hyaena gait: hind feet register close to opposite side's front foot.

WILD DOG

Front left foot — 88mm
Hind left foot — 79mm

Track symmetrical. Large middle toes sit in parallel. Triangular-shaped main pad. Substantial claws. Variable gait. Often trots.

MALE LION

Front left foot — 138mm
Hind left foot — 141mm

Large rounded oval toes and substantial, broad main pad. Posterior edge of main pad rounded.

FEMALE LION

Front left foot — 127mm
Hind left foot — 116mm

Large oval toes and main pad. Main pad leading edge narrower. More negative space than male lion. Main pad posterior edge more angular.

MALE LEOPARD

Front left foot — 95mm
Hind left foot — 100mm

Rounded, oval toes and large main pad. Main pad leading edge is broad, and posterior edge rounded.

FEMALE LEOPARD

Front left foot — 77mm
Hind left foot — 80mm

Oval toes. Main pad leading edge narrower than male leopard (and indented). Main pad more angular.

ANIMAL TRACK COMPARISONS

BLUE WILDEBEEST

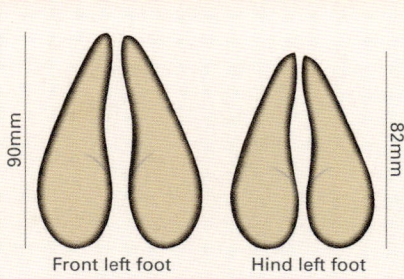

Front left foot — 102mm | Hind left foot — 95mm

Broad track. Square and blunt on leading edge. Straight hoof edges. Wide central ridge. Front track typically rectangular, hind is pointed. Hooves often splay. False hooves show occasionally. Overstep is typical.

Blue wildebeest galloping

TSESSEBE

Front left foot — 90mm | Hind left foot — 82mm

Variable shape: pointed and blunt versions possible. Hoof edges usually straight. Rim-walking – hoof edges are prominent. Hind track narrow. Overstep is typical.

WATERBUCK

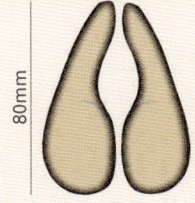

Front left foot — 80mm | Hind left foot — 75mm

Pointed, narrow and occasionally heart-shaped track. Cloven hooves close but do splay when slippery. Hind more pointed. A step is possible. Gap between hooves causes a small mound of soil. Variable gait, but a small overstep is common.

BUSHBUCK

Front left foot — 45mm | Hind left foot — 38mm

Rounded hoof edges. Hooves usually tight. Hoof tips often mismatched. Walk on tiptoes – hence scuffing of hoof tip common. Widest near middle. Hooves face outwards, slightly. Tracks typically register.

STEENBOK

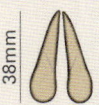

Front left foot — 38mm | Hind left foot — 40mm

Narrow and pointed track with straight hoof edges. Prominent and proportionately wide central ridge. Step is possible. Hind track hoof edge is concave. Tracks typically register.

COMMON DUIKER

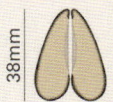

Front left foot — 38mm | Hind left foot — 38mm

Highly variable in shape. Usually symmetrical. Narrow central ridge. Hooves tight. Hoof edges curved but a straighter version is also possible. Widest near posterior edge – creates a V-shape. Tracks typically register.

SHARPE'S GRYSBOK

Front left foot — 25mm | Hind left foot — 26mm

Neat triangular-shaped track. Very pointed on leading edge. Hooves may be narrow. Wide on posterior edge. Tracks typically register.

ANIMAL TRACK COMPARISONS

BUFFALO

Front left foot — 170mm / 122mm
Hind left foot — 126mm / 200mm

Broad, curved symmetrical track, almost circular in shape. Gap between hooves varies but usually appears small – creating a narrow central ridge. Hind slightly narrower. False hooves occasionally make an appearance. Gait varies. Register is common.

GIRAFFE

Front left foot — 195mm
Hind left foot — 190mm

Long, broad cloven hoof track. Front rectangular. Hooves tight. A central mound of soil or narrow central ridge is common. A significant overstep is typical.

ELAND

Front left foot — 127mm
Hind left foot — 115mm

Curved with noticeable gap between hooves. Hoof tips often mismatched (asymmetrical). Oval-shaped hind markedly narrower than front. A very broad version of the front is common. False hooves don't show. Typically register. Longer stride than buffalo.

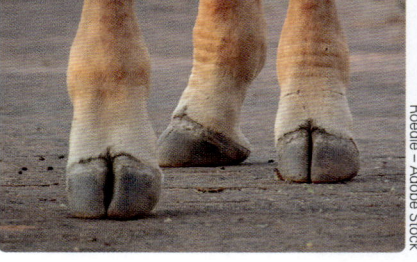

Giraffe hooves

Roedie – Adobe Stock

WHITE RHINO

Front left foot — 290mm
Hind left foot — 275mm

Overall box-shaped track with three prominent toes. Outside toes close to middle toe. Sole creases in little block shapes are common. W-shaped indentation on posterior edge. Variable gait. Understep is common.

BLACK RHINO

Front left foot — 240mm
Hind left foot — 230mm

Overall circular-shaped with three toes. Outer toes located further away from middle than white rhino. Shallow indentation on posterior edge. Less sole creases and smaller toes than white rhino. Direct register is typical.

ANIMAL TRACK COMPARISONS

WATERBUCK

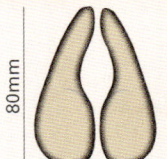

Front left foot — 80mm
Hind left foot — 75mm

Pointed, narrow and occasionally heart-shaped track. Cloven hooves close but do splay when slippery. Hind more pointed. A step is possible. Gap between hooves causes a small mound of soil. Variable gait, but a small overstep is common.

KUDU

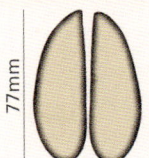

Front left foot — 77mm
Hind left foot — 77mm

Neat rugby-ball-shaped track with rounded hoof edges. Blunt on leading edge. Cloven hooves tight, creating a narrow central ridge. Widest near the middle. 'Irons the ground' – walks flat-footed. Typically register.

NYALA

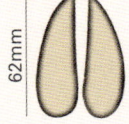

Front left foot — 62mm
Hind left foot — 54mm

Rounded edges with characteristic gap between hooves, prone to splaying. Hoof tips blunt. Widest near the middle. 'Irons the ground' – walks flat-footed. Typically register. Shorter stride than kudu.

BUSHBUCK

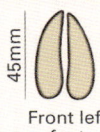

Front left foot — 45mm
Hind left foot — 38mm

Rounded hoof edges. Hooves usually tight. Hoof tips often mismatched. Walks on tiptoes – hence scuffing of hoof tip common. Widest near middle. Tracks typically register. Hooves face outwards slightly.

RED HARTEBEEST

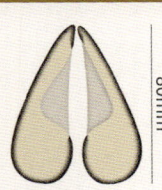

Front left foot — 87mm
Hind left foot — 80mm

Triangular-shaped. Front foot broad on posterior edge. Often leaves oval-shaped mound of soil, or prominent central ridge. Straight hoof edges. Occasionally shows a step. Overstep is typical.

GEMSBOK

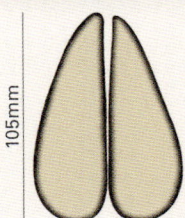

Front left foot — 105mm
Hind left foot — 90mm

Large, flat-footed, symmetrical track. Roughly triangular. Broad front foot is curved, and pointed hind is straighter. Cloven hooves tight – narrow central ridge is distinctive. No step. Digging may change shape of front foot. Overstep is typical.

SPRINGBOK

Front left foot — 50mm
Hind left foot — 54mm

Sharp on leading edge and broad on posterior edge. Prominent central ridge. Hoof edges usually straight rather than curved. Front foot often broad. Hind foot hoof edges can be concave. Step is possible. Overstep is typical.

Springbok pronking

Alta Oosthuizen – Adobe Stock

ANIMAL TRACK COMPARISONS

IMPALA

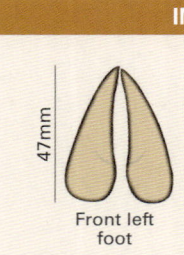

47mm — Front left foot
47mm — Hind left foot

Pointed and triangular shaped with convex, straight, or concave hoof edges. Front foot is broad. Prominent central ridge. Rim-walker: hoof edges often distinctive. Often creates a step. Overstep is typical.

SOUTHERN REEDBUCK

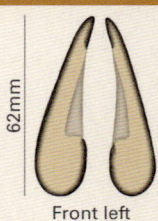

62mm — Front left foot
62mm — Hind left foot

Proportionately long, narrow, sharp, and pointed. Distinctively straight hoof edges. Gap between hoof tips and clear central ridge. Occasionally shows a step. Hooves prone to splaying. Overstep is typical.

SPRINGBOK

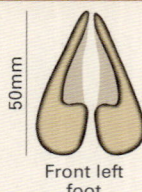 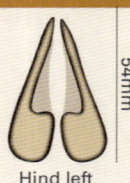

50mm — Front left foot
54mm — Hind left foot

Sharp on leading edge and broad on posterior edge. Central ridge varies. Distinct hoof edges usually straight rather than curved. Front foot often broad. Hind foot hoof edges can be concave. Often flat-footed. Overstep is typical.

COMMON DUIKER

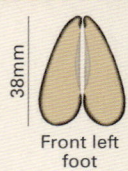 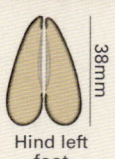

38mm — Front left foot
38mm — Hind left foot

Highly variable in shape. Usually, symmetrical. Hooves tight. Hoof edges curved but a straighter version is also possible. Widest near posterior edge – creates a V-shape. Tracks typically register.

RED DUIKER

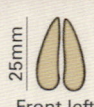 

25mm — Front left foot
30mm — Hind left foot

Straighter hoof edges are common. Narrow central ridge. Tracks typically register.

BLUE DUIKER

26mm — Front left foot
23mm — Hind left foot

Typically rounded. Front foot may splay. Hind foot straighter and more pointed. Central ridge is prominent. Tracks typically register.

SUNI

20mm — Front left foot
20mm — Hind left foot

Very small and round. A straighter, more pointed version is common. Central ridge narrow. Can easily be overlooked. Tracks typically register.

COMMON DUIKER

38mm — Front left foot
38mm — Hind left foot

Highly variable in shape. Usually symmetrical. Hooves tight. Hoof edges curved but a straighter version is also possible. Widest near posterior edge – creates a V-shape. Tracks typically register.

ANIMAL TRACK COMPARISONS

ROAN ANTELOPE

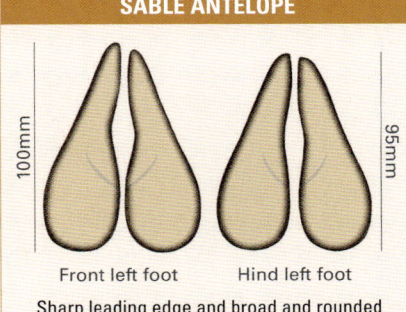

Front left foot   Hind left foot

105mm / 95mm

Large, robust track that is broad on the posterior edge. Hind foot can be very sharp. Narrow central ridge. A significant gap between front hoof tips is common. Overstep is typical.

SABLE ANTELOPE

Front left foot   Hind left foot

100mm / 95mm

Sharp leading edge and broad and rounded on posterior edge. Narrow version common. Hoof edges straight or concave. Cloven hooves tight, although front may splay. Often shows a step. Rim-walker: hoof edges often distinctive. Overstep is typical.

TSESSEBE

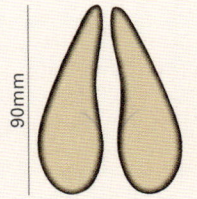

Front left foot   Hind left foot

90mm / 82mm

Variable shape: pointed and blunt versions possible. Hoof edges usually straight. Rim-walker: hoof edges are prominent. Hind track narrow. Overstep is typical.

Roan antelope fighting on their 'knees'

BUSHPIG

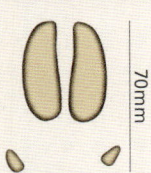

Front left foot   Hind left foot

75mm / 70mm

Front foot rounded and very splayed on leading edge, resembling the shape of mopane leaf. A less splayed version is also common. Hind foot hooves tighter, and rectangular in shape. False hooves may show. Variable gait, with a register being common. Tracks more rounded than warthog.

WARTHOG

Front left foot   Hind left foot

80mm / 70mm

Box-shaped and blunt on leading edge, particularly front foot. Hind foot is more curved and pointed. Prominent central ridge. Widely set false hooves show in deep substrate or when moving quickly. Often drags feet. Variable gait. Tracks smaller than bushpig.

Glossary

aestivate – when animals enter a dormant state during a hot, dry period, to conserve energy and minimise water loss (as opposed to hibernation, which is in winter)
anterior – towards the front
arboreal – inhabiting trees
bachelor – a male animal living by itself
bachelor herd – a group of males (usually young) living together
browse line – clear line in the vegetation marking the level at which herbivores have browsed
browser – an animal that feeds off the leaves of trees and shrubs
carnivore – a flesh-eating animal
carpus (wrist) – a group of small bones connecting the forelimb to the paw or hand. The carpus provides flexibility, stability and support to the limb, allowing for a wide range of movements and dexterity. It acts as a transitional joint between the forearm and the metacarpal bones, enabling animals to perform tasks such as grasping, manipulating objects and maintaining balance during locomotion.
carrion – decaying meat
cloven hoof – a hoof that is split into two 'toes'
crepuscular – active at dusk and dawn
cud – partly digested food that is regurgitated into the mouth of ruminants for re-chewing and swallowing again
deciduous – describing trees or other plants that shed their leaves at the end of the growing season
defecate – to drop faeces
detritus – organic waste or debris
digit – a finger or toe
direct register – describing an animal's hind foot imprinting directly on top of the front foot track as it walks
diurnal – active during the day
dominance – social status that allows privileged access to resources

ecotone – a zone of transition between two distinct ecosystems or ecological communities, often serving as a habitat for various animal species as these zones can offer a diversity of resources
ectoparasite – an external parasite
endemic – occurring only in a certain area
faeces – animal droppings
forb – herbaceous flowering plant (not a grass)
gait – the way that animals walk and run
gland – an organ in the animal body that secretes particular chemical substances either for internal use or for discharge into the surroundings, such as for territorial marking
grazer – an animal that eats grasses
gregarious – living in groups
habitat – the environment in which a plant or animal lives in its natural state
hallux – toe number 1 (hind toe) in birds
harem – group of breeding females; found with a dominant male that drives off other males
herbivore – an animal that feeds on grasses, leaves and other vegetable matter
home range – the undefended area in which an animal lives year-round
horns – the hard, often sharp, bone-like protuberances growing permanently on an ungulate's head, consisting of a core of bone encased in a keratin sheath
humerus (arm bone) – the bone found in the forelimb, the upper arm, connecting the shoulder (scapula) to the lower arm, such as the radius and ulna in mammals, or other corresponding bones in different animal groups. The humerus provides support and facilitates a range of movements and functions, including walking, running, flying or swimming, depending on the species.
insectivore – an animal that eats insects
juvenile – an animal that is past infancy but not yet an adult

GLOSSARY

lateral display – behaviour shown by males in which they turn side-on to impress the competition and establish dominance by virtue of their size

latrine – a place where animals habitually deposit faeces

metacarpus – lies between the wrist (carpus) and the digits (fingers or toes). In mammals, such as humans, the metacarpus comprises the bones that form the palm of the hand, connecting the wrist bones to the finger bones.

midden – a particular spot where droppings are regularly deposited for the purpose of territorial marking

monogamy – a mating system whereby each animal has only one partner, either for the season or for life

muzzle – the part of the face in front of the eyes

nocturnal – active at night

oestrus – the period during which a female is sexually receptive

omnivore – an animal that eats both meat and plant material

osteophagia – chewing of bones by herbivores to address a deficiency in phosphorus

overstep – the registration of an animal's hind foot ahead of its front foot while walking

pace – a single step when walking or running; the speed at which an animal is moving

passerine – a bird with feet that are adapted for perching

pellet – a small, solid animal dropping

phalanges – the individual bones that make up the digits (fingers and toes) of terrestrial vertebrates including mammals, birds and reptiles

plastron – underside of tortoise and terrapin shell

posterior – towards the back

pre-orbital – in front of the eye, often referring to a scent-marking gland

radius and ulna (forearm bones) – the paired bones found in the forearm of animals. They run in parallel. The radius, on the thumb or outer side of the limb, and the ulna, on the inner or pinky side, work together to provide stability, support and facilitate various motions such as flexion, extension, rotation, and weight-bearing. The radius-ulna complex is essential for tasks like walking, running, climbing, swimming, or manipulating objects, depending on the species.

register – the placement of an animal's hind foot directly on top of its front foot track as a result of its gait

rhizome – the continuously growing horizontal underground stem of a grass plant

ruminant – an animal that regurgitates and re-chews partly digested food (cud) that has been fermented in the rumen and reticulum chambers of its four-chambered stomach

rut – annually recurrent sexual excitement in a male antelope; the period during which this occurs

savanna – open grassland with trees spaced widely enough not to form a canopy

scat – animal droppings or dung

scavenger – an animal that feeds on other dead animals

spoor – the trail of an animal, notably its tracks but also other signs of its passage

step – a feature in some hooved animal tracks indicating the presence of a ridge or an intersection between two different substrate textures created by the hoof

straddle – the distance measured from the outside of the left foot to the outside of the right foot

stride length – the distance between two consecutive steps taken by an animal

strike rate – a quantitative measure used by scientists in the field that expresses the success or efficiency of a predator in capturing prey

substrate – the underlying ground or surface

succulent – a plant that has thickened, fleshy parts adapted for retaining water

territory – the area in which an animal lives and which it defends

understep – the registration of an animal's hind foot behind its front foot while walking

ungulate – a hooved animal

Bibliography

Carruthers, V. 2016. *The Wildlife of Southern Africa. A field guide to the animals and plants of the region*. Struik Nature, Cape Town, South Africa.

Ginn, P.J., McIlleron, W.G. & Milstein, P. le S. 1989. *The Complete Book of Southern African Birds*. Struik Winchester, Cape Town, South Africa.

Grainger, M.J., Van Aarde, R. & Whyte, I. 2005. Landscape heterogeneity and the use of space by elephants in the Kruger National Park, South Africa. *African Journal of Ecology* 43(4), pp. 369–375.

Gutteridge, L. 2012. *The Bushveld including the Kruger Lowveld: A South African Field Guide*. 30 Degrees South Publishers (Pty) Ltd, South Africa.

Halfpenny, J.C., Thompson, R.W., Morse, S.C., Holden, T. & Rezendes, P. 1997. Snow Tracking (Chapter 5) in J.E. Harris & C.V. Ogan (eds), *Mesocarnivores of Northern California: Biology, Management and Survey Techniques, Workshop Manual, August 12–15, 1997*. The Wildlife Society, Arcata, California.

Hes, L. & Mills, G. 1997. *Complete Book of Southern African Mammals*. Struik Nature, Cape Town, South Africa.

Liebenberg, L. 1990. *A Field Guide to the Animal Tracks of Southern Africa*. David Philip Publishers Ltd., Claremont, South Africa.

Liebenberg, L. 2008. *A Photographic Guide to Tracks and Tracking in Southern Africa*. Struik Publishers, Cape Town, South Africa.

Murray, K. 2011. *Scatalog – Quick ID Guide to Southern African Animal Droppings*. Struik Nature, Cape Town, South Africa.

Newman, K. & Newman, V. 2010. *Newman's Birds of Southern Africa*. Struik Nature, Cape Town, South Africa.

Picker, M., Griffiths, C. & Weaving, A. 2008. *Field Guide to Insects of South Africa*. Struik Publishers, Cape Town, South Africa.

Sinclair, I. 2004. *A Photographic Guide to Birds of Southern Africa – Fourth Edition*. Struik Publishers, Cape Town, South Africa.

Sinclair, I., Hockey, P., Tarboton, W. & Ryan, P. 2005. *The Larger Illustrated Guide to Birds of Southern Africa*. Struik Nature, Cape Town, South Africa.

Skaife, S.H. 1979. *African Insect Life*. Struik Publishers, Cape Town, South Africa.

Skinner, J.D. & Smithers, R.H.N. 1990. *Mammals of Southern Africa*. Pretoria University, South Africa.

Smithers, R.H.N. 1996. *Smithers' Mammals of Southern Africa: A Field Guide*. Southern Book Publishers, South Africa.

Stuart, C. & Stuart, M. 2013. *A Field Guide to the Tracks & Signs of Southern, Central & East Africa*. Struik Nature, Cape Town, South Africa.

Van Heerden, K. & Shearing, D. 1994. *Karoo – South African Wild Flower Guide 6*. Botanical Society of South Africa, Claremont, South Africa.

Van Wyk, B. & Van Wyk, P. 2013. *Field Guide to Trees of Southern Africa*. Struik Nature, Cape Town, South Africa.

Useful websites

CapeNature – **capenature.co.za**
Gaits – Gait foot-fall patterns – **vanat.cvm.umn.edu/gaits**
IUCN Red List – **iucnredlist.org**
Kruger National Park – **sanparks.org/parks/kruger**
South African National Biodiversity Institute – **sanbi.org**

A leopard tortoise comes to drink.

James Tyrrell

A young male leopard is treed by a buffalo herd.

Index

A
aardvark 195
aardwolf 84
ACCIPITRIDAE 319, 320
Acinonyx jubatus 58
Actophilornis africanus 305
Aepyceros melampus 170
Afrotis afra 312
Alcelaphus buselaphus caama 174
　A. lichtensteinii 176
Alopochen aegyptiaca 303
Amaurornis flavirostra 305
Anas undulata 301
antbear 195
antelope, roan 189
　sable 191
Anthropoides paradiseus 313
Anthus caffer 339
Antidorcas marsupialis 168
antlion 340
ants 341
ANURA 268
Aonyx capensis 236
ARACHNIDA 348
Arctocephalus pusillus pusillus 130
Ardea alba 296
　A. cinerea 295
　A. goliath 295
　A. melanocephala 294
Ardeotis kori 311
Atelerix frontalis 207
Atilax paludinosus 221
avocet, pied 299

B
baboon, chacma 243
badger, honey 238
beetles 342
blesbok 187
Bostrychia hagedash 300
BRADYPORIDAE 345
Bubo africanus 327
　B. lacteus 326
Bubulcus ibis 296
Bucorvus leadbeateri 332
buffalo, African 112
Buphagus erythrorhynchus 334

Burhinus capensis 310
　B. vermiculatus 310
bushbaby, southern lesser 247
　thick-tailed 249
bushbuck 145
bushpig 125
bustard, black-bellied 312
　kori 311
　Ludwig's 311
Butorides striata 294
butterflies 345
buttonquail, common 315
　kurrichane 315

C
cane rat, greater 259
Canis adustus 76
　C. mesomelas 76
CAPRIMULGIDAE 328
caracal 65
Caracal caracal 65
cat, black-footed 71
　small-spotted 71
caterpillars 344
Centropus superciliosus 325
Cephalophus natalensis 151
Ceratotherium simum 103
Chamaeleo dilepis 273
chameleon, flap-necked 273
Charadrius marginatus 309
　C. tricollaris 309
cheetah 58
CHELONIOIDEA 288
Chlorocebus pygerythrus 245
Ciconia ciconia 297
　C. episcopus 299
　C. nigra 297
civet, African 200
Civettictis civetta 200
Clamator glandarius 330
COLEOPTERA 342
COLIIDAE 331
COLUMBIDAE 323
Connochaetes gnou 131
　C. taurinus 133
coot, red-knobbed 303
cormorant, white-breasted 291
corn cricket 345
CORVIDAE 337

Corythaixoides concolor 324
coucal, Burchell's 325
courser, bronze-winged 308
　double-banded 308
crabs 353
crake, black 305
crane, blue 313
　wattled 313
crocodile, Nile 282
Crocodylus niloticus 282
Crocuta crocuta 90
crows 337
crow, Cape 337
　house 337
　pied 337
cuckoo, great spotted 330
Cynictis penicillata 226

D
Damaliscus lunatus 193
　D. pygargus phillipsi 187
dassie 241
DECAPODA 353
Dendrocygna viduata 301
Diceros bicornis 99
dikkop 310
doves 323
dove, African mourning 323
　Cape turtle 323
　emerald-spotted 323
　laughing 323
　Namaqua 323
　red-eyed 323
duck, white-faced whistling 301
　yellow-billed 301
duiker, blue 153
　common 148
　grey 148
　red 151

E
eagle-owl, spotted 327
　Verreaux's 326
eagles 320
eagle, African fish 320
　African hawk 320
　bateleur 320
　crowned 320
　martial 320
　tawny 320

INDEX

earthworms 351
egret, great 296
  little 296
  western cattle 296
Egretta garzetta 296
eland, common 118
elephant, African 94
Ephippiorhynchus senegalensis 298
Equus quagga burchellii 123
  E. zebra zebra 121

F

Felis nigripes 71
  F. silvestris cafra 68
fishing owl, Pel's 326
flamingo, greater 292
  lesser 292
FORMICIDAE 341
fox, bat-eared 80
  Cape 82
francolins 314
francolin, coqui 314
  crested 314
frogs 268
Fulica cristata 303
fur seal, brown 130
  Cape 130

G

Galago moholi 247
Galerella pulverulenta 219
  G. sanguinea 216
GASTROPODA 352
geckos 271
gemsbok 155
genet, large spotted 202
  small spotted 202
Genetta genetta 202
  G. tigrina 202
GERBILLINAE 266
gerbils 266
Giraffa camelopardalis 115
giraffe 115
go-away-bird, grey 324
goose, Egyptian 301, 302, 303
  spur-winged 302
grasshoppers 346
grebes 303, 304
ground squirrel, South African 255
grysbok, Cape 163
  Sharpe's 162
guineafowl, crested 316

helmeted 316
gull, kelp 290
Guttera pucherani 316

H

Haematopus moquini 290
hadeda 321
hamerkop 300, 321
hare, Cape 251
  scrub 253
hartebeest, Lichtenstein's 176
  red 174
hedgehog, southern African 207
Helogale parvula 211
heron, black-headed 294
  Goliath 295
  green-backed 294
  grey 295
Herpestes ichneumon 231
Himantopus himantopus 308
hippopotamus 108
Hippopotamus amphibius 108
Hippotragus equinus 189
  H. niger 191
HIRUNDINIDAE 329
hoopoe, African 336
hornbill, southern ground 332
  southern yellow-billed 333
hunting dog, Cape 73
Hyaena brunnea 86
hyaena, brown 86
  spotted 90
hyrax, rock 241
Hystrix africaeaustralis 261

I

ibis, African sacred 300
  hadeda 300
Ichneumia albicauda 224
Ictonyx striatus 205
impala 170
IXODIDA 347

J

jacana, African 305
jackal, black-backed 76
  side-striped 76

K

klipspringer 177
Kobus ellipsiprymnus 136
  K. leche 138
  K. vardonii 180

korhaan, red-crested 313
  southern black 312
kudu, greater 139

L

LACERTILIA 271
Lamprotornis australis 338
lapwing, African wattled 307
  blacksmith 306
  crowned 306
  Senegal 307
Larus dominicanus 290
lechwe, red 138
leopard 52
LEPIDOPTERA 344, 345
Leptailurus serval 62
Leptoptilos crumeniferus 298
Lepus capensis 251
  L. saxatilis 253
Leucorchestris 349
lion 44
Lissotis melanogaster 312
lizards 271
Lophotis ruficrista 313
Loxodonta africana 94
Lycaon pictus 73

M

MACROSCELIDEA 266
Manis temminckii 198
martins 329
martin, rock 329
meerkat 233
Mellivora capensis 238
millipedes 351
mongoose, banded 209
  dwarf 211
  large grey 231
  Meller's 214
  Selous' 229
  slender 216
  small grey 219
  water 221
  white-tailed 224
  yellow 226
monitor, Nile 277
  rock 275
  water 277
monkey, vervet 245
Motacilla aguimp 335
  M. capensis 335
mousebirds 331
mousebird, speckled 331
  white-backed 331
Mungos mungo 209

374

INDEX

MURIDAE 266
murids 266
MUTILLIDAE 347
MYRMELEONTIDAE 340

N

Neotis ludwigii 311
Neotragus moschatus 158
nightjars 328
Numida meleagris 316
nyala 141

O

OLIGOCHAETA 351
Onychognathus morio 338
Oreotragus oreotragus 177
oribi 160
ORTHOPTERA 346
Orycteropus afer 195
Oryx gazella 155
ostrich, common 317
Otocyon megalotis 80
Otolemur crassicaudatus 249
otter, Cape clawless 236
Ourebia ourebi 160
oxpecker, red-billed 334
oystercatcher, African 290
    black 290

P

pangolin, Temminck's 198
Panthera leo 44
    P. pardus 52
Papio ursinus 243
Paracynictis selousi 229
Paraxerus cepapi 257
Pedetes capensis 264
Pelea capreolus 185
Pelecanus onocrotalus 293
pelican, great white 293
PELOMEDUSIDAE 286
penguin, African 289
Phacochoerus africanus 127
Phalacrocorax lucidus 291
PHASIANIDAE 314, 315
Philantomba monticola 153
Phoenicopterus roseus 292
pipit, bushveld 339
Platalea alba 291
Plectropterus gambensis 302
plover 306
    three-banded 309
    white-fronted 309
Podiceps 304
polecat, striped 205

porcupine, Cape 261
Potamochoerus larvatus 125
Procavia capensis 241
Proteles cristatus 84
Pterocles bicinctus 322
puku 180

Q

quails 315
Quelea quelea 339
quelea, red-billed 339

R

ravens 337
raven, white-necked 337
Raphicerus campestris 165
    R. melanotis 163
    R. sharpei 162
Recurvirostra avosetta 299
Redunca arundinum 183
    R. fulvorufula 181
reedbuck, mountain 181
    southern 183
rhebok, grey 185
rhinoceros, black 99
    hook-lipped 99
    square-lipped 103
    white 103
Rhinoptilus africanus 308
    R. chalcopterus 308
Rhynchogale melleri 214
rodents, small 266

S

Sagittarius serpentarius 318
sandgrouse, double-banded 322
Scopus umbretta 321
SCORPIONES 350
scorpions 350
sea turtles 288
secretarybird 311, 318
sengis 266
Seothyra 349
SERPENTES 279
serval 62
shrews 266
sitatunga 143
skinks 271
slugs 352
snails 352
snakes 279
SORICIDAE 266
SPHECIDAE 347
Spheniscus demersus 289

spiders 348
    buckspoor 349
    white lady 349
SPIROSTREPTIDAE 351
spoonbill, African 291
springbok 168
springhare 264
spurfowls 314
spurfowl, Natal 314
    Swainson's 314
SQUAMATA 271
starling, Burchell's 338
    Cape glossy 338
    greater blue-eared 338
    Meves's 338
    red-winged 338
steenbok 165
stilt, black-winged 308
stork, black 297
    marabou 298
    saddle-billed 298
    white 297
    woolly-necked 299
Struthio camelus 317
suni 158
Suricata suricatta 233
suricate 233
swallows 329
swallow, greater-striped 329
Sylvicapra grimmia 148
Syncerus caffer 112

T

Tachybaptus 304
terrapins 286
TESTUDINIDAE 284
thick-knee, spotted 310
    water 310
Threskiornis aethiopicus 300
Thryonomys swinderianus 259
ticks 347
toads 268
Tockus leucomelas 333
tortoises 284
tortoise, African leopard 284
    Speke's hinge-backed 284
Tragelaphus angasii 141
    T. oryx 118
    T. scriptus 145
    T. spekii 143
    T. strepsiceros 139
tree squirrel, African 257
tsessebe 193
Turnix sylvaticus 315

INDEX

U
Upupa africana 336

V
Vanellus armatus 306
   V. coronatus 306
   V. lugubris 307
   V. senegallus 307
Varanus albigularis 275
   V. niloticus 277
VESPIDAE 347
Vulpes chama 82
vultures 319

vulture, Cape 319
  hooded 319
  lappet-faced 319
  white-backed 319

W
wagtail, African pied 335
  Cape 335
warthog 127
wasps 347
waterbuck, common 136
wild cat, African 68
wild dog, African 73

wildebeest, black 131
  blue 133

X
Xerus inauris 255

Z
zebra, Burchell's 123
  Cape mountain 121
  plains 123
zorilla 205

Ian Thomas

The taloned feet of a white-backed vulture charge in to a rapidly vanishing impala carcass.